BEYOND THE DARKNESS

Cult, Horror, and Extreme Cinema

By Phil Russell

A Bad News Press book
First published by Bad News Press in 2012
Beyond The Darkness: Cult, Horror, and Extreme Cinema
Text copyright © Phil Russell
This volume copyright © Phil Russell 2012
Design & layout: Phil Russell
Cover image courtesy of ContraFilm.
The moral rights of the author have been asserted.

All rights reserved. No part of this book may be reproduced, stored on a retrieval system, or transmitted, in any form or by any means, electronic, mechanical, photocopying, recording, or otherwise, on earth or in space, this dimension or that, without prior permission in writing from the author/publisher.

Author's Acknowledgments: Many of the people below helped in so many ways I'd have to create a new chapter just to describe how much they mean to me. Jonny Eyres, Jenny Sinclair, Mike at MYO, Ronny at FilmBizarro.com, Mitch Davis at FantAsia, Tyra Yeabsley, Chad West, Carlos Lopez, Kimberly Davis, Tomas Olsen, and all at BD. David Kerekes at Headpress, Johannes Schonherr, Nick Zedd, Asia Argento, and the folks at Amazon.com. To all of you, thank you so much!

    ISBN – 13: 978-1481865128
    ISBN – 10: 1481865129

This book is dedicated to the memory of Ken Russell

1927 - 2011

BEYOND THE DARKNESS

Cult, Horror, and Extreme Cinema

By Phil Russell

CONTENTS

Introduction – Page 7

Reviews – Page 13

Interview With Nick Zedd – Page 22

The Fall of George Romero – Page 158

The CAT III Phenomenon – Page 176

Mondo Movies and Shockumentaries – Page 337

Subversive! Spanish Horror Under The Franco Regime – Page 510

Is Censorship Still Relevant? – Page 516

The Vanishing Point of Cinema – Page 535

INTRODUCTION

Mainstream movies have always struck me as bland, boring, safe, predictable, and prudish. However, the mainstream is also necessary for cult movie fans as a point of distinction between 'us and them'. One of the great pleasures of being into this kind of stuff is to seek and ferret out new cinematic treasures, and for that reason I have resisted the urge to compile a comprehensive guide. Generally, this book concentrates on the darker side of film; the controversial, the shocking, and disturbing. It serves as a gateway into extreme cinema rather than a complete guide. The intention is to give readers an idea of what is out there, but by no means is the territory fully mapped-out in these pages. Rather than being content to seek out random, directionless entertainment, as mainstream film fans do, devotees of the darker side of cinema are more willing to discover these oddities for themselves. For example, it was only a few short years ago when the usually reliable IMDB listed just a handful of films by Japanese provocateur, Hisayasu Sato. But the last time I checked that number had grown to more than 50! Barely any of his films have had a DVD release in the

West, but with the recent success of Rampo Noir, cult movie fans are quickly catching up with the filmic output of this extraordinary director. Some of his films are covered in this book, including one of the most fucked up movies you'll ever see, Lolita Vibrator Torture. As for the rest, you'll have to discover them for yourself.

There are a number of films covered here that have barely been written about before, not even online, such as First Transmission, The Video Diary of Ricardo Lopez, Love To Kill, and Molester's Train: Dirty Behaviour. This is not an entry-level book. It is assumed that the reader will be somewhat familiar with the world of film and the horror genre in particular, and be open to alternatives. It's not a complete overview of extreme cinema (a complete A-Z guide would include almost 3000 titles!). But hopefully you'll be introduced to a few gems you have never even heard of before. And if I can convert just one person to the sleazy joys of a CAT III movie, I'll consider this book job done.

Everything from big-budget Hollywood flicks to micro-budget amateur crap is covered here, and everything in between. The style of the reviews are also varied; some are short and straight to the point, others are more in-depth attempts to engage with a film. Some are strictly objective in approach, whereas others offer a more personal, subjective point of view. Most were written in a sober frame of mind, but there were one or two written under the influence. I also attempt to explain my own interpretations of some of these films but many will probably be widely off the mark. But hey, don't mind me.

There are some people out there who prize certain films depending on the levels of gore, violence, or sexual depravity on display that the more mainstream types of films don't deliver. If that's your main interest in film then perhaps you should join a relevant web forum and compare top ten lists of favourite decapitations with fellow geeks because this book will have little interest for you. Likewise, if you're just interested in the real stuff. Mondo movies and shockumentaries are covered in these pages but the coverage isn't all that extensive. Although I have watched a fare few of these types of films over the years, I generally draw the line at the genuine stuff. If you've become so jaded that even the grisliest and goriest of special effects have no effect on you then by all means go check out the fully illustrated Color Atlas of Forensic Pathology, or the AP photos of the Liberian Civil War, or the police recovery footage of the corpses under John Wayne Gacy's house, because let's face it, there's no hope for you in fiction. That stuff might just bring it on home to you the cost of human destruction.

Films like Pasolini's Salo, however disgusting it may be, had a point to make about the reduction of man to pieces of meat in the world of late capitalism, and John McNaughton's Henry-Portrait of a Serial Killer is a gruelling character study that effectively shows how vulnerable we could be to an unreasoning psychopath. But the celebration of these films should not be at the expense of the more gratuitous and exploitative side of shock cinema. Koji Shiraishi's Grotesque may not offer anything even resembling a social and/or political standpoint, but is a darn good piece of torture porn, nonetheless. William Lustig's Maniac may not offer the same psychological insight as the anti-hero in McNaughton's film, but it remains one of the most brutal and harrowing slasher movies ever made. Sometimes the horror and the gruesomeness and the sleaze is reason enough to watch these films, and there is nothing wrong with that. It's perfectly natural to express an interest in the dark and the forbidden; we shouldn't need to justify our viewing pleasures by relying on some 'moral message' or serious subtext. If a filmmaker decides to use shocking and disturbing imagery in order to make a point about where we're heading as a society, then that's great. And if the same director decides to make a film that is gratuitous and for the sole purpose of shocking and amusing his audience, then that's also fine by me. After all, we're responsible adults and we should be free to decide for ourselves what we would like to watch. Cinema as pure spectacle is accepted in the form of the musical or the big-budget action film, but the censors always make a point of cutting and banning this kind of thing in the horror movie equivalent; the violent set-piece. A recent example is The Human Centipede 2 which was briefly banned in the UK in 2011 for being utterly gratuitous.

The Devils, Peeping Tom, and Scum have never been easy viewing and had caused much controversy and scandal on their initial releases, but at the same time these are among the finest British films of the post-war years. Nagisa Oshima's Ai no corrida is considered a masterpiece but has been banned and censored across the world. Even the former head of British censorship, James Ferman, admired the film (and this is the same man who seemed to have a personal vendetta against The Exorcist and The Texas Chainsaw Massacre, both of which he happily banned in this country). But while many of the films covered here have their own artistic and social merits, an equal amount of coverage is given to films that possess no such thing. Such then is Beyond The Darkness, a book that juxtaposes the highs of the arthouse cinema with the lows of the scuzzy underground flicks, and much in between. You're just as likely to read about the work of despised filmmakers such as Fred Vogel, Andrey Iskanov, and Uwe Boll, as you are the films of such vital artists as Abel Ferrara, David Cronenberg, and Lars Von Trier.

My unshakeable enthusiasm for the most bizarre, deformed, and outrageous cine-life-forms has sometimes led me down some dubious paths - Hentai anime, Japanese AV crap, and even German amateur gorefests - There are so many genres and sub-genres to explore that it's easy to get lost and find yourself completely alienated from the reasons why you love movies in the first place. However, it's the willingness to explore the nether-regions of the world of

extreme cinema and to dig through all the crap, that forms the ethos of this book. I don't expect to stop taking unwise detours in the film jungle any time soon. I remain utterly and foolishly in love with movies. And I hope you are too.
Enjoy!

Phil Russell, January 2012.

phil.russell81@hotmail.com

REVIEWS

ABNORMAL - THE SINEMA OF NICK ZEDD (1980-2001)

Dir: Nick Zedd / USA

This 2-disc set from the man who coined the term 'Cinema of transgression' includes a dozen short films mostly shot on 8mm that span twenty years of his career. They're presented chronologically but in reverse order for some reason, and are a hit and miss collection displaying the difficulties of being a super low-budget filmmaker whose main objective is to shock, provoke, and push the boundaries.

Tom Thumb In The Land of The Giants (1999) was shot in Copenhagen and is fashioned in a faux trailer style (a la Jim Van Bebber's Chunk Blower and Richard Gale's The Horribly Slow Murderer With The Extremely Inefficient Weapon). A child is running through a graveyard and is followed by a being in black. The voiceover is very tongue-in-cheek and sells the film well. The kid (played by Zedd's son) crawls into a huge vagina at the end. Running time: 3 minutes.

Ecstasy In Entropy (1999) 17 mins. This looks like a tribute to the old grindhouse movies of the 60s with its gritty style and constant barrage of tinny pop music. A bunch of strippers get into a fight and a man receives a blowjob before unloading half a bucket of (fake) spunk onto a woman's face. Then we switch to a colour scene where someone dressed in black and wearing a mask strips and attempts to rape a woman (Annie Sprinke), but she fights back and amusingly drops some huge tit-bombs on his head while she rides on his back.

Why Do You Exist (aka Screen Test) (1998) 16 mins. This starts out quite fun and entertaining but outstays its welcome by a good ten minutes. It basically presents a group of people in front of the camera; a large woman puts squirty cream allover her tits along with cinnamon and cherries, and then licks it off (or as Zedd puts it, "consuming a picnic on her tits"). More people posing and smoking a lot. The woman painted in blue and strumming an acoustic guitar (the 'Blue Lady' Kembra Pfahler) was another highlight but overall this isn't up to much. The film also features other underground personalities, including Brenda Bergman and Dr. Ducky DooLittle.

War Is Menstrual Envy (1992) Perhaps the highlight of the whole set. This excerpt from Zedd's feature film ranks among the finest work he has ever achieved. A woman painted almost entirely in blue (except for the pink nipples, reminiscent of Barbara Steele in Curse of The Crimson Alter) unwraps a mummified figure to reveal a man who has severe burns to his head, face, torso, and arms. It's quite clear that this guy is a real burns victim, and this makes the clip uneasy viewing. This sequence is played out to a light flute arrangement like from an old Disney movie, and this gives the proceedings a dark fairytale edge. Then we cut to the next scene in which the man is encountered by the infamous fetish porn actress, Annie Sprinkle, and she dresses him in a gun holster, a head scarf, and a pair of shades, takes them off again, and then kisses and licks his melted flesh. The man then sucks her tits for a while and tries to caress them, but finds it difficult because all his fingers have been melted together, and he struggles to make that lustful contact he so desires. I'm not sure what this clip means but it's mesmerizing stuff. The end credits are displayed with graphic footage of real eyeball surgery.

Whoregasm! (1988) 12 mins. A short collage/experimental film which juxtaposes images of hardcore sex and war footage through a process of tricky and inventive editing and overlapping techniques. Perhaps Zedd's most technically impressive film to date. Again, there's no narrative here to speak of but it's quite engaging and much more interesting than some of the crap that gets passed off as experimental. Includes graphic shots of fellatio, explosions, in-and-out penetration close-ups (some performed by Zedd himself), more explosions, and an image of a young boy whose hand is being held by a man who has an erection (whether this is a 'doctored' image or a real one I've no idea but it certainly adds to the transgressive nature of the film), a transvestite sucking a foot, a policeman screaming into the lens (that shot was taken from Zedd's previous short, Police State), and the transvestite receiving a blowjob from a woman.

Police State (1987) 18 mins. This micro-budget slice of punk nihilism could have been so much better, but as it stands it's a scrappy and uneven piece that at least adds a few nuggets of interest on repeat viewings. Perhaps the most disappointing film of the set due to the potential at its disposal, Police State is about a young man (played by Zedd himself) who is cornered and harassed for a while by a cop before he is taken to the station, interrogated, beaten by more cops, and is eventually castrated. It shows an obvious disdain for the police and an Orwellian warning about where we're at as a society, sleep-walking into totalitarianism, which is a valid point to be made, but the acting, camera work, and script could have been so much better. According to the interview on the second disc, Zedd and his cohorts were almost caught by the cops vandalising police cars with spray paint during the making of the film.

Kiss Me Goodbye (1986) Another disappointing short but at least this one only takes up three minutes of your time. A man (again played by Zedd) wanders into a room to find a woman reading a book. He kisses and then strangles her. The end. Zedd appears as B.D. Shane, a 'dead star' and he apparently strangles one of his fans.

Go To Hell (1986) 11 mins. This one isn't much better. Zedd wanders around and sees a woman dressed in white and some junky shooting up into his arm. The junky follows the woman and beats her unconscious, and then Zedd shows up and kisses her as an atomic bomb blast goes off in the background. Music by The Swans who sound like an 80s version of The Doors.

Thrust In Me (1985) 8 mins. Things improve a lot with this one. This time Zedd plays two roles. Co-directed with Richard Kern (it's also included on Kern's Hard Core Collection). A tranny reads a book on suicide. Zedd walks the streets. Tranny gets into the bath and slashes her wrist. Zedd enters the apartment and takes a shit without noticing the bloody corpse in the tub. He takes a picture of Jesus off the wall and wipes his arse on it, and then notices the dead tranny. He then fucks the corpse in the mouth and squirts half a gallon of spunk on its head. He walks out onto the rooftop of the apartment and gazes at the New York skyline. Aww, who said romance is dead. It's a shame that Zedd and Kern ended their friendship over a "misunderstanding" as this film shows potential. Yes it's childish and you get the impression that they're trying really hard to offend you whilst at the same time pretending not to care what you think. But there is an undeniable power to this clip that probably stemmed from a competitive streak between the two. It would have been interesting to see more collaborations. A stunt porn star was also used.

The Wild World of Lydia Lunch (1983) 20 mins. Someone once dubbed this 'The Incredibly Dull World of Lydia Lunch', and to be honest I can't argue with that. Even many of Lunch's fans find this a crushing bore. It starts in a dark room where she reads a letter from someone complaining about being stranded in London with increasing money problems. Then it cuts to scenes of Lunch walking the streets of London (well, we see a red phone box so I assume it's somewhere in England), and a voiceover talks a lot of nonsense. She teases a cute dog, hangs out in the park, stands on street corners, and stares a lot into the camera lens. It's as if she is trapped in some kind of post-punk-pre-goth limbo.

The Bogus Man (1980) 11 mins. A satirical pseudo-documentary with weird clips of rehearsed and repeated voiceovers. A man in a ski mask tells of his warped ideas about the American President being a clone. He explains his conspiracy theory and shows us some footage of a doctor under interrogation who shoots himself when asked why he has blood on his hands. We also see footage of the kidnapped President (actually, some dude in a Jimmy Carter mask). He is tied to a strange vaginal chair that has phallic prongs sticking out at either side, and someone cuts his finger off. We're told that the tissue from each finger will be used to generate more clones... The most disturbing scenes though are the ones featuring the woman (or is it a man?) in a full body suit dancing around in a room with an American flag displayed in the background. One of the freakiest things you'll ever see. This film is also notable as an early outing for special fx legend 'Screaming Mad George' of A Nightmare On Elm Street and Society fame.

1 of K9 (2001). This last clip is in black and white and lasts just a couple of minutes. There looks to be an orgy going on in the background and a woman takes hold of a dog's face and starts kissing it on the mouth with tongues and everything. The Doberman doesn't look to be too happy about being slobbered on (I suppose it makes a change, it's usually the dogs who slobber on us), and looks to be on the verge of chewing her face off at any moment. But then a man enters the frame, shoves the woman out the way, and then he starts to kiss and lick the dog's mouth; he almost has his tongue down its throat at one point. An amusing clip but I've no idea what it means.

So there you have it, 12 shorts that vary in terms of quality and re-watchability set over a twenty-one year period of filmmaking history. None of them can really live up to the scummy triumphs of Zedd's debut feature, They Eat Scum (1979), but there are a few clips here that are worth a re-visit from time to time. It's a good place to start if you want to know what all the fuss was about in the New York underground. I should also point out that the extras on the second disc includes a very strange interview with Zedd taken from some old cable TV show. See it to believe it.

  Nick Zedd made his debut feature, They Eat Scum, in the late 70s. Starring Donna Death as Suzy Putrid, she leads her Death Rock band, The Mental Deficients, to world domination when she kills her family and causes a core meltdown at a nuclear power station. The film features murder, cannibalism, bestiality, and a girl being forced to eat a live rat. It was broadcast on cable TV in 1982 causing much controversy when the Wall Street Journal condemned the screening with a damning front page article. The following year Zedd returned with his second feature film, Geek Maggot Bingo, Or, The Freak From Suckweasel Mountain. Coming on like a twisted take on the Universal monster cycle of the 1930s, Geek Maggot Bingo saw the return of Donna Death along with Brenda Bergman and Richard Hell, and depicts an evil doctor who uses a slave to procure victims for his fiendish experiments.

In 1985 Nick Zedd wrote The Cinema of Transgression Manifesto for his fanzine, The Underground Film Bulletin. Written under the pseudonym Orion Jericho, Zedd calls for a rejection of traditional film theory and instead declares that he and his fellow underground filmmakers, including Richard Kern, intend on breaking every taboo they can in the name of freedom.

His next feature, War Is Menstrual Envy, appeared in 1992, and is the first of his full-length films to break away from traditional narrative storytelling.

THE CINEMA OF TRANSGRESSION MANIFESTO
(Reproduced here with the kind permission of Nick Zedd)

We who have violated the laws, commands and duties of the avant-garde; i.e. to bore, tranquilize and obfuscate through a fluke process dictated by practical convenience stand guilty as charged. We openly renounce and reject the entrenched academic snobbery which erected a monument to laziness known as structuralism and proceeded to lock out those filmmakers who possessed the vision to see through this charade.

We refuse to take their easy approach to cinematic creativity; an approach which ruined the underground of the sixties when the scourge of the film school took over. Legitimising every mindless manifestation of sloppy movie making undertaken by a generation of misled film students, the dreary media arts centres and geriatric cinema critics have totally ignored the exhilarating accomplishments of those in our rank - such underground invisibles as Zedd, Kern, Turner, Klemann, DeLanda, Eros and Mare, and DirectArt Ltd, a new generation of filmmakers daring to rip out of the stifling strait jackets of film theory in a direct attack on every value system known to man.

We propose that all film schools be blown up and all boring films never be made again. We propose that a sense of humour is an essential element discarded by the doddering academics and further, that any film which doesn't shock isn't worth looking at. All values must be challenged. Nothing is sacred. Everything must be questioned and reassessed in order to free our minds from the faith of tradition. Intellectual growth demands that risks be taken and changes occur in political, sexual and aesthetic alignments no matter who disapproves. We propose to go beyond all limits set or prescribed by taste, morality or any other traditional value system shackling the minds of men. We pass beyond and go over boundaries of millimeters, screens and projectors to a state of expanded cinema.

We violate the command and law that we bore audiences to death in rituals of circumlocution and propose to break all the taboos of our age by sinning as much as possible. There will be blood, shame, pain and ecstasy, the likes of which no one has yet imagined. None shall emerge unscathed. Since there is no afterlife, the only hell is the hell of praying, obeying laws, and debasing yourself before authority figures, the only heaven is the heaven of sin, being rebellious, having fun, fucking, learning new things and breaking as many rules as you can. This act of courage is known as transgression. We propose transformation through transgression - to convert, transfigure and transmute into a higher plane of existence in order to approach freedom in a world full of unknowing slaves.

POSTSCRIPT: INTERVIEW WITH NICK ZEDD
Conducted via email on 1st February 2012

"I believe you must be obsessed to produce anything of lasting value in this world...My commitment was total"

– Nick Zedd

PR - Tell us about your childhood and where you grew up.

NZ - I grew up in Hyattsville, Maryland, watched a lot of TV as a kid, went to drive-in movies, had a big imagination, played out having a television network in my head, produced, wrote, directed and starred in my own movies and television programs on a daily basis. I read a lot of comic books, Famous Monsters of Filmland, Castle of Frankenstein. I produced and performed scenarios with puppets for my brother and myself as a kid. This was all a rehearsal for making real movies later in life.

Many filmmakers started out with Super-8 as youngsters, such as Jim Van Bebber and Sam Raimi. Did you get to play around with cameras as a kid?

Yeah, I made my first 8mm movie when I was 12, animating GI Joe dolls. I produced and directed a series of science fiction films and their sequels from the age of 14 to 16, using friends as actors.

I've always been fond of They Eat Scum. How did that project come about? Must have been pretty daunting to set out making an apocalyptic punk movie on such a miniscule budget.

It started with a script I wrote while in film school after I moved to New York. I produced, wrote and directed it using people I knew, met or auditioned from the punk scene. It was made with almost no input from the film teachers or film students, like an outside project. I left
school before it was finished. I financed it by sweeping floors in a wood shop part time. I used miniatures and stock footage shot off a TV screen for the more expensive effects or location shots.

It was just an extension of my directing style which I'd begun 9 years earlier in Maryland; do-it-yourself, don't get hung up on money or "professionalism," don't let anything stop you, just do it. Things come out better when you keep it personal, working with amateurs, with people who aren't motivated by money; inspired to be part of something new. My enthusiasm must have been infectious because I always could get people to work for free.

The year I premiered it, I was invited to show it in San Francisco and was flown there to screen it at some punk venues with good local publicity and big crowds. Some place in Berlin also showed a video of They Eat Scum in 1979 which amazed me. There was immediate interest as soon as it came out. A local NY paper gave it a great review.(Fortunately one of my film teachers wrote movie reviews.) The other local paper gave it a scathing review, dismissing it along with Gordon Stevenson's Ecstatic Stigmatic, another brilliant and legendary super-8 film made at the same time, so I was in good company.

Who was the burnt guy in War Is Menstrual Envy?

Ray, who was Annie Sprinkle's boyfriend at the time. He was a drummer who got burned in a camping accident as a teenager.

Who was it who was dancing around in the body suit in The Bogus Man? I found those scenes to be quite disturbing.

That was Grier Lankton, a friend of Donna Death who made costumes as sculpture and later had a sex change and became female.

Johannes Schonherr held screenings of your films in Nuremberg in 1990, and apparently feminists attacked the event and threw cat shit at the screen. And you were subjected to some front page tabloid infamy. In the UK (and America) it's usually the conservatives who picket and protest at cinemas, but in Germany, according to Schonherr, it's more often than not the leftists who are the most intolerant of daring and challenging films. Can you share some of the most memorable reactions to screenings of your work, both the good and bad?

When I showed War Is Menstrual Envy at Anthology Film Archives in 1993, a guy fainted and had to be carried out of the theatre during the scene with Ray the burn victim and Annie.

In San Francisco in 1979 when I showed They Eat Scum, enraged punks were heckling and screaming at me so I shot them with a water pistol.

On Nuremburg in 1990 the Rote Zora feminazis threw garbage and cat shit over the audience and threw acid on the movie screen, blew whistles and threw tracts in the air, protesting the "provocation" of the program notes describing the movies, which I hadn't read. I locked myself in the projection booth when I heard a stampede of feet from the theatre and people pounding on the door, but Johannes opened the door anyway and fortunately the feminists had left.

In Gothenberg, Sweden in 1993 I was arrested upon arrival at the airport, then the police spent 3 hours examining my movies and held me in a cell, threatening to put me in prison. Afterwards they let me go, but warned me to never show them because they were "sick" and "immoral." A week later, police raided the apt I was staying in, arrested me and took me to the station where I spent another 2 hours in a cell while they looked at all my movies. The chief of police told me the government instructed him to let me go, but warned me to never show the movies in Sweden.

In Canada, my films were confiscated in 1988 and later returned 4 months later by mail to NYC. In 2007, I was removed from a train entering Canada by the police, who escorted me over the border after looking at my films which they declared "borderline criminal material" and told me I was banned from the country for ten years.

Best recent reaction was last year in Mexico City when I showed Geek Maggot Bingo at the Cinetequa, and a big audience loved it and asked for autographs and lined up to have pictures taken with me. This movie was not popular when I originally showed it in 1983.

This morning I saw a news report claiming that scientists have learned how to read minds by monitoring brainwaves as a way of decoding inner voices. It brings to mind Orwell's Thought Police and also your film Police State. Do you feel that society is heading towards totalitarianism?

Of course. Surveillance is everywhere. Now that people spend most of their time on computers they can be monitored and tracked thru social networking sites. The populace has been made docile with superficial distractions like text messaging, virtual reality sites and video games. A massive dumbing-down is taking place all over the world. But totalitarian control is being short-circuited by occupy movements using technology against the global elites, organizing online and with cel phones, taking to the streets and rendering bogus electoral systems irrelevant. Parliamentary cretinism has been revealed as a false construct by mass passive resistance and organized protest world-wide. Corporate media and their puppet masters are dumbfounded at this turn of events which is a good sign that things are changing. People are fed up all over the world and want their freedom back.

It seems you take inspiration from all kinds of areas, not just filmmakers. Who do you consider to be the biggest influence on your work?

Whoever I'm in contact with at the moment. That changes from week to week. The more isolated I become the more I influence myself. I'm not really that inspired by anyone at the moment.

What do you make of John Waters' early films?

They're fabulous.

How was it working with Richard Kern? Thrust In Me seemed to bring out the best in you both. Would you agree that there was a competitive streak between you and Kern?

Sure. We were all competing with each other as filmmakers in the early days. Later, I was competing with my main collaborator Rev Jen, from 2001 to 2009. Creative competition is a great catalyst. It's unfortunate that inflated egos and insecurities can turn creative collaborator/competitors into mortal enemies. I always thought that producing end results far outweighed holding grudges and being on pointless ego trips but you'd be astounded at the level of assholism in most artists. They're some of the worst people in the world to deal with; vicious, petty, mean-spirited hateful creatures...It's unfortunate when they also have some talent waiting to be exploited, but I've become an expert in utilizing that talent until it dissipates into self-destructive narcissism. Then it's time to move onto the next "star" and break new ground. So much can be accomplished when people put their egos aside and can see the bigger picture. It's that narcissistic egotism that kills so much creative potential, destroys creative alliances that could produce historic art. I've seen it happen again and again.

What's the New York underground scene like nowadays? Is there anything interesting going on?

No, it's dead.

Tell us about Electra Elf.

That was a superhero comedy series I produced, directed and co-wrote with Rev Jen from 2003 to 2009, shown on NYC public access and syndicated to some cities in other states, ultimately released by MVD as a boxed set of twenty episodes. It was really sugar-coated subversion designed to activate certain sexual fetishes while attacking the status quo through political and social satire. Some episodes completely deconstructed conventional narrative in order to jolt the viewer awake with xenomorphic shock therapy disguised as family friendly entertainment. It was an exercise in anti-Simulation free thought. I loved making that series as much as a cultist might love a new religion...It was my reason for living for six years...I believe you must be obsessed to produce anything of lasting value in this world...My commitment was total.

What's the most shocking or disturbing film you've ever seen? And what was it about the film that disturbed you?

The 9/11 inside job, perpetrated by traitors in the US shadow government and facilitated by brainwashed imbeciles in corporate media who collaborated in promoting the greatest hoax in human history (aside from the Christ and Mohammad myths.) This Big Lie enabled the illegitimate Bush crime family to jump-start two disastrous wars of aggression that bankrupted our economy and extended the profit margins for war profiteers and fossil fuel conglomerates while expanding the global control grid of an elitist blood-line (the

Rockefellers and the Rothschields) whose tactical agenda is world genocide. The current administration is a continuation of the same illegitimate neo-con lunacy. The false-flag 9/11 event and its promotion by corporate media to millions of conspiracy dupes disturbs me as much as the Kennedy assassinations, which similarly were covered up and mythologized by corrupt fascists peddling disinformation to the masses. The decline of everything positive in our lives can be traced back to these pivotal events, orchestrated by the most evil men in history.

What's your favourite book, and why?

Totem of the Depraved, because I wrote it, and it's a great series of true stories. I'm the world's best living writer. No lie, just fact.

Finally, what's next for Nick Zedd? Do you have any future projects lined up?

That would be telling... It's better to surprise the world...

THE ADDICTION (1995)

Dir: Abel Ferrara / USA

In Abel Ferrara's earlier film, Bad Lieutenant, Zoe Lund suggests that drug addicts are like vampires, and that "vampires are lucky, they can feed on others. We have to feed on ourselves". It was only natural that Ferrara would eventually tackle the opposite: Vampires in the clutch of addiction. He teamed up once again with his long-time writing partner, Nicholas St. John, and together they came up with a vampiric tale that contemplates the nature of eternal guilt.

The plot concerns Kathleen (Lili Taylor), a postgraduate philosophy student who is pulled into a dark alley and bitten by a glamorous vampire, Casanova (Annabella Sciorra).

After having her wounds checked out at the local hospital, Kathleen comes to realise that she is now addicted to human blood. This affliction brings on a new outlook on life and has a tremendous effect on her thesis. And when she thirsts for the red stuff, she uses an oddly ethical approach to her victims, giving them the opportunity to overpower her ("Tell me to go away like you mean it"). But strangely, none of her victims can sum up the willpower to avoid their fates (much like drug addicts in real life who seem to inadvertently will their own corruption and downfall by not being steadfast enough to confront the situation before it takes hold - Avoiding the confrontation, hence Sartre's 'Bad Faith').

Kathleen digs deeper into her studies and wallows in the graphic footage of atrocities at My Lai, Auschwitz-Birkenau, and Srebrenica as a way of coming to terms with her own eternal damnation. Her biggest life-lesson though comes in the form of Peina (Christopher Walken), a wise old vampire who discusses Nietzsche and Burroughs' Naked Lunch before biting into her jugular, and informing her that "Demons suffer in hell".

One of the most serious-minded horror movies of all time, The Addiction is nonetheless disliked by many who are turned off by its harsh philosophical probing and abrasive visual style. The film's central motif is moral responsibility; when Kathleen is first approached by the vampiric Casanova she is given the opportunity to deal with the situation head-on ("Tell me to go away"), but Kathleen can only manage a pathetic "please" in response. In the world of Ferrara and Nicky St. John, this kind of feeble stance amounts to consent. Accordingly, by refusing to face up to evil and deal with it openly, Kathleen and other victims just like her, deserve all they get.

kathleen later succeeds in luring a young student to her place. And after feeding on her blood, she blames the terrified girl, insisting that "It was your decision". The victim pleads "Don't you care what you did to me! Doesn't it affect you?" She replies, "Why didn't you tell me to leave, to get lost like you really meant it? My indifference is not the concern here; it's your astonishment that needs studying." In another scene Kathleen looks in the mirror and muses "Is it wrong for me to draw blood? No. It's the violence of my will against theirs." A comment that also relates to Sartre's Being and Nothingness. Free will is of vital importance to Ferrara and St. John in their idea of evil: If you don't put up a fight then the vampire, the evildoer, takes that as a form of social consent. In this case, in the supernatural world of the vampire film. In addition, this concept of evil also relates to the real life evil in the form of murder, genocide, and drug addiction. The theme of refusing to confront evil recurs throughout the film in its many and varied ways, and also examines attitudes of moral ambivalence and apathy towards evil that exists in modern society.

It's possible that Katleen's blood addiction isn't real. Maybe her obsessive studying has caused her illness through mental exhaustion. Perhaps she is a plain old drug addict, and she fantasizes on vampirism as a way of making light of her condition (and this could also relate the film to George Romero's Martin in that it is never confirmed or denied whether Martin is in fact a real vamp. Martin has flashbacks to times set in old Europe where he drank blood from victims, but those episodes could be plain old fantasy).

Lili Taylor is superb as Kathleen, even surpassing her performance in Mary Harron's I Shot Andy Warhol. Christopher Walken and Paul Calderon (both of whom appeared in Ferrara's King of New York) add some solid support. Still one of the most irredeemable American filmmakers working today, Abel Ferrara has managed to combine exploitation with a high-minded sensibility for more than three decades. From The Driller Killer in the 70s, Ms.45 in the 80s, Dangerous Game in the 90s, and RXmas in the 00s, this native New Yorker has never once compromised on his dark vision, even when working within the studio system (Body Snatchers). The Addiction remains one of his darkest efforts, a black and white gem which asks some important questions and never flinches in its search for answers. Essential viewing.

AFTERMATH (1994)

Dir: Nacho Cerda / Spain

Rarely does a short film attract such global recognition when it is limited to playing only a few film festivals, but Nacho Cerda's Aftermath has become something of a cult classic and has divided its audience down the middle between those declaring it a masterpiece of horror and others a crude and overblown piece of nonsense. But make no mistake, once seen this film is not so easily forgotten.

Aftermath presents a day in the life of a necrophiliac pathologist whose job in the local morgue puts him into close contact with the recently deceased. No sooner have his colleagues left the building when the nameless pervert (played by Pep Tosar) indulges in a bit of 'how's your father' with a female corpse. The film is about as explicit as a non-pornographic movie can be, with the infamous scenes of Tosar defiling the corpse with a knife and plunging the blade in between the legs whilst jerking off, and then climbing on top for a bit of gross penetration. The film is beautiful to look at considering the subject matter, with some impressive photography, an insane performance by Tosar, giving it a sheen of glossiness.

Whereas previous necro-shockers like Lucker The Necrophagous had a cheap and nasty aura about it, Aftermath offers the production values of a Hollywood film (albeit on only a fraction of the budget), at complete odds with the rank and disgusting imagery on screen. Indeed, horror fans didn't get to witness such nasty and perverted scenes in such glossy looking productions until the equally troubling likes of Grotesque and A Serbian Film came along more than a decade and a half later.

The film basically puts us in the company of a sicko for half an hour, during which time the hopelessly defenseless cadavers are opened up and sexually violated with nary a word of dialogue in the whole film. The camera prowls along investigating the lifeless slabs of meat whilst Verdi's Requiem plays out on the soundtrack. It's a film that is tailor-made to kill your spirit; one day it will be your corpse laid out on a slab similar to the ones in Aftermath, and it's that helpless identification with the subject matter that affects viewers the most: It's personal, it makes you feel vulnerable, it presents to you your own mortality that is both natural and open to abuse. And of course, most people don't want to be reminded of such things.

Emerging as part of Cerda's 'Death Trilogy', sandwiched between his black and white student film, The Awakening, and his beautiful shot in scope Genesis, Aftermath premiered at the Sitges Film Festival in October 1994 after seven months of intense work from pre-production to its first screening. It was met with staunchly polarized opinions from both those who were impressed and those who were appalled, and it became one of the most talked about films of the year, leaving similarly themed, big-budget dreck like Curdled for dust.

This word-of-mouth buzz and excitement followed the film across the Atlantic to its North American premiere at the 1997 FantAsia Film Festival in Canada where almost a thousand avid horror fans reacted in wild delight as Cerda's shockfest unspooled before their eyes (the 2003 documentary, In The Belly of The Beast, includes some invaluable footage of this event and also the fascinating reactions of people like Mitch Davis and Jim Van Bebber defending the film as a masterwork, and Chas Balun dismissing it as an over-hyped, pretentious student film).

Aftermath picked up the Public's Prize at FantAsia and Cerda became a cult celebrity in Montreal. The film became a mainstay on the bootleg video circuit (along with Genesis) until it was released on DVD by Unearthed Films. Later, German company Dragon released the Death Trilogy in a metallic box set with a shed load of extras including an anatomical figurine!

AFFLICTION (1996)

(aka Idiots with disgusting hobbies)
Dir: Mark Hejnar /USA

A mondo style film about a bunch of soulless and talentless people who try to shock with their redundant artistic statements. Razorblades, human dartboards, shit, and graphic sex. Basically the purpose of this documentary is to present a barrage of shock images based on extreme controversial personalities (aka Idiots with disgusting hobbies).

There's GG Allin of course in full display demonstrating his coprophiliac fetishes, the idiotic Mike Diana, who got arrested for obscenities, throwing up on a cross and the bible and masturbating with a cross, there's the even more idiotic 'Full Force Frank' who caused a fuss with his ideas on mass-murder and his gun fetish, music clips with extreme bands and stage performances, montages of random imagery and shock footage, self-mutilation, piercings, genital torture, gender benders, and sick or gory hardcore sex scenes. This documentary doesn't take a stance either way except to present it all in what it thinks is an art-piece, but this is humanity at its most absurdly depraved and idiotic. Not for the easily offended or anyone else.

AI NO CORRIDA (1976)

(aka In The Realm of The Senses)
Dir: Nagisa Oshima /Japan

Based on the true story of a woman who in 1936 was found wandering the streets of Tokyo with a severed penis tucked into her kimono, Nagisa Oshima's sexually explicit and deeply disturbing Ai no Corrida became infamous when it was seized by US customs in 1976, delaying its screening at the New York Film Festival.

In 1930s Japan, ex-prostitute Sada (Eiko Matsuda) gets a job at an inn owned by Kichizo (Tatsuya Fuji) and his wife. Kichizo begins an affair with Sada, eventually leaving his wife so that he can be with her. They stay at a geisha house in the red light district and indulge in constant sex. Their shenanigans are enough to even embarrass and shock the other prostitutes. In need of money, Sada agrees to become a prostitute herself and resumes contact with an ex-client of hers, who was once her school principal, and Kichizo has sex with a maid at the geisha house. Their sexual escapades become increasingly bizarre and dangerous, experimenting with domination and strangulation before the grisly finale...

Blurring the line between pornography and art, Ai no Corrida was tailor-made to break taboos. With graphic scenes of unsimulated penetration and fellatio, the film was nonetheless not intended to arouse sexual desire in the audience, and was instead created by writer/director Oshima as a completely honest depiction of encroaching madness brought on by an insatiable sexual mania.

Fuji and Matsudo are haunting in their roles as the doomed lovers, and Oshima takes great care in presenting the scenes in a serious manner with a delicate visual beauty of sparse colour, decor, and composition. And this sensitive approach is aided by an aesthetic which borrows from classical Japanese block prints and Kabuki theatre, combined with themes of sadomasochism and voyeurism. Oshima once remarked on Japanese culture, saying "People hurry to live and hurry to die", and Ai no Corrida ultimately serves as a mirror on the ceremonies of the society which spawned it.

The film premiered in Japan in 1976 with black optical blocks concealing the sexual details on screen (which for many years was a customary part of Japanese censorship). Oshima side-stepped the problems of making an 'obscene' film in Japan by having the footage processed in France, but this didn't stop the authorities from charging him with obscenity, and for years he was left to defend his film and his reputation in the courts.

When Ai no Corrida reached the UK it was denied a certificate by the BBFC but was allowed to play under a club license at the Gate's Cinema Club in Notting Hill in the late 70s for members only. By this point, the head of British censorship, James Ferman, had successfully altered the law with the introduction of the Obscene Publications Act. But even with the new bit of leniency brought in by the OPA, Ai no Corrida was not granted an official BBFC certificate until 1991.

Ferman, who was clearly an admirer of the film (although you certainly couldn't say the same of The Exorcist or The Texas Chainsaw Massacre, both of which he happily banned in the UK), personally approached Oshima for permission to employ an altering to one of the most problematic scenes in the film in which Sada reaches out and tugs at a young boy's penis. The scene caused problems for the British censors because, although Sada's character is clearly insane at that point in the film, the scene could not be passed intact because she grabs the boy's penis for real. With very good reason, UK law forbids any kind of sexual involvement of children in films, however integral to a plot such things may be, but Ferman re-set the scene by zooming in onto the top half of the screen. Thus in his words, "You see her intentions, but you don't see the contact".

Due to the Video Recordings Act, it was almost a decade later when Ai no Corrida was finally passed for a home video certificate in the UK in 2000, with the only form of censorship being the aforementioned optical zoom.

ALEXANDRA'S PROJECT (2003)

Dir: Rolf De Heer / Australia

The wife of a newly promoted business man takes the kids and leaves him. But she also leaves behind a nasty video tape for him to watch... This is a slow-burner but stick with it because there are some cruel surprises along the way. The performances of all involved are very impressive, the characters who seem to have everything are actually struggling to cope with their depressingly empty lives, and the whole scenario has been deliciously thought through
by director Rolf De Heer (whose previous work includes the equally unnerving Bad Boy Bubby and Dance To Me My Song).

Brief exchanges between the husband Steve (Gary Sweet) and his colleagues and neighbours come to mean so much in retrospect. The finger and cucumber speech is quite funny and it points towards some home truths about the mindset of men in general. Overall though, Alexandra's Project is the kind of film that delights in subverting the conventions of feminist tracts. The film never confirms whether Steve is really the scumbag he is accused of being, and in all the time we spend with this character in the film, he seems like a fairly decent kind of bloke. And this leaves us to question the mental state of Alexandra herself; is she justified in her actions, or is she just a sick and twisted nutcase? Well, that is very much left up to the viewer to decide.

Personally, I like to think that De Heer was merely poking fun at audience reactions to films, with many willing to go with whatever scenario is presented to them having only heard one side of the story. He seems concerned with mankind's almost deliberate 'blind spot' for anything that requires us to think for ourselves and make up our own minds.

Reactions to this film has been allover the place since it premiered in 2003. Some believed Steve's character to have been to blame for the evil that comes his way. Others, whilst recognising that Steve could be innocent, were still offended because it never occurred to them that this is exactly what director De Heer was getting at in the film. To put it bluntly, Alexandra's Project is the story of an insane woman who has managed to manipulate a weak-willed neighbour to aid her in getting revenge on her husband. She prostitutes herself and even uses her own body as a weapon against Steve with the help of their neighbour.

Whether the neighbour understands that he is just a pawn in an evil game is never revealed, but in either case it says a lot about the male of the species in that many of us would stoop to some pretty base levels just so that we can get our balls wet. And that the power of sex rests almost entirely with Alexandra.

Regardless of how Alexandra portrays him, Steve seems to be a decent, hardworking father and husband. In fact, he actually serves as a kind of stereotypical role-model of the modern world; he resembles one of those perfectly formed, diligent men who populate TV commercials; suited and booted and prepared to do anything for his family. He even goes to the trouble of stopping smoking because his young daughter asked him to.

The first half hour or so plays like a simple family drama even though we know that things are not okay with Alex (Helen Buday). Not only is she distracted by her 'project' but something else seems to be amiss, and we don't find out exactly how hurt or angry she is while the kids are around. The shock tactics of the film come at you slowly; De Heer preferring to turn up the heat gradually, making sure the revelations hit you where it hurts. And it works. There is a scene where Steve, having paused the tape, mumbles at the screen "I wonder what other tricks you have in that sick little mind of yours", and it's a pivotal moment because we the viewers are thinking the exact same thing.

Not recommended to gorehounds, but anyone who has a taste for the more sublime and sombre type of shocks could do a lot worse. The film also features one of the most awkward striptease moments in cinema history.

ALICE, SWEET ALICE (1976)

(aka Communion; aka Holy Terror)
Dir: Alfred Sole / USA

Alice (Paula Sheppard), a disturbed, destructive, foul-mouthed little girl loves making life hell for her family members and the residents in the area. Her mother (Linda Miller) is a devout Catholic who prepares for her other daughter, Karen's (Brooke Shields) communion. But Alice's nasty streak gets out of hand, and when good girl Karen is brutally murdered in church, the finger of blame is pointed at Alice. Throughout the police investigation and the intervening of nervous relatives suspicious of her, Alice doesn't show a glimpse of sorrow for her dead sister, runs rings around the police, and continues her spiteful attacks on the neighbours (most notably the obese Mr. Alphonso, played by Blood Sucking Freaks' Alphonso DeNoble), and more murderous mayhem ensues...

Through a string of excellent performances, complex plotting, and scenes of brutal violence, Alice Sweet Alice is a merciless attack on Catholicism. It's a film whose sociological viewpoint actively demands viewer participation, despite its roots in low-budget horror. The film's low end scale actually helps the proceedings, with its New Jersey setting offering up some believable locations and a sense of stuffy religious repression and the eruption of household tensions. Organised religion is the film's central target point, with its double-crossings, maliciousness, and ruthless treatment of its characters, randomly picking them off regardless of whether they deserve their fates or not.

The knife attacks are spectacular, as good as anything seen in 70s horror, and it isn't just the special effects that make the stabbings impressive, it's the overall execution of performances, editing, and the build-up, too. Many horror fans of the time would have put money on director Alfred Sole becoming the next big thing in American horror,
but that honour went to John Carpenter instead, even if his first big hit, Halloween, owes much to Sole's masterpiece. It's a shame there wasn't room at the top for both of these talented filmmakers. Sole's future genre offerings were scarce with the jokey slasher movie Pandemonium not even coming close to the greatness that is Alice Sweet Alice.

The film was originally released theatrically as Communion, then on video in edited form as Holy Terror. Alfred Sole was never happy with the cut of either of those presentations, and was eventually given the chance to tighten up his film in the editing room. But this new version has caused controversy with some fans annoyed at the deletion of a scene where Dom receives a phone call from his latest wife. The Anchor Bay DVD reinstates the footage, offering something of a definitive cut, and thus making everyone happy.

AMERICAN HISTORY X (1999)

Dir: Tony Kaye / USA

The leader of a white supremacy gang must face up to the effects of his lifestyle and the consequences it has on his family... Told from the perspective of an admiring younger brother (the superbly cast Edward Furlong), American History X charts the development of Derek Vinyard (Edward Norton), a smart young man who becomes a neo-Nazi after his father is shot dead by a black thug. He shaves his head, has a swastika tattooed on his chest, and rallies the local disaffected youth into joining him in his racist crew before he kills a pair of black thieves who attempt to steal his car. When Derek is released from prison after serving three years of his sentence, his younger brother, whose boyish looks bely his own racial hatred, is shocked and offended to discover that Derek is a reformed man who not only has grown back his hair but also wants to make amends for his previous crimes. Needless to say, his new perspective on life is not shared by the vicious gang he has left behind...

  Films which deal with racism, especially those churned out by the Hollywood system, tend to generalise the subject and rely on cardboard character types in order to drive the point across to the viewers that "racism is not good". And this approach to the touchy subject leaves no room for the complexities that are sometimes found at the roots of racism. And though American History X does have its problems as a film, such as relying on easy stereotypes and an uncomplicated morality, it does at least have the courage to explore the subject-matter in all its ugliness before delivering the expected moral message.

Edward Norton is magnetic as Derek, and is easily the most complex character in the film. We watch his development as a young man and the dangerous shifts in his ideals. His fierce rhetoric is perhaps the most important aspect of the film, and it's easy to make comparisons with the fiery hatred of right-wing radio hosts in America. It's the kind of poisonous bile that goes for the heart and not the head in its way of recruiting people into this reductive way of thinking. And American History X as a film is also guilty of these kinds of simple tactics.

Derek's racism is shown to have started when his father complains about the faults of preferential treatment in the workplace while the family have dinner. And later, Derek realises the error of his ways when he befriends a black man in jail. Such simple mechanisms offered to the viewers as a way of showing a young man embarking on a new way of life, and indeed seeing the error of his ways, remains unconvincing. And the black man also happens to be funny and serves as perhaps the only source of humour in the whole film; are we supposed to think 'oh look at him, a black guy... but he's a funny black guy so he must be a good guy really, and maybe I should have some sympathy for him'? These are just a couple of examples of the film dispensing with the complexities of real life racism and resorting to the clean and easy filmic methods of telling a story.

While Derek is in prison it is a character called Cameron (Stacy Keach) who takes over as leader of the gang, and he serves as a typical tyrant, a man who leeches onto the simmering rage of the local youth and turns them on to the 'joys' of racial hatred - He ultimately gives them a direction in life. The film is all the more interesting for having a scumbag character like Cameron, because despite the needless simplicity of much of this film, Cameron's character actually serves as a more honest and realistic hate monger. And his existence in American History X seems to shield the other kids from being directly to blame for their recruitment into such a gang. Cameron's main method of grabbing new skinheads is through the raw power of hardcore punk music; he allows aggressive bands to make a racket at his house, and the youngsters can't get enough. It's a well-known fact that in real life hardcore has been successful over the years as a source of recruitment for neo-Nazi/White power gangs because the aggression of it often rings home in bored, disenfranchised youth. It's the simple and uncomplicated noise that wins the hearts of these kids; that's their hearts, not their minds.

The film was directed by Englishman Tony Kaye, who had previously made TV commercials. He had a very public falling out with the studio over final cut of the film which he was unhappy with, and some commentators more or less accused him of cutting off his nose to spite his face. But as it stands, American History X is one of the better films that deals with racism. Lookout for some superb set-pieces including one of the most vicious acts of violence of any film made in the 90s. There's also a brutal attack on a convenience store, an argument at the dinner table that erupts into violence, and a gruelling prison rape.

AMERICAN PSYCHO (2000)

Dir: Mary Harron / USA

Not since the days of Joseph Ruben's The Stepfather (1986) had a major American film tackled social satire in the form of a slasher movie, and not since the days of Kathryn Bigelow's Near Dark (1987) had we seen such a violent film directed by a woman. Patrick Bateman (Christian Bale), a good-looking, wealthy Wall Street banker, tries to alleviate his soul-crushing boredom by engaging in ferocious acts of murder. Prostitutes, homeless bums, or even his colleagues are fair game for his senseless wrath and lack of conscience. No one around him suspects a thing as Patrick effortlessly blends in to the shallow narcissism and petty one-upmanship of big city life. We're left smirking at Bateman's monologues which detail his meticulous hygiene habits, snooty materialism, and ridiculous taste in music in between bouts of stylish slayings until he loses his sense of sanity altogether...

  Attempts to bring Bret Easton Ellis's outrageous novel to the big screen was never going to be easy; published in 1991, American Psycho the book was met with much controversy as it was widely misinterpreted as a nasty misogynist tract that wallowed in extreme violence and torture disguised as a thinly-plotted social satire. Mary Harron (who had previously directed the underrated I Shot Andy Warhol) does a fine job of replicating the antiseptic and blackly hilarious feel of the book. Unfortunately, the horrendous tortures of prostitutes in Ellis' original (which left me despairing for the evils of mankind when I read them) are not really touched upon in the film; Harron is a well-known feminist so maybe that's why she avoided depicting those gruelling chapters, and instead stays with the satirical vibe of the book.

Bale's Bateman is a touch more anxious and comical in the film than in the original, but the 'business card' scene is almost spot-on same as the book, and Bateman's loathsome yuppie monster and his world of literal cutthroat capitalism is fairly well portrayed overall. Andrzej Sekula's scope photography is a marvel, almost every frame can be taken out and used in a glossy haute couture magazine (except for the bloody bits, of course), and John Cale's modernist score keeps things from becoming too cosy.

American Psycho was met with problems both during and after production; Bale left the set when Leonardo DiCaprio expressed an interest in playing Bateman, but returned (along with Harron) when DiCaprio changed his mind. Lions Gate had no idea how to market the film and released it as they would a major blockbuster, which led to many mainstream movie-goers (who were used to the likes of The Sixth Sense and Hollow Man) scratching their heads at the ironies of an art film which unspooled before their eyes. It also ran into trouble with the MPAA who demanded lengthy cuts to the threesome frolics and the first axe murder scenes (they were later reinstated on the unrated region 1 DVD by Universal). In the UK and elsewhere in the world the film was untouched by the censor's chainsaws and all region 2 releases are uncut.

ANGEL HEART (1987)

Dir: Alan Parker / USA

In 1955 New York a mysterious boss of a law firm, Louis Cyphre (Robert De Niro), sends a seedy private eye, Harry

Angel (Mickey Rourke), to investigate the disappearance of a popular singer who is in debt to him. Angel heads off in search of the crooner and meets an odd bunch of occultists and weirdos from New York to Louisiana where he eventually discovers that the missing person had opted out of a pact with the devil. He then seems to plunge quite literally into hell.

Based on the novel Falling Angel by William Hjortsberg, Angel Heart was met with shock and awe by film fans and critics at the time who were expecting just another Faust knock-off, or something similar to Wes Craven's Serpent and The Rainbow. The pervading grimness, graphic bloodletting, and spooky twists and turns, however, seemed to be too much for everyday movie-goers. Often accused of being thoroughly unpleasant in detail, which it is, but devotees of the darker side of horror should get a kick out of this scorching hot tale of eternal damnation. It's quite simply one of the greatest horror movies of the 80s.

The MPAA demanded cuts to the scene where Rourke and Lisa Bonet writhe on the bed covered in chicken blood, but the same scene has been reinstated in its entirety on all DVD editions. It's always a sick pleasure to see the innocent Cosby kid Bonet getting naked and covered in chicken blood, so fans of celebrity skin watch out for that.

Resembling a cross between a gritty detective yarn, film noir, and full-bloodied horror, Angel Heart failed to make much of an impact at the box-office. It raked in around $17 million, just about breaking even with its budget costs.

However, it was on home video where the film quickly established itself as a cult classic with fans around the world appreciating the grim tone and mish-mash of genres.

ANGST (1983)

(aka Fear; aka Schizophrenia)
Dir: Gerald Kargl / Austria

lack that self-consciousness. One of the most disturbing and realistically executed killer movies of all time. In this straight forward story we follow a nameless criminal who has just been released from prison for stabbing his mother. But there's not a trace of guilt or remorse at all. In fact quite the opposite; in a series of fascinating but twisted voiceovers we soon learn that this creepy little man has no thoughts of trying to build a new life; the only thing that's on his mind is the search for new victims.

 'Addicted' to and aroused by the fear he sees in his victms eyes, we're challenged to tag along with this maniac as he goes about his work. He gets into a taxi and eventually tries to strangle the female driver. But because of his suspicious behaviour before-hand, she seems ready for anything and manages to fight him off and escape. So he wanders through the woods until he arrives at a large family home. He breaks in and snoops around and discovers a man in a wheelchair who appears to be both physically and mentally disabled ("I knew I would kill him but not immediately"). And when the rest of the family get back from a shopping trip, they're completely oblivious to the monster who is lurking in their home. The maniac then sets about a series of deeply unpleasant murders - The disabled son is slowly drowned in the bath tub in a truly agonising scene, the middle-aged mother is strangled, and the young daughter is repeatedly stabbed up and mutilated. He then rapes her bloody corpse in a frenzy (in the first full-on depiction of necrophilia in film history). And all of this is shot more or less in real time.

Unsurprisingly, this film is often referred to as 'Europe's answer to Henry-Portrait of a Serial Killer' (even though it pre-dates that film), but unlike John McNaughton's masterpiece, we get to see everything in unflinching detail in Angst. It's also based on the crimes of convicted mass murderer, Werner Kniesek, who killed three people in Slazburg, Austria in 1980 (and who, incidentally, made a failed escape attempt during the film's production). Quotes are taken from real life killers throughout; "I just love it when women shiver in deadly fear because of me. It is an addiction which will never stop." Those are the words that Kniesek used when addressing the Judge in court. Quotes are also used from the true confessions of the 'Vampire of Dusseldorf', Peter Kurten (true crime buffs will also spot similarities in the film relating to the latter case of Jack Unterweger).

Erwin Leder's central performance as the crazed killer is so full of bug-eyed, manic energy and unpredictability, it reminded me of Klaus Kinski at his nuttiest or even an actor from the silent era. It's the shifty and erratic behaviour that draws so much attention to this character, and is ultimately his downfall. And Leder captures that fear and twisted excitement so well. In real life, psychopathic killers are usually very good at concealing their sickness to appear quite normal to the everyday public. Even moments after committing the most horrendous crimes, the psycho killer can revert back to outward normality in a flash. But the killer explored in this film seems to lack that self-consciousness.

A major influence on Gaspar Noe, especially his Seul Contre Tous, Angst features a soundtrack which is more well-known than the film; Klaus Schulze of Tangerine Dream provides the ominous electronic score, of which the track 'Surrender' seems to be playing constantly, complimenting the ice-cold set decoration, colouring, and lighting of the film. Kudos to Zbigniew Rybczynski, whose handheld camera work was really quite innovative for the time. In fact, his work is so impressive that it's easy to forget that much of the film was indeed shot in real time. He also co-wrote the script and edited the film (according to French filmmaker Pascal Laugier, he even directed the movie too! Apparently 'Gerald Kargl' was just a pseudonym used by Rybczynski so that he could avoid facing responsibility if the film were to cause outrage! Unfortunately, I've been unable to verify this as fact).

Angst was released theatrically in Austria in the early 80s to some good reviews, but made no money and disappeared pretty fast. It then turned up in France on VHS under the title Schizophrenia and even garnered a bit of a cult fan base. In the UK it was the 'video nasties' era and potential distributers felt it would be a waste of time and money to release it here only to see it banned immediately, so the film was deemed 'too outrageous' and distributers wouldn't touch it. In America the film was slapped with a XXX rating, usually given to hardcore porn titles, so the market potential there was pretty slim... Over the next couple of decades Angst became a much talked about but little seen film, with awful looking scuzzy bootleg videos being the only way for horror fans to see it. Barrel Entertainment announced that they would release Angst uncut on DVD but the company went bust soon after, and it wasn't until 2005 that we saw a significant release of the film when German DVD label Epix Media issued the full uncut version in a very satisfying transfer.

Kargl (or Rybczynski, or whoever he is) fully financed the film on his credit card, and after completion he found himself stuck making TV commercials for years while he paid off his debts. He sacrificed a potentially great career to bring us this masterpiece.

POSTSCRIPT: THE REAL KNIESEK

Kniesek's psychiatrist described him as "extremely abnormal but not mentally ill". The real life Kniesek was mixed race but is white in the film. When released from prison, he drove to a town called Poelton, broke into a villa owned by a widow, Gertrud Altreiter, and found the son in a wheelchair. Later the mother and daughter returned from a shopping trip. He tied them up and gagged them, and dragged them into different rooms in the house. The daughter actually tried to seduce him as a way of softening him up but he was having none of it. He strangled the son and displayed his corpse to the mother and daughter before strangling the widow. The 25 year old daughter was then tortured and raped for hours before she too was murdered. He also killed the family cat, whereas in the film it's a pet dog which he takes with him and treats nicely. He also spent the night in the house with the bodies.

"I killed them simply out of lust for murder", he claimed, "I even gave the elder woman some medicine so that she would live longer". He tried to commit suicide in his prison cell but failed. A few years later he made an escape attempt, but failed.

ANTICHRIST (2009)

Dir: Lars Von Trier
/Denmark/Germany/France/Sweden/Italy/Poland

Lars Von Trier grew up in a very liberal Danish household in which his parents didn't believe in setting rules, and he was basically given free reign to do whatever the hell he liked. Some critics and psychologists have suggested that this kind of boundless freedom is the cause of his supposed depression and neurosis in later life, and the reason why he now seems to suffer from every phobia known to man, and why he insists on making films designed with maximum mischief in mind. If this is so, then it follows that we who lived a more normal childhood with rules and punishments have developed a fascination for all that is wild and chaotic and forbidden. Well, at least in my case that's certainly so.

Thus, judging by this kind of logic, Antichrist should be absolute bliss for a horror fanatic like myself. It seems like the perfect match; the work of an artist at a complete distrust of the world projected from a screen into my own retinas that lens a mind that yearns for the darkness and the forbidden and the horror. Except, of course, that Antichrist is not really a horror movie, at least not in the way that most of us expect a horror movie to be.

Antichrist opens with a monochrome prologue shot in stylish slow-motion. It shows a man and a woman having sex in the shower (Willem Dafoe and Charlotte Gainsbourg, with a little help from a couple of porn actors standing in for the graphic penetration shots). In the bedroom, their young child, Nick, climbs out of his cot and lifts himself up onto the sil to watch the falling snow from the open window. And just as his parents reach orgasm, he falls to his death.

After collapsing at the funeral procession, Charlotte is hospitalised for a month (I'll be using the actor's names, Charlotte and Willem, because the character's names are not mentioned on the credits or in the entire film). Willem visits her daily and she mentions that "Dr. Wayne said my grief pattern is atypical". It seems odd and a bit sarcastic for her to use psychological terminology to express her state of mind. The words sound cold and clinical the way her emotions and raw grief are labeled like stages on a chart; it doesn't seem natural to put a medical spin on her deep sorrow, even if the words did come from Dr. Wayne originally. Perhaps she used the words because Willem is a trained therapist and has a good understanding of terminology and psychological states, or maybe she used the words because they offended her, and she passes them on to her husband as a way of making him angry at Dr. Wayne for addressing his suffering wife in such a cold and clinical way. If so, it seems to have worked. For, though he doesn't confront Dr. Wayne, he criticises the doctor's treatment of her and checks her out of hospital the very next day. But in the meantime Charlotte blames herself for Nick's death. He tries to deflect the grief away by reminding her that he was with her when he died and that he should be just as much to blame. It's a comment which she later uses against him.

The next day when he checks her out of hospital with the intention of treating her in his own way, she accuses him of being arrogant. He argues against that by saying "No therapist can know as much about you as I do", and tries to assure her that he is doing it because he loves her. He takes Charlotte back to their apartment where the therapy can begin.

Her grief gets worse, and she understandably resents the fact that her husband is treating her like a patient. She lashes out at him as a way of trying to break his cold medical manner; "You've always been distant from me and Nick. Now that I come to think of it, very very distant." He doesn't react in the way she wants - that of a loving father and husband - but as a psychologist; "Ok. Can you give me some examples?" he asks. She tries again, "I never interested you until now that I'm your patient."

A man of Willem's profession should have known it would be a bad idea to attempt a treatment of his wife at such a difficult time. Her reactions are cruel and hurtful, and obviously disastrous to their relationship. She wouldn't have had that kind of ammunition or personal connection to her designated therapist had she stayed in hospital, and Willem probably recognises this but stubbornly sticks to his guns, no doubt as part of his male pride - He knows what's best for his wife. He stays unmoved even when she interprets his cold manner as proof that he isn't grieving; "You're indifferent as to whether your child is alive or dead. I bet you have a lot of clever therapist replies to that, haven't you?"

Charlotte's grieving gets worse, or at least much more physical and aggressive. Dafoe is there with her every step of the way, helping her through her night terrors and nightly panic attacks, but he insists on keeping the strict doctor-patient role. He also uses terminology to explain her state of mind; according to him, Charlotte has reached the "anxiety stage" of her mourning, and this echoes the earlier words of Dr. Wayne (the 'atypical grief pattern'), which probably offended her, and now sees her husband monitoring her in the same clinical way like a slide under a microscope. She later pounces on him for sex in a frantic and hysterical manner; he pins her down to the bed and jokes "You should never try to screw your therapist". He's actually only half joking. He knows they were having sex the moment their son died, and will be aware of how much guilt and resentment it would later cause if they were to give in to their physical desires at that moment.

Willem takes Charlotte out to Eden, a place of country wilderness and isolation where she was supposed to have taken Nick on a holiday. Eden connotes an obvious biblical reference, but also, as the couple trek through the woods to their cabin, she complains that "The ground is burning", a clue to her new hellish perspective on life and nature. Willem goes off alone through the woods while Charlotte rests and he sees a deer in a clearance; the deer is in the process of giving birth, but the birth has gone wrong and the fawn hangs from the doe's behind, swinging from side to side in the embryonic sack, at the mercy of nature and its elements. The deer's eyes have that look of bewilderment and confusion, a frightened animal in the midst of nature, and when the camera zooms in on Willem's eyes, we can see that he shares that same haunted look; it's a shot that reminds us that he's in pain too, not just his wife, and for all his knowledge and expertise in psychology, he doesn't really hold the answers, and the environment is just as harsh and unforgiving to him as it is to everyone else.

Eden brings the couple face to face with nature. Even when they are out in the open air their voices sound strangely echoed; this perhaps reflecting the enclosure and isolation of their grief. Mother Nature is shown in all its stark reality; its harshness and obliviousness as dead animals decay in the earth. Nature doesn't care, nature just is.

The unimaginable pain of losing a son is made all the more difficult to accept in an environment that is unmoved and unsympathetic. Charlotte hears Nick crying and she races through the wilderness and the woods calling his name - This is not a nightmare sequence, it's a real waking moment, and it goes to show how even her own mind is part of this unforgiving nature; the pain and the torment in her heart is just as brutal and unsympathetic as the space and sky that surrounds her. She wants to lash out at the injustice of it all, but who can she blame? She first attacks Willem and accuses him of being arrogant once again. She then attacks nature itself, explaining that everything she thought was beautiful about Eden has now become "hideous" to her. Acorns rain down onto the cabin making a loud clattering sound and she describes the noise as "cries", and concludes that "Nature is Satan's church".

Eden was supposed to help Charlotte, but her exposure to the place is having the opposite effect; it seems she connotes the screams and 'cries' of nature with that of her own son whom she thought she heard crying earlier that day - Nick, her own flesh and blood, had no more significance in the world than a spilled acorn; just another piece of nature's debris. These backward steps into negativity are of much concern for Willem, because her new perspective on life goes against his own training and male rationality. He tries to counter this by stressing that "Thoughts distort reality, not the other way round", but his words only seem to confirm the opposite (as they will do again later in the film), and serve as an illustration of how men and women are very different. And this is perhaps the first true sign of misogyny in the film.

For Willem, his relationship is of paramount importance to him even though he is systematically wrecking it in his own bullish and pig-headed way of trying to do what's best. He seems to have put his own grief on hold in order to help his wife get through the worst of her pain. Charlotte treats him as part punch bag, part crutch, part shoulder to cry on, part therapist, and part husband. She lashes out and attacks him just as much as she needs him; she even bites him at one point and draws blood, perhaps as a direct way of testing his strength, of testing how much room she has for her emotions to manouevre. But it's important to remember that it was Willem who put himself in that position by checking her out of hospital in the first place. Meanwhile, Charlotte's emotions are back and forth; happy one moment and explosive the next.

Late one night while she sleeps, Willem browses through Charlotte's research papers. She had been writing a thesis on gynocide throughout the ages, and something written in those pages causes him deep concern. Charlotte's initial feminist stance in studying the history of misogyny had eventually led her to the opposite opinion; she concludes that because nature is fundamentally evil, and that women's bodies are governed by this nature through menstruation and pregnancy, then women as a whole must be evil too. The later scene where Willem confronts her about this the following morning is very pivotal and is the most important scene in the film. But later that night Willem makes the big mistake of sleeping with Charlotte, and thus opening that can of worms, guilt, on her part which will come back to haunt them both. It's ironic how Willem's natural bodily urges causes the final breakdown of their relationship, and also goes to confirm - at least in this instance - that nature has indeed had a destructive and seemingly evil effect on both his and Charlotte's well-being. And perhaps Charlotte recognises this; before sex, she demands to be hit, and when Willem refuses, she accuses him of not loving her. She then storms off and masturbates by a tree in the woods. Willem the psychologist then disappears completely, and what we're left with is Willem as his true self; a confused and bewildered animal in the midst of nature who ultimately has no more understanding of the world and its mysteries than that poor deer he saw in the woods earlier. The unruly spark of nature's ways are everywhere all around him; a fox even looked him in the eye and uttered the words "Chaos reigns", but still he resisted to acknowledge it until now. He approaches Charlotte outside by the tree and he fucks her and he slaps her as many times as she wants him to because he has now given himself up to the chaos; he is now in her world and his slaps are a cry for help just like the clattering of acorns on the cabin roof, and she will show him how evil nature can be.

With the sunrise Willem thinks himself to be back in control. It is hinted throughout the film that the daytime represents the world of the masculine with calm, order, clear sightedness and rationality, whereas the evening is the realm of femininity, a world of darkness, mystery, and the irrational (an idea also explored in Dario Argento's Suspiria). The next scene is a key point in the film. Willem confronts Charlotte about her thesis; he tells her "Good and evil, they have nothing to do with therapy. Do you know how many innocent women were murdered during the 16th Century alone just for being women? I'm sure you do. Many. Not because they were evil". Charlotte's reply is resigned but shielded, just blase words of agreement uttered by millions of women over the centuries under the domination of the masculine rationale, "I know. It's just that sometimes I forget". Willem continues, "The evil you talk about is an obsession. Obsessions never materialise, it's a scientific fact. Anxieties can't trick you into doing things you wouldn't do otherwise; it's like hypnotism, you can't be hypnotised into doing something you wouldn't normally do, something against your nature. Do you understand me?... You don't have to understand me, just trust me". There is a desperate pleading in his voice as if his own convictions are crumbling in the face of the opposite that he sees all around him. Indeed, he even CONFIRMS that Charlotte is evil by his own statement.

In the autopsy report it is mentioned that Nick had a slight deformity in his feet, but that it was "nothing significant". Dafoe believes the deformity to have been caused by Charlotte who would sometimes put his shoes on the wrong feet. He shows her a photograph of Nick sitting in the grass with his shoes on the wrong way round and she still doesn't notice until he points it out to her. Now, director Lars Von Trier is clearly trying to 'put the boot in' here with regards to offending the fairer sex; the whole sequence may seem to be 'nothing significant' but this is just a ploy to make the implied accusations seem less significant than they really are (everything is significant in this film to such an extent that even the main character's names are not even mentioned because they represent men and women as a whole). With this scene Von Trier implies that women are bad mothers, that they harm their children in a series of small and insignificant ways, until the accumulated damage results in your typical adult. In my experience it has always been the mothers who are quick to notice when their children have their shoes on the wrong feet, and I've certainly never known any mother to have even accidentally put their kids' shoes on the wrong way round. But there is also some ambiguity here relating to the earlier scene where Willem sees the deer in the woods; sometimes nature goes wrong, sometimes the birthing process goes wrong, sometimes children have slight deformities at birth that have nothing to do with how they are raised. The implication that the 'evil' of women is just an extension of the 'evil' of nature itself. Thus Von Trier is suggesting that if nature doesn't get you then your mother will.

Earlier in the film, Willem drew up a pyramid chart and asked Charlotte to list the places where she would feel the most afraid and exposed. She placed Eden near the top of the chart. But later on Willem comes to the conclusion that Eden wasn't the true answer; he scribbles out the word and replaces it in thick marker pen with the word 'ME'. It's nightfall, and he has once again entered the world of the feminine; only now is he willing to fully acknowledge that Charlotte is indeed evil and that she fears herself more than anything else in the world. She immediately attacks him in a hysterical frenzy, beats him unconscious, jerks him off, and then bores a hole through his leg with a hand drill before attaching a heavy iron lock onto him by hooking it through the wound and tightening it with a wrench. She then wanders off and throws the wrench under the cabin porch.

Willem comes to in agony and manages to crawl outside to the woods and slide himself into a fox hole that is hidden in the roots of a tree. Charlotte returns to find him gone and then charges through the woods looking for him and calling him a bastard. In a blackly comic scene, nature is shown to be on Charlotte's side when a black crow squawks loudly in the fox hole giving away Willem's presence. He tries to silence the pest by grabbing its beak but this doesn't work. In the end he resorts to beating its head in as a way of putting an end to the squawks, but it's too late; Charlotte knows where he is and she uses a garden spade to beat him and jab at him, causing the earth to crumble in around him. Poor Willem has had a bit of a rough night; he's been knocked out, mutilated, beaten with a spade, and buried alive. Way to go Doc! Nice therapy you've got going there, looks to have worked a treat!

A remorseful Charlotte later returns to the scene and digs him up. She drags him back to the cabin and continues in her misogynistic observations ("A crying woman is a scheming woman"). She masturbates using his hand. This brings out her guilt - as shown with flashbacks to the night their son died - and she takes a pair of scissors and snips off her own clitoris. For Willem, enough is enough; he ends up slaying the beast and burning her body out in the open. And in a strange epilogue, he is descended upon by hundreds of blank-faced women.

Antichrist was met with cries for it to be banned wherever it played. It's dark, violent, sexually and emotionally explicit, and undoubtedly misogynistic (even the film's title logo, with the T in Antichrist displaying an O on top reminiscent of the female symbol, implying that femininity is connected to evil). But the film is also expertly made and offers two stunning performances from Dafoe and Gainsbourg. Von Trier's films have never been beautiful to look at but Antichrist is an exception; Anthony Dog Mantle's superb camera work is a marvel to behold, and the stylish slow-motion shots in Eden are nothing short of breath-taking (the film looks astonishing on Blu-Ray).

The film is a mix of the sacred and the profane, good and evil, darkness and light, art and artifice; it borrows heavily from the horror genre - The cabin in Eden looks very similar to the cabin in The Evil Dead, and the subliminals are clearly taken from The Exorcist. Von Trier also uses horror influences to create that eerie atmosphere and dark demonic imagery. But perhaps the biggest influence came from Andrzej Zulawski's Possession; this underrated masterpiece also explores the fundamental differences and incompatability of men and women, and also boasts a superb performance from Isabel Adjani as the hysterical and shrieking woman, and sticks to a cold blue-ish colour scheme and themes of darkness, and the enigma of nature and the feminine, and possession.

Von Trier claims to have been depressed when he wrote and directed the film, but it's difficult to take anything he says seriously anymore. In an earlier film, The Boss of It All, he claimed that it was shot in 'Otomovision', a computer technique that was "A principal for shooting film developed with the intention of limiting human influence by inviting chance in from the cold". As ridiculous as this may sound, many film critics took it seriously and went into great detail about this 'technique' when reviewing the film.

As for Antichrist, it's very much up to you to decide how seriously you take it. Von Trier opens himself up for accusations of misogyny by linking womankind with the cruel and chaotic 'evil' of nature. But Gainsbourg's character, after all, is meant as a symbolic representation. The overall message is a troubling one, and seems to be that nature was created by an evil and irrational Antichrist, and the only way for man to get through this hell is to live by violent domination, not rationality. Only then can he get to grips with nature and fruitfully pro-create.

ASSAULT! JACK THE RIPPER (1976)

(Orig title- Bôkô Kirisaki Jakku)
Dir: Yasuharu Hasebe /Japan

A young couple agree that they both feel sexually aroused by the act of murder and bloody mutilation, and so embark on a sex and killing spree. I'm not sure what Jack The Ripper has to do with any of this, but hey, the Ripper still sells, right? This couple seem to get along fine until the boyfriend (Yukata Hayahashi) ventures out alone for his own thrill-kills, and leaving his girl behind (how selfish!).

The roof-top crotch-stabbing and unplanned escape debacle says a lot about a killer's complacency and arrogance that sets in if they're not careful. The girlfriend sees news reports of his murders on TV and goes ape shit until she realises she may lose him, then calms down a bit. The absurdity of this sequence is that she feels so jealous of missing out on the action (not necessarily the violence, but missing out on HIM, knowing that he's been out there getting his sick kicks without her) that it feels like a dark send-up of the dynamics of the modern relationship. She tries to show him what he's been missing and unbuttons his jeans; we're expecting a nice blowjob scene but she pulls out his murder blade instead (symbolic?).

Before long it becomes clear that it's the boyfriend who has the real murder-lust, and the girl just agrees and tags along with him out of a desperate and deranged love (shades of Brady and Hindley, moreso than Jack The Ripper). We get oodles of soft core sex scenes which usually get pretty boring in this type of fare, but here they're done quite well, and the girlfriend (played by Tamaki Katsura, who was requested to sport an afro hairstyle for the film by director Hasebe) has the most beautiful breasts which makes it all the more easy on the eyes. The body count rises dramatically at the film's finale and we're even offered a warped tragedy of sorts (although I'm sure many viewers certainly won't see it that way).

Emerging as the second part of Hasebe's 'Violent Pink Trilogy' which kicked off with Rape! and concluded with the notorious Rape! 13th Hour, Assault! Jack The Ripper was received the most positively by the critics. It was still treated as an outcast movie by the mainstream public, but the producers at the Nikkatsu studios were so happy with the critical appraisals of their film that they decided to up the ante and push the rape theme into overdrive with their next Roman Porno offering, Rape! 13th Hour. It was a move which backfired horribly when 13th Hour was widely deemed to be one of the most offensive movies of all time and almost ruined the Nikkatsu Corporation. The fact that the very same critics who hated 13th Hour for its ugly misogyny but were happy to write lovingly about a film which depicts a pair of deranged sex killers beggars belief.

Assault! Jack The Ripper is arguably the best in the trilogy, and includes many odd little quirks that make Japsploitation all the more interesting, like the connection between food and sex that is always hinted at throughout the film, the scene in the abandoned bowling alley - Was that an actual police car siren, or was it the filmmakers inventing their own sound effects on the cheap? Also, the crazy self-mutilating girl in the taxi at the beginning - perhaps a little homage to The Texas Chainsaw Massacre? And the crotch-stabbing scenes give Giallo a Venezia a run for its money.

AT MIDNIGHT I WILL TAKE YOUR SOUL (1963)

(Orig title: A Meta-Noite Laverei Sua Alma)
Dir: Jose Mojica Marins / Brazil

Welcome to the strange films of Jose Mojica Marins, a heady mixture of gothic horror and desolate cruelty, wanton surrealism and German Expressionism, Catholic guilt and Nietzschean nihilism. He wrote, directed, produced, and starred in Brazil's first ever horror movie, and created that country's most infamous character, the cackling gravedigger known as Ze do Caixao (or 'Coffin Joe').

His horror career began in 1963 with At Midnight I Will Take Your Soul, which offers up two introductions before the film itself begins; one from Coffin Joe himself and another from an old gypsy woman who urges viewers to leave the theatre before it's too late... Coffin Joe is the undertaker of a desolate village who attacks the residents for his own warped amusement. He keeps the local women in bondage and tortures them with deadly spiders, picks fights in bars, eats meat on Good Friday, and cuts off someone's finger with a broken bottle. Turns out that Coffin Joe is looking for the perfect female to be the mother of his son, but the residents don't seem to offer any suitable candidates, that is until the beautiful Terezinha shows up.

Shot in thirteen days, At Midnight is a remarkable achievement for a home-made horror movie. Taking its inspiration from the Universal horror cycle of the 30s and the EC comic books of the 50s (especially Tales From The Crypt), it also bares a close resemblance to Mario Bava (the graveyard scenes in Black Sunday), and Terence Fisher (whose 50s Hammer horrors were also a big influence on Marins). All of the actors used in the film were non-professional, either friends or relatives of the director, and they did a remarkable job, especially the young women who underwent all manner of discomfort and humiliation in the making of the film.

It is Marins himself though who deserves the bulk of the credit for single-handedly creating the Brazilian horror genre and creating its most infamous son, the maniac with long curly fingernails, top hat, and piercing eyes (you only have to look at pictures of Coffin Joe and Strewel Peter to know who Freddy Krueger's parents really are). At Midnight became a huge hit with audiences in Brazil where it played non-stop for sixteen months in Sao Paulo alone while Catholics complained of its blasphemous content. But this kind of interference from the nation's Catholics did nothing to quell Marins' thirst for the forbidden; he would return a couple of years later for the even more outrageous This Night I'll Possess Your Corpse.

AUDITION (1999)

(Orig title: Odishon)
Dir: Takashi Miike /Japan

"Kiri, kiri, kiri". When Audition made its Western premiere at the Edinbourgh Film Festival in 2000, most of those in attendance had never heard of Takashi Miike or the fact that he was fast becoming one of the most outrageous filmmakers on the planet. And when the projector bulb dimmed at the end, some of those lucky enough to have caught the film wished they hadn't as it turned out to be a completely different filmic experience than what they had expected, and were unable to rid their memories of the sadistic tortures they had just witnessed.

  Mainstream horror doesn't get any more stomach-churning than Audition, an almost perfectly crafted venus flytrap of a movie that runs like a quirky romantic drama for an hour, and features a man in the middle of a mid-life crisis searching for love. However, what he finds instead is the ultimate Sadean nightmare in the flesh. So if you still haven't seen this film yet then I urge you to stop reading now and go and check it out.

After the death of his wife Yoko, Aoyama (Ryo Ishibashi) raises their son alone. His movie producer friend knows all about Aoyama's loneliness and suggests that he hold an audition to find his next beau. Realising how much of a hassle dating is to a middle-aged man, Aoyama agrees, and together they set up a fake film audition. The girl of his dreams appears in the form of Asami (Eihi Shiina); young, beautiful, and artistically talented, they begin their tentative relationship, but she remains very vague when asked about her personal life and past relationships. Even those who knew her are less forthcoming about her mysterious past. And then things take a turn for the worse...

This is the film that propelled Takashi Miike to global notoriety, but those expecting a flashy and gory piece of ultra-violence like Dead Or Alive or Ichi The Killer may be disappointed because Audition is not that kind of film. It's a slow-burner that takes its time in its build up before it shows its teeth, but trust me, it bites. And it works best on those who have no idea of what's in store (like the fans and critics at the Edinbourgh Film Festival).

Many interpretations have been bounded around concerning the subtext of the film, from feminist revenge fantasy, a comment on modern dating rituals, to postmodern genre-blending, and even as a cross between Fatal Attraction and Misery! Some critics have seen similarities with Joseph Conrad's Heart of Darkness in Audition's portrayal of a man's complicit relationship with Hell. Dressed in ghostly white, Asami has been deemed a mental emanation of Aoyama's rather than an actual woman. But the most interesting interpretation centres on the cerebral aspects of dream distortion.

The final reel of the film is a physical illustration of the mixture of guilt and fear that Aoyama feels towards both his ex (Yoko, who died), and the mysterious Asami. The horrific scenes at the end of the film are all a dream. That is, all that happens between Aoyama being covered with a sheet after going to bed with Asami and his waking up for a glass of water is all dreamt. The dream continues when he goes back to bed. His new beau's 'baggage' is, of course, only alluded to, but it's enough for Aoyama's imagination to work into a terrifying expression of his own fears and personal sense of guilt via dream distortion. Two thirds of the movie are played out straight forward like a conventional drama; it's only near the end when events take on a disturbing and surreal tone. Freud wrote that the ego works as a censor and relaxes somewhat while you sleep, but is still at work repressing unconscious drives. If your dream becomes too explicit in its meaning then the censor hasn't been sufficient enough in distorting the dream and the whole thing is just wiped from your memory (we supposedly dream all the time, night after night, but we can only remember the occasional dream after waking). The interesting thing here is that Aoyama perhaps won't even remember his nightmare the next day, it's just too revealing for his ego to acknowledge. Much of it will be repressed, edited, or wiped from his consciousness altogether. And his unconscious will continue to throw up its symbols of baggage, guilt, fear, helplessness, and torment - We are the monsters and agents of our own nightmares.

As for Takashi Miike, he has gone from strength to strength, becoming one of Japan's most bankable filmmakers with subsequent fare like Visitor Q, Izo, and Imprint, and breaking box office records with Kuroozu Zero II and Yatterman (both of which raked in more than three billion yen, out-selling even the most popular of mainstream releases in Japan). A truly staggering feat for an artist who has never once compromised on his edgy vision. Only in Japan is it possible to become a household name by continually rattling your audience and bombarding them with some of the most extreme imagery of the decade.

AUSCHWITZ (2011)

Dir: Uwe Boll /Canada/Germany

Uwe Boll became infamous for a series of ineptly made video game adaptations like Alone In The Dark and House of The Dead which have been described as cinematic train wrecks but still managed to garner a bit of a cult following. More recently he has taken the indie route with a string of disturbing low budget films focusing on the dark side of human nature in Seed, Stoic, and Rampage, all of which were reviled by international censors and critics but adored by his growing army of fans. But, perhaps driven by the desire to be taken seriously as a filmmaker, Boll has also tried his hand at films based on true events, with the interesting Tunnel Rats, Darfur, and most problematic of all, Auschwitz.

Those expecting a quick exploitationer based on the worst atrocity of the 20th Century will be in for a surprise here as Boll makes it clear in the film's introduction that he is undoubtedly very passionate about that time in history, and also angry that many people (according to Boll, at least half the world's population) have no idea about the Nazi death camps. His mission statement is clear: People should never forget what happened at Aushcwitz.

First up we get documentary footage of college students being interviewed on camera about their understanding of the death camps. It soon becomes apparent that their knowledge is hazy at best. Then we're shown a dramatised account of a train load of Jews arriving at Auschwitz. They are changed out of their clothes and then marched to the gas chamber. Boll himself cameos as an SS officer who guards the doorway (perhaps his small role serves as a reminder of his indirect complicitness with the Holocaust, simply for being German? A nation's guilt personified?). The film as a whole is very sensitive to the suffering of the victims, unlike Andrey Iskanov's Philosophy of a Knife which seems to wallow in the gruesome torture and ethnic cleansing of World War II. Boll's film is certainly no easy ride though; we see people being gassed, corpses pushed into the ovens and licked by the flames of modern barbarity, little boys are shot in the back of their heads. Real archive footage of piles of bodies awaiting mass burial is also inserted into the film lest the audience should fail to comprehend the horrors played out before
our eyes. Even the deliberate and methodical way the Cyclon B is poured into the air ducts is chilling. As the

deadly fumes fill the chamber and the victims scream and bang on the iron doors with their fists, we can hear the arrival of another train load of doomed souls at a nearby station. The bored soldiers sit around casually discussing their work whilst looting through a mound of personal possessions belonging to the Jews. Boll closes the proceedings with a little speech in broken English; here he justifies the making of the film: "We have to make sure that crimes doesn't happen. We have to make sure that something like this is not getting forgotten or that somebody can repeat it".

The original teaser trailer for Auschwitz caused a storm on the web as it graphically shows the corpse of a child being pushed into an incinerator, and people were accusing Boll of gross exploitation on such a sensitive subject even before the film itself had been released. Auschwitz was then rejected by the Berlin Film Festival which resulted in the director threatening to sue the programmers for 'breach of trust and unfair competition in its selection process'. When the film finally did see the light of day the critics weren't too kind, and they labeled it a shoddy exercise in bad taste. In an attempt to defend his film, Boll commented "If you see all the Auschwitz movies made in a row, from Schindler's List to The Boy In The Striped Pyjamas, in all those you will not see what actually happened in Auschwitz [...] It's not a movie about heroes or survivors, it's a film about the daily routine of a human slaughterhouse. And I think it is important that one movie actually shows what really happened at Auschwitz". That's all well and good a comment but it was soon to backfire on him as people then went to see the film expecting detailed historical accuracy in the minutae of everything from the uniforms, sets, and methods of execution, including exactly how many Jews were put into the chamber at each time, etc. And of course, those hoping for a film with that kind of detailed accuracy came away disappointed too.

Boll was also under fire from people who accused him of exploiting the Holocaust in a previous film, Bluberella, in which a gun-toting overweight woman goes to war against the Nazis. Boll claims that Bluberella was made simply as a way of securing the funding for Auschwitz.

AUTO FOCUS (2002)

Dir: Paul Schrader /USA

The story of Bob Crane, a Californian DJ who became a star when he landed himself a role in the US sitcom, Hogan's Heroes, and then descended into sex and drugs debauchery and eventually hit rock bottom as his marriage disintegrated and was found bludgeoned to death in his own bed.

Writer/director Paul Schrader is at the top of his game here as he continues in his fascination with sex as a substitution for a life of substance, the seduction of porn, and reckless characters who add to their own corruption and downfall. Schrader doesn't flinch from depicting the sexcapades that made up Bob Crane's life. Schrader remains completely committed and non-judgmental in his approach to telling the sad story, unsentimentally cutting open Crane's addictions to fame and technology and sex (the latter nowadays referred to as 'sex addiction', a term that I have never agreed with; sex is a biological need, you can't become addicted to it. Some have a stronger sex-drive than others - and more opportunities, that's all), and clinically exploring these matters like some kind of cinematic autopsy.

Also on top form is actor Greg Kinnear whose performance here surpasses anything he has ever done in his career, before or since. He manages to make Crane likable even as he spirals way out of control, never asking the audience to sympathise with this stupidly oblivious sleaze ball. And he is aided by the brilliant Willem Dafoe, who plays the gadget man, Carpenter, who is a master at pathetic seediness and neediness. The mutual dependency between these two characters forms the core of the movie as Carpenter provides the contacts and Crane the star power. The scene where Crane learns of a wandering finger after an orgy is hilarious ("You put your finger in my ass?!!!").

AVERE VENT'ANNI (1978)

(To Be Twenty) Dir: Fernando Di Leo / Italy

Two beautiful young women meet on a beach and discover that they both have something in common - They're both "Young, hot, and pissed off", so they head off to Rome and their attitude gets them into all kinds of adventures. They stop by at some commune of low-life hippies and indulge in sex, fights, tantrums, and lesbianism (but this is 70s lesbianism which basically means lots of kissing and stroking and little else). Whilst staying at the commune they're asked to pay their way, so they reluctantly agree to go door to door selling encyclopedias, and this leads to more fun and games. It's supposed to be a comedy but the gags are old and worn out for the most part. The 'La la la la la' on the soundtrack becomes annoying very quickly, as do the two young leads (Gloria Guida and Lilli Carati). Much of the film plays like a tourist's travelogue. Anyway, after cavorting with stoned radicals and a pretentious filmmaker, the commune is raided by the police, and the girls are ordered to get out of Rome or face being arrested. So they decide to leave, but on their journey home something dreadful happens...

There seems to be some kind of vague political/sociological message here but it's never made clear (perhaps a comment on the death of 60s idealism and a rude wake up call to the violence and cynicism of the 70s?). The ending of the film is notorious, but be sure to catch the uncut version because the American version has a completely different ending, apparently. The last ten minutes are very dark but it's not enough to save it.

AXE (1974)

(Orig title: Lisa, Lisa; aka California Axe Massacre)
Dir: Frederick Friedel / USA

Not your typical video nasty. For, although it was made on a tiny budget of $25,000 and is a fairly grim and downbeat affair, Axe is nonetheless an atmospheric mood-piece that possesses genuine artistic merit, despite its lurid title.

Three criminals are on the run after a killing and a bungled robbery. They race their getaway car to a remote farmhouse where they intend to hideout until the dust settles. The people who live in the house - the wheelchair-bound mute grandfather, and a disturbed teenage girl, Lisa - seem like easy prey to the trio of hoodlums, but this kind of cocksure bravado overlooks just how dangerous Lisa is...

Axe was written and directed by former fashion photographer Frederick Friedel who was just 25 years old when he shot the film. His naivete and inexperience ironically helped rather than hindered the proceedings; he kept the production on a miniscule basis, with just a handful of sets and characters, and his way of stretching the running time to meet the 'feature length' requirements was frankly ingenious - He allowed the scenes the space to breathe in the editing room and allowed the end credits to run their full course, creating an intense atmosphere to prevail throughout, and it also offered composers George Newman Shaw and John Willhelm the chance to shine with their fantastic score that plays uninterrupted at the end. The result is a beautiful, poetic mood-piece that is unlike anything else ever shown at a drive-in theatre. Friedel (who cast himself in the role as Billy, one of the crims) is also aided by some decent performances from Jack Canon who plays the leader of the gang, Leslie Lee who plays the withdrawn Lisa, and Douglas Powers as the grandfather whose mute and crippled existence limited his role to his intensely expressive eyes.

All was going well for the film when it played a few dates under its original title, Lisa Lisa, until Friedel secured a distribution deal with Harry Novak and his Box Office International company. Lisa Lisa, along with Friedel's follow-up film, Date With a Kidnapper, had their titles changed immediately to Axe and Kidnapped Coed, respectively. Novak was also skilled at ripping people off, and Friedel barely saw a penny of revenue from the film's modest success at the drive-ins. Stung and disillusioned by the experience, Friedel backed away from the movie business and was unable to pay back his financiers, and this resulted in family members of those who bankrolled the film committing suicide, and Friedel wanting to murder Novak. That's the tragic side of indie filmmaking for you (see Stephen Thrower's excellent book, Nightmare USA, for the full story).

In the UK, Axe found itself on the 'video nasties' list and was kept out of our homes for years until the BBFC relented and passed it uncut in 2005, allowing us to finally lay eyes on this idiosyncratic gem. Sometimes referred to as 'America's answer to Repulsion', Lisa Lisa works best at night in a hazy frame of mind. Don't expect a traditional 'join-the-dots' type of narrative, but a dark and troubling dream, and you're on the right track.

BAD BIOLOGY (2008)

Dir: Frank Henenlotter / USA

Bad Biology sees the welcome return of writer/director Frank Henenlotter after a 16 year break from directing, and the results are typically unpredictable in keeping with the native New Yorker's track record. Basket Case (1982) was a grim and twisted tale of familial love, Brain Damage (1988) was a bizarre psychedelic trip on the dangers of drug addiction, Frankenhooker (1990) was an insane cartoon update on Mary Shelley's classic novel, and the Basket Case sequels (1990, 1992) were coying and sentimental freakshows. Even the style of each of his films had its own unique flavour, and Bad Biology is no exception.

Aspiring photographer, Jennifer (Charlee Danielson), is not your average kind of girl. For a start she is equipped with seven clitorises which makes her a nightmare to deal with in bed, as many men realise to their horror as they are quite literally banged to death while she takes polaroid snapshots of their death throes. Her strange biological makeup is somehow super-charged, and she gives birth to mutant babies only moments after conceiving. She then quickly and efficiently dumps the screaming spawn into trash cans, the bath tub, or wherever she happens to be at the time. Jennifer's ferocious sexual appetite goes unmatched until she has a chance encounter with Batz (Anthony Sneed), a young man who is also the victim of his own bad biology after a gone-wrong circumcision at birth; all his life he has tried desperately to self-medicate his manhood with all manner of experimental drugs and steroids, and now his cock is a huge aggressive monster with a mind of its own, and this makes Batz a very unsociable person. You would think that Jennifer and Batz are a match made in heaven, but things aren't that simple...

Bad Biology offers all the hallmarks of Henenlotter's previous work - warm colourful settings, the exaggerated cartoonish style, outsider characters with dark secrets, etc - but this latest offering also treats us to a harsh, nasty, and cynical black humour several shades darker and meaner-spirited than all of his previous works combined. It's an approach which may disorientate some of his regular fans, but I thought it worked well and is definitely in keeping with the cynical times we live in. He also shot the film in 35mm and not the HD video that many expected, and that's a welcome relief. Charlee Danielson isn't a great actress but her game attitude and keen energy more than make up for her sometimes stilted line readings, and Gabe Bartalos' wild special effects work is as crazy and impressive as anything seen in Henenlotter's films; the mutant babies and huge killer cock in particular.

Early screenings of Bad Biology were shown via video projection for some reason. It went on to wow fans at the festivals and one-off screenings before showing up in the UK on its first DVD release by Revolver, untouched by the hands of the BBFC (it was also released uncut in France under the title Sex Addict!). Shriek Show eventually unleashed the film on disc in America in its most impressive print to date, uncut and with a shed load of extras missing from the UK and French versions.

With the moderate success of Bad Biology we can only hope that Henenlotter will be encouraged to get back into the director's seat very soon.

BAD LIEUTENANT (1992)

Dir: Abel Ferrara / USA

"I'm sorry. I'm sorry I did so many bad things". After causing much controversy in the 70s and 80s with a pair of notorious video nasties, Driller Killer and Ms.45, director Abel Ferrara shocked the world once again in the 90s with Bad Lieutenant, an intelligent and fiercely uncompromising journey into the pit of human darkness, boasting a riveting, uninhibited performance from the brilliant Harvey Keitel.

Taking its inspiration from a newspaper headline about the rape of a nun, Ferrara co-wrote the script with Zoe Lund (formerly Zoe Tamerlis who starred in Ms.45 as the angel of vengeance), and together they fashioned a tale about a New York cop who self-destructs on drink, drugs, and gambling. The nameless cop becomes even more troubled when he discovers that the nun has forgiven her attackers, and the Lt. must try to put aside his own desperate need for vengeance if he is to save his wretched soul...

The resulting film was met with outrage from the press, so much so it even surprised Ferrara himself who was certainly no stranger to cinematic controversy. For, although Bad Lieutenant is a raw exercise in requisite shocks, it's also a classic tale of Catholic redemption. The BBFC recognised this and passed the film uncut for a British cinema release after seeing the light at the end of a very dark tunnel. But when it came to home video classification, Ferrara's film didn't make it through unscathed; a minute and a half of cuts were imposed by the censors due to an altering of legislation that stemmed from the original Video Recordings Act (which Ferrara's films, Driller Killer and Ms.45, ironically helped usher in).

In America the MPAA imposed an NC-17 rating on the film which resulted in Blockbuster Video refusing to stock it, and instead oversaw a drastic re-cut that was so empty and incoherent it has since been referred to as 'The really not that bad at all lieutenant'. The video release was also beset with contractual problems over the Schooly D soundtrack; Jimmy Page of Led Zeppelin had allegedly watched the video and noticed that his song Kashmir had been sampled without permission in the song Signifying Rapper. A lawsuit followed which resulted in the removal of all home video editions of the film. I think that's a bit cheeky of Jimmy Page, after all Led Zepp ripped off plenty of classic blues numbers themselves back in the day, but I digress.

In the year 2000 Film Four broadcast Bad Lieutenant in the BBFC-approved version with the Schooly D track restored.

Other video and TV prints include an acoustic track 'Bad Lieutenant', written and performed by Ferrara himself. But it's Harvey Keitel's stunning performance which saves the film and stops it from falling by the wayside. Even with the camera following him and rarely leaving his side for most of the running time, his method master class basically carries the film from start to finish. Whether he's shooting up heroin, jerking off in front of a couple of girls, walking around stark bollock naked whilst drugged up to the eyeballs, or wailing like a sick parrot, he somehow manages to add a touch of humanity to the role which, for many viewers, has made Bad Lieutenant just about tolerable.

Look out for the late great Zoe Lund as Keitel's junky mistress, and Ferrara's buddy Paul Hipp who makes a cameo appearance as Christ himself. Despite some of the knee-jerk reactions to the film, and despite what the Washington Post's Desson Howe said about it ("A notch nicer than Satan"), Bad Lieutenant has had many good write ups over the years. Martin Scorsese claimed it to be one of the finest films of the 90s. What more encouragement do you need?

THE BEAST (1975)

(Orig title: La bete)
Dir: Walerian Borowczyk / France

Talented Polish painter Walerian Borowczyk moved to France in the 60s taking with him a Bunuellian sense of mischief and a strong desire to use erotic cinema as a way of attacking and undermining bourgeois values. His early films were animated and well received (The Theatre of Mr. and Mrs.Kabal, 1967), but he soon moved onto live action with his impressive Goto, Island of Love (1968), and the ambitious medieval epic, Blanche (1971).

He returned three years later with Immoral Tales (1974), a quartet of erotic stories which earned him a solid reputation among the arthouse elite. But all of that positive acclaim came crashing down with his next film, La bete, which features a sequence in which a pretty young woman is chased through the woods and ravished by a well-endowed hairy beast, complete with wild prosthetics and cum shots.

The story of La bete focuses on Lucy Broadhurst (Lisbeth Hummel), an English woman who travels to the L'Esperance estate where she intends to marry the brutish son, Mathurin (Pierre Benedetti). Whilst the family await Lucy's arrival, members of this deranged household have sex and plot murder, all in the guise of social respectability. Lucy is welcomed to the estate by the sight of horses copulating on the driveway and she takes a polaroid snapshot for herself. After finding an illustrated diary belonging to the lady of the estate, Romilda, Lucy has a nightmare of being chased through the woods by a humongous beast with a huge erection. Mathurin dies the next day just as Lucy's sexuality awakens. And when the Cardinal arrives explaining his own ideas on bestiality, Lucy is sped away in her chauffeur-driven car.

A horny and explicit piece of incendiary filmmaking, La bete explores the sexual subtexts of classic fairytales like Little Red Riding Hood and Beauty and The Beast. The infamous 20 minute segment featuring the monster in the woods was originally envisaged as being part of Borowczyk's previous film, Immoral Tales, but instead seemed to develop a life of its own and became the centrepiece of an entirely new film. Whether seen as a horror film, a satire, dark fantasy, or erotica, Borowczyk clearly delights in stripping away the facade of polite convention. It's a film that uncovers the bestial nature of polite society, as seen in the horses breeding on the drive, and taking inspiration from Luis Bunuel for an amusing comedy of manners spiked with a subversive edge. The Spanish surrealist's The Discreet Charm of The Bourgeoisie looks to have been used as a healthy template.

The film caused an almighty stink when it first hit screens, and found itself banned and censored all across the world. The critics who had previously championed Borowczyk's work turned against him and felt personally insulted by the film, and for years it was almost impossible to see in anything even resembling an uncut copy. An English language version appeared on VHS under the title Devil's Ecstasy, but most of the offending footage had been removed (including the horses). An uncut French print played at UK and American arthouse cinemas in 2001 in a limited run, but on DVD it was Cult Epics who came to the rescue with a 3 disc set of La Bete in a Director's Cut which is actually missing around four minutes of dialogue that Borowczyk himself cut out of the film (the third disc presents the original fully uncut version with English hard subs).

THE BEAST IN HEAT (1977)

(Orig title: La Bestia In Calore; aka SS Hell Camp)
Dir: Ivan Katansky (Paolo Solvay aka Luigi Batzella) /Italy

After a short-lived video release in Britain, The Beast In Heat was swept up in the moral panic that was the Video Recordings Act 1984, and has been an outlawed 'video nasty' in the UK ever since. But its 'Banned' status may be just down to the fact that no distribution company has submitted the film for classification in this country since those draconian days. In any case, I wouldn't expect a deluxe Special Edition of this title to hit the shelves anytime soon.

The haphazard 'plot' to Beast In Heat centers upon a Nazi torture chamber run by the fiendish Macha Magall with the aid of an aphrodisiac-fuelled troglodyte, all in the name of science, whilst a group of resistance fighters struggle against the Nazi Stormtroopers in the surrounding countryside. If the film lacks coherence overall, that's because it's basically two movies spliced together; director Luigi Batzella recycled some footage from his 1970 war film, When The Bell Rings, added the new sequences featuring Magall, and bingo, he had a sleazy new cine-product on his hands. The old footage takes up around 60% of the film's entire running time, but it holds together quite well, much better than many would have you believe (heck, we've all sat through Marino Girolami's Zombie Holocaust which was pasted together in a similar fashion). The intro credits come and go whilst a red swastika is flaunted before our eyes accompanied by wonky sounding electronic music. This most despised symbol of the 20th Century seems to linger on the screen forever before the movie starts proper; and it's then that we're led into the torture chamber where the evil Dr. Kratsch commands the tasteless and ludicrous proceedings (the old UK video version is amusingly dubbed and offers up some insane dialogue). We get rape, baby shooting, a woman being eaten alive by rats, another woman tortured with electrodes attached to her vag, a fat hairy man strung upside down and whipped (long rumoured to have been played by the film's producer, Xiro Papas!), and a young woman having her fingernails ripped off; but the real show-stopper is Sal Boris who plays the caged troll forced-fed on aphrodisiacs; it's basically a reprise of his similar role in Tinto Brass' Salon Kitty (1975), taken to the extreme. It's one of the most ludicrous performances in the history of shock cinema, and makes this film essential viewing for that reason alone. As punishment, women are thrown into the cage where the eponymous 'Beast' attacks and rapes them with gusto. At one point he gets so carried away in his frenzy, he even rips out a bunch of pubic hair from his victim and proceeds to eat them, leaving behind a raw bloody patch.

The DVD is available uncut on Region 1 under the title SS Hell Camp, in Italian with English subs. This is Nazisploitation at its nuttiest.

BEAUTIFUL GIRL HUNTER (1979)

(aka Star of David - Hunting For Beautiful Girls)
Dir: Norofumi Suzuki /Japan

A twisted war veteran intrudes on a home, ties up the couple who own the place, robs them of their savings, and then subjects the woman to forced deep-throating and penetrative rape. Later, when the ordeal seems to be over, the partner cruelly lashes at the woman with a bull whip, accusing her of enjoying the experience. And his rage only intensifies when she reveals to him that she is pregnant with the rapist's baby...

A few years later and the household is fast deteriorating. The 'father' can barely look at the youngster because he reminds him of the rapist, and constantly slaps, threatens, and abuses the boy, much to the dismay of the mother. He often subjects his wife to brutal S&M sessions, involving another woman whom he ties up, whips, abuses, and forces to urinate on each other. The boy, Tatsuya, witnesses much of this by spying through the keyhole. Wife can't handle it anymore, and she commits suicide by plunging her own throat down onto a blade (similar to the suicide of a murder suspect in David Cronenberg's The Dead Zone, in which a man plunges himself face-first down onto a pair of opened scissors).

Not surprisingly, Tatsuya grows up to become a deeply disturbed sadistic sex maniac, partly because of his traumatic childhood experiences, and (according to the film) partly due to his own wretched gene pool. He spikes a lady's drink and then carries her unconscious body down into his basement that he has renovated into his own secret torture dungeon that resembles the spacious lab in Paul Morrissey's Flesh For Frankenstein. He strips and rapes her, and when she regains consciousness he berates her and blames her for his own emotional turmoil. His deranged activities go unchecked, even using his own birthday party as an alibi so that he can escape down into his basement to indulge in his sick urge to rape and murder his captives.

Meanwhile, Tatsuya's biological father is still up to his old tricks. He may be older but he still has no trouble in overpowering young girls and savagely raping and strangling them out in the wilderness. And like father like son, Tatasuya becomes bolder in his kidnapping antics, and in a scene which serves as a chilling reminder of the crimes of
Ted Bundy, he approaches a high school girl pretending to be a photojournalist and manages to lure the poor girl into his car. Back at the basement she is abused and forced to masturbate.

Through a series of short flashbacks we get some more backstory on Tatsuya; as a school student he became obsessed with the Nazi's and Auschwitz, and is seen jerking off to images of Jews being hung and gunned down by firing squads (Ian Brady displayed similar traits). He deflowers the school girl and she eventually becomes completely subservient to him, willing to do absolutely anything for her 'master'. It's interesting to note here that director Suzuki composes the sex scenes in such a way that there is no need for those distracting 'blurs' that crop up all the time in Japanese sex movies. Here Suzuki pushes as much as he could get away with in this type of soft core fare.

Next up, Tatsuya kidnaps a pop star (Hiromi Namino, who was Miss Japan at the time in her first film role in which her nudity caused much fuss in the Japanese press) and her assistant. By treating the pop star like shit and treating her assistant with a bit of care and kindness, he succeeds in exposing a knot of resentment between the two, and the master-slave dynamic is reversed when the assistant bullwhips the pop star to within an inch of her life.

In perhaps one of the most offensive sequences in the film, Tatsuya seems to take pity on the schoolgirl and he dumps her on a beach in the middle of the night. And in a later scene he spies on her while she's back at school, and she seems to have rebuilt her life - Not only is she more popular than before, but she seems to have developed a new lease of life; she's happy, smiley, care-free, and the centre of attention. The implications of this scene are very dubious. And dangerous. To suggest that her awful experience at the hands of a madman who had deflowered and turned her into a nervous subservient wreck, and then showing her to have gained from it and even to have appreciated the experience - This sequence gives the film one of its most authentic notes of misogyny.

Anyway, the pop star makes an unsuccessful escape attempt. And while an injured Tatsuya is dealing with her, the assistant manages to escape from the house. But in a cruel (and ludicrous) twist of fate, she runs straight into the arms of Tatsuya's father. Cue a long-overdue family reunion as father and son meet for the first time and team up for more depraved fun involving the captives, an Alsation, and of course, rape, torture, and murder.

Throughout the film, Tatsuya has been courting a pretty young girl; they go on dates, go horse riding, and generally spend a lot of time together. He tells her that he keeps birds in his basement and the girl is keen to see them but he always avoids taking her home. Indeed, viewers are not sure whether Tatsuya is just luring her along as part of another of his twisted games, or whether he genuinely cares for her. But in a nasty and cruel finale, we discover that yes he really does care about her, but he has a funny way of showing it... But as it turns out, this girl has her own warped agenda to deal with involving her faith, incest, and the star of David. A touch of redemption maybe? I don't think so!

When asked why his films contain so many images and references to Christianity, director Norifumi Suzuki replied "I suppose sacred things are actually quite erotic. The idea of defiling something sacred like a nun or a nurse or a schoolteacher is very erotic". Certainly, if you look through the films of Suzuki (Truck Yaro and School of The Holy Beast, for example) you'll find that the defiling of sacred things is an ongoing theme in his work, and Beautiful Girl Hunter is no exception. Having worked for the Toei studio for a number of years, Suzuki was eventually head-hunted by the Nikkatsu Corporation who offered him bigger budgets and a free choice to make whatever kind of film he liked, just as long as it would fit in with the 'Roman Porno' tradition. Suzuki settled on Star of David, a Manga by Masaaki

Soto, and in just 19 days he had written, directed, and edited the film in a flash. The result is a vile and misogynistic piece of trash that perhaps isn't supposed to be taken seriously. But it's also beautifully shot with neon-lit photography, and permeates a dark and brooding atmosphere, and boasts some fantastic performances. For all the shocking and disagreeable elements the film may possess, it's certainly never boring and is expertly made; in today's PC climate nobody makes big-budget shock films like this anymore. Suzuki once described Beautiful Girl Hunter as a film which "deals with the joys of being evil".

BEAUTIFUL TEACHER IN TORTURE HELL (1985)

(Orig title: Oniroku Dan: Bikyoshi jigokuzeme)
Dir: Masahito Segawa / Japan

Beautiful Teacher In Torture Hell is a typical entry in Nikkatsu's Roman Porno series of the time. It's simple premise sees a newly recruited teacher, Ran Masaki, subjected to a barrage of nasty goings on from both the pupils and the teachers, including violence, rape, and imprisonment. Masaki is picked up on her first day at the train station by a fellow teacher, and their drive through the isolated mountain roads is blocked by a group of thugs who attack the women. Masaki just happens to be a fencing teacher, and she puts her sword skills to use by beating off two of the thugs with a stick. She then rescues the other teacher from rape by beating the third yobbo into submission.

Despite the incident on the journey to her new job, Masaki seems to settle into her new role. That is until she is bopped on the head and knocked unconscious in the basement. She awakens in a hospital ward surrounded by a pupil and a couple of creepy looking teachers, but she has no memory of what happened to her. She has marks on her wrists which suggest she has probably spent some time tied up somewhere. She settles at her friend's house to recuperate but the event has clearly affected her deeply. The two women then get naked and have a sexy bath time together, but Masaki rejects her friend's sexual advances. She wakes up in the middle of the night to find her housemate in an S&M session with the creepy looking dude. She spies on the action for a while until she is spotted, and then goes back to bed.

  Back at school the following morning, the creepy dude enters Masaki's classroom and hands her an envelope containing naked photos of her that were obviously taken while she was unconscious in the basement. She flees the school premises and confronts the young pupil, Yuki, about the incident and to find out who is responsible for her ordeal, but to no avail. After burning the photos, she enters the gym one night after school to find Yuki being tied up and tormented by the thugs who attacked her on the mountain road at the beginning. They threaten the girl with a knife and cut off her panties. Yuki pleads with her teacher to help her and Masaki reluctantly obeys the boys demands that she take off her clothes and have a fencing duel with one of the thugs. After beating the thug's arse with the stick she is set upon by the other boys and gang raped whilst a third records the event on film.

After the ordeal, Masaki takes the girl home and ends up staying the night at her house. However, it soon becomes clear that Yuki's father is the school headmaster and the whole episode that night was just a ploy to get her to the house. Yuki, the gang of thugs, the creepy guy, and even her own housemate were in on the conspiracy. Masaki is then trussed up in the basement for more depraved fun where everyone gets in on the act; bondage, tit-slapping, forced fellatio, vibrator fun, an enema, and a hanging. Even the young pupil gets in on the action when she climbs into an aquarium for a bit of teacher molestation.

With a running time of just over an hour, Beautiful Teacher In Torture Hell is a silly piece of brainless exploitative garbage. But if you're a fan of Japanese Pink films then you'll probably lap it up anyway as this is no better or worse than the usual Nikkatsu fare of the time. The script was written by Nikkatsu veteran Oniroku Dan, and the visuals are typically stunning and put most American and Italian exploitation pics to shame with the beautiful lighting, textures, framing and photography. The story is deliberately stripped down to its basic essentials so that we're basically left with a string of sleazy sex and bondage scenes. And it's this latter element that perhaps puts the film into context as a precursor to the whole 'Torture Porn' movement of recent years.

Even by the Japanese standards of the time this is an extremely cynical and pessimistic film. We can't even rely on the innocence of youth here as the young pupil Yuki turns out to be just as fucked up and debased as the adult characters. The film is populated almost entirely with sly and manipulative scumbags, and the only decent character is subjected to all of the vile abuse! Even many of the most disreputable Pink films of the era had their bad guys getting their comeuppance at the end, but not so here; actually quite the opposite; in the coda we see another young teacher arrive at the train station, and it's clear that this new recruit will be subjected to the same abuse.

THE BEYOND (1981)

(Orig title: L'Aldilà; aka Seven Doors of Death)
Dir: Lucio Fulci /Italy

Italian gore maestro Lucio Fulci is best known for his quartet of extremely violent and gory zombie movies, which includes Zombie Flesh Eaters, City of The Living Dead, House By The Cemetery, and of course, The Beyond. It's a series of films in which all of the elements come together in a perfect way, and everyone involved in the making of the films were at the top of their game; from the performances of the cast, to the stunning photography and lighting effects of Sergio Salvatti, the gruesome and innovative special effects of Gianetto De Rossi, Dardano Sacchetti's nightmarish scripts, Fabio Frizzi's haunting music, and the meastro himself, Lucio Fulci, tying it all together in a masterful way. And even among such grisly company as Zombie Flesh Eaters and City of The Living Dead, The Beyond remains not only the finest film Fulci ever made, but also a landmark of Italian genre cinema. And of all the spaghetti horrors out there, only Ruggero Deodato's Cannibal Holocaust can rival The Beyond's grim spectacle and gut-punch nihilism.

The film opens with a sepia prologue set in 1927 Louisiana in which a torch-carrying lynch mob enters the Seven Doors Hotel, make their way to room 36, and chain-whip the room's occupant, Schweick, a painter and "ungodly warlock", before they nail his wrists to the wall and pour acid in his face. While this is going on, a woman reads from the Book of Eibon (pronounced 'A-ban'), an occult text that catches fire as Schweick's face dissolves into an acidic mess.

Cut to modern day 1981 where the long-abandoned hotel has been inherited by New Yorker Liza (scream queen Catriona MacColl). One of the workers helping to renovate the building falls from the scaffold after seeing a pair of evil eyes, and John McGabe (exploitation favourite David Warbeck) arrives on the scene to try and keep things under control. Strange occurances and more nasty goings on begin to happen in and around the hotel, including an unfortunate plumber who has his eyeball ripped out, dead bodies rising in the morgue, and an extended spider attack in the local library. Liza first meets Emily (the woman reading from the Book of Eibon in the prologue) on an eerily deserted stretch of road, but Emily's eyes have turned a milky white. Turns out that the book holds a dark secret concerning the gates of hell which are located somewhere within the Seven Doors Hotel. Soon enough, Liza and John are fighting off hordes of walking corpses, and this leads to the film's stunning finale in which the characters seem to plunge into hell.

As with many of Fulci's films, The Beyond is often accused of being a confusing mess, especially by those who rely on mainstream storytelling where everything comes together with a satisfying 'click' at the end. Fulci has little concern with traditional filmic manners or the niceties of character development or rationality. However, true fans of Italian terror and Fulci in particular, know that those odd peculiarities are what makes these films so interesting and so different. If you want proof that Fulci was a talented filmmaker, you only have to look at the last few minutes of The Beyond. Everything in the Fulci cannon suddenly makes perfect sense in the film's finale; a nightmare logic that spirals into hell as the heroes find themselves eternally trapped in a dark netherworld.

In the prologue we're led to believe that Schweick was an innocent painter hunted down by a superstitious lynch mob.

The themes of good and evil are muddied though when we see that the hellscape at the end looks identical to Schweick's painting. This supposed innocent painter, it turns out, really was responsible for opening the gates of hell. At the beginning and end of the film we're shown two forms of evil; the physical and the metaphysical. The lynching and the walking corpses represent physical evil and earthly horror, whereas the closing scenes of the film shows evil as a vast nothingness. The blank eyes of Liza and John express an existential terror rather than physical horror at their comprehension of an infinite emptiness. And this idea is made clear in the film's grim voiceover that declares "And you will face the sea of darkness and all therein that may be explored".

Fulci's masterpiece was neglected for years with a heavily censored American VHS under the title 7 Doors of Death was the only way for fans to see it. In the UK it was added to the video nasties list and banned until 2001 when the BBFC finally passed it uncut, by which time the film's reputation rocketed thanks to the uncensored Japanese laserdisc and American midnight screenings by Grindhouse and Quentin Tarantino's Rolling Thunder Pictures. For the first time fans were at last given the chance to fully appreciate Giannetto De Rossi's stunning visual effects which include an eyeball being ripped out of a plumber's head, an Alsation biting a chunk out of a woman's throat with blood gushing out of the gaping wound, a little zombie girl getting her head blown off, and a bunch of creepy-crawly tarantulas chewing on a man's face. It was only then that the film secured its long-overdue status as a cult classic. Oh, and Fabio Frizzi's excellent score was reinstated too.

BEYOND THE DARKNESS (1979)

(Orig title: Buio Omega; aka Buried Alive)
Dir: Joe D'Amato / Italy

A morbid and graphic shocker from the king of sleaze, Joe D'Amato, Beyond The Darkness follows the exploits of a disturbed young man, Frank (Kieran Canter), who has recently lost his girlfriend. Taxidermy just happens to be his favourite past time, and so he tries to preserve his beloved by embalming her. But, as in any self-respecting horror movie, Frank's plans to live happily ever after with his doll are quickly dashed when stragglers and strangers become suspicious of his weird behaviour, and pretty soon he finds himself on a graphic and gruesome murder spree, wiping out those who may know too much. Cue burnings, dismemberments, fingernail-ripping, eye-gouging, and an acid bath.

   Boasting a creepy and morbid atmosphere and a downbeat soundtrack courtesy of Goblin, Beyond The Darkness marks one of the highlights of D'Amato's long and varied career. For years this film was really only available in horrible looking VHS bootleg copies where the picture quality was so dark and scrappy that many of the scenes were barely visible, and reviewers trashed it as a cheap and nasty piece of garbage (the video version was also cut). However, the DVD release was something of a revelation as the original source materials were used to re-master the footage. Not only were the legendary gore scenes reinstated and now clearly visible, but also other more subtle qualities could be appreciated for the first time for many viewers, including the beautiful interiors of the inherited villa where Frank lives, and Enrico Biribicchi's creative and intriguing camera work.

Beyond The Darkness ultimately stands as a tragic and twisted love story with a necrophiliac edge (though Frank doesn't have the time to get too intimate with his girlfriend's corpse because he's too busy murdering and dismembering those who enter his life). It's an insane and desperate love that spirals out of control, and not even his dead mother's housemaid (with whom he has a perverse sexual relationship, and who helps him to dispose of the bodies) can talk him into letting go of his beloved Anna. Joe D'Amato perfectly combines the fever dreams of Edgar Allan Poe with the down-at-earth morbid realism of Marijan Vadja's Mosquito The Rapist for a true nightmare on film. Younger horror fans who are more accustomed to the flash-trash style of many modern films will probably find it difficult to deal with the laid back tempo and eerie mood, but they sure don't make 'em like this anymore. British filmmakers George Dugdale and Peter Mackenzie Litten later explored similar territory in blackly comic style with Living Doll in the early 90s.

BLACK CHRISTMAS (1974)

Dir: Bob Clarke / Canada

"Ho ho ho, shit!" An icy gem of a film that continues to scare the hell out of each new generation of horror fans.

It's Christmas Eve and a group of college girls are preparing for the holidays. The festivities are soon spoiled when they're pestered by obscene and threatening phone calls - possibly the creepiest and most disturbing phone calls in film history; the killer's voice yelps and shifts tone so crazy and spouts incomprehensible gibberish of pure maliciousness it'll put you on the edge of your seat right away - One of the girls is murdered and dumped in the attic. The police are quick to link her disappearance to a spate of attacks on young girls in the local area, but as is the way with any seasonal slasher, the killings continue...

There are lots of jump-out-of-your-seat moments in Black Christmas, and along with Mario Bava's A Bay of Blood, this served as a blueprint for the slasher movies that followed in the late 70s and early 80s. The spooky close-up shots of the killer's eyes recalls taut classics like The Spiral Staircase and Profondo Rosso. John Carpenter's Halloween takes credit for kick-starting the slasher boom but that film owes a huge debt to Bob Clarke's underrated masterpiece. It is also laced with a biting sense of humour that also inspired the later unfunny slasher imitators; the ongoing fellatio joke ("I know, it's something dirty ain't it"), and the killer's obscenities on the phone ("Let me lick it! Let me lick your pretty pink cunt!"). It was also an influence on another underrated gem, Fred Walton's When A Stranger Calls in 1979.

THE BLANCHEVILLE MONSTER (1963)

Dir: Alberto DeMartino /Spain

Emily has a lot of growing up to do. She returns to her family castle after completing her studies to discover that her home life has drastically changed. Her brother is now in charge of the estate, the servants and maids whom she knew for years and were almost part of the family have died and been replaced by new members of staff who are cold and unfamiliar. Her father, Count Blancheville, has been horribly disfigured and lives secluded in one of the castle's isolated towers. Count Blancheville believes that the family curse will be lifted if Emily dies before her 21st birthday (some kind of ancient 'prophecy'). Emily is 20 years old and her birthday is only 5 days away. To make matters worse, her father escapes from the tower and disappears, only to show up trying to convince Emily to embrace 'sweet death'.

  This underrated and rather obscure Spanish oddity still hasn't received its due on DVD but is worth hunting down for fans of Eurohorror and the cine-bizarre. It has an eerie atmosphere and a grand gothic setting reminiscent of Roger Corman's Poe adaptations of the early 60s. Emily returns home as the picture of youth; one can only guess how much fun she had while away at college, making new friends and having the space and the freedom to shape her own ideals and identity with her whole life ahead of her. Time brings inevitable changes to any household, and in this film those changes are exaggerated. Death has taken away the servants from old age, her father has been "horribly disfigured", but in a metaphorical sense this disfigurement is simply old age. Many youngsters are forced into adulthood due to circumstances beyond their control; debilitating terminal disease and death itself can alter family life beyond recognition (the new members of staff are blank faced and unfamiliar, and this could represent a personification of this change).

Much of the film centres around the struggle of Emily to stay young and irresponsible and fight against the changes which demands her to grow up and allow her youthful spirit to die. The 'family curse' is of course death itself, the curse of every family. The bed-ridden father sends out a phantom shape of himself to stalk and harass Emily, trying to lure her by guilt and pity into giving up her life to care for him and to keep the family unit going. It seems appropriate that the father's method of 'killing' Emily are by poisoning, because in situations where youths are expected to take on the responsibilities of adulthood, many feel they are being poisoned with duties and burdens. When the doctor informs Emily's brother that she has been poisoned, he adds "It's not her body that is threatened, it is her spirit". Whilst in bed sick with the delirium brought on by the poison, her fever dreams represent the adolescent battle between freedom and responsibility. In these dreams Emily wanders around the desecrated ruins of the castle dressed in a swirling and virginal white dress, seemingly looking for a way to escape, but instead she always bumps into her father who whispers things like "You have reached the eternal lair; you are dead Emily, you are dead".

It all ends in the nightmarish finale where Emily is comatose at her own funeral. Not literally dead but spiritually nullified. "Why can't you hear me?" she calls out to the mourners, "I'm alive! I'm alive!" She is then entombed in the mausoleum in a splendid metaphor of the painful birth of the adult; we are always forced into adulthood. And of course, the 'family curse' continues... In the coda, Emily escapes from the nightmare of the mausoleum, but finds herself in wedlock; her youth and vitality gone, replaced by conformity and boring old adulthood.

The film can also be read as an attack on the Franco regime that ruled over Spain at the time (see the Subversive! article at the back of this book), in which the adults, the 'ruling elite' instill madness on the youth as a way of holding onto their own corrupt power (as seen in The Bell From Hell), and women are subjected to the chauvanist rule of patriachy where the freedom and sexual awakening of young women is seen as the ultimate evil of Catholicism (as seen in The Blood Spattered Bride).

BLOOD AND SEX NIGHTMARE (2008)

Dir: Joseph R. Kolbek / USA

This shot on video shocker was something of a unique entry in the slew of amateur gore movies that were being churned out of North America in the late 00s, because for a start, the film actually lives up to its title.

Nick is horny. Nick is frustrated. Nick really needs to get his end away. So when his girlfriend Amy returns from a family funeral in Japan, he manages to twist her arm into agreeing to spend a few days with him at a sex resort in the country. When they arrive at the Pleasant Mountain Adult Retreat, Nick expects to find a haven of campfires and swingers, but the place seems eerily deserted. They book into their cabin and are visited by the local handyman, Walter. But Walter's creepy manner and leering eyes sets the couple on edge. And when a pair of fellow swingers are butchered in graphic detail nearby, Nick and Amy must put aside their sexual frustrations and get the hell out of there... But who's the murderer? Could it be weird Walter or the sex maniac killer who died in the woods years earlier?

Coming on like a spare change remake of Porno Holocaust and shot on a cheap video camera with a miniscule cast and crew, Blood and Sex Nightmare at least delivers on its title promise. The performances and script are kind of average at best, but the bloody FX are quite impressive, and the whole show flies by in a brief but brilliant 81 minutes. Indie trash regular Tina Krause supplies the obligatory T&A, indie rapper Eyez The Filmmaker Emcee cameos as an unfortunate victim, and the DVD was released by Bloody Earth, making Kolbek a household name among DIY film lovers everywhere.

BLOOD FEAST (1963)

Dir: Herscell Gordon Lewis /USA

The first gore movie ever made. With a budget of $24,000, director Herscell Gordon Lewis and producer David F. Friedman scored a tremendous hit on the drive-in circuits of America in the early 60s and became exploitation legends overnight. The plot of Blood Feast concerns a young woman, Suzette, who dates the local shit-for-brains cop, Pete. They attend a lecture on Egyptian cults; meanwhile, young women are being murdered by the local caterer, Faud Ranses, who sets his eye on Suzette becoming his latest sacrifice to the Egyptian God, Ishtar.

Blood Feast is funny and revolting, the acting is terrible, the lighting is flat; cheap and nasty amateur time. But the film does have at least one positive aspect to talk about, and that's the defiantly in your face, gore-for-gore's-sake attitude - Tongues are ripped out, legs are cut off (see the newspaper headline!), tabletop eviscerations, skulls are ripped open, entrails fondled in loving close-up, etc. American audiences had seen nothing like it before, and punters queued for miles to see it. Movies had always shied away from showing gruesome death before Lewis and Friedman showed up. Banned in Britain during the video nasties era, it was then passed with 23 seconds of cuts in 2001. Available uncut on Region 0 DVD.

BLOODY MOON (1981)

Dir: Jess Franco /Germany

This Halloween-inspired Euro-slasher would sit perfectly on a bouble-bill with Juan Piquer Simon's Pieces, a film which in turn owes a chromosone or two to this deranged offering from cult legend Jess Franco.

Facially-disfigured Miguel is an unwelcome lurker at an evening pool party. The object of his affections rejects him in favour of another guy, so Miguel dons a Micky Mouse mask and tries it on with her. Not knowing who he is, she succumbs to his advances, and pretty soon they're back to her room for some fondling on the bed. But when she removes the mask, she is horrified when she discovers who she's been canoodling with. Outraged by this indignity, Miguel grabs a pair of scissors and stabs her to death.

A few years later and the disturbed young man is released into the care of his sister, Manuela, who along with their wheelchair-bound mother, operate the day to day running of a language school. Pretty soon we learn that Miguel and his sister had an incestuous relationship before the murder, and when little sister refuses to rekindle their sex frolics, poor mother meets a fiery death. Meanwhile, another pretty girl, Angela (Olivia Pascal of Behind Convent Walls) is being stalked by Miguel, and no one believes her when her hot young student friends are offed in grisly fashion.

The most shocking thing about this film for many viewers was the fact that director Jess Franco delivered a pretty solid body count movie. Having earned himself an unflattering reputation as being one of the most prolific but incompetent filmmakers of all time, some dismiss his entire filmography on the basis of having seen only one or two of his movies. But true fans of this maverick of schlock know that his back catalogue (which at the moment stands at around 169 features) contains dozens of surprisingly accomplished films, and even a handful of absolute gems. And it has become something of a rites of passage for Franco fans to wade through all the crap to find the treasures.

Bloody Moon is far from being a masterpiece but is entertaining from start to finish, with a barrage of T&A, inventive murder scenes, ludicrous dialogue ("So, where's the cadaver, honey?"), and tributes to John Carpenter's

Halloween. One topless chick is stabbed in the back and the blade exits her body through the nipple, another woman is tied down onto a rock and sent hurling into the path of an oncoming circular saw. A young boy tries to save her but the maniac scares him away, and the woman is decapitated complete with blood spurting from the neck wound (this scene was inserted into the gore montage in Pedro Almodovar's Matador a few years later). The young boy is squished when he runs in front of a passing Mercedes. Another of Angela's friends is strangled with a pair of fire tongs, a snake is unnecessarily decapitated with a pair of shears, and a man is brutally cut wide open across the chest with a chainsaw.

After an extremely limited theatrical release, Bloody Moon was released on VHS at the dawn of home video, but uncut copies weren't available for long in the UK due to the arrival of the video nasties fiasco. All of the tapes were removed from circulation when the film was prosecuted and banned. The Canadian VHS by CIC was uncut but difficult to get hold of on these shores. UK fans had to make do with the diluted version by Vipco (which was missing 80 seconds of gore) until it was passed uncut by the BBFC in 2008. The Severin DVD is the best option to date with the best transfer from the original negative, the complete cut of the film, and a fantastic audio commentary by Franco (who cameos early in the film as the psychologist).

BLUE VELVET (1986)

Dir: David Lynch / USA

It seems incredible now to think of him as the savior of 80s American cinema, but David Lynch emerged on the scene with Eraserhead in the late 70s, a surreal and disturbing dream of dark and troubling things. It was a midnight movie favourite that became an international cult classic and allowed him to head towards the mainstream with his follow-up, The Elephant Man, which in turn earned him a BAFTA and an Oscar nomination. The Hollywod A-list seemed to be within his grasp for a while until he helmed Dune, a multi-million Dollar disaster which could have ended his career. But two good things came out of Dune: Actor Kyle MacLochlan and producer Dino De Laurentis. De Laurentis never lost faith in Lynch and gave him $6 million to make his next film. And while Coppola was skint, Scorsese tired, and Spielberg adapting literary works, David Lynch quietly went about filming his own script, Blue Velvet, a nightmare voyage through the underworld of suburbia.

College student Jeffrey Beaumont (MacLachlan) heads home after his father suffers a heart attack, and whilst walking through a clearance in the woods he discovers a severed human ear. He takes the evidence to the police but his curiosity overwhelms him and he teams up with sweet-natured school girl Sandy (Laura Dern) to help him find out more about the ear, and who it belonged to. Their sleuthing leads them to nightclub singer Dorothy Vallens (Isabella Rosselini). Jeffrey sneaks into her home in search of clues but ends up having to hide in the wardrobe as Dorothy's psychotic 'boyfriend' shows up. Frank Booth (Dennis Hopper) subjects Dorothy to bizarre sexual games and sadism, and Jeffrey has to play peeping tom through the slats in the closet doors while all of this is going on. It soon becomes clear that Frank holds a terrible secret over Dorothy...

The late great Dennis Hopper steals the show as Frank. His daring performance is a stunning creation; terrifying, perverse, and brutal. His snarling delivery and child-like tantrums are enough to put viewers on the edge of their seats almost three decades later. Lynch picked up his second Best Director nomination at the Oscars, his long-time composer, Angelo Badalamenti, provides the grandiose Hermann-esque score, and film fans the world over were relieved that, at last, a true filmmaker was back to his full strengths, leaving the likes of contemporary hits like Top Gun and Back To The Future paling into insignificance. But it wasn't all praise from the critics; horror expert Mark Kermode was physically assaulted in a pub after he wrote a damning review of Blue Velvet, and stateside critic Roger Ebert famously hated it, and argued that the scenes of sexual despair should have featured in a sincere film, not a bubblegum pop movie. He did at least acknowledge the film's strong sexual horror, but was angry that the power of the scene was squandered in its half-arsed context.

Blue Velvet opens with a superb visual metaphor as we see the white picket fences, green lawns, and friendly neighbourly faces passing by and tending their gardens. It's a dream-like sequence of middle America perfectly encapsulated. But then the camera dips and we're suddenly faced with the underbelly that is crawling with insect life.

Dorothy's character is perhaps the most haunting in the film; we discover that her husband and child have both been kidnapped by Frank, and he blackmails her into playing along with his strange sadomasochistic games in order to save the lives of her loved ones (he has already cut off one of her husband's ears). Some have suggested that Dorothy takes a masochistic pleasure from her encounters with Frank, and she certainly does seem to be playing along, but is it genuine or is she just playing it safe and giving Frank what he wants so as to save the lives of her family members? Even during the most intense scenes with Frank, there's something not right; she seems totally withdrawn and distanced from herself, perhaps as a way of turning herself into a passive object so that the abuses can almost have the effect of happening to another person, and not herself.

The theatricality of that scene has led psychoanalysts to suggest that the intensity of that S&M session stems from Frank's impotence. His loud, aggressive manner is almost comical in an old 'arch-villain' way. He bellows "Don't you look at me!" and it seems fairly obvious that he doesn't want to be looked at because he is ashamed; there is nothing there - No erection. He fakes these crazy 'sex' sessions so as to conceal his impotence. All the shouting and wildness and sexual gestures serve as a mask to conceal the fact that he can't get it up! He apparently has no idea that Jeffrey is hiding in the closet and spying on them, but at the same time he seems to be in some kind of exhibitionistic performance; but for whom? He doesn't know about Jeffrey, and he doesn't want Dorothy to look at him, so we can only assume that he is simply performing for himself, so that he can convince himself of his potency with a strange game of sexual charades.

Another late great, Jack Nance (of Eraserhead), and Brad Dourif (who provides the voice of Chucky in the Child's

Play movies) lend good support as members of Frank's gang, and Dean Stockwell plays the doomed detective. But film fans often need reminding that Blue Velvet is not perfect. Sure, it's one of the best of the 80s but Lynch has improved in almost all areas in his subsequent efforts. Twin Peaks was more effective in exploring the small-town underbelly, and its villain, Leland Palmer, is more dangerous than Frank Booth simply because he conceals his evils and appears quite normal, even friendly, on the outside. In Blue Velvet the characters only get into problems when they venture into unknown areas, whereas in Twin Peaks evil is everywhere; it's all a part of the character's families and their home lives - a much more disturbing idea. Blue Velvet's take on sexual obsession, identity, and even its garish musical numbers were all done to better effect in Mulholland Dr. and Lost Highway.

Blue Velvet is best viewed today as a Hitchcockian greatest hits package: The aforementioned Hermann-esque score, nods to Shadow of a Doubt, MacLochlan's voyeuristic character reminds one of James Stewart in Rear Window, and the sexual obsession with Dorothy strays into Vertigo territory. This tribute to Hitchcock's greatest achievements is also alluded to when Sally says to Jeffrey, "I can't figure out if you're a detective or a pervert".

BODY SNATCHERS (1993)

Dir: Abel Ferrara / USA

"Where you gonna go? Where you gonna run? Where you gonna hide? Nowhere, because there's no one like you left".

With a slight difference on the previous entries in the Body Snatcher's series, here we have an environmentalist who is investigating chemical waste on an American military base. Meanwhile his unsettled family are slowly falling apart due to a 'wicked' stepmother and constant in-fighting. But there's also something genuinely sinister going on among the local soldiers and it's up to the daughter, Marti, to save her family from the invading aliens who are taking over the bodies of the residents and turning the entire community into a mindless conformity.

Jack Finney's 1955 novel The Body Snatchers was originally filmed by Don Siegel in 1956 as Invasion of The Body Snatchers, a classic of conformity which was a thinly veiled attack on the communist witch hunts of the McCarthy years.

It was remade in 1978 by Philip Kaufman (and coincided with the release of George Romero's blackly comic satire on mindless consumerism, Dawn of The Dead). This latest update by Abel Ferrara continues with the series' addressing of the universal, political, and personal fears of the loss of identity, and a smart move of the filmmakers was to shift the action to a military base where the commonly held attitudes of 'patriotism', 'discipline', and 'duty' become enmeshed in paranoia, at constant odds with the idea of the military as a fighting force for freedom. It thus becomes even more difficult for the film's heroes to differentiate between the mindless drones of the alien invaders and the mindless drones of the local marines. The military setting also allows for an explosive finale with guns, bombs, and even an Apache helicopter getting in on the action.

Body Snatchers had a complicated production history with no less than five writers credited with the screenplay. It was B-movie legend Larry Cohen who wrote the original script (based on Finney's idea, of course), and that version was initially given the green light for shooting. Writer Denis Paoli and director Stuart Gordon (the pair behind Re-Animator and From Beyond) were hired to polish up on some of the dialogue, but ended up creating whole new scenes and ideas along the way. Stuart Gordon was originally set to direct, but due to the unorganised situation during pre-production, his patience ran out and he decided to head off to Australia to direct the Christopher Lambert vehicle, Fortress, instead. Body Snatchers once again found itself in limbo for a while until Warner Brothers took a chance and roped in bad boy director Abel Ferrara whose dark imagination would no doubt take the project to where it needed to be. Every smart director has a writer, and Abel had Nicholas St. John, a man who is often referred to as the angel to Ferrara's demon. Nicky St. John managed to rescue the abandoned script by solving the narrative problems, and after much delay the film was ready to shoot.

With a budget of $20 million, Body Snatchers was Ferrara's most expensive film to date, shot in beautiful scope by Bojan Bazelli, and including the spine-tingling alien scream that was purloined from W.D. Richter's script for the 1978 version. Gabriel Anwar is serviceable as teen heroine Marti, Forrest Whitaker is as you've never seen him before as the increasingly 'delusional' odd man out, and Meg Tilly's stepmother Carol adds a dark foretaste to the horrors of the invaded family. The film also boasts plenty of creepy and disgusting special effects courtesy of

Phil Cory, with probing tendrals, dissolving carcasses, and slimy pods being a real treat for horror fans. Also of note is the excellent theme tune by Ferrara's regular composer, Joe Delia.

Warner Brothers felt uncomfortable with the end result and had no idea how to market the film. They basically sat on it for almost a year unsure of how to proceed. Ferrara managed to get a screening at the Cannes Film Festival where the critics were willing to take him and his film seriously, and this led to many positive reviews. Bolstered by this good reception, Warner Brothers put the film out on the festival circuit and it became an instant cult classic at the Dylan Dog Horror Festival in Milan where thousands of hardcore horror fanatics appreciated the sharp satire and dark imagination at work. This overwhelming response saved the film from its 'straight-to-video' hell and was given a moderately successful theatrical run in America.

BRAINDEAD (1992)

(aka Dead Alive)
Dir: Peter Jackson / New Zealand

The final part of Peter Jackson's celebrated 'splatter trilogy' which kicked off with Bad Taste and continued with Meet The Feebles, is also the funniest and goriest. The basic plot concerns Lionel (Timothy Balme), whose tarot reading girlfriend, Paquita (the gorgeous Diana Penalver) joins him for a date at the local zoo. But Lionel's mother Vera (Elizabeth Moody) disapproves of their relationship because she believes the girl to be "experienced", and does all she can to disrupt their date until she is bitten by a Sutran rat monkey and transformed into a contagious zombie. Lionel takes her home but is unable to stop the spread of the undead, and pretty soon he has to deal with a zombified nurse, priest, and a very annoying zombified toddler. And then all hell breaks loose.

Braindead is a bloody spoof which takes a nostalgic look at 50s New Zealand, subverts it with a sharp social satire, and then adds a whole lotta blood. It's a film which marks the zenith of extreme movie gore whilst at the same time is a lot of fun, coming on like a feel good family comedy that just so happens to have sick jokes, hungry zombies, and a lawnmower bloodbath at the end. It's a bizarre mix that has delighted global audiences over the years, but not so much the critics, many of whom failed to see the funny side, like The Daily Mail's Christopher Tooky who sniped "It's a good job the director grew out of making this stuff". Yeah, so that he could bombard us with utter tosh like Lord of The Rings, King Kong, and Lovely Bones? No thanks, I'd settle for Braindead any day. Another critic labeled the film "The end of civilisation as we know it". High praise indeed!

With the international cult success of his homemade debut, Bad Taste, Jackson struggled for a long time to find anyone willing to finance Braindead, and eventually set out to work on Meet The Feebles instead, a strange puppet parody which became the focus of his frustrations as a filmmaker, and the result was a very nasty piece of work which attacked everything from showbiz, to war veterans, to AIDs victims. But all of that spiteful aggression is nowhere to be seen in Braindead, which despite the high levels of violence and sick gore, is a very upbeat experience. And with this film Jackson seems to have exorcised some kind of demon from his psyche, because after Braindead he seemed to have matured and moved on to more adult-orientated projects like Forgotten Silver and Heavenly Creatures before selling out to Hollywood.

Incredibly, the BBFC passed Braindead uncut whilst films like Straw Dogs and Reservoir Dogs were still being refused home video certificates. The film did, however, cause much controversy in America when the MPAA cut it to ribbons for an R rating (it was also re-titled Dead Alive to avoid confusion with the Bill Pullman film of the same name). The morons at Blockbuster Video refused to stock the unrated version, so video company Vidmark supplied them with the R-rated cut which is just as silly and incoherent as the Blockbuster versions of The Cook, The Thief, His Wife, and Her Lover, and Bad Lieutenant.

It's a testament to Peter Jackson that he stuck to his guns and made exactly the type of movie he wanted to make without compromise, leaving viewers slack-jawed in amazement as Lionel gets out his lawnmower for the bloody showdown. Often topping polls for being the goriest movie ever made, but there is also a lot of heart here, even if you do have to pass through an avalanche of blood, guts, and body parts to get there.

BRANDED TO KILL (1967)

(Orig title: Koroshi no rakuin)
Dir: Seijun Suzuki / Japan

Japan has produced many risque and unique filmmakers over the decades, from Koji Wakamatsu (The Embryo Hunts In Secret), Teruo Ishii (Horrors of Malformed Men), and Norifumi Suzuki (School of The Holy Beast), to latter day saints like Shinya Tsukamoto (A Snake of June), Takeshi Kitano (Violent Cop), and Takashi Miike (Gozu). But nowhere will you find a more unique talent under such restricted conditions as Seijun Suzuki, an uber-prolific artist who was as inventive as anyone working in the medium, and who was producing up to four movies per year at the height of his powers whilst maintaining a distinctly wacko style all of his own.
   Branded To Kill is his finest hour, a strange nihilistic hitman movie made in the late 60s for the Nikkatsu Corporation, Japan's biggest film studio who released a couple of new movies every week due to their frantic schedule. Nikkatsu demanded that their filmmakers have only one week for pre-production, three weeks to shoot the film, and three days for editing. Ironically, working under such hectic circumstances seemed to bring out the best in Suzuki who thrived on a spontaneous approach to filmmaking, and he would add all kinds of surreal and perverse touches to his pictures, much to the annoyance of the execs at Nikkatsu who had continually warned him against it. But the great Suzuki would just carry on regardless.

The plot of Branded To Kill concerns lone hitman, Hanada Goro (Jo Shishido), who is ranked third in his assassination organisation but is under some stiff competition. He becomes obsessed with Misako (Annu Mari), a femme fatale who has her own fixation on dead birds and butterflies. She recruits him for a seemingly impossible contract killing, and when he fails in his mission due to some blackly comic timing, he becomes the target of the Number One ranked hitman known only as The Phantom, whose methods of hunting threaten Goro's sanity just as much as his life...

Branded To Kill borrows elements from classic American noir, French new wave, and the expressionistic style of The Cabinet of Dr. Caligari, but Suzuki blends those disperate elements into something fresh, exciting, and original. It's a confusing tale for many, but it's also astonishing to look at; almost every frame in the film is perfected to Kubrick-esque proportions, even if many of those frames contains images of demented sexuality and shockingly casual violence. The result is a feast for the eyes and the brain, as beautiful as it is outrageous, seductive and repulsive, entertaining and appalling.

The executives at Nikkatsu were not impressed with Suzuki's freewheeling style, and they immediately fired him for making "movies that make no sense and no money". But in the meantime he became something of an icon among the counter-culture movement, and after much prompting from fellow filmmakers, like-minded students, and the general public, Suzuki successfully sued Nikkatsu for wrongful dismissal. Suzuki was henceforth blacklisted and unable to direct another feature for years.

Branded To Kill's reputation has gradually flourished over the decades into cult classic status, and is generally considered to be an 'absurdist masterpiece', and has achieved a certain level of international arthouse acclaim, with luminaries like Jim Jarmusch, John Woo, and of course Quentin Tarantino all citing Suzuki's film as being an influence on their own works.

THE BROOD (1979)

Dir: David Cronenberg / Canada

Controversial psychiatrist, Dr. Hal Raglan (Oliver Reed), has created a treatment called Psychoplasmics whereby his patients are taught how to manifest their anxieties into physical mutations spawned through the pores of their skin.
Sometimes the teachings of this method brings out sores and cancers in his patients, and his treatment of Nola (Samantha Eggar) unleashes mutant killer humanoids who murder those responsible for the 'mother's' rage. Her ex-husband, Frank (Cindy Hinds of Black Christmas fame) becomes suspicious of Raglan and his methods, and he attempts to find out why his daughter is covered in bruises and why people are falling victim to a clan of pint-sized killers. He eventually discovers that Nola can project her hostilities in physical form by giving birth to furious mutant offspring, and the showdown begins...

The Brood presents a typical Cronenberg scenario; a mad doctor creating radical new techniques that goes badly wrong and have an ambiguous effect on the human body. I use the word 'ambiguous' because the body horror elements that Cronenberg unleashes on his characters aren't necessarily destructive of the human host, but serve rather as an altering of the biological make-up of the victim. The disease sits in its own warm human shell, beyond good and evil, and unleashes its life-force as needs must. In Shivers it was a slug-like parasite that invaded the human body and turned its hosts into sex-crazed maniacs; there was no real damage done to the hosts other than wanting to have sex all the time. In Rabid it was a spike which emerged from a woman's armpit and fed on the blood of her victims with the unfortunate aside of infecting her 'partners' with rabies; she still wanted 'intercourse', but her idea of sex had become radically different from the rest of society, and crucially, her new biological disposition didn't really do her any harm. The virus, or disease, or (in the case of The Brood), the physiological mutations taught by Raglan are only evil in relation to other humans (and their nervous systems), and their attempts to hit back against the alienating condition and resist the 'orgy'. But beyond that, Cronenberg always treats his body horror scenarios and bizarre diseases with respect. He famously proclaimed "I am syphilis" whilst promoting Shivers a few years earlier, and has since commented that he would be interested in seeing a beauty contest based on the internal organs of humans and a reality TV show of terminal patients angled on the perspective of the cancer (and Cronenberg is one of the sanest and most intelligent directors in this book!).

Cronenberg wrote the script for The Brood in an agitated state in the middle of a nasty divorce and custody battle. And it's these autobiographical details combined with his obsessions on the bizarre mutations of the human body that led to the birth of his most quintessential film. Amazingly, The Brood was originally only a side project; he was supposed to be working on a script called The Sensitives (which later became Scanners), but because of his ongoing divorce and parental strife, he found it difficult to concentrate on writing it, and instead tried to deal with his anxieties by developing a whole new screenplay that was much more in tune with the way he was feeling at the time. He has since described The Brood as "My version of Kramer Vs. Kramer", adding that he seriously wanted to kill his ex-wife.

What follows is a nasty and poignant little movie set in the bleak of winter. It's a much more character-driven piece than his previous work, but there are still some fantastic set-pieces of brutal carnage, such as the murder by mallet and the scene where a playschool teacher is beaten to death in the presence of her traumatised pupils. Reed is as good as ever as Raglan, Hinds is likable as the concerned father, and Samantha Eggar is superb and way over the top in her role as the dangerous mother, Nola. Also lookout for Cronenberg regular, Robert Silverman, as a disgruntled ex-patient, listen out for Howard Shore's modest but effective score (the first of many for Cronenberg), and marvel at the dark subtext concerning familial anguish, child abuse, domestic hell, and of course, the revolt of one's own body.

THE BUTCHER (2010)

Dir Kim Jin-Won /South Korea

Remember the scene in The Texas Chainsaw Massacre where Marilyn Burns is strapped to the chair surrounded by the crazy cannibal clan at the dining table? Well, this Korean effort is a feature-length tribute to that classic scene. The director represents the father, the maniac in the pig mask represents Leatherface (he even gets to play with a chainsaw), and the lad in the red t-shirt represents the idiot self-mutilating son. Unfortunately, there's no Grandpa in this one.

The Butcher is your typical 'Torture Porn' offering; the gimmick here being that we get to watch the action mostly from cameras that have been attached onto the heads of the victims. We get the usual warehouse/mill setting, a small group of characters, most of whom are there to scream and beg for their lives, and of course, lots of blood and gore. The film would have worked much better as a short, or at least trimmed down to an hour or so because it's quite over-stretched and time-padded in places. If you have a sick sense of humour, however, you'll probably find much to enjoy here. The director treats his assistants almost as harshly as the victims, and bellows orders like "Pull the shit out of her stomach and make 'em eat it!!!" Yeah, eat your heart out Mr. Spielberg.

The mounted 'photography' gets annoying at times; I know this was meant to create a verite effect but it does become nauseating after a while. It's also a dark film, not just in terms of subject-matter, but the print quality on the DVD is much too dark and it's difficult to see what's going on in some scenes.

The black humour is a treat and is perhaps the film's strongest asset overall. In the middle of some power tool torture, the director gets a phone call from his mum and spends the next few minutes talking to her about church and the bible like a good Christian. And when he hangs up he gets right back to the power tools. There are also some satirical and self-deprecating swipes at the movie business; the director mentions selling the film to America because "they like bloody things", and you can't help but chuckle because the director of The Butcher, Kim Jin-Won, no doubt had similar plans for this film. Also, the young assistant wears a t-shirt that reads 'I Love Korea' in English - Perhaps a cute comment on Western dominance seeping into everything, even corrupting these Koreans through useless commodities and trashy cinema?

It takes a while for the gore to be explicitly shown, but the film makes excellent use of sound design - It's one of the nastier sounding movies I've ever watched. Your neighbours will probably think you're watching a real snuffy. Snuff 102 is still the most disturbing and troubling of all the 'torture porn' films, but The Butcher is worth a look in a less demanding mood, especially for those who have a rank sense of humour. Banned in many countries around the world (even in its native land), this gritty exercise in sadism ultimately has a gleeful sense of fun and mischief about it, like a young child who delights in showing us a mouthful of chewed up food. A cross between The Texas Chainsaw Massacre and Last House On Dead End Street, shot on DV.

CAGED HEAT (1974)

Dir: Jonathan Demme / USA

Roger Corman's greatest contribution to film was his willingness to nurture new talents. In the 60s his AIP studio was crammed with up and coming young directors including Martin Scorsese, Francis Ford Coppola, Peter Bogdanovich, Joe Dante, and Jonathan Demme, filmmakers who would go on to define the age of modern cinema. So just remember, if it wasn't for Corman we would probably never have had Raging Bull, The Godfather, or Silence of The Lambs.

Jonathan Demme's stint as a writer/producer for Corman put him in good stead to make his debut feature, Caged Heat, a women-in-prison title for the drive-in market, whose memorable tagline ('Rape, riot, and revenge. White hot desires melting cold prison steel') sounds very typical of the exploitational angle of many similar types of films. However,

Demme's take on the sleazy genre manages to strike an impressive balance between violence, nudity, and sadistic authority figures, whilst keeping the proceedings in line with the popularity of feminist ideology.

Jacqueline Wilson (Erica Gavin) is sentenced to a spell at Connorville Women's Prison for armed robbery. The institute is run by the crippled Governess, McQueen (Barbara Steele), and her cronies, including her side-kick, Pinter, and a neo-fascist doctor, Randolf. She befriends inmates and together they hatch an escape plan which sees them back on the streets. Together with 'Crazy Annie', an old friend of Jacqueline's, the gang pull off a bank robbery, stealing the thunder from a couple of male would-be robbers. The escapees then decide to return to Connorville to save their captive friends from the sadistic experiments of the evil Dr. Randolf...

All the usual women in prison ingredients are here - the obligatory shower scenes with full frontal nudity, the violence and bitching, the riots and rebellions, and fiendish personel - But Demme expands on this limited genre by centering on a likable bunch of renegade women, and stylistically pushes the boundaries for such fare; legendary DP Tak Fujimoto supplies the eye-popping visuals, John Cale the unorthodox score, Erica Gavin a rousing lead performance, and horror starlet Barbara Steele presents her usual iconic campy quality, all adding to the legitimate proceedings of a prison film which is far greater than the sum of its exploitational parts.

The US drive-in crowd always had a taste for dangerous foul-mouthed women, and this has resulted in a few strange concoctions over the years, such as Russ Meyer's Faster Pussycat, Kill! Kill!, but very few were as interesting or as unique as Caged Heat. I'd settle for this over Silence of The Lambs any day.

CAMERA (2000)

Dir: David Cronenberg /Canada

A short autobiographical film by David Cronenberg which was made to celebrate the 25th anniversary of the Toronto Film Festival. Camera charts the short (six minute) monologue of an ageing man who has become terrified of the movie camera - "Get that damn camera out of here, it will do irreparable damage to us all!" - Voicing his concerns about the camera, "that clunky old ghost", the man (Videodrome's Lewis Carlson) laments on the absurdity and cruelty of a machine that preserves our youth whilst life continues to haggar our flesh. Shot on video and 35mm, this short comes on like a Philip Larkin poem with all the dark cynicism of age and fears of encroaching death; but it's also infused with Cronenberg's traditional obsessions - "It was like I had caught a disease from the movie" - and is shot in his usual cold and detached manner (which is ironic considering how close to the bone this project was to Cronenberg who was approaching his 60th birthday at the time of filming). Camera is available on the Videodrome 2 disc set (Critereon's deluxe edition). Alternatively, you could probably catch it on Youtube.

CANNIBAL (2005)

Dir: Marian Dora /Germany

Armin Meiwes is a German cannibal who achieved global notoriety after cooking and eating a voluntary victim whom he contacted via the web. The two men recorded the whole event on video camera, and parts of that footage were broadcast on a UK TV documentary series, Bodyshocks, in an episode entitled The Man Who Ate His Lover (I'll never forget the scenes of Meiwes cooking the penis and then complaining that it was "too chewy" to eat) .

This bizarre and discomfiting story had a touching poignancy about it; Meiwes was not a sadist, he was quite willing to allow his volunteer, Bernd Jurgen Brandes, to back out of the plan at any time. And though their short-lived relationship seemed sick and debased to most people, there was also something undeniably beautiful in their mutual understanding and willingness to go ahead with their heart's desire, knowing full well of the consequences.

The real life event had an immediate impact on the media, and the intense drama within sent shockwaves across the world. It's no surprise that filmmakers were quick to explore the story, with Grimm Love being a touching portrait of the doomed pair, but ultimately failing to capture the emotional depths at its disposal. Marian Dora's take on the story, Cannibal, takes us even further away from the dark heart of the event, and instead stands as a grim exploitative shockfest.

Unlike Grimm Love, Dora's film doesn't dwell too much on the relationship between Meiwes and his mother; instead we're shown only a fleeting (but vivid) childhood memory where she reads to him that dark fairytale, Hansel and Gretel, at bedtime. A memory which seems to have buried itself deep into his subconscious, and implies that it was those terrifying descriptions of the youngsters who are eaten by the wicked witch that had fascinated him, and became a chief motivation in his life.

Most of the film takes place in Meiwes' unkempt home which looks like a grim backdrop for a Richard Kern photo shoot. Actors Carsten Frank (from Jess Franco's Incubus) and Victor Brandl are adequate in their roles, and clearly have no qualms about shedding their clothes. Dora also serves as cameraman (as he did in Le Petite Mort: Die Nasty), and his directorial style reminded me of Andrey Iskanov in the way he uses up-close and personal camerawork, his willingness to unleash his characters' fantasies and fears in a hallucinatory but physical form, and the use of child-like repetitive chimes on the soundtrack.

Grimm Love is perhaps the better film as it is more believable and more faithful to the true story (though it's certainly far from perfect). Grimm Love was also quite touching and genuinely heartfelt in places, whereas Cannibal isn't; a soppy piano ballad just isn't enough to move an audience. Overall, Dora's take centres much more on the S&M fantasy of the event, and does little to shed any light on the mindset of the characters involved. It's a shame then that Dora doesn't seem interested in exploring the most interesting aspect of the story. On the plus side, he does deliver on the shocks: In particular the infamous cock-biting and severing scenes which are very strong and is the most excruciating genital mutilation seen since Ryan Nicholson's Torched. With that scene I guarantee you'll be shielding your nads for safety.

CHRISTIANE F. (1981)

(aka We Children of Zoo Station)
(Orig title: Wir Kinder vom Bahnof Zoo)
Dir: Uli Edel /W.Germany

Many first encountered this film on the back of the David Bowie soundtrack and had no idea what was in store for them. It is a disturbing classic that has left scores of film fans reeling over the decades as this bleak narrative features youngsters falling to the depths of debauchery with no redemption in sight. Along with Requiem For a Dream, Christiane F is one of the most effective anti-drug movies of all time. The plot is based on the true story of a thirteen year old girl who arrives in Berlin after her parents' divorce, and whose desire to be accepted by the local youths leads her to becoming a desperate junky and street prostitute.

Even before her addiction to heroin, life isn't exactly much fun for Christiane; she lives in a grim tower block that "stinks", her sister moves away to live with their dad, and her mother is rarely there for her. On the positive side, she's a big Bowie fan and she hangs out at a local night club called Sound, a place where fellow Bowie fanatics hang out, do drugs, and watch Night of The Living Dead in a conjoined cinema club.

Christiane soon becomes attracted to Detlev, a young homeless kid who is part of the scene at Sound - he introduces himself to her after she spots a junky on the nod in a toilet cubicle (she thought he was dead). Her relationship with Detlev means she gets to hang out with druggies, wastoids, and punks, and go on petty crime sprees to pay for their kicks. This early part of the film bristles with a positive vibe of youthful optimism. But perhaps inevitably, dropping LSD becomes passe for the group, and when Christiane learns that Detlev and his buddies are hooked on smack, she is tempted to try it for herself...

Christiane (based on real-life counterpart Christiane Felscherinow, on whose autobiography this film is based) dyes her hair pink on her fourteenth birthday and uses her birthday money to buy some heroin and shoots up for the first time using a kit borrowed from a complete stranger.

And it's all a slippery slope from there - street hooking for dirty and abusive scum at Zoo station, shooting up in filthy toilet cubicles, needles clogged with blood, and the nightmares of withdrawal are all par for the course here. We see Christiane transform from a bright and pretty young girl, to a sick and repellent, greasy street bum in less than two hours. Heroin chic it most certainly ain't.

If the powers-that-be were serious about their anti-drug campaigns, they could simply make it mandatory for all impressionable teens in the country to watch this film, because believe me after watching this harrowing masterpiece only the stupidest of the stupid would consider the lifestyles depicted here as cool or hip.

The drug abuse explored in the film is so unglamorous that it makes viewers shake their heads in disbelief when Christiane goes right ahead and gets herself hooked on heroin, despite the degenerate junkies that surround her and who should have made her realise what damage the drugs can do. But having said that, Christiane seems to drift in to her addiction by just going along with the flow, by not having any kind of motivation either way except that she wants to be with her new boyfriend, or as William Burroughs puts it in his classic novel, Junky; "Heroin wins by default". She isn't forced by bullying or by peer pressure into taking drugs; in fact, when Detlev discovers that she has taken H he goes mad and gives her a harsh telling off.

Parental neglect is an issue that is dealt with in subtle fashion in the film by director Edel; Christiane's mother is rarely ever at home and generally has no idea what her daughter gets up to while she stays out all night. Even when she does learn of Christiane's habit (after the girl OD's in the bathroom), her way of dealing with the situation is suspect at best.

The David Bowie soundtrack - which comprises some of his most new-wavy stuff taken from such classic albums as Station To Station, Low, and Heroes - is nothing short of incredible; we have TVC15, Look Back In Anger, Warszawa, V-2 Schneider, Stay, and Helden/Heroes, the latter becoming the theme tune to Christiane and Detlev's co-dependency. Bowie even makes an appearance as himself in a live performance of Station To Station in which he looks to be just as wasted as his audience. And it's a credit to the Thin White Duke that he accepted the role, despite the inevitable controversy of the subject-matter.

Natja Brunckhorst's performance as Christiane is astonishing; she has an assured manner and maturity which far exceeds her years. In fact, the entire cast of young actors in this film do not put a foot wrong - Each and every one of these performances is astonishingly good. The aforementioned Bowie tracks are also perfectly woven into the dark fabric of the film, wearing off as each reel becomes bleaker and more depressing until we reach the equally downbeat ending. Uli Edel's sleek and detached direction is also expertly done, as is Pankau and Jurges' mesmerizing camera work; they manage to make late 70s Berlin look like a neon-lit hellscape. Quite simply one of the greatest movies ever made. Unmissable.

The real Christiane F has been on and off drugs since the late 70s. She was in a band called Sentimentale Jugend with her then boyfriend Alexander Hacke, with whom she appeared in the early 80s cult movie, Decoder, alongside fellow junky William Burroughs and Genesis P. Orridge. She lost custody of her son in 2008 when it was discovered that she was back on drugs.

LA CLASSE DE NEIGE (1998)

(Class Trip)
Dir: Claude Miller / France

A nervous child is driven to his school skiing trip by his father. Having been raised from a young age on terrifying stories about marauding gangs of organ thieves, ten year old Nicolas (Clement van den Bergh) seems prematurely aware of the hidden dangers of life and finds himself trying to deal with his anxieties through a series of disturbing and often violent fantasies. Meanwhile, a youngster has gone missing on the trip, and Nicolas' father may have something to do with it...
   La classe de neige is a chilling tale based on Emmanuel Carrere's best-selling novel (itself based on a true story), and went on to win the Jury Prize at Cannes. The film is chock-full of stunning performances from the youngsters whose youthful faces nevertheless provide an inner-maturity and nuance which far exceeds their years. Director Claude Miller, who was a protoge to Francois Truffault for many years, is best remembered in the English-speaking world for his 80s thriller, Garde a vue (which was remade in Hollywood as Under Suspicion), lends a cold eye to the chilly proceedings and flits around the dark heart of children's fairytales like Hansel and Gretel, Sleeping Beauty, and The Little Mermaid, and updates those allegories to an unnerving effect. Indeed, he even treats us to a re-telling of W.W. Jacob's classic horror story, The Monkey's Paw, in a particularly bloody and gruesome fantasy sequence.
   American filmmaker Larry Fessenden would later try his own hand at depicting the disturbing daydreams of traumatised youth in his underrated Wendigo, which also borrows the ice-cold look of Miller's film.

Often compared with Neil Jordon's The Butcher Boy and Atom Egoyan's The Sweet Hereafter, La classe de neige is a grim but subtle fairytale shocker which has its roots in that most unacceptable of modern taboos. It's a film where childhood is anything but sweet.

CLEAN, SHAVEN (1993)

Dir: Lodge Kerrigan / USA

A journey into the mind of a paranoid schizophrenic; do you really want to go there? Often described as the closest thing to experiencing schizophrenia on film, Lodge Kerrigan's Clean Shaven follows Peter Winter (Peter Greene), who escapes from a mental institution and heads off in search of his daughter, and seems to leave a trail of bodies behind. En route, we get to witness his torment through heard voices, screams, and self-mutilation, and the soundtrack is one of the most challenging and abrasive you'll ever hear.

Coming on like a less exploitative version of Romano Scavolini's Nightmares In a Damaged Brain, the film is bleak and convincing in its portrayal of mental suffering, and features a solid central performance from Greene. There's an awful sense of loneliness and isolation in the dread-ridden atmosphere, and the auditory hallucinations are spine-chilling; even though most of the words can't really be heard properly, the tone and volume of this demanding voice is enough to put viewers on edge. But what tips them over is the self-mutilation; the scene where Peter cuts himself with a razor in the shower is hard enough to watch, but later in the car when he convinces himself that there is a transmitter implanted in his fingertip, and then uses a pen knife to dig up his fingernail. Even the hardiest of extreme movie devotees have squirmed in their seats at this scene.

Amazingly, this film was partly financed by Warner Brothers! God knows what they thought they were investing in. Clean Shaven played theatrically on the underground circuit in America in the early 90s, and then vanished. It has since found its way onto DVD enticing an international audience to take the dread-ridden journey into psychological hell.

A CLOCKWORK ORANGE (1971)

Dir: Stanley Kubrick / USA

Tagline - "Being the adventures of a young man whose principal interests are rape, ultra-violence and Beethoven".

Stanley Kubrick's most controversial film follows Alex (Malcolm McDowell) as he leads his gang of young rogues through nightly rounds of "ultra-violence", with beatings, rape, stolen cars, and breaking and entering, all for kicks. They wear white jump suits, codpieces, and black bowler hats, and communicate in a strange lingo made up of broken Russian and cockney slang called "nadsat". Alex dislikes school but has a passion for Beethoven and sexual violence. The victims include subversive writer (Patrick Magee) who is severely beaten before his wife (Adrienne Corrl) is gang-raped.

After violently dealing with insubordination among his "droogies" (Russian for friends), Alex is smashed in the head with a milk bottle and left for the police during a raid on a house. In police custody he learns that his beating of a woman with a huge phallus has resulted in her death, and pretty soon Alex finds himself in prison. In order to shorten his sentence, he volunteers to undergo a radical new treatment for violent criminals, or 'Aversion therapy'. The treatment is still in its experimental stages, and although Alex has a torturous experience, by the end of the therapy he does seem to be cured. He still has the violent urges, but those feelings are countered by extreme nausea.

Released back into society, Alex is no longer a natural being with free will, but a technologically manipulated drone (hence 'A Clockwork Orange' of the title), and even the thought of his beloved Beethoven is enough to make him physically sick. The outside world suddenly becomes very menacing to Alex, where vengeance is visited upon him by his ex-droogies who are now policemen, and his old victims (including Magee, who has some special payback in mind). After a suicide attempt, the media make Alex into a celebrity and the shadow Prime Minister uses him as proof of a broken society in a cynical ploy to win votes. But perhaps the biggest cynic is Alex himself, whose phrase "I was cured alright" ends the film on a morally dubious note.

Kubrick's free-thinking, anti-authoritarian take on Anthony Burgess' novel on Catholic redemption is extremely effective, regardless of what allegorical take you put on it. It's visually astonishing, disturbing, ever quotable, and featuring one of the most memorable portrayals of evil in the history of film. With his lurid narration which is at once intimate and engaging, it's difficult not to feel sympathy for Alex, especially when you consider the dreary leap-frog games going on around him in the political sphere, with power-hungry parasites using him as a pawn in their reckless antics.

With A Clockwork Orange, Stanley Kubrick even surpasses the directorial virtuosity that he displayed in his previous film, 2001: A Space Odyssey; almost every trick in a filmmaker's arsenal is utilised, with fish-eye lenses, beautifully choreographed set-pieces, expert use of lighting and arrangement, fast motion, slow motion, etc. McDowell puts on the best performance of his career, gleefully reeling off Burgess' self-invented slang terms (good is "Horrorshow", sex is "The old in-out-in-out") with a sadistic glint in his eye, and perfectly capturing the faux-innocence of youth ("It wasn't me, brother, sir").

A Clockwork Orange was released in the UK in January 1972, not long after the controversies which met Ken Russell's

The Devils and Sam Pekinpah's Straw Dogs. A wave of media-led controversy shot the film to box-office success, and this in turn led to some imitative behaviour among young fans who started wearing the white boiler suits and bowler hats as a way of emulating their anti-heroes. The media leapt onto 'copycat' crimes, such as a Dutch tourist who was gang-raped by youths who sang Singin' In The Rain (a song Alex sings during a gang-rape in the film) whilst they did it. And the case of a 16 year old youth who kicked a homeless man to death. The press described the kid as being fascinated by A Clockwork Orange, although it later turned out he was obsessed with the book and had never seen the film.

The controversy escalated when the British censors were seen to be lenient on the film, and unlike The Devils and Straw Dogs, A Clockwork Orange was passed uncut with an X rating. This led to calls for the head of censorship, Stephen Murphy, to resign. Even the government got involved when the Home Secretary, Reginald Maudling, demanded to view the film at the BBFC headquarters before its release, and this led to accusations of state censorship. However, while all this hassle was going on, something very strange happened; director Stanley Kubrick simply banned the film himself due to concerns of copycat violence, and that ban remained in force for almost 30 years until he died in 1999. Still a hot topic today, no film fan should miss it.

COMBAT SHOCK (1986)

(aka American Nightmare)
Dir: Buddy Giovinazzo / USA

"Today's one of those days where everything that can go wrong, does". Combat Shock is a grim and repellent little movie that was eventually picked up by Troma and given a theatrical and home video release, becoming a cult classic among 80s videophiles in the process.

The DVD box art makes this look like some all-action, gung-ho heroic war movie, but anyone buying or renting the DVD who were expecting a Rambo clone or a Platoon would have been shell-shocked at what they actually got for their money.

Without a doubt, Combat Shock is one of the nastiest, bleakest, most depressingly downbeat movies ever released by Troma; and it also happens to be a near-masterpiece of zero-budget filmmaking. Imagine Taxi Driver remade by John Waters with a bit of Eraserhead and The Deerhunter thrown in, and you should have some idea of what to expect here, but nothing can really prepare viewers for how ugly this movie is...

The Director's brother, Ricky, stars as Frankie, a down-on-his-luck, severely traumatised 'Nam vet who lives in a rank and grubby tenement block with his shrieking wife and mutant baby. They have no money and no food, and he receives a letter from the landlord informing him that his family have been evicted and should vacate the premises by 6pm. To make matters worse, he is in debt to a trio of local thugs who constantly hassle him and beat him up, and his best friend is a sick junky who has resorted to robbing lone women at gunpoint as a way of feeding his addiction. Plagued by constant flashbacks to his traumatic experiences in a makesift POW camp, and being hunted through the jungle by the Vietcong, this deeply troubled ex-marine - a trained killer - crumbles psychologically, and this leads to one of the bleakest and most shocking movie endings of the 80s.

Combat Shock is a labor of twisted love; director Buddy G filmed most of the Vietnam scenes on Staten Island, and to be fair it's almost a perfect illusion; had he decorated the close-ups with exotic plants, those scenes would have been much more convincing as a Vietnam warzone, but he nonetheless captures that sense of hostile terrain perfectly. Buddy earned his living at the time as a music teacher, and most of the cast members (even the extras) were his drum students who agreed to appear in the film in exchange for free drum lessons. So he got his music students to dress up and run around Staten Island with fake guns. Love it. The only downside is that most of the amateur actors aren't really good enough to convey the severity and desperation their roles needed, such as Mike Tierno who plays the junky and who uses a rusty wire coat-hanger to manually insert heroin into a raw wound on his arm because he doesn't have a syringe at hand. Also, the hoodlums were a bit miscast and look about as tough as The Village People (they were probably decent drummers though).

On the plus side, actress Veronica Stork who plays the annoying wife is superb in her grating role, and leading man, Ricky G, whose burned-out stare and grubby clothes make him one of cinema's most memorable budget-psychos (he also contributed the quirky and eccentric music score). Director Buddy G shows remarkable visual flair with some interesting camera work, tightly-paced editing, and a real knack for picking out shooting locations - We have scenes shot in genuine urban cesspools of grime and squalor, which seems to mirror the fractured state of mind of our troubled protagonist. Needless to say, if you're accustomed to such Troma crappola as Fat Guy Goes Nutzoid or Surf Nazis Must Die, then Combat Shock will come as something of a nasty surprise.

Originally shown on the festival circuit under its original title, American Nightmare, it played well at the grinders in New York's Times Square district before Lloyd Kaufman and Michael Herz of Troma offered a distribution deal. The MPAA demanded cuts to the film but the folks at Troma decided to push their luck and release it uncut. They were eventually found out and ordered to remove the more graphic shots or face a hefty fine (in the book version of Sleazoid Express, Bill Landis claims that this kind of practice was fairly common for Troma who would release the uncut versions of their films into theatres, regardless of what the censors had to say on the matter). Troma also added the stock war footage which definitely improves the film, especially during the opening credits.

And while we're on the subject of Troma, it's worth pointing out that their DVD release of Combat Shock includes an excellent audio commentary by Buddy G, and he is joined by European gorehound Jorg Buttgereit for a fact-filled, laugh-out-loud funny audio track that is worth the price of the disc alone.

Buddy G continues today as a music teacher and he occasionally teaches video production classes at New York's School of Visual Arts. His career as an indie filmmaker has been marred by frustrations since his promising debut; he got the gig to direct the legendary Maniac 2 but the project fizzled out when actor/producer Joe Spinell died suddenly. Also in the late 80s he wrote a screenplay called Dead and Married for Vestron. It was a dark comedy but in the finished cut of the film all the sick jokes had been watered down to such an extent that the finished product (re-named as She's Back) didn't work.

Numerous self-written scripts remain unfilmed, such as the intriguing Dirty Money, the controversial 123 Depravity Street, and even the relatively commercial Jonathan of The Night. He has written short stories, poetry, and even novels, the third of which he adapted to the screen himself under the title Life Is Hot In Cracktown. The crowning achievement of his career so far is undoubtedly No Way Home (aka Life Sentences) in which, by a mad miracle, he managed to cast Tim Roth, James Russo, and Deborah Unger in his film which is about a man who is released from jail and who must face the daily grind of poverty, drugs, and violence.

COME AND SEE (1985)

(Orig title: Idi i smorti; aka Kill Hitler)
Dir: Elem Klimov /Soviet Union

Produced to mark the 40th anniversary of Russia's victory over the Nazi invaders in World War II, and based on the novella The Khatyn Story by Ales Adamovich who was a partisan himself during the conflict, Come and See follows young teenager, Flyora, who joins the Soviet partisans in the woods near his home. With a naive sensibility Flyora reckons on being a hero with an easy triumph over the Nazi's, but as the film progresses we witness his descent into trauma and madness as the Byelorussian holocaust literally tears his world apart. It's a horrendous coming-of-age story, from naive innocence to blind hatred to costly experience, his face physically alters throughout the film from fresh youth to haggard old war veteran.

Made during the Perestroika period, Come and See is perhaps the most brutal and emotionally draining war film you'll ever see. Director Elem Klimov was obsessed with authenticity in the making of his film and went to some alarming extremes in order to replicate the harsh environments of war - The explosions weren't created with safe pyrotechnical trickery, they were real. The bullets were also real. And it's astonishing to see lead actor Aleksei Kravchenko running around with real explosions going off around him, sometimes as close as three feet away. In some scenes he has live rounds just missing his head by centimeters. All weapons used here (guns, bombs, flame throwers, etc) are genuine. Even the uniforms in the film are 100% authentic originals. Adding to the realism is Aleksei Rodiomov's handheld camerawork which gives the proceedings an intimate edge. Real footage showing the aftermath of Nazi atrocities in the area is inserted into the film to drive the authenticity home.

Originally entitled Kill Hitler, Come and See is a hallucinatory, heartbreaking, traumatic, and uncompromising experience - Not for all tastes. There's a scene where civilian villagers are rounded up and forced into a barn by Nazi soldiers where they await their fate with dread. An officer appears at the window offering the chance for anyone to leave, but on condition that the children are left behind. Of course, no one is prepared to desert their children to die alone. And unlike the Jews in Spielberg's Schindler's List, there's no respite at the final moment. No, the barn is then merrily set on fire by the Nazis. And while the civilians are screaming and burning alive, the Nazis shoot at the barn with machine guns and flame throwers, and we are forced to watch all of it.

For a while this film was used as propaganda to warn citizens of the Eastern Block about the dangers of fascism, but it certainly wasn't made with propaganda in mind. There's no nationalistic one-upmanship to be found here, the 629 villages decimated are well documented. There's no communist rhetoric either, and many of the partisan heroes in the film are flawed characters. It's a film about the suffering of ordinary people during wartime. In fact I would say there is ten times as much propaganda in films like Saving Private Ryan.

In the UK, Come and See was given an uncut 15 certificate, which may puzzle some readers, but it's one of those films that really ought to be seen by the largest possible audience, even school students. However shocking the film may be, it's never gratuitous and certainly not exploitative, and the British Board of Film Classification have recognised this.

The Kino DVD release is disappointing - It looks to be a rushed job presented with very little care in full screen format and appears to have been lifted from the VHS version with no attempt at re-mastering. The film is also split over two discs which means having to change discs midway through viewing. Such an important film treated in a cheap and shoddy fashion is not good enough. Hopefully a much better presentation of Come and See will be released in the near future.

THE COOK, THE THIEF, HIS WIFE, AND HER LOVER (1989)

Dir: Peter Greenaway / UK

"I'm gonna kill him, and I'm gonna... EAT HIM!!" Perhaps Greenaway's finest film to date, and one of the highlights of 90s cinema, The Cook, The Thief, His Wife, and Her Lover centres on Le Hollandais, a lush restaurant owned by gangster Albert Spica (Michael Gambon) whose wife Georgina (Helen Mirren) has an affair with Michael (Alan Howard), a mild-mannered bookish type, before all hell breaks loose. The film boasts excellent performances all round but Gambon steals the show as Mr. Spica, a foul, obnoxious, ignorant brute whose verbal tirades are blackly hilarious and whose poisonous presence soils the atmosphere of any room he's in. Every time he opens his mouth something vulgar comes out (an accusation he amusingly levels at one of his cronies). There's superb camera work courtesy of veteran DP Sacha Vierney, Jean Paul Gaultier provides the costumes which compliments the decor of each luschious room in the restaurant, and Michael Nyman contributes one of his finest scores.

Due to the outrageous violence, sex, and nudity, this film (along with Pedro Almodovar's Tie Me Up! Tie Me Down!), was one of the first to receive an NC-17 rating in America, prompting those idiots at Blockbuster Video to destroy all of their uncut copies and replace it with the R-rated alternative which loses a whopping thirty minutes of footage. Now the R-rated version implies a more perverse ending than Greenaway intended; during the cannibalistic finale in which Georgina forces her husband at gunpoint to eat Michael's dead body, she suggests that he "try the cock, you know where it's been", then there's a cut showing Spica eating a piece of meat from a fork with the audience believing that he is eating Michael's penis. Whereas in the uncut version we know that that particular
piece of meat came from Michael's hip area (David Cronenberg's The Brood suffered a similar glitch in narrative when British censors demanded cuts to the scene where Samantha Eggar gives birth to a furious humanoid creature and proceeds to lick away the blood, with the cut version implying that she is eating her child!). But all censorship

hassles are over now and The Cook is widely available on DVD in all its uncut, NC-17 glory.

CRASH (1996)

Dir: David Cronenberg / Canada

Disaffected couple James and Catherine Ballard (James Spader and Deborah Unger) have a jaded sex life and only seem to get excited whilst listening to each other's stories of sexual escapades. One day James has a head-on car collision with Helen Remington (Holly Hunter), whose husband is killed in the accident, and the pair are treated at the same hospital. The two eventually discover that the crash was sexually arousing, and this is when they are approached by Vaughan (Elias Koteas), a mysterious man posing as a doctor so as to get pally with crash victims to fuel his own obsessions. Turns out that Vaughan is also turned on by car wreckages and mangled humans, and he takes James and Helen on a voyage of discovery where they get to meet more members of this shadowy subculture, get to witness the re-enactment of the fatal crashes that killed Jayne Mansfield and James Dean, and sink further into the cold and dreamy perversion for everything flesh and metal that is mangled on the highways.

Based on the cult novel by JG Ballard (described by Jean Baudrillard as "The first truly hyperreal novel"), Crash sees the return to form for David Cronenberg after the disappointing Naked Lunch and flat M. Butterfly. It's not an easy film to get to grips with in one viewing but there is much to be enthralled and appalled by here as we're presented with technology that becomes an extension of - and deconstruction of - the human body. The characters are like human crash test dummies; there's no psychology, no erogenous zones (at least, not in the old sense); the human body is physically altered and transformed, revealing new sex organs in the process (check out the scene where James has penetrative sex with a wound on Rosanna Arquette's leg). Like Ballard's book, Cronenberg chooses not to get involved with the events on screen and keeps an observers distance from the characters - There's no real desire among them, no libido, no death drive; just the plain banality of the anomaly of death. Vaughan's body is a reflection of the twisted and dented metal stained with sperm: No orgasms, just ejaculation. And for many viewers it's the cold and necrophiliac vibe of Crash that unnerves the most.

The film was met with anger and walk-outs when it played at the Cannes Film Festival, but still managed to win the Special Jury Prize. It also won the Genie Award in Canada where it was the most successful domestic film of the year.

Glowing reviews and healthy box-office led many to believe that Cronenberg had tamed down the extremes of Ballard's book, but the hassle really began when Crash hit the UK. After its screening at the London Film Festival, Heritage Secretary Virginia Bottomly demanded it be banned (she hadn't even seen it), the London Evening Standard went to town on the film describing it as being "beyond the bounds of depravity", and Westminster City Council banned it immediately. With its subject-matter it was inevitable that it would be largely misunderstood and cause offence among moralists. Film critics led by Alexander Walker were also campaigning to have the film banned, and The Daily Mail's Christopher Tookey got his knickers in a twist complaining that the film "Promulgates a twisted morality of its own: namely that life is about the pursuit of sexual gratification, whatever the consequences. It is the morality of the satyr, the nymphomaniac, the rapist, the paedophile, the danger to society." If that wasn't idiotic enough, he also took the time to condemn the film's positive depictions of gay and lesbian sex, and sex with the physically handicapped, which did more to expose his own right wing agenda more than anything.

The BBFC remained completely unmoved throughout the whole Crash debacle, and they even held screenings of the film for lawyers, forensic psychologists, and disabled groups, and concluded that "Rather than sympathising or identifying with the attitudes or tastes of the characters in the film, the average viewer would in the end be repelled by them, and would reject the values and sexual proclivities displayed". It was subsequently released uncut in the UK which led The Daily Mail to condemn the decision, commenting "All the psycho-babble in the world cannot refute the simple fact: The film is sick. It should not be shown".

The message of Crash is a grim one indeed about the direction human sexuality is heading in. It's also beautifully shot and is perhaps Cronenberg's best looking film since Videodrome, and Howard Shore contributes the eerie, guitar-based theme tune to stunning effect. Although you can never beat the experience of seeing Crash in the cinema (or the drive home afterwards), DVD editions look fantastic. It's just a pity that the Cronenberg commentary track (available on the Criterion laserdisc) is still missing in action.

DANGEROUS GAME (1993)

(aka Snake Eyes)
Dir: Abel Ferrara /USA

Harvey Keitel stars as Eddie Israel, an increasingly unhinged filmmaker struggling with his latest project, Mother of Mirrors, an autobiographical film based on the collapse of his own marriage. Madonna stars as Sarah Jennings, a bad actress whom Eddie guides through scenes as his fictional wife. He also hires Frank Burns (James Russo) to play his self as Sarah's drunken and abusive husband. But, as things turn out, Frank is drunk and abusive to Sarah for real, both on and off camera, and events from Mother of Mirrors soon spills out into real life...

What makes Dangerous Game so remarkable is that Eddie's character is clearly based on director Abel Ferrara himself. Those paying attention will notice that the clapperboard for Mother of Mirrors will sometimes read 'Abel Ferrara' instead of 'Eddie Israel'; Eddie's stories and anecdotes about his experiences with sex and drugs are based on Ferrara's own past; Ferrara's wife, Nancy, plays Eddie's wife in the movie, and his ways of screaming at his cast and crew are allegedly based on Ferrara's own aggressive directorial methods.

Basically, the film has three layers - The film itself (Dangerous Game), the film-within-the-film (Mother of

Mirrors), and the real life drama that enshrouds the proceedings and can only be guessed at. It was originally titled Snake Eyes but was changed when Brian De Palma took the title for his own movie - A much more appropriate
title in fact. Characters in Dangerous Game sometimes shout out for the attentions of Ken Kelsch and Nicholas St. John; Ken Kelsch served as DP and Nicky St. John wrote the script, but neither of them were actually in the fictional film! It would have been nice if Ferrara himself had made an appearance to guide Harvey Keitel in his tough moments, just as Eddie intervenes in Mother of Mirrors to help his cast members, but perhaps that would have pushed the boat too far. As to what is fact and what is fiction; well, Ferrara's fans have been arguing about that for the best part of two decades. But one thing's for sure; this is a rewarding, sometimes shocking and compulsive viewing experience.

DAS KOMABRUTALE DUELL (1999)

Dir: Heiko Fipper / Germany

"WARNUNG! This film contains extreme violence, and isn't suitable children or viewers under the age of 18. Kids, pregnant women, and psychologically unstable men might suffer severe mental trauma from watching this movie. The HF team takes no responsibility!"

Made in the late 90s but not released on DVD until 2008, Das Komabrutale Duell opens with segments that were shot in 8mm. And to be fair it looks alright; in amongst all the jumbled gore footage of mangled humans, including women's faces that have been smashed in and their tits cut off (this is a bit odd and random because there are next to no female characters in the entire film!). We do get a brief backstory - A vicious gang of sadists called The Eightlets Mafia are in the middle of a street war with the Bandera family. Problem is, the Bandera family are near immortal, and all attempts to do away with them is doomed to failure as the Bandera clan just keep on coming back for more...

And that's basically it; the rest of the pic is shot on video and shows how the Bandera's are chased, captured, brutally beaten, cut up with chainsaws, shot, stabbed, have their heads smashed in with sledge hammers, but they will not die. This all sounds like a gorehound's dream but the special fx are mostly quite lame and never even remotely realistic. The blood looks like watered-down tomato puree, the victim's being beaten and shot and dissected are obviously plaster mannequins (perhaps an homage to Lucio Fulci?), and the whole project seems to have stemmed from the imagination of an extremely disturbed eight year old. The fact that the cast and crew are made up of grown men in their 20s and 30s only adds to how ridiculous this film is, but there's no doubt that these guys enjoyed making this movie, they're clearly having a great time.

A bloody awful film then, but it is at least more watchable than other German amateur jobs like Familienradgeber and Hunting Creatures, but that isn't saying much. Included on the end credits is a warning from the filmmakers; "Don't even think of pirating this movie, or you'll be the next coma-brutal duel" - HF Pictures 1984-1999. Interestingly, I have never seen this film available on any illegal download site so I assume the threat must have worked! Maybe other production companies should follow suit. Das Komabrutale Duell was also banned in its native Germany in 2007.

DAUGHTER OF DARKNESS (1993)

Dir: Ivan Lai Kai Mingh / Hong Kong

Daughter of Darkness is part of producer Wong Jing's loose trilogy based on lurid news headlines that also includes Brother of Darkness and Red To Kill. Anthony Wong plays the police chief who is investigating the brutal murder of an entire family. The film begins as a silly comedy with the police breaking into a house to discover the bodies. Wong's experience on the job means that he is used to the sights and smells of crime scenes, but his younger colleagues are tentative when entering the building. Three battered bodies are found in the living area. Wong heads upstairs and finds a further corpse in the bath tub. He fondles the dead girl's breasts claiming it's a useful way to get an idea of how long the victim has been dead for. The local press has descended on the scene with their cameras and notebooks but are kept at the doorway. Wong accepts a bribe and allows a reporter inside to take snapshots. In a macabre and silly scene, Wong displays an insensitive and twisted humour when he starts posing with the dead bodies during the photo shoot.

The only relative to have survived the massacre is Amy (Lily Chung, who played Ming Ming the retarded girl in Red To Kill), and Wong immediately puts her and her boyfriend under suspicion. And in a scene reminiscent of Hitchcock's Rear Window, he follows the couple to the boyfriend's flat and watches them have sex in the apartment from an opposite balcony. Cue more silliness as a guy falls from the baloney into a skip, Wong indulges in a bit of bra sniffing (which causes him to sneeze!), and a steamy sex scene in the shower. The young couple are questioned at the station and it soon becomes apparent that the girl is responsible for the murders. And in a series of disturbing flashbacks, Amy tells the whole story of how she felt driven to commit the massacre due to a long and sustained period of abuse.

The wacky humour soon dissipates once Amy tells her story; one night she and her boyfriend are walking home after a date and they catch her father sleeping with another woman. The father (played by Brother of Darkness' Ho Ka-Kui), slaps her and has an altercation with the boyfriend. She goes home and is scolded and humiliated by her mother and jealous siblings. Later that night the father gets up to take a piss and winds up peeping on Amy through the keyhole as she takes a shower. He jerks off. Amy opens the door and catches him at it, so she goes and tells her mum, but mum doesn't believe her, and the whole family converge on her once again to scold and lecture her about 'telling tales'. The father is especially pleased with himself during this little episode.

Amy returns home one day to find her father frolicking with another woman in the house. Father doesn't seem to mind being caught in the act and continues to toe-fuck the woman with his big toe. He then gets out the camera and takes a few pictures of his naked floosy, much to her annoyance, and she takes her belongings and storms out. Left alone and horny, daddy then turns his attentions onto his daughter; he bursts into her room drunk and starts taking snapshots of her in her transparent nightdress. He then rips the dress off and rapes her in her bed. Mother then returns home from her own bit of extra-marital fun and suspects that another woman has been in their bed. Mum and dad then have a blazing row.

Wong and his assistant conducting the interview at the station are shocked and saddened by the story so far, but the tale only gets worse... Amy runs away from home and stays at her boyfriend's flat. A while later her dad shows up at her work place and hands her an envelope which contains the naked pictures he took of her. He then cruelly scatters a handful of the pictures across the floor of the workshop and she has to scurry around trying to retrieve them all before any of her workmates can see them.

It's Amy's birthday, and after a long and steamy sex sesh at her boyfriend's place, she grabs a knife and heads off home for a bloody massacre. She walks in to find dad sitting on the couch watching TV with a pair of panties on his head, and a lit birthday cake on the coffee table. She slashes him with the knife but he manages to wrestle it away from her. He then ties her hands to the ceiling, strips her, and rubs her body in cake before licking it off. He then bends her over the dining table and rapes her from behind. Amy's sister comes downstairs and sees what's going on but she doesn't do or say anything, she just turns and heads back up the stairs.

Boyfriend suddenly kicks the door down, charges in and attacks the father. A violent struggle ensues and the boyfriend pistol whips him unconscious. But just as the couple embrace and the ordeal seems to be over, dad gets back up and beats him with a long piece of wood. Amy then shoots her father at close range, and he staggers backwards onto the floor begging for his life. She shoots him a further five times in the groin. She collapses to her knees in the middle of the room, and this is when mother and brother return home. They immediately try to calm her down but she is giggling and has clearly lost her mind. Mother begs for her life but is shot dead on the spot. Brother makes a run for it up the stairs but she catches him and drags him back down and stabs him to death. She then goes upstairs to hunt for her treacherous sister and finds her hiding in the wardrobe. She drags her out and drowns her in the bath tub in a long and harrowing sequence.

Amy then returns downstairs and sits in stunned silence at the enormity of her crimes. Dad then suddenly sits up, Michael Myers-style, and attacks her, pinning her on the ground and strangling the life out of her. She manages to reach a broken Buddha ornament and stabs him in the throat with the sharp end.

Wow, what would Jeremy Kyle have to say? Daughter of Darkness is a quintessential CAT III movie in that it includes all the typical ingredients that make these films so bizarre and outrageous. The slapstick and darkly comic interludes that set up the story, the leering and exploitative angles, the faux-Hollywood erotic thriller template, the bright colourful settings, the factual basis, and extremely violent finale, it's all here. The film also does much to expose the facade of the modern nuclear family where, despite appearances, no one really knows what goes on behind closed doors in the average family unit. Director Ivan Lai also seems to have a snipe at the useless conformities of organised religion, especially in the scene where the father returns home one night and lights an incense stick for his Buddha statue and offers a blase prayer; he seems to do this purely because it's a 'done thing' and not because he has any religious convictions - Actually, he doesn't seem to have a spiritual bone in his body, and instead runs on a purely animalistic instinct to satisfy his mad primal urges. Quite a statement for a low-budget exploitation movie! (And this Buddhist sham has also spread across the world in recent years as many Westerners consider it cool and chic to have a Buddha in their homes to create a facade of spirituality, but this type of thing seems to be embraced the most by idiotic 'culture vultures' and the most shallow and soulless cretins of society).

In court, Amy is sentenced to death by firing squad, and she gives birth to a baby boy while on death row. The baby is immediately taken away from her. She is then led down a corridor and out into the open where she says her goodbyes to her boyfriend and their baby before she is executed.

DAWN OF THE DEAD (1978)

Dir: George A. Romero / USA

In the late 60s a zombie movie called Night of The Living Dead changed the face of modern horror forever. With its mixture of creepiness and a sharp social satire, this lurid black and white classic introduced audiences to a new master of horror, George A. Romero. Across the decades Romero would occasionally return to his living dead roots, and alongside such classics as The Crazies and Martin, he would add to his zombie series, and each one seemed to pick up on some social dislocation that was relevant for the time, and as a whole these films served as a cracked mirror reflecting back on the era in which they were made.

In the 60s with Night of The Living Dead, it was the Vietnam war and the civil rights struggle which was strongly hinted at (despite Romero himself who has always denied that he intended any such 'messages' in the film). In the 80s, Day of The Dead presented scientific progress being hijacked by the military for the purpose of conflict and destruction. Land of The Dead (2005) focused on the callous conservatism of the Bush administration, Diary of The Dead (2008) on the information overload of the Youtube generation, and Survival of The Dead (2010) on man's lack of progress since the days of the 'wild west'. But it was in the 70s with its mindless consumer culture that Romero offered up the blackly comic gore-fest, Dawn of The Dead.

The film opens on a chaotic scene in which a TV station struggles to make sense of the situation as they see the living dead chomping their way through civilization. Fran (Gaylen Ross) and her helicopter pilot boyfriend, Stephen (David Emge) decide to flee before the mayhem takes over. Meanwhile, a brutal SWAT team including Peter (Ken Foree) and Roger (Scott H. Reiniger) launch an assault on an infected housing project, which expands upon themes in NOTLD in which, in the eyes of the law, there is no difference between racial minorities, political radicals, and flesh-eating zombies; they are all gunned down in cold blood.

Pretty soon Peter and Roger join Fran and Stephen (or 'Flyboy') for a chopper flight into the wilderness where they hover above fields crawling with gun-toting rednecks before settling down in a huge shopping mall. It's here that the gang of human survivors stay put surrounded by zombies who are seemingly drawn to the comforting consumer paradise by a faint nagging memory that continues to possess them, post mortem. Interestingly, the zombies here aren't as menacing as they are in NOTLD; they're slow, pathetic parodies of humanity, stumbling around dazed and confused and falling into water fountains whilst instinctively gnawing at useless consumer products. The survivors aren't much better; they winge and argue amongst themselves endlessly in their materialistic haven as they load up all the products they can until a marauding biker gang turns up and spoils all the fun. And then the situation spirals completely out of control...

In a market swarming with glossy Hollywood horrors, Dawn of The Dead was something of a controversial hit. The film's huge success in Europe and Asia put other horror efforts of the time (like Nightwing and Prophecy) to shame. Romero's sly take on 'retail therapy' and the pleasure of blowing lots of cash still rings true today. It would make a great double-bill with Philip Kaufman's remake of Invasion of The Body Snatchers (1978) which was made around the same time and also touches upon themes of mindless conformity
(or even a triple-bill with Willard Huyck's Messiah of Evil which pre-dates Dawn and also has much to say on the subject, too).

It's also worth noting that Dawn was the first film to fully explore the concept of a man being bitten and slowly turning into a zombie himself. Night of The Living Dead hinted at the idea with the sick girl in the basement, but Dawn presents us with the slow, harrowing details, from delirium to the cooling down, to death and transformation. And this idea has been duplicated in countless zombie movies ever since. But even here, Romero remains disinclined to reveal whether the zombie pandemic is something that affects a human corpse, or is a contagious disease that affects the blood. Decades later, when new classics like Danny Boyle's 28 Days Later and Zack Snyder's Dawn remake hit the screens, this idea had become so confused that, technically, the 'zombies' weren't really zombies at all. Almost every single zombie movie has to tussle with this idea to a certain extent, to gauge its path and find its feet in zombie lore.

Dawn of The Dead exists in at least three different versions, all of which were the subject of controversy with the censors. The European print, which was put together by none other than Dario Argento, is the shortest, but ironically, caused the most offense to the BBFC. This version concentrated more on the gore and dropped much of the satirical stuff, and for this reason it was heavily censored. Romero's preferred 128 minute final cut was treated less harshly but still it didn't escape unscathed. For although the censors seemed to 'get' the joke, they remained insistent on locking out some of the more extremely gory moments. This same version was released unrated in America as Romero feared the MPAA would give it an X rating (to most Americans an X means porno). A longer 'Festival Version' was shown at Cannes and did the rounds in 16mm format. This version includes many extended and alternate sequences but the Goblin soundtrack is missing, and it runs for 140 minutes.

On home video the film has suffered a lot with the UK censors, with the 'Director's Cut' being shorn of a few seconds up until 2003 when it was finally passed uncut. Say what you will about Mr. Lucas' many re-releases and special editions, but as far as George's go, it's actually Romero who takes the biscuit with endless DVD repackaging. After numerous bootlegs and not-quite directors' cuts (including that in the Trilogy of The Dead box set), the fully uncut edit of his zombie masterpiece is here in all its glory. Okay, so those extra few seconds of gore don't make much difference to what was already one of the finest horror movies ever made, but it's a welcome addition to any self-respecting horror fan's collection, nonetheless. With a budget of $1.5 million and boasting the very graphic head-popping special effects by Tom Savini (who also cameos as the leader of the biker gang), DOTD went on to become one of the most profitable indie movies in history. Essential viewing.

Black Friday is an exciting day for consumers in America, as on the day after Thanksgiving the nation's superstores dramatically reduce the prices on all of their snazzy products, and the public arrive in droves to take advantage of this special day on the calendar to load up their shopping baskets with mountains of gadgets, LCD TV's, and designer label clothes. In November 2011 we witnessed a more crazy Black Friday than usual; in addition to the stampedes and fisty-cuffs and hair pulling and general greed, one woman resorted to using pepper spray on her rival consumers, and one man, when cornered by armed robbers in an outside car park, refused to hand over his precious bargains, he was shot dead on the spot. Say what you want about the rampant consumerism of the 70s but things nowadays have escalated to the point where people are willing to die over a few cheap products; what can you say about a culture in which a man feels that his shopping goods are more important than his life? George Romero has said that the scariest thing about Dawn of The Dead was watching an American audience 'getting off' on the fantasy of running riot in a shopping mall, and it was only then that he realised how raw a nerve he had struck with his film.

POSTSCRIPT: THE FALL OF GEORGE ROMERO

Unfortunately, Dawn of The Dead seems to have marked the high point of Romero's creativity and artistic control. The Pittsburgh native has found it increasingly difficult to find funding for his projects, and when he has, the results have often failed to impress his fans. He still comes up with interesting concepts but they're usually let down by a bland, middle-of-the-road directorial style, perhaps more suited to TV than the big screen.

The trouble began with Creepshow (1982); Stephen King wrote the screenplay, an uninspired anthology of shorts which Romero couldn't do much with. King may have ruled the paperback market, but his film scripts have never been up to much. The film itself is nothing more than a silly distraction, a throwaway piece aimed at youngsters.

Day of The Dead (1985) was Romero's last truly satisfying film, a gruelling masterpiece that can stand shoulder to shoulder with his finest work even though the film went through some production problems with the financiers wanting him to trim down the gore. Monkey Shines (1988) was suspenseful in places and has some decent performances, but overall it suffers from that awfully safe, TV vibe that has marred quite a few of his films. The same sort of problems returned again when Romero teamed up with Dario Argento (the pair became friends during the making of Dawn of The Dead) for Two Evil Eyes (1990). Argento's half of the film was great; a mixture of several Poe stories that presented a new take on the macabre. Romero's half, The Facts In The Case of M. Valdemar, however, totally lacks any kind of menace and has a bland music score and a flat TV movie vibe; it's about as scary as Murder She Wrote.

Another Stephen King adaptation, The Dark Half (1993), had a very interesting concept, but Romero doesn't dig deep enough; had he fully explored the roots of King's novel and the real life events that inspired it, he may have had another masterpiece on his hands. My main criticism of the film though is that it seems he was just trying to cash-in on King's name alone. Bruiser (2000) was Romero's first self-written work in more than a decade and remains one of the most disappointing efforts of his career; it's a badly written mess of cliches and mundanity.

After a long time trying to secure funding, Romero was at last able to return to his living dead series in 2005 with Land of The Dead. And although the film was met with muted applause from fans and critics, it was Romero's best film in a long time. It does have its problems; it fails to capture the epic quality of his initial trilogy, it offers up a cliched villain and an unlikable, bland hero, and is basically more of a sketch of a film than a finished piece. The main problem, I find, is that in this fourth installment, the zombies are now the sympathetic ones but this angle isn't explored in any kind of detail - A black zombie's facial expressions cannot carry the bulk of a movie's plot, it was never going to work.

Diary of The Dead (2008) began the annoying trend of pushing the zombies to the background while Romero concentrated on his 'progressive aspect' by exploring the topic of the day; in this case the internet and 24 hour news coverage. The characters were more bland than ever and the film also suffered from a very inconclusive ending.

Survival of The Dead (2010) was released straight to video in all territories, but ironically, it is the finest entry in the series since Day of The Dead twenty five years previously. While again the zombies are hidden away in the background for much of the film's running time, Romero treats us to a bunch of characters who are forced to be ruthless to each other as an essential part of the survival instinct. We are thus transported back to the lawless days of the wild west. All in all though, it's at a loss compared to the grim nihilism and rough edges of his earlier work.

Romero's films are often left of centre in outlook: ethnically and sexually integrated, pro-feminist, gay-friendly, anti-macho and skeptical about capitalism, they represent the 'progressive aspect' of the horror genre (an aspect that mainstream critics love to sink their teeth into as a way of justifying their love of violent splatter movies!). Recent interviews with Romero show a man who feels uncomfortable with the violent and ideological excesses of his earlier films, and who seems to be more concerned nowadays with peace and love, and is as far away from wanting to push the envelope of horror cinema as one can get. It's a real shame that this once great filmmaker chooses to play down the darkness and bleakness of his best work and instead attempts to soften the blow with his most recent output. It's an attitude which continues to disappoint his fans.

DAY OF THE DEAD (1985)

Dir: George Romero / USA

The third installment in George Romero's living dead series is a moody, claustrophobic gem set almost entirely in a huge subterranean storage compound in Florida that serves as a makeshift laboratory and military base. The army have been ordered to protect a small group of scientists who are trying to find a solution to the zombie pandemic. Hordes of walking corpses have been penned into an enormous cave, and the scientists use them as guinea pigs for their research. The chief scientist, Dr. Logan (Richard Liberty), nicknamed 'Dr. Frankenstein', tries to domesticate the zombies so that the human survivors (who are now outnumbered by 400,000 to one) can keep them under control. One zombie, 'Bub', shows promise and responds to various influences like music and hand gestures, and offers hope to the ever-dwindling civilisation. But the army, led by Captain Rhodes (Joseph Pilato), puts an end to the research and takes over with reckless abandon, ultimately leaving themselves exposed to the millions of hungry zombies who are waiting outside...

George Romero's initial living dead triptych offers up three of the greatest zombie movies ever made. Night of The Living Dead (1968) was the first truly modern horror film with its verite ambience and savage social commentary. Dawn of The Dead (1978) attacked the mindless consumer attitude of the 70s and beyond, and Day of The Dead (1985) took us underground to explore the pseudo-scientific engineering being hijacked for murderous military deeds. The film also follows on from his earlier efforts like The Crazies and Martin in the way it addresses the lack of communication as being a big problem to any kind of solution.

Romero originally intended to create an epic three hour movie of Day, but financiers would only pay up if he agreed to tone down the blood and gore (1985 was the year that the MPAA started clamping down on movie violence). Fortunately, Romero saw sense and slashed his budget and script in half, brought back effects maestro Tom Savini, and delivered hell on earth as mankind makes its last stand against the living dead.

Looking back, it's incredible how Romero decided to scrap his "mainstreamed" idea for the script and plunge into a much more darker and bleaker territory of the film, because not only was his third installment set to compete with his earlier Night and Dawn, but there were also a couple of contemporary zombie movies competing at the box office around the same time, Dan O'Bannon's Return of The Living Dead and Stuart Gordon's Re-Animator. And, as mentioned before, the MPAA was tightening its restrictions, and its interference would have a negative effect on those who enjoyed watching violence on the big screen for years to come (notice how slasher franchises became increasingly silly and 'comedic' in the latter half of the 80s, the Friday The 13th and Nightmare On Elm Street sequels, for example).

Fans and critics treated the film with disdain on its initial release and Day of The Dead quickly died at the box office, only to break out of the grave as the film earned a huge cult following thanks to home video and late night cable screenings. It is now generally regarded as one of his finest, with many hardcore horror fanatics ranking it in their top five greatest movies of all time. It's interesting how opinions can change like that; from disappointment to admiration in a few short years. Indeed, Romero's latest trilogy of the dead, consisting of Land of The Dead, Diary of The Dead (dubbed 'Diarrhea of The Dead' in some circles), and Survival of The Dead have been treated non too favourably in recent years, and perhaps that too will change a little further down the line. In Romero's defense, it's important not to forget that he no longer has complete control of his finished films anymore; his latest efforts have been studio financed, thus he has the bigwigs to answer to nowadays. Even a masterpiece like Martin was greeted with boredom and confusion on its initial release.

It's no coincidence that Day of The Dead was made right after Creepshow. The characters in Day seem to have stepped out of an E.C. comic strip with the sly, nasty, perverted bad guys meeting their grisly fates. Romero perhaps wasn't through with that side of things. And how could he be? Creepshow is a piece of juvenile garbage and a waste of Tom Savini. But rest assured, Savini sure wasn't wasted on Day of The Dead, he really went to town on this one; characters are literally torn apart before our eyes, arms are hacked off, heads blown to pieces, and guts are literally spilling out onto the floor.

Although the film has been available uncut in the UK since 1997, the BBFC initially snipped out 30 seconds of gore for both film and video, including the shot of one of the soldiers having his back bitten by a female zombie, the close-up shot of the machete cutting through Miguel's arm when he has his limb amputated, the scene where a zombie is decapitated with a shovel, a soldier having his fingers bitten off, and the zombies feasting on the innards of Captain Rhodes.

DEADGIRL (2008)

Dir: Marcel Sarmiento and Gadi Harel / USA

Wow. A pleasant surprise. We need more teen comedies like this. Ok, this isn't a comedy per se, but there's lots of sick and twisted humour here... Two high school students discover a zombified girl in some deserted basement, and she becomes a sex slave to a group of horny outcasts. The film stumbles at the beginning with idiotic characters and some awful dialogue, but once it gets going this is actually a pretty decent little film. The character JT becomes an increasingly unhinged psychopath in his determination to keep their secret safe (he's also in danger of becoming cool, especially when he comes out with lines like "Jail is full of motherfuckers like us"), and the main character, Ricky, is infuriatingly incompetent - He is supposed to be the film's moral conscience, but like the young lad in The Girl Next Door, he does too little too late to help the damsel in distress; so there goes his credibility (amazingly, in a move that makes me wonder what on earth the filmmakers were thinking, Ricky encourages the school jock to partake in a bit of forced fellatio with the deadgirl; we know it's all part of a revenge plan whereby the girl will bite off his cock, but still, it does seem a bit morally dubious when the film's 'hero' looks to be actively contributing to her woes). The film has much to say on the destructive power of adolescent sexuality and gets darker and more twisted and interesting with the passing of each reel.

DEAD OR ALIVE (1999)

(Orig title: Hanzaisha)
Dir: Takashi Miike / Japan

Tagline - "WARNING: This motion picture contains explicit portrayals of violence; sex; violent sex; sexual violence; clowns and violent scenes of violent excess, which are definitely not suitable for all audiences".

Takashi Miike is in typically outrageous form with Dead Or Alive. It's a basic cop vs. crims scenario but Miike, in his own way, manages to keep things fresh and exciting. Ryuichi (Takeuchi Riki) leads a small gang of outcasts who, because of their Chinese heritage, have no place in either the Yakuza or triads, and so they wage a street war against both. Detective Jojima (Aikawa Sho) is on their heels, but he also has some personal problems of his own to deal with. His wife is having an affair, and he cannot afford to pay for a life-saving operation for his dying daughter. He urgently needs 20 million Yen and his allegience to the law is seemingly swept aside...

Dead Or Alive is a nice slice of cinematic excess which kicks off with an incredible opening sequence montage; a naked woman falls from a high-rise building clutching a bag of cocaine; also strippers, bloody shootings, gay sex, throat stabbings, arterial spray, freaks, gangsters, clowns, and a man snorting what must be the world's longest line of coke. The film is also typical of Miike's fast and makeshift shooting style with a very loose and improvised feel. Those who are only familiar with Miike's Audition will be surprised by how chaotic and undisciplined this film is, as Audition was so much more tightly constructed. However, if you enjoyed Gozu and Ichi The Killer then chances are you'll find much to savor here too.

The story of how the film came into being is an interesting one. Miike was approached by money-hungry film producers who offered him two male lead actors and a basic plot structure. He was given free reign to create whatever the hell he liked just as long as he stuck to the basic plot requirements. The producers felt safe in the knowledge that their actor's star power alone would be enough to secure a hit. Miike's reaction was to purposely make an anti-mainstream film with as many crude and offensive scenes as he could get away with, knowing full well that it would be aimed at mainstream audiences. I wonder what those two producers must have thought of the end result; they can't have been too dismayed though because Dead Or Alive eventually did become a hit across the world and not just in Japan. It also spawned a couple of well-behaved sequels, too.

People often criticise DOA for being directionless, claiming that it can't decide what kind of film it wants to be and so ultimately fails to satisfy on any level. I think that's a bit harsh; you only have to see a couple of Miike's films to know how much he likes to play around with genre conventions, and like his other work, such as Gozu, there's a real anything-can-happen-next vibe in DOA which far outweighs anything the critics have to say. Just take a look at the final showdown between the two lead actors; both Tekeuchi Riki and Aikawa Sho were big stars in Japan and it would have been sacrilegious for fans of either actor to see their hero being killed off by the other, a seemingly no-win situation you would think. However, Miike's way of dealing with fan expectation is so sarcastic and over the top that the ending must be seen to be believed.

Direct to video in all territories including Japan, in America DOA was released in both R-rated and unrated versions. The R-rated version loses a whopping 9 minutes of footage including the throat stabbing and subsequent blood gushing over the two men having sex, a guy being shotgunned in the back and the noodles he just ate exploding out of the exit wound in his stomach. Also animal porn, genital licking, a woman being drowned in paddling pool of diarrhea, semen spitting, a severed hand, more bloody shootings, and a guy ripping his own arm off. Be sure to catch it uncut.

DEAD RINGERS (1988)

Dir: David Cronenberg / Canada

Dead Ringers offered solid evidence of David Cronenberg's maturity and development into a truly great filmmaker, and builds on his previous character study, The Fly, and combines it with his interest in the metaphysical, to ultimately create yet another milestone in his exotically extreme ouevre. Stunningly powerful, deeply moving, and loaded with bizarre and disturbing ideas, Dead Ringers' expose of male fantasies has much to say on the fragility of masculinity and is presented in the director's usual cold, detached, and unflinching manner.

Based on the book Twins by Bari Wood and Jack Geasland (which was in turn inspired by the real life story of respected twin gynecologists, Steven and Cyril Marcus who in 1975 were both found dead in their littered New York apartment, a double suicide by overdose brought on by their addiction to barbiturates), Cronenberg presents Elliot and Beverly Mantle, a pair of outstanding gynecologists who open a brand new state-of-the-art fertility clinic and share a luxurious apartment. Although physically identical, the twins have very distinctive personalities; Elliot is a self-assured lady magnet, whereas Beverly is shy and introverted. Elliot is happy to procure women for Beverly by seducing them, having his wicked way, and then passing them off to his brother when he's done, unbeknownst to the women. When famous actress Claire Niveau (Genevieve Bujold) enters the clinic for help with her infertility, she also brings trouble in the form of jealousy; for although both brothers take turns in bed with her, Beverly falls in love, thus driving a wedge between them...

Not your average horror roller-coaster ride then, Dead Ringers' shocks are much more suggestive this time, but no less horrifying. Gone are the more openly grotesque and spectacular shocks of the exploding head (Scanners), gaping stomach cavities (Videodrome), and squeamish fingernail ripping (The Fly), and in their place are disturbing questions on the nature of identity, masculinity, narcissism, eroticism, and misogyny; a far cry from contemporary horror hits like Friday The 13th Part VII or A Nightmare On Elm Street Part IV, which were more concerned with churning out bloodless kills and corny one-liners (actually, the biggest screen monsters of the time were the MPAA whose tough new stance on movie violence was strangling the life out of the genre). The censors though couldn't touch Dead Ringers, for although it explores some dark and disturbing themes and subject-matter (misogyny, drug addiction, and um, custom-made gynecological apparatus for 'mutant women', to name but a few), Cronenberg's quietly devastating horrors were simply censor proof.

The true star of the show is Jeremy Ions whose double role as the twins offers a nuance so perfected that viewers can tell immediately which twin he is playing without him resorting to bug-eyed dramatics or cliched characteristics. And he is aided by Bujold whose striking performance stops her role from becoming a mere plot device.

DEEP THROAT (1972)

Dir: Gerard Damiano / USA

The world's first porno blockbuster, Deep Throat tells the tale of Linda Lovelace who visits her doctor (Harry Reems) complaining that she cannot reach orgasm. After some tests Reems discovers that the reason is because her clit is located deep down in the back of her throat. Cue much hilarity as a newly cured Lovelace gobbles every cock in sight and has that long sought after orgasm after all...

  Not exactly the best place to start if you're getting into 70s porn, for although Deep Throat is one of the most well-known pornos of all time, the film itself looks bloody awful. The lighting and sets are flat and completely uninteresting, and as for the sex scenes themselves, they're all rather boring. The film serves as nothing more than a curiosity nowadays. To have it available on DVD is surprising because I can't imagine why anyone would want to watch this more than once. The sex scenes are also ultimately a turn-off after hearing the awful rumours and allegations concerning the making of the film, such as the rumour that Lovelace was under-age when the film was shot, and the alleged practices of Chuck Traynor. The DVD presentation is disappointing with print damage and speckles galore. It was shot for $22,000 and the cast and crew had to hitch hike from New York to Miami where the shooting took place.

  The film has a sinister dark side due to the involvement and practices of Lovelace's then husband/manager, Chuck Traynor, a hate figure not only among the anti-porn movement and feminists, but even among long-time porn fanatics and many who have worked in the industry. Lovelace later spilled the beans and accused Traynor of beating and coercing her into selling her body and appearing in porn films. Feminist author Andrea Dworkin helped Lovelace to put a case together and took the matter to court where she accused pornography of being a violation of women (see also her scathing book on the subject; Pornography: Men Possessing Women). In a 2000 documentary for Channel 4 entitled The Real Linda Lovelace, Traynor was interviewed and confronted with the allegations that he had ordered his own wife's gang rape and had forced her at gunpoint to have sex with a dog on camera in a Miami motel room. His reaction to these claims was horrifying; he seemed basically nonplussed by the idea and acted like it was no big deal, and didn't really deny anything.

As for Linda Lovelace, I think her sad story has more to do with the fact that she had found herself in an awful relationship rather than being a victim of porn per se. She married a man who battered and abused and exploited her for a couple of years, ironically making her a star. To put a ban on porn won't make it go away, it will only make it more difficult to regulate and drive it underground. Nor will it put an end to the violence and abuse of women.

THE DEVIL'S EXPERIMENT (1985)

(aka Unabridged Agony; Orig title - Za Ginipiggu: Akumano Jikken)
Dir: Hideshi Hino /Japan

Devil's Experiment was the first entry in the Guinea Pig series from Japan, and one of the first shot on video shockers ever made. Nowadays 'torture porn' is everywhere, a cheap and simple way for filmmakers to make an impact, rather like the power chord in punk rock. With the advent of the camcorder which became widely available in the early 80s, the everyday public was able to contribute to the medium with home-made amateur epics like Boarding House, They Don't Cut The Grass Anymore, and Black Devil Doll From Hell. Over in Japan meanwhile, there was a growing market for micro-budget shot on video dreck; the burgeoning AV (adult video) market was becoming ever popular, with specialist superstores filled to the brim with amateur and very small production companies filling the shelves with assembly line trash. These videos were mostly porno products, but with the natural evolution of the horror genre, it was only a matter of time before a company came along and injected a bit of grue and nastiness into the market.

At the auspice of producer Satoru Ogura, Devil's Experiment was made back to back with the second in the series, Flower of Flesh and Blood, and like that film it's a plotless exercise in cheap and nasty sadism. And although Hino's Flower of Flesh and Blood is open to interpretation as far as those interested in subtext are concerned, there's really none of that to be found here. What we get is quite literally torture porn in its most stripped down and obscene basics. Three young men kidnap a woman and spend the next 40 minutes torturing her before finishing her off with some nasty and graphic eyeball needling. The eyeball trauma is the single most impressive and realistic looking scene in the entire Guinea Pig series, but the rest of the film ranks among the poorest, too.

The film's insistence on scene after repetitive scene of slapping the captive woman across the face becomes irksome very quickly; the oft-quoted "Banality of evil" is in full force here as we're witness to a seemingly endless display of slaps (the actors are clearly seen just slapping their own hands, and it's so lame and unconvincing) that reach an almost nullifying effect on the viewer. But rather like the scene in Mariana Peralto's Snuff 102 in which a woman is repeatedly punched in the face, this silly and clearly unrealistic violence ultimately curtails the edgy nature of both films, and instead serves as a disturbing realisation that we the viewers are simply wallowing in the lowest detritus of 'shock video', for better or worse.

Oh, but it definitely gets worse; the three lads put the woman in a swivel chair and spin her around. And around, and around. She is also kicked around on the floor, has the skin on her knuckles twisted with a pair of mole grips, is forced to listen to white noise on headphones at very high volume for 20 hours, has her finger nails ripped off, is hung from in a tree in a hammock, is burned, covered in maggots and animal guts, is cut open with a scalpel, and then the nasty eyeball trauma. And that's it.

It's interesting how Japanese censorship forbids the sight of pubic hair, and yet has no problem with the most vile and misogynistic nonsense like this (another example is Tamakichi Anaru's Tumbling Doll of Flesh which mixes pixelated sex scenes with graphic tongue torture!). Along with the rest of the Guinea Pig series, Devil's Experiment became an underground cult collector's item in the west, but I'm sure that many of those who hunted high and low for the bootleg VHS would have been disappointed with the end result. The whole series is available uncut from Unearthed Films.

DIARY OF A SERIAL KILLER (1995)

Dir: Otto Chan Juk-Tiu / Hong Kong

A notorious serial killer recounts his tale to cellmates in a Hong Kong prison the night before his execution. He starts out as a sex maniac whose busy wife can't keep up with his insatiable libido. He turns to hookers for violent sex. He gets a bit carried away one night and ends up killing one of them in mad lust, decides he enjoys the thrill of murder, and so continues killing more. He also indulges in kidnap and torture to satisfy his sick urges whilst keeping the 'family man' bullshit going for a while before the whole shithouse crumbles around him.

Judged alongside similar Asian atrocities, such as Men Behind The Sun or the infamous Guinea Pig series from Japan, Diary of a Serial Killer is either a fearless challenge to established cinematic limits or a reckless descent into the abyss, depending on your point of view. Photographed with stunning visual flair and expertly edited, the film alternates scenes of naive sentimentality with eruptions of graphic horror, taking time to establish the groundwork before unleashing the forces of hell against its audience.

With lots of softcore sex and violence, Diary of a Serial Killer is your typical CAT III shocker of the mid-90s. It is also awash with that strange candy-coloured lighting so typical of Hong Kong cinema of the time and makes the proceedings look like it could have been made ten years earlier (see also Robotrix and A Chinese Torture Chamber Story for more 90s CAT III movies that look like they could have been made in the 80s). The killer is a nasty piece of work, displaying all the sick characteristics you've read about in true crime books. He takes souvenirs from his victims; the tits usually, and he also uses string tied around the wrists and ankles of his victims to make macabre puppets of their corpses and has 'conversations' with them to amuse himself. He seems to love his wife and child very much but doesn't show any signs of remorse for his crimes until his murderous urges strike closer to home. The writers have obviously studied the characteristics of real life killers and have heaped all of this stuff into the script making for a very cliched type of killer with the old textbook traumas and all that, but the film is still quite entertaining.

The killer is very protective of a naive young woman. She may as well have the word 'victim' stamped on her forehead, but he somehow manages to suppress his urge to kill her, perhaps because she reminds him of more carefree and innocent times. She refers to him as "brother" and their (sibling?) relationship is quite sweet and innocent until they have a sex sesh in the back of his car!

Allegedly based on a true story, and hugely indebted to Doctor Lamb.

POSTSCRIPT: THE CAT III PHENOMENON

In 2010 a CAT III movie came along entitled Dream Home which focused on the extreme lengths that one crazy woman will go to secure her ideal living space. The fact that the film was also loosely based on a true story only added to the viewer's discomfort as Josie Ho went about her goal with a ruthless single-mindedness.

At its core, Dream Home represents a frustrating aspect of Hong Kong life; the poor, cramped living conditions, and busy, almost ruthless lifestyle of its citizens. Of course, all big cities have their daily grind and bustle, but in Hong Kong the environment is more concentrated than your average city. And it's these harsh unnatural conditions and the relentless hyper-capitalist mindset of its inhabitants that make Hong Kong one of the most chaotic cities of the Far East. Anger, madness, and violence is rife, and the tabloid papers are often strewn with lurid headlines detailing the bizarre and shocking crimes of those who cannot handle the pressures of life anymore.

With no safety nets of social housing or even a minimum wage, it's the poor who feel the worst effects of this kind of lifestyle, and they're often the first to crack under the pressure cooker of Hong Kong life. It's hot, humid, competitive, cramped, and hostile. The streets are a frenzy of traffic and stressed out commuters, the bright neon-lit city scape is littered with thousands of signifiers and advertisements all vying for your attention, becoming an illuminated blur of capitalist calamity. And even when you get home you can't really relax due to the crowded living conditions with families sharing tiny apartments in high-rise tower blocks with barely enough room to stretch their legs. Such breakneck speed and intolerable conditions leave behind a debris of madness and murder.

The main reason for all of this chaos is fairly obvious. In 1947 the British 'borrowed' the island of Hong Kong on a 50 year lease as a way to have access to the 'Tiger economies' of the far East. Shortly afterwards, mainland China fell under the rule of Communism. Hong Kongers knew that in 1997 their land would be handed back to the Chinese, but very few of them relished the idea of living under Communist rule. And after Margaret Thatcher failed to secure anything in the way of the British having a say in the running of the island once it was to be handed back, the race was on for the citizens to make their fortunes and escape the territory before the handover which would commence on the 1st of July 1997.

This rush to get things done seeped into everything; the day to day running of the city, the financial sector (Hong Kong was one of the world's fastest growing economies), and especially in the cinema. Whether it be the hyper-kinetic Kung-Fu vehicles of Jackie Chan, the fast and furious gunplay of John Woo's action epics, or the lightning speed of the production schedules of the sleazy CAT III movies, this race against time was clear to see in the nation's cinematic output.

Although there had been a few outre films released in the 80s, such as Dangerous Encounter of The First Kind and Devil Fetus, the CAT III rating wasn't officially made law in Hong Kong until 1988. The idea was to give filmmakers the room to produce sex, violence, and horror films with the encouragement of cashing-in on the export (and domestic) potential of such films. A slew of extreme Hong Kong productions hit the screens soon after and caused a scandal the world over.

The CAT III rating is similar to the American equivalent of the NC-17 - No one under 18 years of age was permitted to see these films (whereas the NC-17 forbids anyone under the age of 17). In America, films are often drastically cut to avoid the stigma of the NC-17 rating, but in Hong Kong the sleaze and the controversy was worn like a badge of honour, and at their height these films made up around 39% of the country's annual output.

Early CAT III releases were dominated by sexy thrillers such as Erotic Ghost Story, Robotrix, and Naked Killer - basically violent softcore films. But just around the corner was a new breed of gruesome ultra-violent killer movies like Doctor Lamb, The Untold Story, and Daughter of Darkness, and these films starred such legends as Simon Yam, Anthony Wong, and Lily Chung. Doctor Lamb tells the tale of a psychotic taxi driver who rapes and mutilates young women before taking photographs and hiding the bodies in the confines of his house. The Untold Story focuses on the confessions of a man who murdered his restaurant owner boss and his family before serving up their bodily remains to the locals in the form of 'BBQ pork buns'. And Daughter of Darkness puts us in the shoes of a young woman who resorts to murdering her entire family after years of rape and abuse from her parents and siblings. All three of these films are spiced up with grim and repulsively dark comedy, and all three are also based on true newspaper headlines.

The Category III ratings system applies to films produced anywhere (the French horror Haute Tension received the CAT III rating, for example), but the ones produced in Hong Kong have often been clubbed together and treated as a genre in itself. Thus many international cult classics, such as Run and Kill and Ebola Syndrome, are referred to under the umbrella term 'CAT III' movies. The significant cultural impact of these titles cannot be overestimated; there is no such umbrella term for the NC-17 movies in the West, perhaps because they constitute only a fraction of the sheer number of their Hong Kong equivalents.

On the 1st of July 1997 the British handed back sovereignty of Hong Kong to China, and it was around this time that the production of CAT III titles started to dwindle. Hong Kong has since been given some autonomy by the mainland, and been allowed to continue in its capitalist drive, but many citizens have complained that freedom of speech has taken a steady decline ever since. For more than a decade since the handover in '97 Hong Kong has continued to release the occasional outre film, such as Naked Poison, There Is a Secret In My Soup, Gong Tau, and Revenge: A Love Story, but the CAT III industry is a shadow of its former self. A recent trend in the Hong Kong film industry is to imitate the cinema of the mainland where romantic comedies rule the roost (if a film is a hit in China it can rake in millions in revenue that just isn't available in Hong Kong). Also, the Chinese have a strict censorship, and horror movies are generally outlawed there, which is perhaps another reason why CAT III movies have dwindled since the handover.

It's doubtful that we'll ever see a resurgence in the production of sleazy and extreme horror in Hong Kong while the mainland continues to frown on such films. But with the miracles of the internet and DVD, and indeed VCD (on which format many CAT III titles found a release for home viewing), we at least have a rich and diverse back catalogue to explore with more than twenty years of frantic and outrageous filmmaking at our disposal.

DIVIDED INTO ZERO (1999)

Dir: Mitch Davis / Canada

A short 34 minute film by Mitch Davis with heavy use of symbolism, grotesquerie, unsettling soundscapes, madness, and catharsis, and also boasts a very dark and grim atmosphere... A troubled serial killer recounts his life story, from self-mutilating youth to fully-fledged perv, he tells all in a calm and matter-of-fact way. Doesn't deliver quite the

same lasting effect as his later collaboration with Karim Hussain, Subconscious Cruelty (although it does share similarities with that doomy masterpiece and wouldn't be out of place as a segment in that film), but you'll find much here that is enthralling and appalling in equal measure, such as the notion that nature is a destructive evil (later hinted at
by Charlotte Gainsbourg's character in Lars Von Trier's Antichrist), and the gruesome revelations that give the film its splendid title. Reminded me of Jorg Buttgereit's Schramm, minus the humour and blatant violence. Recommended.

DOGTOOTH (2009)

(Orig title: Kynodontas)
Dir: Yorgos Lanthimes / Greece

An eccentric father keeps his wife and children locked in the grounds of their home and is determined to raise them so that they'll never need to know about the evils of the outside world. But of course the kids are growing up fast and the father begins to lose control.

This strange little film can be summed up in the scene where the father goes to collect his dog that is in training with the police force; "A dog is like clay" he is told, "Our job here is to shape it. We teach them how to behave. And we are here to determine what behaviour the dog should have. Do you want a pet, or a friend or a companion? One that obeys orders?" Whether you see this film as a comment on the overprotectiveness parents often put on their kids in the name of love, or as others have said, a comment on the Greek government's (and indeed western government's) treatment of its citizens (people as pets), it's important to remember that the film also works on a very literal level.
    Cats as demonizing propaganda, suspicion of outsiders, the beating of the daughter over the head with the naughty video tape can be read on many different levels. The wordplay censorship reminded me of Doublethink and 2+2=5 from George Orwell's 1984 ("A cunt is a large lamp", "A zombie is a small yellow flower"). The household is very much a patriachy - It's a shame we never get to hear the mother's side of the story; she seems totally out of it and depressed.
    The kids have reached adolescence and have begun to question everyone and everything around them - The attempted brainwashing can't keep them down for very long. The cast are totally game but Aggeliki Papoulia who plays the sister steals the show with her deranged performance in which she does a Rocky Balboa, a crazy dance, and even punches her own teeth out in one scene. She deserves a ton of respect, especially as her role was all but ignored at film festivals. The chloroform game is extremely dangerous and fucked up, as is the 'evil' kitty getting the shears, and the father's insistence on keeping the game running as smoothly as possible. The graphic incest scene surprised me because it wasn't used as a way to show the kids' rebellion but as a simple and natural curiosity!
    Dogtooth immediately gained a large cult following after it was denied top honours at Sitges and other film festivals.

The fans feel that the film's often graphic and provocative nature was the only reason why many ignored it and tried brush it under the carpet.

THE DRILLER KILLER (1979)

Dir: Abel Ferrara / USA

The Driller Killer became infamous in the UK in the early 80s as a principal title on the video nasties list. But was the film really all that bad? Well, the answer is simply no because despite all the negative attention heaped on the film at the time, and the original VHS cover which graphically shows a man being drilled through the forehead, The Driller Killer actually bares a closer resemblance to the art films of Andy Warhol rather than a sleazy stalk and slash epic.

However, the film nonetheless got swept up in the controversy and was prosecuted under the 1984 Video Recordings Act, a farcical piece of legislation which Ferrara's film ironically was partly responsible for bringing about, and which affected home video viewing in the UK for the best part of two decades.

Often wrongly listed as Ferrara's debut feature (he actually directed and performed in the earlier XXX porno, Nine Lives of a Wet Pussy), The Driller Killer stars Abel Ferrara himself as Reno, a struggling artist living in a squalid apartment in New York surrounded by bums, druggies, and a noisy rock band next door. His lack of concentration drives him to madness, and he eventually goes on a killing spree with a portable power drill.

Many have dismissed the film (including Ferrara himself on the Cult Epics DVD commentary), mainly because it doesn't pander to any notions of popular taste or commercial manners (slasher or otherwise). The film instead makes great use of gritty realism and a DIY punk aesthetic in the harsh natural light, improvisation, and location shooting which no doubt has left many slasher movie fanatics scratching their heads over the years. But all this is really just bleak window dressing, and what Ferrara and his writing partner, Nicholas St. John, really concentrated on was the crumbling psychological state of Reno's mind.

The painting of the buffalo is a work in progress - Reno's art represents his mind's eye. As the painting develops, incidents which annoy or distract Reno have a direct effect on the painting. Early in the film, Ferrara employs quick-fire edits between the drill and the buffalo's eye; these cuts express the simmering rage that is gathering in Reno's head. The buffalo also represents Reno as he would like to be; a wild, free, and careless animal instead of a starving artist in a crummy apartment. When he fantasizes on future success, the buffalo is proudly displayed in the background like a thought-bubble on the verge of breaking free. But in reality, Reno is faced with tensions from the other members of the household, an art dealer who doesn't understand his work and refuses to buy his paintings, a dreadful rock band who live next door and insist on rehearsing late into the night, financial troubles, and the homeless bums (one of whom is Reno's father) who are a constant reminder that he too could soon be joining them on the streets. And of course, at this stage the painting becomes increasingly frayed and off-balance, reflecting the building tensions in his mind.

When the painting reaches its conclusion, the distractions and annoyances continue to irritate Reno, and instead of starting afresh with a new canvas and a new painting, he snaps - and this is the most important part of the film - The urges and demons which he channeled into his art have now broken loose into reality. And he immediately sets forth to drill those who represent his fears and anxieties. The beast breaks out of the painting and onto the seedy streets of New York.

The Driller Killer was originally promoted with lurid artwork and posters which implied that half-dressed bimbo's would be drilled by an unhinged psychopath, but this exploitational tease couldn't be further off the mark. For a start, all of the on-screen killings are dealt out to male victims, and overall the film stands as a rumination on the sometimes torturous process of creativity and as a study on encroaching madness. It's a film that is actually closer in spirit to Roman Polanski's Repulsion than to big apple sleaze like William Lustig's Maniac. Indeed, Ferrara's follow-up to The Driller Killer, Ms.45 (which also found itself on the DPP's nasties list), revisits similar territory from a female perspective.

The film was re-released in the UK in the late 90s with 54 seconds of violence cut by the distributers themselves. The BBFC's chief censor at the time, James Ferman, suggested that the uncut version probably would have been passed had the film been submitted to the board intact. And it wasn't until 2003 that The Driller Killer finally received an uncut 18 certificate. The film's salacious reputation has roped in many horror fans over the years only to leave many of them disappointed with the overall lack of bloodshed (there are a couple of great scenes of violence in the film though, such as a bum being drilled through the forehead that looks very realistic; but I suppose it's the scene where Ferrara eats a pizza that remains the most disgusting), but The Driller Killer is not the film many think it to be.

ELEPHANT (1988)

Dir: Alan Clarke /UK

A ruthless and relentless comment on the troubles in Northern Ireland, Elephant is a short 39 minute assault to the senses depicting the seemingly unstoppable tit-for-tat murder and counter-murder in that troubled part of the world at the time. With no real narrative to speak of, the film presents a series of chilling shootings, back to back, with nothing to explain what's going on. Instead we're shown the sickening violence with no context other than the bloodshed itself.

Whether each killing is revenge for another, or a pre-emptive strike, or a punishment is not made clear, nor whether the shootings are being carried out by Loyalists or Republicans or both. Each deadly scenario is played out to such a spot-on and chillingly accurate way it makes big-budget Hollywood gunplay look kind of silly in comparison. With no music on the soundtrack and no dialogue to distract us from the relentless onslaught on screen, director Alan Clarke doesn't allow for a moment's respite from the horrors.

It's also ironic how a film which strives to avoid all artistic notions and entertainment value boasts such superb performances from both the killers and the victims; these 'sketches' of characters nonetheless offer vivid portrayals of cold-blooded killers and desperate victims, the most memorable of which are the shootings at the taxi rank, the football field, and the large abandoned warehouse complex (reminiscent of the warehouse cum squat in Geoffrey Wright's Romper Stomper, a later film which was influenced by Clarke's work).

Each scenario is also rehearsed and directed to within an inch of its life; in fact, it might just be the most perfectly directed film of Alan Clarke's career. From a horror fan's perspective, Elephant resembles the stripped-down kill-a-thon antics of a lurid slasher movie; but instead of 'stalk and slash' we get 'stalk and shoot'. And the special effects are amazingly realistic and unflinching with trickling blood and exploding squibs adding to the senseless onslaught of this extraordinary body-count movie. All the details concerning the build-up to the killings are discarded as a way of exposing the evil practice of murder. But even the most bland and mundane of the slasher movies had some kind of narrative as a way of 'joining the dots' and making the 'pay off' seem cinematically justified when a dumb jock or bimbo cheerleader meets the sharp end of a blade or axe. Alan Clarke didn't need to play that game, the narrative of his 'story' was headline news, day in and day out.

The slasher film is often accused of being grim and irresponsible - an outcast genre. And Clarke takes that disreputable template and turns it into a political statement that says more about the troubles in Northern Ireland than a dozen other movies. And the reason for its success is simple: Just like the bastard slasher movies, Elephant is a purely visceral experience, it is designed to affect viewers on a primeval level, make them gasp, make their skin crawl and their hearts race as the film's perspective changes from predator to prey from one sequence to the next. It's certainly not a popcorn movie, and you won't hear any bad jokes or see any sex scenes or drug taking before the killings start. No, Clarke used the slasher template because it's the most effective way of expressing the startling hunting ground of life and death on the big screen, with the 'boogeymen' often wearing black ski masks and invading the lives of others and taking them out with the cold and precise manner of a gun. And the audience walks away wanting no part of that in their lives.

EMPEROR TOMATO KETCHUP (1970)

(aka King Ketchup Tomato)
Dir: Shuji Terayama /Japan

This cinematic attack on Japanese state policies and culture of the time is wild, shocking, and even a bit dull in places. However, some of the imagery here is jaw-droppingly risque... It's a film about an imaginary revolution where the children have seized control of the country and have condemned their parents to death for restricting their free-expression and sexual freedoms. Many themes that subsequently cropped up in Terayama's later work are also included here - Adults raping young boys, white powdered faces, clocks, and studio sets falling apart. Many scenes of disturbing and playful decadence look to be ad-libbed and were probably drawn from Terayama's own experiences in the theatre.

In the opening sequence we watch people doing seemingly random and mundane things like climbing up buildings, pulling an old boot out of the toilet, dancing in a garden, someone standing in the middle of a sun dial, body builders flexing their muscles, a goat wandering around aimlessly in some bleak and desolate wasteland. This intro lasts for about ten minutes and has a green tint on the lens. The soundtrack is brooding and rhythmic like we're anticipating something to happen.

Next we get a pink tinge on the lens for the opening credits which involve still images of historical figures, children in school photos, and artist's impressions of historical events played out to traditional Japanese music, presumably as a way of showing a bygone era. Then the screen turns black for a few seconds and we can hear a high-pitch noise. Something's wrong, but what is it?

Well, there are street riots, and historical faces are crossed out with children's crayons (Karl Marx, et al), and a jangly guitar on the soundtrack culminating in victorious kids standing on street corners in military uniform, waving flags; the winners of some kind of revolution. The rest of the film is tinged in a dull sepia tone as the kids have taken over and are now in power. The adults are stripped, tied up, and used as sex slaves.

The most notorious scene in the film is undoubtedly where a trio of women pin a young boy onto a bed, strip him, and stroke, tickle, and roll around with him on the bed whilst they too get naked and simulate playful sex positions. It is a scene that will offend and infuriate many, and should make any normal person feel uncomfortable. And it's hard not to conclude that the kids were exploited by the adults in the making of the film in the same way the adults were exploited in the film by the kids, making any message that Terayama intended to convey all the more difficult to accept.

At the end of the film, three youngsters put on fake beards and mustaches as a way of making themselves seem more grown up and authorititive, and putting their mark over the new regime. This looks like a shoddy and pointless recap of Orwell's Animal Farm, with the revolutionaries exploiting the situation for their own self-interests in a similar way as the animals in Orwell's book who gradually expose their hunger for power by adopting human traits; the very same 'evils' that they had successfully overthrown in the revolution.

There are two versions of this film doing the rounds; a black and white 'highlights' version which was produced in Germany for the European market (under thirty minutes running time), and Terayama's full version which runs for about a hour and is mostly in sepia. This latter version also has two short films spliced into the footage, bringing the total running time to around 88 minutes. Those shorts are The Cage and Paper-Scissors-Rock-War which plays out the destructive finale.

Director Shuji Terayama (1936-1983) was also a poet, playwright, essayist, and theatre director with a healthy interest in all that is strange and chaotic. He made a number of films in the 70s and his style and attitude matured considerably during that decade, becoming one of Japan's most revered artists. He was involved in naive revolutionary provocations for many years (Emperor Tomato Ketchup was only a part of it), and preferred practical knowledge rather than books, which is strange coming from a writer. Pastoral: To Die In The Country is a Fellini-esque mix of childhood memories, symbolism, and bizarre surrealism, and is generally considered to be his masterpiece, although a case can be made for Fruits of Passion (1983).

EMANUELLE IN AMERICA (1977)

(aka Brutal Nights)
Dir: Joe D'Amato /Italy

Sex, nudity, hardcore sex, more nudity, bloody violence, bad dubbing, groovy music, censorship troubles, snuff footage, torture, hairy porn, bad acting, bad clothes and bad hair, bestiality, lesbianism, orgies, sleaze, blowjobs, penetrations, secret brothels, freakish fantasies - This film has everything you could possibly want from 70s exploitation.
  Exotic beauty Laura Gemser stars as the nympho Emanuelle who embarks on her international jet-set lifestyle as a globe-trotting photo-journalist doing all she can to find the latest scoop. No danger is too great for her if it means getting hold of a good story or two. En route, she witnesses all manner of lusty perversions, from horny aristocrats to sleazy snuff movie dealers, but her 'undercover' work is about to get her into big trouble...
  Emanuelle In America is part of a range of Italian exploitation pics that were made to cash in on Just Jaeckin's

1974 film Emmanuelle, which was an international box-office success in softcore erotica. The Italian versions were often made by Joe D'Amato and starring Laura Gemser in the lead role, and these films were much more exploitative, adding all kinds of bizarre elements and hardcore sex into the mix.

The film stomps through the narrative with very little method, but D'Amato wasn't famous for his pacing skills, so the film's series of mini-structures allows him to get away from traditional narrative constraints. Some may still find it plodding of course, but in the vast jungle of 70s exploitation you could do a hell of a lot worse. D'Amato never claimed to pursue any artistic notions in his epics, he always made his intentions clear: To entertain the fans. And this remains the sleaze standard to which all exploitation aims to match.

Made during a time when filmakers were free to explore the darkest areas of human behaviour and have the results played out on the big screen in glorious 35mm celluloid, EIA is still a jaw-dropping experience for jaded fans today. The hardcore scenes, the castration, gyno shots, orgy dinner parties, gruesome and graphic snuff footage, 2 on 1 interracial action, cumshots, and even a pornstar (Paula Senatore) jerking off a horse; all these sequences are shown so casually from one scene to the next in D'Amato's usual blase manner - Just another day on a movie set! The only disappointment is that we never see Gemser in any hardcore action.

Controversy surrounded the film while it was still in production; legend has it that one actress was so distressed by the awful screams coming from the snuff set that she thought it was real and informed the police. The producers had to prove that no one was being hurt or killed on the sets. The snuff footage looks amazing; the dirty, grainy shots of girls having nipples hacked off, meat hooks inserted into vaginas, and huge dildos filled with red hot tar forced down their throats; it has that awful air of authenticity about it and looks exactly the way you would imagine a snuff movie to look. Not pretty (and these brutal sequences are said to have influenced David Cronenberg's Videodrome). D'Amato himself has said that the snuff footage was shot in 35mm and then the negative was scratched to make it look rough, printed in 8mm, and then blown up again.

Look out for sleaze veteran Lorraine de Selle (Cannibal Ferox) as the lesbian in the steam room, and Gemser's real life husband, Gabriele Tinti, as the host of the decadent party at the Venetian mansion. The 100 minute full uncut version is available on DVD from Blue Underground and looks tons better than those old bootleg tapes. Included are interviews with D'Amato and Gemser (the latter is audio only).

ENTER THE VOID (2010)

Dir: Gaspar Noe / France

A two and a half hour audio-visual extravaganza from the man who brought you Seul Contre Tous and Irreversible.
Enter The void opens with an extraordinary credits sequence created by German experimental filmmaker Thorsten

Fleisch in which the assorted cast, crew, and composer's names are embellished on the screen in a dazzling variety of big, bright and colourful logos against a black background, and played out to a thumping electro tune by LFO. It reaches a crescendo of psychedelic intensity as the credits flash away on the screen so fast that it's impossible to focus on the names of those involved in the making of the film.

The plot is simple: An American drug dealer in Tokyo is shot dead by the police. His spirit then rises from his body, reflects on his troubled life and relationships, and is then seemingly reincarnated as the son of his sister Linda and his best friend Alex. But what makes this film special is the way Gaspar Noe tells the story.

The film is viewed entirely from the perspective of lead character Oscar (Nathaniel Brown), with the camera permanently mounted at his viewpoint. It's incredible to think that this technique has rarely been done before in film, because, after all, that is the way we experience life, in the first person. And it also serves as an obvious way of merging the director's vision, the lead character's journey, and the viewer's gaze, as all three come together at a specific meeting point to enquire about what happens to us when we die.

Oscar is reunited with his sister Linda (the beautiful Paz de la Huerta) after years apart due to being raised by different foster carers after a nasty road accident killed their parents. Oscar's good friend Alex (Cyril Roy) has lent him a copy of The Tibetan Book of The Dead, and the passages from the text have an influence on his drug-induced hallucinations; strange organic patterns and psychedelic snowflake shapes accentuated by the downbeat ambient sounds of Coil and Throbbing Gristle. Bizarre CGI effects that resemble blooming symmetrical smoke clouds in a faint luminous glow of reds and amber dominate the screen to illustrate the intoxicated mind of the lead character.

With a long tracking shot in real time we pass through the dark neon-lit streets of Tokyo as Alex and Oscar head for the nightclub, The Void, to make a simple drug deal. This scene - in which the characters discuss their latest experiments with DMT and other hallucinogens, and Alex relates to the high as being similar to the spiritual passages in The Tibetan Book of The Dead - has a strong documentary feel, but also has its own kind of spatial awareness and is nicely composed. It has a verite vibe with its city sounds and passing vehicles, and people seemingly unaware of the characters or of Noe or of a film called Enter The Void. It's a scene that reminded me of Hitchcock's Vertigo with James Stewart stalking the ice-cold blonde, or later in Brian De Palma's Body Double in which Craig Wasson stalks the brunette; both these sequences show the respective directors exploring the environment - with its bright clean surfaces and weatherless atmosphere; real streets become toys; movie sets - just as much as the narrative which is temporarily put on hold.

Alex doesn't enter The Void, he hangs back and waits outside, presumably because he knows how risky it is to be carrying drugs in Japan where the laws are very strict. Oscar enters the club to sell to a friend but is confronted by cops instead. So he locks himself into a toilet cubicle and frantically tries to dispose of the drugs down the bowl but the flush doesn't work. The police hammer at the door and Oscar in his panic stupidly shouts out that he has a gun and is going to shoot. The hammering stops, but moments later Oscar is shot through the door.

With a gasp of shock and pain he sinks to the ground, his hands covered in blood, and we get to listen to the confused last monologue in his head (rather like The Butcher character in Seul Contre Tous in which Phillipe Nahon holds a loaded gun to his head in a serious contemplation of suicide, his finger squeezing at the trigger and his thoughts flaring off into a web of anger, confusion, and nihilism); "This isn't happening, I'm tripping", "I'm dying. I'm dead". His voice drifts off into silence, and his spirit lifts out of his body and up towards the light. Time seems to have momentarily paused. It slowly revolves in the light and looks down at its own empty shell, a pitiful young corpse slumped in a public urinal. The police enter the cubicle and we can hear screams. Oscar's spirit floats over the club and out into the street in a bird's eye view. The police cars, the ambulance, the sirens, the crowds, the confusion; the aftermath of his own death. Alex flees from the scene and the camera swoops down behind him as he sprints down a dark backstreet.

The spirit then enters another nightclub where Oscar's sister, Linda, works as a stripper. Benoit Debie's camera acrobatics are in full force here as the bird's eye view observes Linda's beauty as she poses and gyrates on a lit stage before floating across the tops of backstage rooms looking down on the lives of strangers (and this recalls another of Brian De Palma's films, Snake Eyes, in which the camera pans just above ceiling level over the rooms of a hotel floor), before settling on Linda's dressing room where she has sex with her exploitative Boyfriend, Mario. Oscar's spirit embodies Mario while he's fucking her and lingers with an incestuous curiosity towards her (and it isn't the first time incest has cropped up in Noe's work). Mario buttons up and leaves, and this is when Linda switches on her phone and receives a message from Alex informing her of her brother's death.

There is a beauty in the bird's eye view in the way it presents Tokyo as looking like a huge expansive toy train set. But it's also infused with a forboding sense of danger and anxiety, perhaps fear on the part of Oscar and his sudden alienation from life - The film presents a dark Disneyland quality to viewers with its bright neon lights illuminating the darkness and scenes of nightlife and hedonism and drug taking forming an ambience of mild pulsating pyschedelia. The film strolls along at a leisurely pace, the narrative feels like it is moving along in real time on first viewing, and this gives the viewers the space to formulate their own thoughts on the matter, and also gives the (very limited) plot all the time it needs to reach its 'conclusion'. Indeed, this is as far away from

mainstream filmmaking as one can get. Oscar's spirit dwells upon events from his past - Him and Linda playing on a swing as children, and then a cut to the startling head-on collision with a freight truck that killed their parents. Another childhood memory where Oscar and Linda are seperated into different foster homes, with Linda screaming and refusing to be seperated from her brother, but to no avail.

Things that impressed Oscar and made an impression on his life are re-formulated into a surreal blend of sensations in his out-of-body experience. The film becomes increasingly hallucinatory when a scale model of a cityscape seen in a friend's flat later becomes a real living bustling city in which his spirit floats and seems to regard with a heavenly perfection (the scenes were filmed with complicated crane shots and by helicopter above Tokyo, but were digitally manipulated in post-production to look strangely toy-like and artificial); there's no wind, no weather, no cracks or potholes on the roads or pavements; it resembles a plastc perfection like a child's idea of utopia. The toy model of the city seen in the flat is also the origin of the Love Hotel which later becomes the centre of paradise where the occupants get to indulge in their sensual fantasies.

This vortex of sounds and visions feels hallucinogenic; the surreal imagery and the chugging beat of the music sticking to its rhythm carries the viewer along as if in a drug-induced state. It's a film as pure feeling, pure experience - Not intellectual. It's a film to be felt rather than understood, much like David Lynch's Eraserhead. Is it pretentious? Sure. But it's also steadfast in its direction and is totally uncompromising when it comes to telling the story in its own expansive way. And with such a long running time the film doesn't meander, despite looking at first glance to be an undisciplined and sprawling mess. The film is actually presented exactly the way it needs to be for maximum effect, much like Stanley Kubrick's 2001: A Space Oddyssey, from which it takes its biggest inspiration. If Kubrick's film is about mankind's struggle with technology over the centuries, Noe's film is about mankind's struggle with the meaning of life and the idea of perception itself. It's very much up to the viewer to interpret what's happening on screen.

Gaspar Noe creates bizarre, narratively unorthodox films, and some have suggested that the reason he does so is because he lacks skills with dialogue and even the most simple narrative simplicity, and that he conceals this by presenting his stories in a fractured and aggressive style (indeed, the 'script' for Enter The Void was a one hundred paged 'description' with no written dialogue). Others have argued that Noe is simply bored by the more conventional forms of narrative and is driven by the desire to shake things up and present us with a more challenging and unusual approach. All three of his feature films so far have their own unique and radical forms of trajectory (which is more than can be said of such staunchly independent filmmakers such as Gregg Araki, Catherine Briellat, and Bruno Dumont, who all stick rigidly to the old tried and tested methods of straight forward storytelling).

Seul Contre Tous (I Stand Alone) is broken up with lengthy misanthropic monologues, on-screen captions, and comes across almost like a non-fiction polemic or manifesto of hate; Irreversible is a rape-revenge film told entirely from back to front - It starts with the end credits and continues with the revenge attack, then the rape itself, and ends at the beginning with the peaceful morning before the anger and heartache begins - Thus only falling into context for viewers once the film has finished. Enter The Void presents its action strictly from the first-person perspective, but this doesn't make it isolated or solipsistic, because the viewers are right there to go along with it and invest their own thoughts and feelings, and is actually Noe's most inclusive film to date as far as its audience is concerned.

Oscar's spirit looking down on his corpse in the morgue is a powerful scene and perhaps represents the epitome of alienation, but at least Oscar is there in the experience; existence hasn't necessarily been extinguished for him, at least not in the way that athiests and nihilists would suggest. At the end of Michelangelo Antonioni's The Passenger, Jack Nicholson's character dies on a bed in a hotel room, and the camera - if not embodying his spirit - lingers on the scene, gently easing towards the open window and soaking up the everyday enormity of life in a small village - Life continuing without him. In Enter The Void we're witness to a similar but more concentrated form of the same idea. Cinema is perhaps the most effective artform to capture those scraps of reality (dead film stars like James Dean and Steve McQueen are still right there in life-like form in Rebel Without a Cause and Bullit), and is the closest thing we can get to experiencing non-being; a world without you, without me, and without Oscar.

The last 20 minutes of Enter The Void are amazing. We (that is we via Oscar's spirit) drift over the toy world city-scape of Tokyo looking directly down on all the bright lights, and the tiny cars passing by, and the ant-like efficiency of the modern world; it's a perspective that is at once beautiful and unsettling, alienating. Life continuing in all its calamitous beauty and delicacy. The sex scenes in the Love Hotel are offset by a grim and depressing ambient soundtrack and flickering lights. The scenes weren't shot out of focus but are difficult to see properly because of the numerous digital layers added in post-production. It floats along with an eerie dream-like quality. Lots of couples having sex, their genitals illuminated in a glowing radiance as if to express the life-affirming potency in all its glory. Alex, who has been a long-time admirer of Linda, finally gets to make love to her, and Oscar even embodies his old friend during the act so that he too can experience that carnal togetherness he has desired from his sister for so long. He then passes into Linda's womb and watches from inside as Alex ejaculates into his sister's vagina. He follows the sperm as it reaches the egg and finds a gateway back into life just like in The Tibetan Book of The Dead. Oscar is reborn once again, reincarnated, and the cycle of life continues. The film fittingly has no end credits.

EVIL DEAD TRAP (1988)

(Orig title: Shiryo no wana)
Dir: Toshiharu Ikeda /Japan

Baring no relation to Sam Raimi's Evil Dead movies, Evil Dead Trap became something of a cult favourite on the bootleg video circuit in the 90s before being passed surprisingly uncut by the BBFC in 2003.

Television host Nami receives a package in the mail that includes a video tape showing the gruesome murder of a young woman. Desperate to improve the viewer ratings on her show, Nami gathers together a bunch of colleagues to serve as her camera crew, and they venture out to the location where the snuff tape was shot (a large derelict warehouse complex) in order to report on the crime and to look for clues as to the killer's identity. But, of course, things go badly wrong, and the TV crew are picked off, one by one, by the mysterious killer in spectacularly brutal fashion.

The second half of the film takes a detour into supernatural territory, borrowing themes of twisted familial love from classics like Basket Case and Psycho, and horror fans have always been divided on which half of the film they like best. Slasher fans love the first half with its gruesome and stylish slayings, whereas those who prefer oddball plotting, shunting body horror, and the climactic fireworks of CAT III movies, prefer the latter half. But there are also those, myself included, who enjoy the whole show!

It's very much a feature length tribute to Western horror at its best with the main theme tune reminiscent of Fabio Frizzi's work on Lucio Fulci's The Beyond, and John Harrison's synth score on George Romero's Day of The Dead. The candy-coloured lighting and gorgeously brutal murder set pieces are very Argento-esque; Suspiria and Tenebre being the most obvious influences (he even recycles the maggots-from-the-ceiling scene from Suspiria). Director Ikeda, who had previously stunned audiences with his entry in the Angel Guts series, Red Porno, bombards his audience with set-piece after blood soaked set-piece, all mired in a moody ambience making this feel like a video nasties greatest hits package - We get severe eyeball trauma, rape, impalements, death by crossbow, a shocking strangulation over the roof of a car, and a very gory demon birth. The Synapse DVD includes an audio commentary with Ikeda and special effects guy Shinichi Wakasa. It's one of the strangest and most absurd chat tracks you'll ever hear; unintentionally hilarious!

A sequel came along soon after, Evil Dead Trap 2, which is vastly different from the original film and features a strange mix of femme fatales, a creepy child ghost, perversities, and surreal nightmare visions. The story seems to be based on guilt caused by abortions, but it's all quite incomprehensible. Also a lonely, overweight projectionist who holds some dark secrets, and a celebrity seems to be extremely envious of the projectionist for some reason. It's visually striking, suitably atmospheric, and has a creepy atmosphere, but these are the only things it has in common with the original.

EYES WITHOUT A FACE (1959)

(Orig title: Les yeux sans visage)
Dir: Georges Franju / France

Les yeux sans visage is one of the most shocking and beautifully poetic horror films ever made. Scalpel-sharp and soft as velvet, its twisted charms have been hugely influential over the years. It's a black and white masterpiece which puts the hokey horrors of contemporary hits to shame with its morbid atmosphere and graphic bloodshed. Forget the flash-trash of modern-day hokum, this is the real deal in hair-raising terror, a true landmark in post-war Eurohorror. Prepare to be blown away by the grim elegance of Eyes Without a Face.

Adapted from Jean Redon's novel by Pierre Boileau and Thomas Narcejac (the pair who wrote Vertigo and Les Diaboliques), Les yeux sans visage was director Georges Franju's most ambitious film to date. Having started his career as a subversive documentarian with the unforgettable Le sang des betes, which juxtaposed the beauty of Paris with the graphic animal butchery of the city's slaughterhouses, Franju felt ready to tackle a feature film. The French critics had always been down on horror and Franju claimed he wanted to add a seriousness to the genre, to help lift it out of its silly rut of ridiculous space monsters and creaky sets, and to add his own unsettling blend of compassion and cruelty, terror and tenderness, and cold blunt visuals. Suffice to say he succeeded. But alas, the critics weren't ready for such stark realism, and they panned the film on its initial release (much like Charles Laughton's earlier film, The Night of The Hunter, which is also considered a masterpiece nowadays but was given a harsh critical drubbing in its day).

The plot concerns a guilty surgeon, Genessier (Pierre Brasseur), who crashed his car, severely disfiguring his daughter's face, and who runs his own sinister clinic with the aid of Louise (Alida Valli, who would later show up in Dario Argento's Suspiria). Genessier attempts to restore his daughter's beauty with disastrous skin grafts, but he can only continue in his guilt-racked obsession by procuring skin donors. Louise powls the streets of Paris and kidnaps pretty young girls whose faces Genessier surgically removes and places onto his daughter Christina (Edith Scob) with increasingly reckless results.

The film caused much controversy in Europe; L'Express magazine noted that viewers "dropped like flies" during the graphic face removal scene. The French critics were united in their disgust and condemnation of the film. Elsewhere, seven people collapsed during its screening at the Edinbourgh Film Festival, prompting critic Isabel Quibly to brand it "The sickest film since I started film criticism". In America the film was cut, dubbed into English, and given a new title, The Horror Chamber of Dr. Faustus, as a way to bring in some revenue and distance it from its reviled status in Europe.

The long and lingering surgery sequence is still quite shocking today, but it's also a master class in tension-building and editing. There are also more subtle moments in the film which disturb and haunt viewers long after the end credits roll, such as the opening scene where Louise drives a corpse out into the wilderness and dumps it in the river (this is played out to Maurice Jarre's bizarre waltzy score). Genessier's misguided love also haunts; he wants the very best for his daughter, but he also wants to ease his own guilt by throwing himself into his research. His desire to restore the innocent beauty of Christina sends his moral compass into haywire; his ice-cold mannerisms and facade of dignity and professionalism dissolves into a slushy mess of heartache and torturous guilt whenever he is in his daughter's company. Christina, in turn, doesn't openly blame her father for the incident which destroyed her face; she's just fed up and depressed at being hidden away in her room the whole time. But it's clear that Genessier blames himself for his daughter's miserable situation. Also, Alida Valli's twisted smile as she lures the young women to their deaths is not easy to forget; it just adds to the overall unsettling atmosphere of the film. Franju himself described the film's unease as "Anguish... it's a quieter mood than horror... more internal, more penetrating. It's horror in homeopathic doses".

Incredibly, it was only in the late 90s when the film was finally released uncut in the UK. And horror fans who for years knew nothing about the film other than the precious write-up in Phil Hardy's Aurum Encyclopedia of Horror finally had the opportunity to see the faceless horror icon Edith Scob, whose blank mask had influenced Jess Franco's The Awful Dr. Orloff and John Carpenter's Halloween. The film's influence spread further, with its heart-rending storyline imitated in Anton Guillio Majano's Atom Age Vampire and Franco's Faceless, and the sailing white doves and graphic face removals updated to stunning effect in John Woo's Face/Off. Quite a legacy indeed, but very few filmmakers have managed to match Franju's classic, which along with Psycho and Peeping Tom, laid the foundations for the sleazy slasher boom which became all the rage a couple of decades later.

FIRST TRANSMISSION (1982)

Director Not Credited /UK

I still don't know what to make of this. Maybe if I was able to ascertain the facts concerning the making of this film, and who exactly was involved, and what's real and what isn't, then it would probably be easier to make sense of the whole thing. However, considering how little information there is out there, and how even some of the most basic 'facts' about the film are constantly being debated three decades after its release, then perhaps the ins and outs of these tapes will be shrouded in mystery forever.

All I know for sure is that First Transmission offered me one of the strangest, most mesmerizing, freakiest, and disturbing viewing experiences in my life so far. It's not a 'good' film by any stretch of the imagination, but even with the truly objectional images on display here (and their supposed authenticity), it cannot be shrugged off as useless junk like so many other shockumentaries out there. If Videodrome wasn't made in the same year as this I would have sworn it had influenced Cronenberg's film. But here, it isn't just the traditional mondo stuff that's disturbing, but also the weird attempts at trying to brainwash the audience by showing mysterious logos that appear on screen for minutes at a time.

Whatever the intention was of including those images, it had an almost hypnotic effect, alluring and off-putting in equal measure. There's an image of the Virgin Mary with a radiating heart and a dark shadowy halo behind her head that became freaky after a while; simultaneously sacred and profane in both spiritual and symbolic terms, it was perhaps the uneasy balance between the innocence of love and the blasphemy of pure evil that became uneasy. The radiating heart became like the Leviathan in Hellraiser 2; it can expose the blackness of your own heart, and the words 'Psychic TV' suddenly made sense to me! Or maybe I just get freaked out by religious iconography. Whatever, it made me feel as uncomfortable as watching a young man volunteering to have his dick cut off.

First Transmission was a collection of video tapes that were made available through Psychic TV's mail order system in the early 80s. Fans of the band had to own all of the albums in order to qualify to be given the videos as a gift. The tapes consisted of almost four hours of footage assembled by the band members themselves, and included an initiation ritual of a new member into the cult of Thee Temple Ov Psychick Youth, of which band member Genesis P. Orridge was a founding member. Thee Temple Ov Psychick Youth (or TOPY) was founded in the early 80s by members of Psychic TV, Coil, Current 93, and others. They allegedly practiced magik "without the worship of gods", and focused on the psychic energy of "guiltless sexuality".

Cassette no.1 starts with an image of a skull that hovers on screen accompanied by weird and wonky orchestral music. Then we meet a spokesman for Thee Temple who gives a speech concerning strange sexual pressures, the stifling nature of society, and how to use your body wisely. We then cut to the initiation ritual; shot on video, it looks more like an underground S&M clip more than anything. It depicts a man whose hands are chained to the ceiling and who has a black sack on his head. He is covered in blood but it's difficult to see where his wounds are. Some dude rubs his cock into another dude's eye. More guys walk around naked and covered in blood; they are aroused and chanting some kind of mantra or incantation. By this point the soundtrack has changed from a piano ballad to something that sounds like a dozen moaning trumpets.

The inductee is unchained from the ceiling and tied to a bed and has talc powder rubbed onto his genitals. He is then subjected to needle torture/pleasure (he doesn't resist or even flinch, so I assume he likes that kind of thing). Symbols are scratched onto his torso with a knife and the blood is smeared across his body. The man with the knife then turns the blade on himself. And after some genital torture it's time for some good old fashioned fucking. It's then the turn of a young woman to experience the cutting blade, and she doesn't mind letting out a few moans of pain/pleasure. The ceremony wraps up with an enema and close-ups of injections (of what I don't know), whipping, dildo play, and the inductee gets pissed on.

The clip finishes with anal sex and lots of blood. This whole sequence is dark, disturbing, and difficult to watch in places, and is undoubtedly 100% real. Then comes the aforementioned Virgin Mary scene before we cut to a shot of a guy or girl pulling down their panties to reveal... erm, I don't know what! Some have said it's a girl with an unfortunate protruding labia, which may well be so, but it could just as easily be a guy showing off an ugly cock stump after castration.

Cassette no.2. According to a caption on screen, this footage came from 'contacts' in San Diego. We're in a car driving through the city. Then we arrive at some hotel room. This footage was shot on 8mm and the cameraman stands in front of a tall mirror and exposes his cock. Back outside again at some California skate park with shots of youngsters whizzing by on their skateboards. Now we reach the most problematic scenes in the whole film; we see a bunch of drowsy kids laid out on beds in the hotel room with what look to be needle wounds in their arms. At first we're thinking junky children, but between more random cuts of driving on the freeway, an older man appears wearing a white surgical overcoat, similar to the kind worn by surgeons and lab technicians. The man cuts into a teenage boy's arm with a scalpel and the kid seems ok with this. He is then connected to an electrical device with a wire that is inserted into the wound, and the man shocks the kid with a few vaults of electricity, causing him to wriggle around like he's having a fit. The kid then uses the device to shock himself, and he keeps on zapping away with the currents until he ejaculates.

In a later scene another kid is laid face down on a table and the strange doc cuts him open at the base of his spine and inserts the electrodes. After feeding him a few currents of electricity, the kid goes limp, presumably dead. The doc packs his stuff away and still the kid doesn't move... (Did I detect a bit of bad acting from the doc here? There's something about his mannerisms during this sequence that looks like he's basically chewing the scenery; theatrically sharpening his posture into panic mode and exaggerating the look of surprise on his facial features like a bad thespian. I don't know about the rest of the scenes on cassette 2, but I'd bet my house that this 'death' sequence is fake).

It's now that we reach the most infamous scene in the entire film: A kid lays on a bed and the reckless and amoral Dr. Benway character enters the frame and proceeds to sever his penis with a scalpel. It's all filmed in one long take with the camera remaining completely static throughout. With blood spurting everywhere, Benway hurries with a rushed stitch-up. Afterwards, the kid explores his cock stump and his testicles are still intact - Stupid boy. He eventually tries to take a piss but finds it difficult and makes a mess (I should also point out that there is no live sound on the San Diego footage. Instead we get a mariachi tune and what sounds like Mexican radio commercials).

Next up is a quirky revolving logo in shades of grey that serves as some kind of subliminal invitation. Created using blocky computer graphics, this hypnotic scene pulsates with a forboding kind of ambience like a TV commercial transmitted from another world. It's very much a product of the 80s, but aesthetically it oozes a warped perfection of its era, with its stark video glow, VHS tracking lines, and cubic vortices combining to produce a timeless glitch of eternity. It genuinely feels like it was created by some 80s retro freaks from the distant future. Absolutely spellbinding, and probably unlike anything else seen from the 80s, completely untouched by the ages of re-mastering and enhancing, it sits in its own dark void of perfection. No amount of modern day tinkering could quite capture that kind of fuzzy analogue magic. It looks simultaneously dated, contemporary, and futuristic; it has a modest and grandiose presence, it moves but stays still, changes but stays the same, fluid but concrete. You look into it and it looks back into you as it sails on its postmodern loop. It belongs in an art gallery (see what I mean about the brainwashing elements?)...

Anyway, next up is a segment entitled 'Brion Gysin's Dream Machine' in which we enter a room filled with Arabic music. A man stares into one of those psychedelic cylinders (the dream machines also appeared in Gysin and William Burroughs' excellent short film, Towers Open Fire). The camera stays focused on the spinning wheel and the whole screen is enlivened with trippy psychedelic colours and random abstract patterns, and the Arabic music picks up in intensity. The whole idea of this clip is to try and induce a hallucinatory experience in the viewer, and I tried to play along, but in the end with those patterns rushing across the screen, I found it difficult to focus on without feeling nausea.

Cassette no.3 starts with a clip called 'Thank You Dad' and features Jim Jones of The Peoples Temple Cult spouting his nonsense. Picture quality is unwatchably bad in this one but the images are quite random and unimportant anyway. Audio is crystal clear though and we can listen to the rantings and ravings of a guy who somehow brainwashed hundreds of people and talked them into committing mass suicide in Guyana in 1978. He had a fake laugh which sounds like Flipper The Dolphin which I hadn't noticed before... Then we go to an 'Intermission' that is basically a short segment in which a woman gets dressed in front of an open window...

Then the skull logo appears on screen once again and a narrator informs us about cognitive brain theory; the individual(s), and our personalities, and the "Traps of time". We are encouraged to describe ourselves as "We" as part of being "multi-dimensional individuals". And this philosophy is basically the raison d'etre of artists like Genesis P. Orridge who reinvented himself from Neil Andrew Megson into the artist-as-metaphor-itself. In the postmodern contemporary world, the metaphorical multimedia artist Genesis P. Orridge was created in order to experientially immerse himself into the artistic formulae, regardless of the results and consequences. Thus, his art must reflect back on himself both physically and cognitively. Unlike previous artists whose paintings cause controversy, the person responsible can sneak away. Not so with Orridge; his art is part of his whole being, and if it goes wrong, or is unpopular, or causes outrage, there is nowhere for him to hide. Thus he is lauded in the underground art and music scenes but demonized in the tabloid press.

The next clip is a strange series of scenes designed to shock with its grotesquely surreal and sexual symbolism. Masked faces, weird pictures, a woman sitting on a toilet and snipping her pubes. A man blows smoke out of his eyes. The woman puts a long black centipede onto her vag... We see some pretty graphic photos of genitals with venereal disease... The centipede is not impressed and wanders off onto the floor... So the woman pokes herself with a vibrator instead. Image of skull shattering on ground. Woman lubes herself up and inserts a long stick-type thing into her cooch... A guy with a massive hole in his cock uses a hooked metal instrument to pick at the hole - He pulls out a bunch of live maggots from the wound... Effigies are burned... The end. This is all played out to an ambient/industrial soundtrack reminiscent of Throbbing Gristle, and sounds like rhythmic factory machinery. And I understand that most of the action in this clip was performed by members of the COUM Transmissions, a group of performance artists with close links to Throbbing Gristle, Psychic TV, and Orridge himself was also a member.

Cassette no.4 opens with an excerpt from a BBC documentary on Psychic TV. Genesis and Peter 'Sleazy'

Christopheson are interviewed before we're shown a short clip from a music video. Then there's more discussion on the 'multi-personality' aspect of Thee Temple Ov Psychik Youth (Psychic TV were allegedly considered to be the propaganda wing of the cult)... 'Psychoporn' is another music video with strange tribal rhythms and colourful abstract imagery. When specific images do come into focus we can make out various sexual positions. A psychedelic blowjob and penetration shots are also included; this latter piece was most definitely not part of the BBC coverage.

A paraphrase from Nietzsche appears on screen, "Those who don't remember the past are condemned to repeat it", and then we're introduced to some kind of experimental music video that basically serves as the band's manifesto - The Burroughs influence is apparent again as the words 'The Naked Lunch' are displayed, and then the tape reaches a crescendo of sounds and visions from the previous cassettes arranged into a 'cut-up' style montage with the moaning trumpets, the face of Jim Jones, the emblematic skull, the electric orgasm device, and various other bizarre imagery crops up again. The tape ends with the re-appearance of the spokesman with some final words.

I mentioned earlier that First Transmission reminded me of Videodrome, and if you consider that Orridge and other band members were involved in radical performance art as part of the COUM Transmissions troupe, the subject inevitably brings us back to Cronenberg. For years Cronenberg has worked on a screenplay entitled Painkillers which centres on a group of performance artists. The script still hasn't been filmed as yet but it's interesting to know that Cronenberg has had a fascination with this shadowy subculture. He felt compelled to write Painkillers after a friend told him the story of how a man surgically removed his own hand in the name or art. Cronenberg's research into the minutae of this kind of activity would no doubt have led him onto the COUM whose public performances have become the stuff of legend. And this would have led him onto Orridge, Psychic TV, Throbbing Gristle, Thee Temple Ov Psychik Youth, and perhaps even First Transmission.

The release of Videodrome in 1982 coincided with First Transmission, and although it seems unlikely that Cronenberg's film could have taken inspiration from those tapes, there are nonetheless some interesting comparisons to be made. Both films attempt to induce a hallucinatory experience in the viewer through the manipulation of the electronic cells on your television screen (and it's important to note that Videodrome built up its considerable cult following by its regular broadcasts on late night cable TV); some will argue that Videodrome is a metaphorical piece of sci-fi/horror make believe, which of course is true, but if you consider the implications of that metaphor and the overall meaning of Cronenberg's film (namely that it's an exploration and a prophetic look at how 'reality' can be manipulated in the minds of others, for good or evil), the implications aren't too dissimilar. Indeed, whilst watching First Transmission you'll probably feel a bit like Max Renn who has stumbled upon a strange and violent broadcast from a pirate satellite, and you'll be asking yourself similar questions like who's behind this? What's real and what isn't? And Where did all this footage come from?

First Transmission was created and compiled by people who were influenced by artists and writers such as Brion Gysin, William Burroughs, and JG Ballard; and they in turn have had a big impact on Cronenberg's work. In First Transmission a kid has electrodes inserted into the base of his spine, and in Cronenberg's eXistenZ characters are injected with 'Bioports' in the same sensitive/dangerous area. Also, characters in eXistenZ are hooked up to 'fleshy game pods' through an attachment of organic wires, and they manipulate the pods with their fingers in order to arouse the game into action. Compare this to the scenes in First Transmission where the kids are hooked up to electronic devices which they manipulate with their fingers as a way of increasing and decreasing the voltage in order to arouse themselves, and you'd perhaps be forgiven for thinking of it as a direct influence as Cronenberg's film was released fifteen years later.

British tabloid paper The People published a scathing sensationalist 'article' on Genesis P. Orridge in the 90s, accusing him of corrupting the nation's youth. And among the range of accusations of Satanic rites, sadism, greed, and general foulness, there is a brief mention of First Transmission and it is described as showing "scenes of a pregnant woman being tied to a dentist's chair and raped and a man being urinated on by Orridge". The pregnant woman being raped is nonsense, and although a man does get pissed on in the film, I'm pretty sure it wasn't Orridge who did the pissing. And if this so-called journalist did actually watch the tapes, I'm certain that those scenes he described above would have been the least of his concerns. The infamous 'castration' scene alone would have stolen the headline.

Now, the 'castration' (technically a de-penising as the kid's testicles remain intact) looks to be genuine. In fact, the whole film looks to me to be genuine except for the aforementioned 'death scene' and bad acting of the doc on the second tape. And although there aren't many reviews of this film around (write ups are scarce even on the web), every one I have read so far has assumed the footage to be real. There are rumours circulating, however, that the footage was faked, and that the special FX were created by artist/madman Monte Cazazza, but I've been unable to confirm this. And to be honest, I'm not convinced it was faked (I wish it was!). It would take a dedicated and precise effort to produce that kind of illusion; the transition from the real penis to a prosthetic substitution would have to be absolutely perfect, and there are no cuts or edits (the version I watched had a slight damage on the tape which fuzzed up the screen for a second before the scalpel makes contact, and I know people will say that's all you need to sneak in an edit, but no, I still don't believe it was faked). The craft of special effects in those days weren't really up to much unless you had a Hollywood-sized budget and a good team of technicians, but for a cheap bit of shock footage shot on 8mm with no chance of financial reward, the chances of creating something that has that awful air of authenticity (even with someone like Cazazza on board) are pretty slim. Even today with the best FX team on the planet working with unlimited resources would struggle to replicate that scene. So if that footage does turn out to be faked then I'd be absolutely gobsmacked.

If the people involved in First Transmission weren't so tight-lipped when it comes to discussing the film then maybe things would be much clearer - Its makers would then either be in jail or in Hollywood giving Tom Savini and Screaming Mad George some FX tips. But strangely, the rumours and hearsay surrounding the film elevate it into that uneasy blur between fact and fiction, a place where all the Blair Witches and Texas Chainsaw Massacres in the world can never hope to situate themselves. Not even the power of the internet can disspell the myths concerning this fucked up little film, and the mystery deepens...

One of the most ludicrous rumours surrounding First Transmission is that Orridge had to flee the UK because the police were onto him about the tapes. Now, I'm no expert on international law, but he only emigrated to the USA, and it wouldn't be difficult for the British authorities to have him extradited.

FLANDERS (2007)

Dir: Bruno Dumont / France

Dumont's most violent and extreme film to date. A bunch of guys from a small French village are all played by the same crazy slut. They're conscripted into the army to fight some unspecified war in North Africa, and they all find themselves in the same regiment. There's lots of seething resentments between the men but nothing spills over - Instead they take out their frustrations on the locals by way of rape and murder. Meanwhile, the slut stays behind and has a mental breakdown. The film starts off slow (as with any Dumont movie) but once we get to the war scenes it becomes a real atrocity exhibition of anger, resentment, revenge, and the will to survive by a group of soldiers who should be looking out for each other.

   Flanders offers a real change of pace from Dumont's earlier work, such as The Life of Jesus and Twenty-Nine Palms, and here he is afforded a much bigger budget than usual. The war scenes in the desert are expertly done, and he captures that raw panic and nightmare of life in the combat zone of hostile territory.

   In the film's most notorious scene, the boys gang rape a local woman. In a later scene when the soldiers are captured, she identifies those who raped her, and the men are then graphically castrated and are left to stagger around the compound bleeding to death. The only soldier conscientious enough not to join in the gang rape manages to escape his captors with his genitals intact, but he is then hunted through the land and the swamps, and he literally has to flee for his life. Highly recommended but not for the squeamish.

FLOWER OF FLESH AND BLOOD (1985)

(Orig title: Za Ginipiggu - Chiniku No Hana)
Dir: Hideshi Hino /Japan

This is the most notorious entry in the Guinea Pig series, and the only one truly deserving of its nasty reputation. Directed by Hideshi Hino, Flower of Flesh and Blood is a short, 44 minute video about a madman who stalks and kidnaps a young woman and takes her home before dismembering her and placing her body parts in a backroom with the rest of his 'collection'. The film is remembered primarily for its remarkable special effects (which looked so realistic on bootleg VHS that Charlie Sheen thought it was a genuine snuff tape and reported it to the FBI; of which more later), and we get to witness the graphic dismembering in full detail thanks to Nobuaki Koga's FX work.

The tape comes with its own legend: Manga artist Hideshi Hino allegedly received an 8mm snuff film in the post along with a letter and photographs. After alerting the Tokyo police (who took away the evidence), Flower of Flesh and Blood was conceived as an attempt to re-enact the scenes in the snuff tape. This was more than a decade before The Blair Witch Project, and the intriguing backstory was bought wholesale by the Japanese AV addicts, and the tape became a hit (the film was actually entirely fictional and based on Hino's own Manga).

Flower of Flesh and Blood is often accused of being utterly repellent, tasteless, and misogynistic. Others have read it as a journey into spiritual nirvana! Personally, I have always viewed the film as a savage satire on the masculine idea of sexuality: It is often remarked how women seek 'soulmate' qualities in potential partners, whereas stereotypical men are happy with surface requirement (legs, breasts, etc); this goes towards explaining why men are more likely than women to enjoy the visual stimulants of porn. The deranged samurai goes on the prowl; he sees his desired love object in a young woman walking the streets, and decides she will be the satisfactory candidate for a 'one-night-stand'. Of course, our madman will fail to lure this girl with his charm alone, so what better way to win her body than to smother her unconscious with a rag of chloroform?

The samurai helmet represents the 'Bushido' attitude, the warrior mentality (and phallus) of men when it comes to procuring a love object. For all the niceties of courting a female, the man has only one true desire - namely flesh.

After tying her down to the bed, the samurai proceeds to inject her with some kind of sedative to make her drowsy and docile (an alert, intelligent woman has always been the arch nemesis of full-blooded males!); he drugs her at the outset as a way of turning her into a passive object, to rid the room of the other consciousness. What follows is a literal joke of the blackest kind. The graphic dismemberment can be seen as a comment on the male habit of breaking down the attractive female into mental body parts (in fact, the whole film could represent this whole thought process as viewed from inside the male psyche). Laddish comments such as "nice arse", "sexy legs", "gorgeous tits but ugly face", etc, are lampooned in graphic detail. Women often complain that men look at their breasts in conversation like they're floating in space, barely acknowledging the presence of another human being, but transfixed, as if the breasts would be better without the actual woman being there. And the stereotypical 'man-on-the-pull' will indeed treat women as blank canvasses on which hang breasts and buttocks and legs, etc.

"In the love relationship the tendency to break the object down into discrete details in accordance with a perverse auto erotic system is slowed by the living unity of the other person"

- Jean Baudrillard, The System of Objects.

It's worth noting too that although our anti-hero doesn't get sexually intimate with the body parts, he does pause briefly between amputations in order to caress and admire the pieces lovingly as if the segments of her body have become his own personal property; her will can no longer operate or manoeuvre her limbs when they have been sawn off. The samurai, however, now has complete control of them without any possibility of her consciousness resisting (possessiveness taken to the literal extreme).

The blood and gore and drama are simply genre requirements - The essential thing here is the samurai representing the phallus (check out that helmet!), and the phallus as libido, rummaging and ransacking the desired love-object in the male imagination, taking each bodily segment and assessing its sexual value. For the grand finale we are invited to a backroom where we get to view the 'collection': Various macabre artifacts, mutilated corpses, hands, limbs, eyeballs, maggots and worms kept in old fish tanks, jars, hanging on the walls and generally scattered about the place. We are also treated to a poem of sorts about falling to the depths of hell. Can you guess where we are yet? The subconscious of course! We followed the libido back behind the curtain where, to quote the poem, "The darkness is boundless".

Flower of Flesh and Blood was directed by Hideshi Hino, a creator of comic books who has been churning out lurid Manga horror such as Panorama In Hell and Hell Baby for more than forty years. He was approached by cheapjack video producer Satoru Ogura and offered the chance to direct a miniscule horror film based on Hino's own comic, Flower of Flesh and Blood. Hino, whose childhood dream was to direct samurai films, immediately set to work, recruiting actor friends from the underground theatre, and an ambitious team of special effects technicians led by Nobuaki Koga. The tape hit Japanese video stores in the mid-80s and became one of the biggest selling titles of the month (Don't forget, Japan is a country where Faces of Death out-grossed Star Wars at the box-office and Cannibal Holocaust out-stripped E.T.). The Guinea Pig films soon became the subject of much controversy when a serial child killer seemed to be re-enacting scenes from Flower of Flesh and Blood, and the police investigation led to the questioning of the film's makers. But even when the culprit, Tsutomo Miyazaki, was apprehended, the tabloid frenzy only intensified, accusing Hino and his films of being to blame for the depravity and sickness of Japanese society.

Meanwhile over in America, Deep Red fanzine editor, Chas Balun, had VHS bootleg copies of Flower and Slaughter Special (aka Guinea Pig's Greatest Cuts), and as a favour to a writer friend, Dennis Daniel, he agreed to make a compilation tape comprising the bloodiest and most graphic sequences from the films to be shown at Dennis' birthday party. The video played at the party and was a success, but copies were made and swapped hands for a while until one of the tapes came into the possession of Charlie Sheen and film producer Adam Rifkin. They watched it and were horrified, thinking it was real. They contacted the MPAA and the FBI. An investigation was launched and everybody basically snitched and ratted on their friends until the trail led back to Chas. But Chas also just happened to have a copy of The Making of

Guinea Pig, a tape which shows behind-the-scenes footage and outtakes of a smiling actress doing re-takes, and the special effects team demonstrating their cable-controlled illusions, proving once and for all that the 'snuff' video wasn't real. The whole episode became an embarrassment for everyone concerned.

In the UK, 26 year old Christopher Berthould was prosecuted for importing Flower of Flesh and Blood (along with Infant Brain Surgery and Faces of Dissection) into the country. The prosecution at Southward Crown Court knew the contents of the tape was fake, commenting that the film was "so well simulated that [snuff] is the impression it creates". Berthould was given a £600 fine and a ludicrous newspaper headline ("DEATH CRAZE MAN'S SNUFF MOVIE SHAME"). The film is still outlawed in the UK today but is available uncut from Unearthed Films in America. I would say import at your own risk but things have moved on a lot since Berthould's day in the dock, haven't they?

FOOTSTEPS (2006)

Dir: Gareth Evans / UK

A harsh lesson in never judging a film by its cover, Footsteps is graced with perhaps the most enticing and iconic DVD sleeve design in the entire Unearthed Films back catalogue. It depicts a young man standing with his back to us in a neon-lit tunnel brandishing an iron bar; it's just a shame the film itself fails to live up to its beautifully presented promise.

Footsteps follows a young man's descent into violence and tragedy. Following the death of his parents, Andrew becomes increasingly detached from the people around him, including his girlfriend and neighbours. He inadvertently gets himself entangled in the debauched and perverted world of snuff movies when a pair of shady psychopaths take him under their wings. But Andrew isn't a mindless idiot, he has a lot going on upstairs and he decides to use his anger and despair as a way of wiping out a couple of scumbags on his downward spiral.

So the cover looks great and the synopsis sounds interesting, but the actual film is a major disappointment. On the upside the film does feature a couple of decent performances from Nicholas Bool (as Andrew) and Danish actor Mads Koudal as a charismatic psycho, and the snuff gimmick had so much potential to make an audience's skin crawl (the snuff element here takes the 'happy-slap' trend to new levels of barbarity with the use of video cameras, homeless bums, and iron bars).

The downside is the slow and ultimately dull style in the vein of Ken Loach in that characters sit around the table speaking their minimal dialogue in a very slow and labored way like they've been downing sleeping pills or something. It suffers from that very British 'kitchen sink' drama style that has basically helped ruin the UK's filmic output in the last couple of decades. It's such a dull, depressing, and labored film to watch it makes Eastenders seem like an upbeat
fun-time comedy in comparison. Scenes open with shots of water dripping from taps, or Andrew wandering around the dull grey streets of Wales, or having the camera focus on random things like passing traffic, and the whole thing is matched by the soundtrack which repeats single, delicate piano notes like it's trying to emulate some crappy BBC drama.

Now, this incredibly boring style is probably based on great notions such as 'slice-of-life-realism' or 'kitchen sink docudrama' where the grey tones are supposed to mirror the sadness and despair in the mind of the main character, and the cruel death-peddlers fuelling the mounting rage in Andrew's head, but this kind of thing has been done much more effectively in Abel Ferrara's Driller Killer and Buddy Giovinazzo's Combat Shock, both of which were directed by artists who didn't mind injecting a bit of grubby exploitation into their pics in order to push the point across. Clearly Gareth Evans didn't want to make an exploitation film, but he seemed happy enough to sign a deal with Unearthed Films, a DVD distribution company who have unleashed some of the most shockingly exploitative titles of the last couple of decades, such as Das Komabrutalle Duell, Aftermath, and Flower of Flesh and Blood. Talk about not knowing your niche!

Maybe I'm being a bit harsh on first time director Evans, but Footsteps really did have the potential to be a great film had its makers gotten over their Ken Loach infatuations and relished the opportunity of exploring the dark heart of this tale to its full potential. There are one or two moments of panache that suited the film's low-key approach perfectly, and had Evans steered the project more towards the twisted territory of Hisayasu Sato (after all, Sato's films often deal with outsider characters and themes of alienation, violence, and voyeurism, with characters documenting their escapades on video), then we could've had a mini-masterpiece on our hands. A sorely missed opportunity.

FORCED ENTRY (1973)

Dir: Helmuth Richler (Shaun Costello) /USA

The deranged Vietnam veteran has turned up in all kinds of films over the last few decades, from silly comedy-horror (The Vagrant), all-out action movies (Rambo First Blood), and home invasion movies (Naked Massacre), to intelligent horror fantasy (Deathdream), the ultra-obscure (The Ravager), and stomach-churners like Combat Shock. But nowhere will you find a darker, more twisted version of the psycho 'Nam vet than in Shaun Costello's directorial debut, Forced Entry.

With a prologue that opens with stock footage of atrocities in the Vietnam warzone, the film proper begins with gas station attendant Harry Reems (without the moustache), who tricks young women into giving him their addresses. He then follows them home, peeps through their windows, and then forces them at knife or gunpoint to perform sexual favours on him while he cuts them down with speeches of pure hatred before stabbing them to death. It's a lurid horror/porn hybrid with unsimulated sex scenes that is much closer in spirit to Lee Cooper's Wet Wilderness and Costello's own Waterpower rather than Gerard Damiano's Deep Throat, and Reems looks to be relishing the opportunity of playing the bad guy; he's clearly enjoying it but few viewers will be laughing.

Forced Entry does have humour alright, moments where you laugh out loud, such as the scene where Reems has finished raping a woman in the arse and then gets angry, teasing her and screaming "You made my prick all full of shit, didn't you?! You made my prick all full of shit!!!" But it's the laughter of sheer cruelty and you need to be in that frame of mind to go along with it. Also, the seemingly endless repetition of the dubbed line "Fucking hippies coming into my station. Scummy hippies!" is amusing, if not a little bizarre.

Viewers who can't handle the entertainment value of brutal rape and murder are advised to stay away from this one as there is more provocative mayhem here to fill a hundred controversial movies. It has a real bad attitude and stands out like a sore, um, thumb. Even in those glory days before the PC spoilsports came along, this film stood out from the unruly crowd. Amazingly, it was originally marketed as just a typical porno; just what the audience must've thought as this nasty piece of work played out on the big screen is anyone's guess; for me it's about as sexually arousing as sticking my bollocks in a bee-hive, but hey, each to their own and all that...

Completely banned in the UK and something of an underground video title in the States for years, Forced Entry made it to DVD courtesy of Alpha Blue in their Costello/Avon box set. That version looks to have been taken from a muddy VHS transfer. A much better presentation is the Afterhours DVD taken from possibly the only print of the film still in existence. Image quality isn't perfect but it's the best we'll ever see it considering the scarcity of the source materials.

An indefensible horror/porn shocker then, but it succeeds in highlighting the nasty bitterness and anger felt by devalued soldiers who returned from Vietnam only to be treated like garbage after being conscripted into the hellscape of state sanctioned atrocities. You have been warned.

FREEWAY (1996)

Dir: Matthew Bright /USA

"Oh my God, is that you, Bob? I can't believe such a teeny-weeny little gun can make such a big mess out of someone!"

Foul-mouthed delinquent Vanessa (Reece Witherspoon) returns from school one day to find her mother being busted for prostitution, and her creepy stepdad on drug offences. And as they're being carted away, she flees the scene rather than staying around to be shuffled off into foster care. Vanessa then says goodbye to her boyfriend and hits the road in search of the trailer park where her grandmother lives. However, when her car breaks down on the freeway, she accepts a lift from Bob Wolverton (Keifer Sutherland), who seems like a decent fellow, but is actually the 'I-5 Killer', a serial child-killing paedophile. Bob thinks he's onto some easy prey, but he completely underestimates the feisty Vanessa...

Freeway is one of those straight to video marvels which was never shown in cinemas, a film which turned out to be far more daring and entertaining than many of its big-screen counterparts. It was written and directed by Matthew Bright, who began his career as a screen writer on oddities like Forbidden Zone and the Drew Barrymore remake of Gun Crazy, and who should really get back into the director's seat after years of inactivity since the disastrous Tiptoes in 2003.

Not a film for the easily offended, Freeway comes on as a twisted version of the Grimm's Little Red Riding Hood;

Sutherland even disguises himself as grandma and awaits the arrival of an unknowing Vanessa ("Them are some mighty big fuckin' teeth you got there, Bob"). It's trash movie heaven of the highest order that pays homage to a whole range of exploitation genres such as the road movie, the odd couple, rape-revenge fantasies, slasher movies, and even women-in-prison epics, all mired in weirdness and warped humour. Imagine a Tarantino script directed by a young John Waters and you're on the right track.

Witherspoon is fantastic as the street-wise reprobate, out-smarting and out-gunning her would-be killer; her brilliance as Vannessa landed her future roles in films like Election and American Psycho, which in turn helped in her subsequent rise to Hollywood superstardom. I wonder what her mainstream fans would make of her in Freeway as the fucked up daughter of a crack ho. Just curious. Sutherland is also spot-on as the wolf in child councellor's clothing; smooth as silk but also cruel and sadistic when he thinks he can get away with it; a true scumbag.

Lookout for some amusing performances from Amanda Plummer, Dan Hedaya, Sydney Lassick, and Brooke Shields in an uncharacteristic turn as Wolverton's idiotic wife who does us all a favour and blows her head off with a shotgun. Also lookout for real life serial killer Richard Speck in a photograph that Vanessa believes to be her father!

Freeway picked up various awards at film festivals and quickly shot to classic status with people as diverse as Alexander Payne and Mary Harron referring to Bright's pic as having an influence on their films. Bright immediately began work on a sequel, Freeway 2 - Confessions of a Trickbaby, which explored the Hansel and Gretel fairytale, and was even more outrageous, upsetting even those who loved the first film.

The BBFC made a slight cut to remove the sight of one of Wolverton's magazines which had an unpleasant title ('Cock Sucking Toddlers'). Elsewhere in the world the film has more or less stayed intact, except in America where it initially got slapped with an NC-17 rating due to the film's heavy language, but it was slightly trimmed for a later R rating. And this same cut version was originally rejected by the Australian censors (OFLC) who demanded further cuts to the explicit dialogue, and also the shot of Vanessa's dead grandmother.

FREEWAY 2 - CONFESSIONS OF A TRICKBABY (1998)

Dir: Mathew Bright / USA / Canada

Easily one of the most disturbing films of the 90s, this sequel to Matthew Bright's cult classic, Freeway, was universally despised by critics on its release and was also equally detested by fans of the first film. With not a single redeeming factor among the characters, and not a single ray of light or shred of decency anywhere to be found here, Confessions of a Trickbaby can only be recommended to those cinema miscreants who really have no limits to their debased entertainments and pitch-black cynical humour.

Whereas the first film took Little Red Riding Hood and turned it into a trashy piece of satire, here writer/director

Matthew Bright focuses on Hansel and Gretel and doesn't hold back in twisting and subverting the subtext with unprecedented levels of mischief and shock tactics. The plot follows another teenage delinquent, Crystal (Natasha Lyonne), who pretends to be a prostitute so that she can lure unsuspecting johns into deserted alleys where she then beats and robs them. She ends up in prison with the dangerous Cyclona (Maria Celedonio), a psychotic lesbian convicted of murdering her entire family, and together they hatch an escape plan, and pretty soon they're back on the loose in society. Crystal, or "White girl", comes to realise just how insane Cyclona is when everyone they meet winds up being killed due to the voices in her head that compel her to murder, and her pathetically lame excuses for the murders ("He tried to rape me!") do nothing to reassure Crystal. So, leading a path of death and destruction behind them, the two girls head south for Mexico where Cyclona knows they can get help from her childhood custodian, Sister Gomez (Vincent Gallo).

This slimy cesspool of a movie throws in enough mayhem and taboos to fill ten unsavory films, with subject-matter ranging from drug abuse, insanity, transvestite nuns, and bulimia, to incest, necrophilia, and child abuse. It's hard to think of another film which presents such an array of grotesque and deeply unpleasant subjects, except maybe Emanuelle In America or Caligula. And the characters are equally unappealing with the nutcase Cyclona killing an elderly couple and then making out with their corpses, or Crystal who seems to be there just so that the director can subvert and mock the traditions of the 'leading lady', with his 'heroine' constantly and amusingly taking the moral high-ground in dealing with Cyclona, whilst at the same time indulging in her own wrong-headed behaviour. And Sister Gomez, the creepy and softly spoken parental figure who turns out to be an evil child butcherer who runs an empire in gruesome kiddie porn. Even the small details are surreal and disturbing, such as the scene where the girls leave a trail of crack cocaine on the ground and a pair of black guys dressed in tatty old suits with feathers in their hats appear from nowhere to pick up the wraps like pigeons pecking at scraps of bread. But these Lynchian moments did little to earn the film any respectability. And yes, John Landis did make a cameo as the judge.

For all the film's gloom and unpleasantness, there are at least a few people out there who appreciated this awful spectacle (and yes, I'm one of 'em), and Matthew Bright wasn't finished yet with his experiments in cinematic shocks. His next film took him away from the twisted re-telling of classic fairytales and into the bleak biographical details of a real life serial killer whose horrendous crimes and suave charisma were explored in comedic fashion for the utterly distasteful Ted Bundy.

THE FUNERAL (1996)

Dir: Abel Ferrara / USA

Abel Ferrara's foray into the gangster movie focuses on the lead up to the funeral of one of three gangster brothers in 1930s New York. The film explores the backstory to the murder and the surviving brother's desire for vengeance whilst the family mourn at their home. The despair and guilt become too much for brother Chez (Chris Penn), and he has a breakdown which leads to the film's shocking climax.

With its Depression-era setting and relation to genre classics like The Godfather and The Petrified Forest, The Funeral is a film which invites its audience to relate to the drama on screen on a moral basis as it follows the usual gangster themes of loyalty, treachery, and religious anguish. And like all of Ferrara's films, he manages to bring out the very best in his cast which includes Christopher Walken, Chris Penn, Vincent Gallo, Victor Argo, Issabella Rosselini, Benicio Del Toro, and Annabella Sciorra.

Walken is superb as Ray Tempo, the eldest and wisest brother who is just as much concerned with the ethical dilemma of murder as he is with his personal need for vengeance. The scene in which he mourns over his brother's body is especially heartfelt, and has passed into legend as script writer Nicholas St. John had lost his son and seemed to be drawing on his own emotional pain when writing the scenes.

Gallow's performance is also impressive as Johnny Tempo, the deceased brother who, in a series of flashbacks, looked to be the most outgoing and socially conscious of the three siblings. But more striking still is Chris Penn as Chez, the fiery, emotionally unstable brother whose ruthless moral code leads him to raping a young girl in an alley before his mind crumbles altogether. Chris Penn and Ferrara both won awards at the Venice Film Festival, making The Funeral Ferrara's most critically acclaimed film to date. It's just a shame that he and writer Nicky St. John fell out and ended their friendship after this film, and they haven't worked together since.

Shot around the same time as The Addiction, a black and white tale of philosopher vampires, The Funeral echoes some of the ethical themes of that film, such as in the rape scene where Penn offers the girl a way out of the situation before screaming "You've just sold your soul to the fuckin' devil!!" and raping her. The 30s setting is captured perfectly, with the obscure politics, religious questioning, and the soundtrack which includes Billie Holiday's suicidal Gloomy Sunday. Not a cheery kind of film then, but even with this raw, troubling, and extremely powerful work under his belt, Abel Ferrara remains one of the most criminally underrated American filmmakers.

FUNNY GAMES (1997)

Dir: Michael Haneke / Austria

wager. "One of toughest nights you'll ever spend in front of your television". That was how Mark Kermode summed up Funny
Games, a cold and brutal addition to the home invasion sub-genre. Building upon his earlier works, such as The
Seventh Continent and Benny's Video, writer/director Michael Haneke here resumes his preoccupations with his attempts to shock and torture those who are seeking violence and murder for entertainment. So, if you're looking for some big screen mayhem in the form of blood, guts, and spectacular human suffering then Funny Games may come as something of a surprise because, despite being one of the most harrowing films of the 90s, there's very little on-screen bloodshed to be found here.

The plot of Funny Games is chillingly simple; a pair of teenage psychopaths enter a lakeside holiday home and set up a wager with the family therein that they will all be "kaput" within twelve hours. What follows is a raw exercise in Sadean evil; the family dog is beaten to death with a golf club, the father, Georg (Ulrich Muhe), is incapacitated by having his shin smashed in with the same club, and this is just for starters. The unfunny games continue when the mother, Anna (Suzanne Lothar), is forced to strip off her clothes to stop the torturing of her little boy, Schorschi (Stefan Clapczynski). She is then given a couple of options; one, choose whether her husband is to be stabbed or shot; or two, she can volunteer to die and take his place instead.

The games are based on psychological torment and physical torture, and reaches a climax with the shooting of the young boy with a hunting rifle. The killers then momentarily leave the house, and the scene that follows has annoyed the hell out of critics for being overlong and boring; for around ten minutes the camera stays unmoved as Anna and Georg embrace on the floor in the presence of their dead son in a state of utter despair and grief. Regardless of what the critics have said, this is the most powerful scene in the entire film - The performances of Muhe and Lothar are frankly astonishing; and their heartfelt and tortured cries make the scene agonising to watch as their pain feels genuine with a spine-chilling effect. Make no mistake, this is one of the most harrowing scenes in the history of film, played absolutely unsettlingly straight by the two magnificent performers. Soon after this scene, the killers return to finish what they started and make good on their wager.

Another thing that annoyed the critics was the film's breaking of the 'fourth wall' with one of the villains (played by Benny's Video's Arno Frisch) turning to the camera and addressing the viewers on matters concerning the plot, and other 'knowing' elements such as whether the film's running time has reached feature length. At one point when the captives get the upper-hand on the invaders, Frisch picks up a VCR remote control and literally rewinds the scene so that the scenario can start over again with the killers back in control and patching up their mistakes. This obvious didacticism, however unpopular, does much to express Haneke's point about the reality of fiction, and vice versa (and in this sense, Funny Games closely resembles Benny's Video, and of course, the Belgian arthouse shocker, Man Bites Dog).

The true greatness of Funny Games is that Michael Haneke succeeds in disturbing his audience with scenes of abysmal horror without actually showing us the carnage we so desire. "I try to find ways of representing violence as that which it is: as inconsumable", he says, "I give back to violence that which it is: pain, a violation of others". The whole point of this film seems to be as an endurance test, whereby you're actively challenged to see it through, or switch it off.

GIALLO A VENEZIA (1979)

(aka Gore In Venice)
Dir: Mario Landi /Italy

Generally regarded as one of the sleaziest gialli ever made, Giallo a Venezia opens at the aftermath of a double murder on the banks of Venice. A man has been stabbed to death with a pair of scissors, and a woman has been drowned. Not only does detective DePaul have to find the killer, but one of the clues may become clear if he can work out why the woman's body was pulled out of the water after her death. Much of the story is told in flashback, and it's here we learn that the murdered couple were husband and wife, Fabio and Flavia. Fabio was a sex-crazed coke head who got his kicks from the violence and voyeuristic cruelties he inflicted on Flavia. And meanwhile a killer is doing the rounds of Venice.

There's very little suspense in this 'murder mystery'; director Mario Landi seems much more interested in showing dull sex scenes and even duller police procedures. The violence is nowhere near as shocking as some would have you believe (the notorious crotch-stabbing of the prostitute is an exception though); Giordano having her leg cut off, and the burning of Marizia's lover are quite well done, but I personally found the simple and unexpected discovery of a body in a fridge to be more effective - It's such a startling image. The long overdrawn sex scenes are nowhere near as explicit as some have said, either, but the cat 'o nine tails and the cinema scenes are good for a giggle.

Overall it's not too bad a film, but if you watch it having heard all the hype then you may be disappointed. If Landi really was more interested in showing blood and sex rather than a tightly constructed giallo, then he ultimately fails there too. He should have given us more. And the film is still unavailable on DVD.

GONG TAU - AN ORIENTAL BLACK MAGIC (2007)

Dir: Herman Yau / Hong Kong

Not your typical CAT III shocker but worth a look on a slow evening. A practitioner of the black arts has a vendetta against the police and attacks them and their families with the aid of black magic and voodoo, and the hunt is on to find the killer and end the curses.

Gong Tau finds director Herman Yau in much less outrageous form than his earlier outings like Taxi Hunter, The Untold Story, and Ebola Syndrome, but his latest effort still has the power to disturb horror fans, and especially those who are newcomers to the CAT III phenomenon. It's a dark film indeed, but also much more pedestrian and ordinary in its manner and style. This sensible approach also cuts back on the humour to a degree, although the masturbation scene is one of the funniest things I've ever seen in any Hong Kong film.

Overall, Gong Tau is just not the same as the great CAT III's of the 80s and 90s; it looks way too polished and stylized. We also get CGI gore effects, but to be fair they look alright. It generally lacks that unruly spark of craziness that makes the earlier ones so enjoyable. It also seems to be aimed at a mainstream Western audience and I much prefer Asian movies on their own terms. But these are just minor quibbles compared to what I thought of the ending; a shameless cliffhanger to lure us into a sequel (which has yet to be made).

To my mind, a film should always have its own kind of closure even if it's part of a planned franchise. I'm not saying that all loose ends should be tied, but I think that some kind of an 'ending' so that the film can stand alone is important. I remember watching Lord of The Rings - Fellowship of The Ring and being disappointed that the ending was such a cop-out and made the whole thing feel like one big advertisement for the sequel. And Gong Tau left me with the same disappointment.

Imagine a Hong Kong version of CSI but bloodier, much more violent, and with some supernatural elements thrown in, and you've got Gong Tau (although I'm not sure CSI would show a dead baby who has been stabbed a hundred times).

LA GRANDE BOUFFE (1973)

(aka Blow-Out)
Dir: Marco Ferreri /France/Italy

Four middle class men choose to escape the restless futility of city life and retreat to an isolated mansion where they indulge in an experimental feast. An airline pilot (Marcello Mastroianni), a judge (Philippe Noiret), a cook (Ugo Tognazzi), and a TV producer (Michel Piccoli), seem to have everything going for them, but the boredom of modern life has taken its toll on their well-being. They greedily devour mountains of food, sit around watching vintage porn loops, and bring along call girls to quench their lusts. All this indulgence is part of their grand scheme; it's a suicide pact whereby the gentlemen will quite literally die on the excess of pleasure.

This visually stunning film nevertheless picks at themes that should offend everyone at some point or another. The grim tone of the setting and savage humour is dished up with very little in the way of subtlety, much like the constant mounds of food that are offered up for the feast. All four of the men represent an evil of modern life - The corruption of the judicial system (the judge), the wasteful and greedy nature of the West when many in the third world are starving (the cook), the thinly-disguised imperialism of the modern world 'village' which exists purely to conquer and exploit weaker nations, made easier by the miracle of aviation (the pilot), and the mind-numbing emptiness and cultural wasteland perpetuated by television (the TV producer).

The film also boasts four of the finest actors in Europe at the peak of their powers, and they're clearly having a good time misbehaving while entrusting their director's impeccable eye to bring all the chaos together into a sumptuous whole. It's certainly not a traditional kind of film, but fans of subversive cinema will find much food for thought here.

La Grande Bouffe premiered at the Cannes Film Festival and caused an immediate firestorm of controversy and divided audiences down the middle. Mastroianni's girlfriend at the time, Catherine Deneuve, is said to have been so offended at the screening that she wouldn't talk to him for a week. Meanwhile, mass brawls broke out in the cinemas in France between those who loved and loathed the film, and the violence continued in Paris throughout its lengthy theatrical run (ah, the 70s).

Elsewhere around the world, the critics were equally divided in their reactions, with some declaring it a triumph as a fierce attack on the appetites of the bourgeoisie, and others a tasteless sick joke. American critic Terry Curtis Fox famously summed up his reaction to the film in no uncertain terms, "This re-affirms my faith that it is possible to be offended by a film". This kind of blunt opposition between viewers surprised even director Marco Ferreri, but it didn't make him temper his work; his next film, Don't Touch The White Woman!, was released the following year and also taunts the easily offended with its biting humour and twisted allegory on American colonialism (not surprisingly, it wasn't released in America).

The influence of La Grande Bouffe was felt soon after its release when fellow Italian auteur, Pier Paolo Pasolini, paid tribute to the exploding bowels and broken toilets in his equally subversive attack on modern society, Salo, Or The 120 Days of Sodom. But it was perhaps British arthouse favourite, Peter Greenaway, who has provided the most obvious homages over the years with his mixture of sex, death, and food in The Cook, The Thief, His Wife, and Her Lover, in which he replicates the trick of naming his characters after the names of his cast members. He also cast Andrea Ferreol in a similar role in A Zed and Two Noughts. And like Greenaway's The Cook, Thief, La Grande Bouffe was also slapped with an NC-17 rating in America in the late 90s, surprising those who had believed the film to have grown much more mellow with age.

Nowadays while watching La Grande Bouffe, or indeed any of Ferreri's films, the action on screen is always tinged with a touch of sadness that this extraordinary filmmaker has never received his full dues as an artist. His talent was the equal of greats like Pasolini and Fellini, and yet his work is ignored by all but the most adventurous of film fans. When Ferreri died in May 1997 it was the end of an era. He should be considered one of the giants of cinema, yet the event of his death amounted to little more than a brief mention in the obituary sections of a few newspapers. The reason for this lack of respect is a mystery to me; maybe it's because he was an Italian who made most of his films abroad, or the fact that his films were distributed in shoddy fashion (his VHS filmography was a joke with most of the titles hard to find and quickly going out of print, and presented in dreadful pan-and-scan jobs). Some of his films saw no other form of distribution beyond the festival circuits. Who knows. At least with the advent of DVD his back catalogue is slowly reaching an audience, and perhaps one day soon Ferreri will get the respect he deserves.

GREEN ELEPHANT (1999)

(Orig title: Zeleniy Slonik)
Dir: Svetlana Baskova / Russia

A very ugly movie. It centres on a couple of soldiers held in a makeshift military prison who slowly go insane. The first half of the film consists of the soldiers arguing and fighting. Events then take a turn for the worse when one of the guys seems to go mad and shits on a plate and on the floor, eats it, and rubs it onto his chest. He then wakes the other soldier and offers him a turd on a plate as a meal, and the sleepy soldier is not very happy about it to say the least... Soon after, a General shows up and marches the two idiots to an abandoned warehouse and orders them to beat each other up, and ...well, we get a final 20 minutes of utter madness and depravity.

Not a very good film at all. The director, Baskova, rivals Andy Milligan for sheer ineptitude and grubby visuals; the sets are awful, the camera work and lighting is atrocious, as is the editing. But the performances are pretty good! The soundtrack includes a very bizarre version of the riff from Pantera's Slaughtered, and Pantera's own version of Throes of Rejection (and that's probably where 95% of the budget went, if they even bothered to secure the rights).

GRIMM LOVE (2006)

(Orig title: Rohtenburg)
Dir: Martin Weisz / Germany

Based on the true story of German cannibal Armin Meiwes who advertised on the web for a willing victim to eat. There are a few other film versions of the event, including Marian Dora's Cannibal, but this one explores the turmoil in the minds of both the eater and soon-to-be-eaten in a less exploitative but equally frank and non-judgmental way.

I also found it to be quite touching and I really felt for the lead characters (but I can't say the same of Dora's film). It's not a very re-watchable movie, and there's a rather useless character in the form of a young woman who is writing her thesis on the subject (she just serves as a convenient viewer surrogate), but is quite an interesting and well-made film. Not exactly 'all meat and no fat' but worth a look. The film was banned for three years in Germany for violating the human rights of Meiwes, from March 2006 to May 2009.

GROTESQUE (2009)

(Orig title: Gurotesuku)
Dir: Koji Shiraishi / Japan

A rare title to be banned in its entirety in the UK nowadays, Grotesque is easily one of the most sick, twisted, and realistically executed torture porn movies I've ever seen. I would probably rank it in the top 20 most disturbing movies ever list. The 'plot' picks up with a disgruntled loner who kidnaps a young couple and ties them up in his basement. And so begins the torture. But here our anti-hero doesn't just rely on sharp instruments and power tools to inflict his damage, he also uses cruel tricks and soul-crushing mind games on his victims. In one scene, the madman finger-bangs the woman (complete with wet and squishy sound effects) and is the first time I've seen squirty female ejaculation in a film. When he's finished, he notices that the young man is now aroused, so he jerks him off, sending his load flying across the room and landing on his girlfriend's stomach. Good shot!

Early in the film the girl asks her boyfriend if he would die for her, and he flounders, not knowing how to answer. Later in the film though and the madman asks him if he would die for her and this time the answer is a spirited "yes". We get all the usual torture porn elements here with some brutal nastiness and some pretty graphic chainsaw mayhem, but then the maniac does something very different from the usual screen monsters; he seems to take pity on his victims and pleads for their forgiveness, and even nurses them back to health. The victims are suspicious at first but gradually start to believe that they are on the verge of freedom; but this is all just a part of his sick game and pretty soon the doomed couple are back in the basement and the cruelties are more brutal than ever...

To say any more about the plot would be unfair to those who have yet to see this, but the 'survival challenge' near the end would make Jigsaw's chest swell with pride! Excellent performances, top-notch gore and splatter, and the production values are superb. To see a grubby little torture film like this looking so nicely lit and glossy is a rare treat; not since the days of Nacho Cerda's Aftermath have we seen such cinematic crimes displayed on beautiful 35mm celluloid like this.

The British censors banned the film in the UK. BBFC director David Cook claimed "Unlike other recent 'torture' themed horror works, such as the Saw and Hostel series, Grotesque features minimal narrative or character development and presents the audience with little more than an unrelenting and escalating scenario of humiliation, brutality and sadism. In spite of a vestigial attempt to 'explain' the killer's motivations at the very end of the film, the chief pleasure on offer is not related to understanding the motivations of any of the central characters. Rather, the chief pleasure on offer seems to be wallowing in the spectacle of sadism (including sexual sadism) for its own sake".

HARDGORE (1974)

(aka Horrorwhore, aka Sadoasylum)
Dir: Michael Hugo / USA

A young nymphomaniac who suffers from hallucinations is put into a rehab centre, but little does she know that the proprietor is the leader of a Satanic cult who indulge in murderous after hour orgies(!) Well, it's certainly unique!

Running around an hour in length, Hardgore is one of the more well-known horror/porn hybrids of American exploitation of the 70s. None of the actors are very attractive, the soundtrack, though pretty decent in places, has the annoying habit of recycling the same old tune until your ears feel like they're gonna pop. The sex scenes are all rather bland and unimaginative, and the horror sequences are few and far between. The Satanic 'orgies' are almost completely static with very little of interest going on (except for the scene where a woman is guillotined the moment her partner reaches orgasm; that was pretty cool, definitely the highlight of the film for me). The hallucinations are silly and mostly quite laughable (dildos on strings spurting semen?), the leader of the cult wears a red Satanic mask and robe and puts on a deep booming voice which is also unintentionally hilarious ("Nirvana!!!"). The girl does get some revenge at the end in the form of an axe rampage, but even this is quite dull and over before it really starts.

HEADER (2006)

Dir: Archibald Flancranstin / USA

A micro-budget shot on video curiosity that delights in wallowing in its grim and darkly comic subject matter, Header pits a grumpy ATS agent against a small community of warring rednecks who are involved in producing bootleg liquor. The moonshine, however, turns out to be the least of the troubles going on in the backwoods as a bunch of corpses are found with mysterious puncture wounds in their skulls... Turns out an evil clan of hillbillies could be responsible for the murders due an exciting new sex trend that is all the rage in hick town (and also gives the film its title).

  Header is the first screen adaptation of underground horror novelist Edward Lee, whose works in the hardcore horror sub-genre of twisted fiction has produced such anti-classics as Infernally Yours and You Are My Everything; the latter proved to be a major starting point for this film because its central theme is the 'header', an act of sexual debauchery a few notches higher on the perversity scale than the old 'watermelon-in-the-microwave' trick, in which the victim is punctured in the back of the head and the pervert then has penetrative sex with the wound whilst the brains are still warm. And though the film isn't particularly graphic in that respect, there are a couple of scenes that are very strong and take on a leering and farcical approach, such as the bit where a particularly deranged redneck assists his frail old grandpa into getting in on the action ("That's the bestest thing anybody ever done for me in my whole life!").

With much of the film played for sick laughs, there's an appealing sense of fun in Header and it has a very laid back attitude; some of the funniest moments look to be completely ad-libbed, such as the scene where Elliot V. Kotek has finished having his depraved fun with a corpse and then turns his next line of dialogue into a salacious sing-song ("Got to dump this skanky cracker in the woods somewhere").

The budget limitations do let the project down overall, but if you're a fan of Bloodsucking Freaks or The Bride of Frank then you'll probably find plenty of warped shit here to keep you amused. The final minutes of the film are ostensibly sick, and it would be great to have someone like Rob Zombie hop on board for the sequel. Look out for Edward Lee and Jack Ketchum, both of whom appear in cameo roles in the movie.

HELL HOUSE (2001)

Dir: George Ratliff / USA

Hell House is an American documentary that exposes the bizarre practice of evangelicals luring unsuspecting people into what they think is an old-time spooky house, but what they actually get is a spectacular display of melodrama showing how sin leads to hell. It's an approach to keeping people on the 'straight and narrow' that has drawn much criticism, even from within the church community, and Hell House shows viewers just how much time and thought goes into the preparation of these horrific sociological campaigns.

The Trinity Assembly of God Church in Texas prepares the latest Hell House show, which calls for casting auditions, local promotion, music and stage design. We also get to meet various young actors from the church school who are very excited about the project, and through scores of documentary footage we watch them re-enact school shootings, AIDs deaths, drug deals turned sour, and even botched abortions. Yes, it comes across as totally tacky and tasteless, but add the church angle and you've got something genuinely disturbing on your hands.

It amazes me to think that the Church gave permission for an outside documentary crew to enter the fray and chart the organisation of a Hell House event without any restrictions (it reminds me of that Louis Theroux BBC TV special that centred on 'The Most Evil Family In America', in which the Westboro Baptist Church, a fundamentalist Christian sect led by Fred Phelps, are shown picketing at AIDs funerals, shouting provocative slogans like "God hates fags", and generally pissing off the local population wherever possible). As you would expect, the footage is shot and edited in an impartial way, allowing the admittedly strange proceedings to flow and to tell its story of how some people go about trying to make the world a holier place. This fly-on-the-wall style, or if you will, 'Gods-eye-view' of things helps tremendously, and you never feel that you're being preached at or invited to mock the film's subjects, unlike Louis Theroux's documentaries.

Regardless of one's religious views, Hell House is a very well-constructed and fascinating documentary that offers viewers the rare chance to delve into one of the stranger corners of middle America. The DVD includes the short film, The Devil Made Me Do It. Also directed by George Ratliff, it shows the Trinity's re-enacting of the Columbine Massacre, which outraged the local public and helped secure the funding needed to make the feature documentary.

HENRY - PORTRAIT OF A SERIAL KILLER (1986)

Dir: John McNaughton / USA

One of the most harrowing movies ever made, Henry-Portrait of a Serial Killer begins as a sleazy 'stalk and slash' caper before settling down into a raw and edgy character study. Loosely based on the confessions of convicted serial killer Henry Lee Lucas, we're invited to join Henry (Michael Rooker), a lowlife drifter whose job as an exterminator allows him to enter people's homes in search of easy prey.

There's no set method to his killing style; whether it be guns, knives, a broken bottle, or even his bare hands, he systematically sets about his brutal and motiveless crimes by whatever means necessary. Henry moves in with Otis (Tom Towles), a degenerate simpleton whom he met in prison, and when Otis' sister Becky (Tracy Arnold) visits Chicago, she stays with them while she looks for work. Henry encourages Otis to join him in his murderous pursuits, and before long Otis is cackling like a goon as he takes to death and destruction like a duck to water. And this culminates in the notorious home invasion scene in which the pair watch their own crimes on videotape after recording themselves in the act.

Things deteriorate even further when Otis goes completely out of control and tries to rape and strangle his sister Becky. Henry stabs him to death and dismembers his corpse in the bath tub. Becky and Henry then leave the area and spend the night in a motel where they are at last free to kindle their tentative relationship uninterrupted. But anyone expecting a glimmer of hope here are left with a final gut-punch as Henry leaves the motel the next morning, alone.

John McNaughton's stunning debut is a masterpiece of horror which presents its sick characters and the world in which they're bred in a chilling but non-judgmental way. It's a film in which there are no cops or good characters to offer hope to the audience, just pure grubbiness and poverty and ugliness, leaving its viewers emotionally drained and depressed. McNaughton's true masterstroke is the way he presents to us our own vulnerability to an unreasoning psychopath like Henry; an idea few will want to dwell upon. It's a grim view that is at once too awful to be a reality, and yet too life-like to be ignored.

Featuring solid performances from Rooker and Towles, who both went on to bigger projects, and also a very impressive turn from Tracy Arnold (who allegedly went into severe shock during the filming of a particularly gruesome scene), whom to my knowledge hasn't appeared in another film since. Tom Towles as Otis fits into the depraved role with ease, drawing on his background in comedy theatre to add a touch of grim humour to his performance. Otis is such a scuzzy character he even unsettles Henry; his disturbing and erratic behaviour seems to expose Henry's own mask of sanity, something which he feels uncomfortable with - it's clear that Henry doesn't like to face up to the depths of his own sickness, and he alleviates this by putting Otis in line like a father guiding a wayward son with an absurd air of moral authority! ("No Otis, she's your sister")! And it's telling that the most graphic murder in the film is that of Otis who is stabbed to death and beheaded. But no matter how sympathetic Henry may become, he truly is a lost cause.

Unsurprisingly, Henry-Portrait was released unrated in America, but in the UK it was heavily censored, first for its theatrical release and then again for video. The most problematic scene was the 'home invasion' sequence in which Henry and Otis force their way into a random family home and proceed to beat, rape, and murder the occupants (not necessarily in that order). The main problematic area becomes apparent when the camera pulls back, revealing the events to be taking place on a TV screen with the two psychopaths watching their own previous crimes on videotape that they had recorded themselves; watching and enjoying it ("I want to see it again"), thus implicating the viewers who are watching - and at least seeking – entertainment through degradation and death.

It's a scene reminiscent of the sadistic massacre at the end of Pasolini's Salo in which the libertines view the carnage through binoculars, merging their perspective with the audience. But whereas Salo was outlawed entirely in the UK for decades, Henry-Portrait was initially passed with a re-editing of that crucial scene, and lost most of its disturbing and voyeuristic power in the process. The BBFC later relented and granted the film an uncut 18 certificate for home viewing, by which point it had become widely regarded as being one of cinemas darkest horror shows. But even with all the censorship hassles, the film is never exploitative or gratuitous, and even won some kind words from mainstream critics. Don't expect an easy ride then, as McNaughton himself has said, "If it becomes too difficult to watch then Henry-Portrait has probably served its purpose".

HER VENGEANCE (1988)

(aka I Piss On Your Urn)
Dir: Simon Nam Ngai / Hong Kong

Hong Kong's answer to I Spit On Your Grave, Her Vengeance is an ultra-violent rape-revenge thriller from the late 80s. In Macau, a group of drunken rowdy hoodlums are thrown out of a cabaret show, and later that night after her shift, usher Chieh-Ying takes a walk home from work, but is dragged into a graveyard by the five men, beaten and gang-raped. Left bloody and traumatized, Ying's only clue as to the identity of the rapists is a cigarette lighter that was left behind at the scene. She later discovers that the ordeal has left her infected with AIDs. Leaving behind her blind sister, Ying heads to Hong Kong to contact her uncle, Hsiung, with the hope that he will help her to wreak vengeance on the scumbags...

Uncle Hsiung happens to be wheelchair-bound and he owns a popular bar in Hong Kong. He refuses to help Ying and instead advises her to go back home to look after her sister. But Ying vows to stay put until she gets revenge. Tracking down her wrong-doers, one by one, and exacting a bloody and ruthless retribution, Ying succeeds in putting fear in the gang. The men who raped her are part of the criminal underworld in Hong Kong, and they suspect that they are being picked off by rival gangsters. Cue much ruthless retribution of their own against shady underworld characters, but the attacks on them continue. And after one of the men has acid thrown in his face, they discover that it's actually Ying who is responsible for the attacks.

In retaliation, the gangsters head over to Macau and pay a visit to Ying's blind sister. And after the deaths of a couple more people whom Ying is close to, such as her flat-mate Susan and her young admirer Hao, she is at last joined by her uncle Hsiung, and together they hold up in the bar and set dangerous booby-traps and await the arrival of the bad guys for an extremely violent finale.

Unlike many CAT III titles of the time, Her Vengeance is completely devoid of the silly slapstick humour that is very popular in Hong Kong cinema, and is instead played absolutely unsettlingly straight. The world of Her Vengeance is portrayed in a bleak and brutal way; it's a vicious dog-eat-dog existence, or as one of the characters puts it, "It's a villain's world". The rain-soaked neon-lit cityscape is Bladerunner-esque with its dazzling surface veneer of colours and sounds barely concealing the darkness and ruthlessness around every corner. The soundtrack includes a deep droning synth that drops out of tune and is quite unnerving and compliments the sense of decay and the apocalyptic vibe of the film.

In the West, the rape-revenge genre usually sees women acting alone in their quests for violent retribution, and even though in Her Vengeance Ying does spend at least two thirds of the running time as the sole avenger dishing out the just deserts, she is joined by Hsiung in the finale. And although Hsiung is confined to a wheelchair, he turns out to be pretty handy in bar room brawls despite his disadvantage, as an earlier scene indicates. But in terms of the 'sex wars' of cinema (in which the rape-revenge movies play a large part in its discourse), feminist-minded viewers will notice that Hsiung's character, despite possessing the 'manly' qualities of being able to defend himself in violent confrontation, ultimately serves as a man who is symbolically sexless, or 'castrated' because of his confinement to the wheelchair. His disabled existence makes him non-threatening to Ying, and therefore he is accepted as a suitable ally in the fight against the enemy.

Most of the other male characters in the film are depicted as pure evil except for Hao, a nice young man who is completely smitten with Ying, and whose sexual potency she can never accept due to her AIDs infection that he doesn't know about. The fact that Ying can't allow herself to get close to him no matter how much she'd like to, adds one of the bleakest notes to the film. The rapists couldn't take away her heart; but perhaps even worse, they made it so that she can never truly love again.

Be sure to stick with the uncut version available through Deltamac on VCD, as there is an edited version floating around on the Joy Sales DVD label which has been stripped down to a CAT IIb rating (even though the DVD sleeve carries the CAT III logo), and this version places heavy cuts on the rape scene.

A HOLE IN MY HEART (2004)

(Orig title: Ett hål i mitt hjärta)
Dir: Lukas Moodysson /Sweden/Denmark

A father makes porn movies in his living room in the presence of his teenage son, and this causes angst, neurosis, and psychological warfare between the two.

For all the onscreen wonders of this film, the real heart of the matter is in the embittered conflict between the characters; the look of an eye, the issues that remain unspoken, etc. The deep family troubles could be easily fixed with a simple solution, but things seem to have gone way beyond that. The sorrows and resentments have become a spiteful game (the father complains that his son doesn't respect him, and his dumb attempts to appease the situation only makes matters worse). The son destroys himself physically, socially, and psychologically, to spite his father who, in turn, worries only that he is not looked up to like a normal father. But of course he isn't a normal father! So round and round we go...

The adult characters are just as lost, fucked up, and self-absorbed as the angst-ridden teen, and they have no idea of the damage they are leaving behind them in their pursuits of pleasure. There's lots of symbolism, psychoanalysis, and neurosis on display here to drive its message home (the son collects dirt and junk, the 'actress' Tessa dreams of fame and body surgery in the name of beauty, and the father, Richard, craves for acceptance but is off-set by his simultaneous need for escape through drink, drugs, and sex). Almost every scene is open to interpretation, and if you like that kind of thing then this is required viewing.

Director Moodysson didn't write a script for the project, he claimed to have had a single sheet of paper with the word 'exorcism' written on it, and basically invented the scenes as he went along. He even walked off set during a particularly intense scene and left the actors there to continue without him while the camera was still rolling, and apparently the resulting scene made it into the finished cut of the film. Lars Von Trier would be proud! The Dogme-style of filmmaking won't be to everyone's taste, nor the real footage of cosmetic surgery inserted therein, but this difficult little film does a lot to show how we all have holes in our hearts.

HORRORS OF MALFORMED MEN (1969)

Dir: Teruo Ishii /Japan

A film that remains as fierce and offensive now as it did more than forty years ago when it first hit screens in Japan, Horrors of Malformed Men gained an instant notoriety in its native land but sadly saw little exposure anywhere else. Made during the late 60s when 'Pinky Violence' was reaching the heights of its popularity, Ishii's seminal shocker is brimful of grotesque imagery, bizarre plot twists, colour-coded flashbacks, and a gleefully un-PC attitude. The film's scandalous reception did nothing to halt the blazing career of one of Japan's foremost purveyors of exploitation, and is essential viewing for anyone interested in the stranger side of celluloid.

Based on the disturbing novel, The Strange Tale of Panorama Island, by celebrated horror maestro Edogawa Rampo, the film follows medical student Hirosuke Hitomi (Teruo Yoshida) on his surreal journey to trace his doppelganger who died under mysterious circumstances. His search eventually leads to a strange volcanic island populated by deformed and disfigured humans who seem to be under the rule of a mad scientist with webbed fingers. In a series of flashbacks we learn more about this madman who may or may not be Hirosuke's father, and also other bizarre and grotesque bits like evil cross-dressing prison wardens, flesh-eating crabs, incest, and hunchbacked freaks raping imprisoned women.

Right from the get-go the film is a disorientating experience, with the curtain-raiser set in a sexually-integrated insane asylum. The plot throws up some amazing scenes, one after another, with little rhyme or warning, such as the half undressed women being whipped, the graphic scene of a woman having her breasts sliced open with a knife, and the colour-tinted episodes which accentuate the mood of the backstory. Although it's not as graphic or extreme as some of the more outrageous Japanese offerings that flourished in the 70s (many of which were also directed by Ishii), Malformed Men nonetheless boasts some freakish imagery and a whacked-out psychedelic edge. It's perhaps best described as a cross between Freaks and Island of Dr.Maureau, as directed by Seijun Suzuki.

After a very short-lived theatrical release, the film had caused so much outrage it was promptly banned by the Japanese authorities. Even the film's title was something of a cultural taboo but that didn't stop it from being a much discussed hot topic, conferring upon it an almost mythic reputation in the ensuing decades for those who didn't get to see it. And this legendary status was bolstered by the subsequent work of its director who became known as 'The King of Cult' in his homeland after a series of unforgettable entries in the notorious Ero guro sub-genre, such as Shogun's Joys of Torture, and of course, Female Yakuza Tale: Inquisition and Torture.

THE HUMAN CENTIPEDE (FIRST SEQUENCE) (2009)

Dir: Tom Six / Netherlands

The Human Centipede is a horrific black comedy made purely for sick laughs, but many people took it way too seriously upon its initial release and failed to see the funny side.

A misanthropic German Doctor is obsessed with creating a 'human centipede'. His experiments with dogs (Three Dog) wasn't a success but he jumps right into human experimentation anyway, by basically stitching three unlucky people together, mouth-to-anus, and studying the fiendish (and amusing) results...

Horror fans were disappointed with the lack of all-out gore (especially those who had read reports of people walking out of test screenings due to being grossed-out), but the heavy streak of black humour more than makes up for it ("Feed her! Feed her!"). The film became an instant cult classic with those who did get the joke. The "YEAH! I DID IT! HAHAHAHA!!!" is as fine a mad doctor moment as Colin Clive's "IT'S ALIVE! IT'S ALIVE!" from James Whale's Frankenstein. The Japanese fella (Akihiro Kitamura) is hilarious as the unfortunate tourist demanding to be untied, ("The Japanese possess unbelievable strength when backed into a corner").

Some have criticised the performances of the two girls (played by Ashley C. Williams and Ashlynne Yennie), but that's a bit harsh; they weren't necessarily bad. They could be bad actresses for all we know, but this kind of comedy horror is no place to judge acting abilities. There's certainly an exaggerated giddiness in their performances as Lyndsey and Jenny, but director Tom Six probably wanted them to ham it up. Besides, their roles were perfect for the kind of affectionate lampooning that seems to be the film's central focus point.

There are many in-jokes and self-reference points in The Human Centipede, and it's incredible how easily much of this stuff has been overlooked; the scene where the girls arrive on the doctor's doorstep is a case in point: He asks if they're alone and will only allow them inside his house when they confirm to him that they are alone. His face, voice, and posture are suspicious beyond belief, but they still put their trust in him and enter his home (this kind of stupid behaviour is the fault of dumb horror characters, not dumb actresses). The stitching of character's mouths to arseholes is an obvious self-reference point - It was a way to shut them up! Tom Six had simply pre-guessed our annoyance at those bimbo characters and did us a favour. It's obvious that he likes to play around with B-movie cliches and stereotypes, and he does it in a fun and clever way, rather than a smug 'know-it-all' way like Kevin Williamson and Wes Craven (Scream). But many still fail to recognise it.

On repeat viewings the humour stands out even more, like at the beginning when the truck driver pulls over to take a shit and is shot dead, mid-excretion. Or the part when the doctor awakens his 'triplets' after the operation and gets them on all fours (or twelves?); he starts snapping away with his camera and his subjects are crying in pain and despair, but the doc's tears are of pride and joy! This cruel mixture of despair and bliss represents the epitome of black and twisted humour.

Tom Six announced that The Human Centipe is only the first in a planned trilogy (hence the First Sequence in the title). Many have speculated on how the sequels will take shape, but the most interesting and feasible idea is the siamese twin angle: During the film, on the doctor's wall can be seen a piece of artwork depicting conjoined fetuses. Is it possible that the doc has a twin brother whom he was surgically seperated from? It would explain why he was so interested in the subject (and would also be a good excuse to bring back actor Deiter Laser for the sequel). Perhaps this long lost twin will come out of the woodwork and continue with Doctor Heiter's research?

If so, let's just hope that this long lost twin is just as sick and twisted as his brother.

HUSTLER WHITE (1996)

Dir: Bruce LaBruce and Ricky Castro /Germany/Canada

With a plot that borrows elements from Sunset Boulevard and Death In Venice, Hustler White centres on LA hustler Tony Ward, who spends his time dealing with punters and appearing in porn movies in Santa Monica, California. He meets Jurgen Anger (LaBruce), and the pair build a growing rapport surrounded by the diverse sexual shenanigans in the local area.

When Hustler White was released in the UK, it prompted that model of liberalism, The Mail On Sunday, to accuse the film of being "Disgusting, sick, filthy, pornographic, and scary", and then added, "Despite being disgusting, sick, filthy, pornographic, and scary, it's not bad". With its postmodern blend of diverse reference points, from old skool Hollywood, to porn, and S&M, sprinkled with hilarious black comedy, it's a film which, despite the outrageous scenes of perverse sex, is actually at heart a romantic story and a celebration of diversity.

Tony Ward is perfect as Montgomery, whose good looks and pleasant nature helps to steer the film away from its moral ambiguity and makes the film feel somehow less offensive to viewers than it could have been. He reminded me of Joe Dallesandro in the Warhol/Morrisey movies, Flesh, Trash, and Heat. That's not to say that it's an easy ride; no doubt, the uber-offensive humour, extreme bondage, and perversities (including sex with amputees) will be too much for some viewers, especially those who are in any way homophobic. Or claustrophobic (as the cling-film scene will demonstrate).

Writer/director Bruce LaBruce started on his road to infamy in 1987 with I Know What It's Like To Be Dead, and followed it up with No Skin Off My Ass in 1991, and then secured his legend in 1993 with Super 8 1/2, a cult classic which put him at the forefront of controversial Queer Cinema. Hustler White was subjected to cuts by the BBFC who objected to scenes including sexual kicks from razor blades, and the aforementioned amputee fetish. But LaBruce still shows no signs of tempering his tastes. His equally uncompromising Skin Flick (later retitled to Skin Gang) was rejected by the London Film Festival for its graphic scenes of skinhead sex and a particularly gruelling Nazi rape scene. And his later effort, L.A. Zombie was banned outright in the UK in 2010.

If you're looking for a grubby gay porn film then Hustler White will be a disappointment. Likewise, if you're easily offended. It's a film designed to lure in unsuspecting viewers and shock them with unflinching scenes of perversity and sadomasochism, but it's also completely unashamed of itself and ultimately embraces the outer realms of human desire, whilst presenting art as imitating art as imitating art, with its numerous and often obscure cultural references.

THE IDIOTS (1998)

(Orig title: Idioterne)
Director not credited (Lars Von Trier) / Denmark

These are the ten rules of Dogme films:

1) Shooting must be done on location. (No sets, no props)
2) Sounds must never be produced. (No music)
3) The camera must always be handheld.
4) The film must be in colour. Special lighting is not acceptable.
5) Optical work and filters are forbidden.
6) The film must not contain any superficial action. (Violence and sex, etc, must be for real)
7) Temporal and geographical alienation is forbidden. (The film must take place in the here and now)
8) Genre films are not acceptable.
9) The film format must an academy 35mm.
10) The director must never be credited.

After the international success of Breaking The Waves, writer/director Lars Von Trier could have headed off abroad and made a big-budget Hollywood blockbuster. But that has never been his style (not to mention his intense fear of flying), and instead he stayed in Denmark and decided on a low-budget and largely improvised project that resembles a fly-on-the-wall documentary. It was made in accordance with the Dogme 95 'Vow of chastity', a set of rules which severely limit the filmmaker's creativity. The result is a film that is at once shocking, offensive, darkly hilarious, and altogether quite extraordinary.

The Idiots follows a group of middle class dropouts who pretend to be mentally handicapped. Living together in a commune-like mansion, they improvise drooling, belching, and urinating on day trips as a way of causing disruption in public places. They refer to their antics as "spazzing" and do all they can to test the patience of the upper middle class. As a potent mixture of anti-bourgeois protest, performance art, and group therapy, their true purpose is never really made clear.

This strange bunch are joined by the unhappy Karen (Bodil Jorgensen) who meets them during a "spaz attack" in a plush restaurant. Karen's background remains a mystery until the end of the film when she takes the group back to her dad's house for one of the most uncomfortable dinner party scenes you'll ever see. But in the meantime, Karen begins to try and fathom the group's leader, Stoffer (Jens Albinus), and serves as a tender surrogate for the more soft-hearted viewer.

The plot synopsis sounds incredibly silly, but according to press interviews, that was what Von Trier intended, to experiment with ideas that are both "philosophically and artistically radical", and simultaneously "disastrously silly, malicious, foolish, and meaningless". And though the film has received a high number of high-profile critical plaudits over the years, it's difficult not to conclude that Von Trier was perhaps up to his old trickster games once again. Claiming to have been depressed during the conception of Antichrist, and publicly claiming to be a Nazi whilst promoting Melancholia, it's hard to take anything he says seriously anymore. In other words, it's entirely up to you to decide how seriously you take this film.

In his 'Dogme director confessionate test' Von Trier admitted to breaking some of the Dogme rules by altering a light source, feeding the actors, hiring a car, and having someone play harmonica music on set. Most famously, he also admitted to hiring a porn actor for the notorious orgy scene. It was this latter element which could have caused problems with the BBFC, but despite the graphic nature of an ejaculating hardon, the film joined Catherine Briellat's Romance and Patrice Chereau's Intimacy as the latest in a line of sexually explicit films to be passed uncut by the board for both cinema and home video.

The Idiots premiered at Cannes in 1998 and generally had a warm reception. But not everyone was impressed; Mark Kermode was famously thrown out of the theatre for shouting "Il est merde!" at the screen. No doubt the film will cause anger and upset for a lot of people, but it also boasts some incredibly powerful scenes; the sequence at the dinner table at the end filled me with a mixture of conflicting emotions I had never felt before anywhere, whether watching a movie or in everyday life, and for that reason alone it gets a thumbs up from me.

Overall though, The Idiots leaves us with more questions than answers; it's unclear whether Karen's character represents Von Trier himself, and it's equally unclear where this film stands in relation to the rest of his filmography; the anti-individualist demands of the Dogme 95 Manifesto seem to be at odds with his own artistic notions. And if Von Trier's film stands as a critique on the conformity of collective thinking and its inevitable encroaching on the individual, then what are we to make of Dogme 95?

Von Trier later abandoned the Dogme rules, "The more fashionable it has become, also the more boring", he claimed.

"When we originally discussed the vow of chastity, we had no ambitions to change the world, like, for instance, the French nouvelle vague. But if in 25 years some film students accidently excavate the manifesto and find the ten rules interesting, we will obviously be happy, but it was not our initial purpose".

IN A GLASS CAGE (1986)

(Orig title: Tras el cristal)
Dir: Agustin Villaronga /Spain

One of the most intense, courageous, and disturbing films of all time, In a Glass Cage ranks alongside Salo and Cannibal Holocaust as a superbly made shockfest.

Klaus, a Nazi paedophile, suffers pangs of guilt and attempts to commit suicide by jumping from the roof of a building. He doesn't die but ends up paralyzed from the neck down at his family home in Spain where he is confined to an iron lung in need of round-the-clock care. A creepy young man, Angelo, enters the family home and lands himself the job as a full-time carer to Klaus. We soon learn that Angelo is a very disturbed individual and subjects Klaus to near-suffocation by unplugging the iron lung as a way of demonstrating his total power over his new 'employer'. Things become even more desperate when Angelo reveals Klaus' wartime diary and reads aloud the entries where Klaus sadistically abused and tortured young boys in a concentration camp; all this whilst masturbating onto the old man's face. Angelo then turns up the heat by threatening his wife and daughter and bringing young boys back to the house where he intends on re-enacting the most harrowing tortures of the diary - The most appalling of which includes injecting petrol directly into the youngster's heart for a truly agonising scene, before the depraved ending.

Very few films touch on the subject of child murder, and fewer still dare to breach the taboo in such detail as this (such transgressions can be found in Salo and Tenderness of The Wolves, and also in the literary works of the Marquis de Sade and Dennis Cooper, but it's a general rarity). Added to the disturbing subject-matter is the way director Villaronga presents the action; he uses classic genre tricks like intensely claustrophobic chase scenes, graphic murders, and a 'thrilling' soundtrack reminiscent of all manner of stylish 80s horror. He also steers dangerously close to viewer implication as he toys with the dynamics of sadistic and masochistic sexual fantasies; make no mistake, this film has the potential to unleash some dark desires in some viewers: Approach with caution.

The murder scenes in Tras el cristal are very difficult to watch. We're not shown much in the way of blood or violence or gore; it's in the extremely effective build-up to the scenes that make them all the more hard to deal with. The scenes are also cruelly fascinating in the way Villaronga exposes our complicitness with the shocking tortures on screen; through his eyes we're not just watching evil events being played out, we're in fact reminded through our willingness to go along with genre conventions, that the dark side isn't just limited to sadistic murderers, but is present within all of us to a certain degree.

Stylistically, In a Glass Cage is part arthouse exploration and part horror, like a cross between Dario Argento and Luchino Visconti. Thematically, the premise is very similar to Stephen King's Apt Pupil (1981), whether the director was aware of this or not. Apt Pupil is about a teenage boy who blackmails an ageing Nazi war criminal into helping him with a school essay on the nature of evil. King's novel can be interpreted as an interrogation of Satan himself, but in Tras el cristal the two central characters are just as evil as each other. Whatever your opinion is on this film, it is at least a gruelling but vital alternative to those cheap and nasty Naziploitation films of the 70s.

Tras el cristal was shown at the London Film Festival and produced mass walk-outs. It was then shown at a gay film festival in Tyneside, and even billed as a gay-friendly title. Unsurprisingly, the film was met with anger and more walk-outs. It was later discovered on video by adventurous horror hounds (along with Salo and Andrzej Zulawski's Possession) and quickly rose to notoriety on the bootleg video circuit before Cult Epics came along offering the full uncut DVD.

I SAW THE DEVIL (2010)

Dir: Kim Jee Woon /South Korea

This is one of the finest Korean movies I've ever seen, way better than over-hyped tosh like Oldboy and Three: Extremes, despite the long running time and ludicrous plot. It centres on a vicious serial killer, Jon Ki-Du (Oldboy himself, Choi Min-Sik), who is tracked down with dogged determination by an equally ruthless cop, Kim (Lee Byung Hun), whose fiance was butchered by the killer.

Kim uses satellite tracking devices to monitor Jon's movements and plays a dangerous game of cat and mouse with him which puts public safety in jeopardy. He always catches up with the psycho when he's up to no good, beating the maniac and breaking his bones before letting him go free once again. His plan is to gradually torture the killer into madness but there's also the danger that Jon could get wise to the game and go off the rails completely...

Much has been mentioned about the morals of the cop character in this film, and yes the good/evil ambiguity leaves innocent people in peril, but I thought it was a refreshing break from the Hollywoodized norm of focusing on cop characters who are morally faultless. Plus, the film takes Nietzsche's old quote about being careful not to become monstrous when facing a monster, and takes this premise to its most extreme conclusion. It's like the filmmaker's took that quote as a challenge rather than a warning! The film is also brimful of excellent set pieces, such as the gruesome killing in the taxi with the camera frantically circling the action that rivals Dario Argento for visual audacity. But the most shocking thing about the film for me was how different it is in terms of style from Kim's previous work, such as A Tale of Two Sisters; a creepy, atmospheric ghost story which is the total flipside to the hyper-kinetic and unflinching style of I Saw The Devil.

Choi Min-Sik's performance as the killer is superb. He's barely recognisable as the victim in Oldboy, even though it's his same face and hair with no prosthetics; he embodies the character so well that he seems to physically alter into that wretched creature. There are no special effects to exaggerate his evil visage, and he captures that predatory deviousness so well; it's a credit to both Min-Sik and director Kim Jee Woon that the killer didn't become some glamorized maniac or descend into some silly pastiche that no doubt will happen if this gets the Hollywood 'makeover' treatment. The result is one of the most memorable and evil screen monsters in a long long time.

ISLAND OF DEATH (1975)

Dir: Nico Mastorakis / Greece

Christopher's 'girlfriend' Celia refuses to have sex with him, so he goes outside and fucks a goat before cutting its throat. Meanwhile, Celia goes and fucks a guy whom the couple had met the previous evening, a man whom Christopher took an instant dislike to. Christopher spots them having sex in a field and takes a few snapshots with his camera (?). Then with the aid of Celia he pins the man to the ground with nails through his hands before pouring a tub of white paint down his throat. Interestingly, Celia joins in excitedly like it's a game, whereas Christopher feels that the murder is justified because he is helping to "punish perversion".

In an earlier scene Christopher spots an adulterous woman in bed with another man through a window and declares that he would "kill her if she was my wife", and yet he seems to forgive Celia of her unfaithfulness. Indeed, the audience has to wait until the end of the film to discover exactly what the relationship is between these two; are they cousins, siblings, boyfriend and girlfriend, or husband and wife?

In Christopher one can detect a repressed homosexuality that is exaggerated to the extreme, and could account for his crimes. And Celia just tags along with this dominant figure. Tragically, Bob Belling, the actor who plays Christopher, committed suicide not long after the film was made. Director Nico Mastorakis described him as "a deeply disturbed and puzzled, complex individual. He stuck the tube of a propane gas tank in his throat and died this way. He hadn't defined his sexuality".

The scene where Christopher seduces the older woman, Petricia, is interesting because he can't get aroused so he pisses on her instead. At first Petricia seems disgusted, but then she starts rubbing the urine over her body (whether it is genuine pleasure or fear that makes her act in this way is not clear). Christopher is not impressed. He takes the slightest opportunity to end the situation (she snags his dick with her tooth), and then he drags her outside and decapitates her with a bulldozer. His brutal crimes are committed to convince himself of his own warped ideas of what masculinity means. Celia's promiscuity allows Chris to become an avenger, to forget about his own problems and vent his frustrations out on 'perverts' whilst attaining a sense of normality in his own mind, safely heterosexual in all consciousness (and as a couple they are well suited in that sense!). And this equilibrium, this sense of normality is worth many sacrifices; mass murder and bestiality is fair game if it means escaping the demands of a repressed libido.

The scene where Celia is attacked in the bathroom and Christopher shows up and dispatches the would-be rapists is interesting because, in this case, he doesn't revel so much in their murders. He kills them quickly to protect Celia. These killings are instinctive and lack the artistry and imagination of the other murders throughout the film. This is because he was not the instigator in this episode; many people would have responded in the exact same way as Chris in a situation like that. The scene where he kills the two homosexuals with a sword, however, is a different matter; his desire to sexually penetrate the queer is countered by an impulse to eradicate or terminate that drive; so of course, in Christopher's mind, the logical thing to do is to stab, or 'penetrate' the homo with a sword! Penetrated and terminated in one fell swoop!

Towards the end when the couple are on the run, Christopher shows vulnerability by seeking shelter in a shepherd's barn. In Celia's eyes he is no longer that domineering male that she longs for. He affections and loyalties shift to the shepherd when he shows up and rapes them both. Christopher couldn't defend her or himself from being raped, so now Celia has found her new man. The shepherd manhandles Chris with ease and throws him into a lime pit (after cocking a leg and farting at him). Christopher calls out to Celia for help, but she doesn't want to know. His pleading only shows weakness, and she doesn't do weakness. The shepherd is her new protector, and Chris can go to hell.

"It needs a strong man to get you out of there", she says as she leaves with her new man, seemingly turned on by Christopher's screaming "Help me! I'm burning!! I'm burning!!!"

Island of Death reached UK cinemas in April 1976 under the title A Craving For Lust in a heavily censored print. The film later surfaced at the onset of the video boom of the early 80s in an uncut cassette from the AVI label. It then found itself on the video nasties list and was prosecuted under section 2 of the Obscene Publications ACT in 1985. Island of Death was later re-submitted to the censors under the title Psychic Killer 2 and was banned outright. Throughout the 80s and 90s bootleg copies were selling on VHS for as much as £50 each. Vipco released a BBFC-approved version in 2002 which had more than 4 minutes of footage missing, and it wasn't until a few years later that the British censors finally relented and passed the uncut version, available from Allstar Pictures.

THE JOY OF TORTURE 2: OXEN SPLIT TORTURING (1976)

(aka Shogun's Sadism)
Dir: Yuji Makiguchi /Japan

This sequel to Teruo Ishii's classic, Shogun's Joys of Torture, focuses on the persecution and corruption throughout the history of Japan. Christians, adulterers, criminals, samurai, etc. We're treated to a couple of stories from different epochs, but don't expect any soapbox moralising here as this film is just an excuse to indulge in scene after scene of mindless ultra-violence.

The film opens with bizarre moog music and stills of war atrocities, and then we're introduced to snake torture, a heavy mallet to the foot, men and women being burned and boiled alive. In one scene a woman is hung, and while she's still hanging there she is cut in half from the waist with a samurai sword. A 12 year old girl is forced to confess to crimes she didn't commit, but she refuses to talk, so she is beaten and branded across the eyes with a hot iron, blinding her. The film attempts some sub-plots along the way, but all very quickly descend into more torture scenes. The latter half brings on some silly slapstick comedy reminiscent of a CAT III movie. The production values are very impressive too, with lavish sets, great location shooting, costumes, and superbly gruesome special effects.

There's not a single redeeming factor among the characters (except for the good Christian girl who sucks the poison out of a man's arm after he is bitten by a snake), but we do get what the title promises - Torture, and lots of it. Also gang rape, crucifixions, stabbings, burnings, a woman being torn apart by wild oxen, blasphemy, foot-stomp abortion, ears and dick cut off... Fun for all the family!

The Japan Shock DVD looks superb. Someone has obviously taken good care of the negative over the years (if only American and Italian exploitation films were so well preserved). The colours are bold and punchy, and there's not a speck of damage on the print. This is top-of-the-range Japsploitation, essential viewing.

KIDS (1996)

Dir: Larry Clark / USA

"Like it or not, it's a modern American masterpiece". That was the Daily Telegraph's response to Larry Clark's Kids, one of the most controversial films of the 90s. Powerful, infuriating, and fiercely uncompromising, this bleak tale of a day in the lives of a bunch of teenage wasters in New York caused a scandal on its release.

This docu-drama follows a group of shameless delinquents as they hang out, do drugs, spread diseases, and indulge in petty crime and mindless violence. The verite effect discloses many lurid details that are not easily forgotten. The narrative falls into place with Telly (Leo Fitzpatrick), a sweet-talking sleaze bag whose hobby is to deflower young girls ("Virgins, I love 'em! No diseases!"). Meanwhile, Jennie, one of Telly's previous bed-fellows, discovers that she is HIV positive. She spends the rest of the film trying to track him down before the disease can be spread any further.

Whether you're a worried parent or a detached spectator, Kids is a film that demands the viewer to confront the depravity on screen. It's a horror show aimed at adults rather than children, and its potent message is driven home with exceptional directorial skill. If you choose to turn away and ignore, then according to the film's unflinchingly candid view, you're no better than the millions of parents out there who let their kids run wild with no clue as to what they're getting up to with their friends. And this stance was backed up by Variety magazine who declared that "Kids is disgusting and disturbing but that does not stop it from being a work of art. The nice thing about Kids is that it isn't nice at all".

Former photographer Larry Clark teamed up with writer and skateboarder, Harmony Korine, to bring this cautionary tale to the screen. Korine was allegedly only 18 years old when he wrote the script; and it's interesting to know that there was a script at all, because the performances in the film are spot-on for the most part, and their casual line deliveries seem completely ad-libbed. The film itself remains a devastating snapshot of a generation who have sunk so low it would surely have caused Bret Easton Ellis a few sleepless nights.

The only real downside is that the film feels phony in its social context; New York is just like any other big city with its neighbourhoods seperated by race, class, and religion (similar to the racial segregation in the urban areas of Paris, and the 'post code wars' in London, for example); there's no way the kids in Kids would be able to mingle in the park without any trouble erupting between those of differing neighbourhoods, and its simply bogus to suggest otherwise.

The press whipped up a storm on its release, and the BBFC cut a minute and a half of footage under the Protection of Children Act. The film was financed by Disney, and they sought to conceal their financial interest in Kids by having their sub-label, Miramax, release the film under an alias company name, Shining Excalibur Films. Warner Brothers distanced themselves from the film in a pathetic show of moral indignation by banning its screenings at its UK cinema chains (but they were happy to allow it to be shown at their other chains across the world).

As for director Larry Clark, he has continued in his efforts to portray modern wayward youth in his subsequent work, such as Another Day In Paradise, Ken Park (again in collaboration with Harmony Korine), and Wassup Rockers, films which vary in their success and explicitness. There's no doubt he feels very passionate about what he does - I suppose you'd have to be - and he at least is prepared to shine a light into the murkier side of American youth, a place that many of us would rather not know about. But credit to him for going places where very few filmmakers are willing to go, and presenting us with the confrontational truth.

KING OF NEW YORK (1990)

Dir: Abel Ferrara / USA

Christopher Walken stars as Frank White, a New York drug lord who is back on the streets after a prison term. He claims to now be a reformed character, and tries to do some good for society by cleaning the streets of rival pushers and pimps, and uses ill-gotten gains to save a Bronx hospital from closure. He is backed up by his (mostly) loyal gang of black maniacs who are happy to unload their weapons on anyone who gets in the way of Frank's dream. Meanwhile, a group of angry cops with a personal vendetta against White decide to take ruthless vigilante action against him and his gang when their efforts to see them back behind bars fails due to legal chicanery and the deaths of important eye witnesses.

King of New York is Abel Ferrara's first foray into the gangster genre with a bleak worldview penned by Ferrara's long-time cohort Nicholas St. John. It's the kind of film where the entire principal cast are wiped out in the most cold and calculated ways (including a cop who is shot dead at his colleague's funeral), and one man's attempts to redeem himself from the errors of his ways is doomed from the start. But for all the film's bleak tone and ruthless slaughter, this is actually one of Ferrara's most optimistic efforts to date. It's also one of his most accessible, boasting a strong neon-lit photography by Bojan Bazelli and one of the most impressive casts of the 90s which, alongside Walken, also features Larry Fishburne, David Caruso, Wesley Snipes, Victor Argo, and Steve Buscemi.

Interestingly, King of New York tips its hat to vampiric legend; it's a film which owes more to gothic horrors like Nosferatu and Near Dark rather than Goodfellas or Scarface. It's no coincidence that Frank White constantly states that he is "Back from the dead", or that his main enemy is called Bishop; Argo's detective serves as a Van Helsing determined to slay White, the slippery bloodsucker who is never seen in any kind of natural light, and who literally walks on his own grave. Indeed, Ferrara went on to cast Walken a few years later as Peina the philosophising vampire in The Addiction.

This vision of New York is dark and complicated. The jumbled scenery juxtaposes criminality and morality, rich and poor, order and chaos, politics and apathy, business and pleasure to such an extent the result is mind-boggling. It's a concrete jungle of racial and cultural diversities where even the cops and politicians roam around in clan-like groups held together by their own sense of loyalty. Ferrara and St. John know the city inside out; the ethnic areas, the subways, districts, tourist spots, hotels, bars, and restaurants. And all of these elements help give King of New York a fractured but realistic sense of place. A classic.

KISSED (1996)

Dir: Lynne Stopkewich / Canada

This is not a Nekromantik. In fact, director Lynne Stopkewich goes so far in trying to portray the subject of necrophilia in a non-sensationalist manner that she ends up making it seem somehow tasteful. And boring. There's no explicit mortuary scenes here, or corpse-fucking in the old Jorg Buttgereit mode. Stopkewich instead aims for an exploration of the spiritual possibilities in the attraction of death.

Based on Barbara Gowdy's short tale, We So Seldom Look On Love, Kissed centres on Sandra (Molly Parker), a morbid young woman whose fascination with death leads to a job in a mortuary. She meets a handsome young man in Matt (Peter Outerbridge), and eventually reveals to him her dark secret. Sandra's disinterest in the living sees her becoming increasingly attracted to the dead, where she seems to have ecstatic spiritual experiences with corpses... Meanwhile, Matt becomes increasingly obsessed with Sandra, and in a leaf taken from Romeo and Juliet, decides to get pretty drastic in his attempts to win her heart...

The worst thing a movie can be is boring. And Kissed is almost sleep-inducing. Rather than cutting the film down into a short, Stopkewich seemed determined to stretch out the incredibly dull proceedings for a full 80 minutes. There's also very little in the way of psychology to help us understand Sandra's motivations, and what we're left with is a cute and rather naive portrait of a corpse-fucker; all very sweet and quirky! Her disgusting perversion is treated in the same way as a woman with a terminal disease in some daytime TV movie; just another well-adjusted leading lady who just so happens to be a bit different - in this case a penchant for sleeping with dead bodies. I know the film focuses more on the spiritual dimensions of such vile subject-matter, but still I didn't believe a second of this garbage. Some have interpreted the film as Sandra's fantasy, and that would perhaps explain why all the corpses just happen to be handsome young men. All in all though, it's a simplistic and lifeless failure.

Despite nearing retirement, chief censor at the BBFC, James Ferman, had some reservations about the film, but new censor, Andreas Whittam Smith, recognised the film as an exploration, not exploitation, and passed Kissed uncut for home viewing.

THE LAST HOUSE ON DEAD END STREET (1973)

(aka The Cuckoo Clocks of Hell; aka The Funhouse)
Dir: Victor Janos (Roger Watkins) /USA

Upon his release from jail, a minor drug dealer, Terry Hawkins (played by director Watkins under the pseudonym Steven Morrison) is determined to avenge the porno peddlers whom he worked with and who have pissed him off in some way by gathering together a group of low-lives whose job it is to film a string of tortures, disembowelments, and murders. A group of victims are quickly assembled and lured to an old abandoned building where the filmic misadventures begin.

Straight up porno is not good enough anymore, people want their movies to be gruelling and nasty, and Mr.Hawkins decides to give the people what they want... Terry tortures and kills the 'performers' while his female assistants stand by in ghoulish masks. The end result is similar to Joel M. Reed's Bloodsucking Freaks but lacks that film's silly grand guignol style, and opts instead to play up the awful seriousness of a snuff film, for better or worse...

Lots of vileness ensues as the slaughter reaches overdrive - Men and women are tied up, branded, have their faces cut off, and eyeballs skewered. One woman has her leg cut off while she is unconscious, only to be brought around again with the aid of smelling salts so that she can fully comprehend the horror of her situation. She is then subsequently disemboweled. And much of the film is narrated by the psychopaths themselves...

Made on a shoestring budget of $800, this heavy-duty horror of nihilism and misanthropy is told in an icy and clinical way with its low lighting and technical limitations adding to its harrowing atmosphere of dread. It isn't a snuff film, but that kind of nasty, cynical attitude needed to make a snuffy is in full force here as Watkin's performance as the troubled filmmaker is one of the most memorable and evil in all of 70s horror.

Speaking of evil, The Last House On Dead End Street also features one of the most freakishly evil soundtracks in the history of film, made using old classical library music slowed down, played backwards, and channeled through a guitar phasing effects peddle. The result is simply mesmerising. Adding to the hostilities are the artistic flourishes throughout the film; it's cheap and nasty for sure, but there's nothing corny about the performances or script or overall tone of the project, unlike many films of its era. I can't think of any other film that oozes such pure hatred in every frame, except maybe Shaun Costello's horror/porn hybrid, Forced Entry.

The murders become a strange kind of ritual towards the end with the use of knives, mirrors, masks, and other objects. Those familiar with the magickal arts and Satanism will notice that a magick symbol is used as a branding iron and deer hooves are used for sexual excitation in the victims, and Hawkins even wears a God mask during the slaughter sequences.

It may come as no surprise to learn that Watkins was heavily into amphetamines during the making of the film; speed leaves its users in a state of social dislocation, and all feelings of empathy towards our fellow human beings are shut down in that highly-charged state. And that mindset is suitably mirrored in the film's grim and heartless hostility.

The Last House On Dead End Street was completed as early as 1973 under its original title, The Cuckoo Clocks of Hell. That version had an epic running time of almost three hours (and right up until his death in 2007 Watkins had always insisted that that version was the definitive cut). The film was reluctantly cut down to 115 minutes for a planned screening at Cannes which never actually happened due to an actor filing a lawsuit after he was fired from the set. This kept the film in litigation for years until the case was thrown out of court.

Watkins was then finally free to secure some distribution and struck a deal with Warmflash Productions. For a while things seemed to be working out well until he discovered that the company had cut his film down to 77 minutes, re-arranged scenes, created a fake credits sequence, changed the title to The Funhouse, and even added a 'bad-guys-get-their-comeuppance' coda at the end. Understandably peeved and disillusioned, Watkins moved away from feature production and carved out a career in the porn industry instead.

Meanwhile, the 77 minute cut was raking in large sums of money on the drive-in circuit when it was re-titled again as The Last House On Dead End Street to cash in on Wes Craven's classic Last House On The Left title. And then the film simply disappeared, leaving only a handful of rave reviews in its wake. On home video it was released in the States on Betamax and VHS by a company called Sun Video and in Canada by Marquee, but both releases were fleeting and short-lived. Due to the rarity of the film and the mysterious nature of its director (billed as 'Victor Janos') and everyone involved, Dead End Street's reputation began spiraling out of control; some of the more spurious rumours going around were that it was a genuine snuff film, and it wasn't long before the movie had garnered a legendary reputation. Bootleg copies from an awful looking Venezuelan videotape were selling on eBay for as much as $100 per tape, and this led Watkins' then girlfriend Suzanne to post a message on an internet horror forum enquiring about fans of the film. This post caught the attention of Headpress honcho David Kerekes, and the rest is history. He met up with Watkins for a lengthy interview (see Headpress 23) and arranged to get the movie out on DVD.

This holy grail amongst horror movie collectors was then dragged out into the light when Kerekes managed to source an incomplete 35mm print belonging to FantAsia's Mitch Davis. It was missing the extended disembowelment scene but the folks at Barrel Entertainment located a super-rare copy on VHS, and they inserted the scene for a Special Edition DVD release. It isn't the long lost 3 hour director's cut, but Barrel did a fantastic job of rescuing this caustic gem from oblivion, and they should be commended for making an uncut release a priority.

THE LIFE AND DEATH OF A PORNO GANG (2009)

(Orig title: Zivot i Smrt porno bande)
Dir: Mladen Djordevic /Serbia

Largely overshadowed by the release of the notorious A Serbian Film around the same time, The Life and Death of a Porno Gang had to make do with luring unsuspecting viewers into its web of nastiness by word of mouth alone whilst Spasojevic's film sparked global controversy and even graced the cover of Fangoria magazine. You won't see any 'Newborn Porn' in Djordevic's film, but you'll see just about everything else besides as we follow a group of dropout pornographers who hit the road in a Scooby Doo van armed with video cameras. Whilst watching months of old video footage, a survivor of the gang explains what's going on...

The film starts in a light-hearted manner as almost documentary-like, but we soon get a touch of style, surrealism, and humour (much like Koen Mortier's Ex Drummer). We also get to see brief shots of unsimulated sex, a nasty beheading scene with bored soldiers playing football with some poor guy's severed head, a man cuts a goat's throat, and a tranny sucks off a horse. This film also features one of the weirdest rape scenes ever in which the gang are gang-raped by country folk; what makes it weird is that one of the guys being raped starts to laugh uncontrollably, and this laughter infects the other rapees, setting off a chain of giggles which leaves the horny yokels understandably confused (it transpires that the bumpkin rapists have been infected with HIV through their attack, and it's that Gotcha! moment which amuses the gang).

Eventually the porno bande decide that snuff sells so they begin organising the making of one. They start by filming some loon cut himself up with a razor; he then cuts his own throat on camera. One of the gang can't handle his death-croaks and steps in to finish him off by bashing his brains in. They dispose of the corpse and then indulge in a hippy-style orgy. Then we get another snuff movie; a woman called Sofia gives a little strip-tease and then smashes a soldier's head in with a mallet. And then they party some more.

By this point the gang have truly become Mansonesque as the drugs get harder and they become increasingly alienated from society, and resort to kidnapping people for their 'pioneering' snuff efforts (it has long been rumoured that the Manson family made snuff movies, but the footage has never surfaced). The cult begin to fall apart soon after with suicide and disease rampant among them, but not before they attempt to stage "the first snuff theatre in the world". But it doesn't finish there; we get a tripple-whammy of bloody surprises before the end credits roll...

LOLITA VIBRATOR TORTURE (1987)

Dir: Hisayasu Sato / Japan

Notoriously difficult to find in any English language version, Lolita Vibrator Torture follows the escapades of a sick voyeuristic maniac who likes to 'cuff young girls to his bed, titillate them with a vibrator, pour acid into their mouths, and take snapshots with his camera as the girl's throats are burned out. Pretty nasty stuff. A typical predatory paedophile, the man (Takeshi Ito) grooms and sweet-talks his potential victims on the streets, gains their trust, and then unleashes hell on them.

When he captures one particular girl (Kiyomi Ito), he discovers that she is already carrying around her own vibrator that she keeps down her panties! He proceeds to assault her and smears the bloody joy stick across her chest. After the ordeal he seems to take pity on her and keeps her alive so that she can become his accomplice. Another girl is defiled with spray paint, stripped, covered in shaving foam, then given the old buzz-stick treatment and raped. His little helper then takes over the vibrator duties and really goes to town, ramming the victim with all of her little might. Then comes the acid and the camera, and young Ito poses with the bloody corpse as the madman starts clicking away with a photo shoot from hell. The pictures are then used to decorate the walls of his lair -
A freight container perched on the top of an apartment block. This couple build a rapport based on sex and secrecy, but perhaps inevitably, things are due to end very badly... and those pesky vibrators just keep on buzzing away.

Even by Sato's sleazy standards this wretched piece of celluloid crosses some serious boundaries. And you thought Maladoloscenza and Emperor Tomato Ketchup were at the cutting edge of under-age exploitation? Well, wait until you clap eyes on this, because for once, the title of the film actually lives up to expectations. And then some. The national age of consent in Japan is just 13 years old, but from a Westerner's perspective the bombardment of school uniforms, bloody vibrators, and deranged black and white stills of children in their death throes amounts to some truly pathological images.

Unsurprisingly, the film hasn't been officially released in any form outside of Japan, and out of the hundreds of Pinku eiga films that were made over the decades, this is perhaps the most shocking and outrageous (though not the best) of them all. Even the Japanese themselves were outraged, with some claiming it to be the most repulsive film of all time. The film does, however, have its share of supporters, most notably Pinky legend Yuji Tajiri who praised it as being a major inspiration behind his own directing career.

Made as part of Kan Mukai's Shishi Productions and released by Nikkatsu as part of a Roman Porno triple-bill, Lolita Vibrator Torture features the debut of actor Takeshi Ito who would go on to become one of the most successful Pink film actors of his era, winning the first ever Best Actor Award at the Pink Film Grand Prix for his role in Toshiya Ueno's snappily titled Keep On Masturbating: Non-Stop Pleasure. And incidentally, actress Kiyomi Ito (no relation) won Best Actress at the same event for Sato's unforgettable Dirty Wife Getting Wet. The original title for Lolita Vibrator Torture was The Secret Garden (Himitsu no Hanazono) under which name it was released on DVD in Japan in 2003.

LOS OLVIDADOS (1950)

Dir: Luis Bunuel / Mexico

By the mid-1940s Luis Bunuel had spent 15 years in the cinematic wilderness. When the civil war broke out in Spain, he found work as a spy in Spain and France, spent some time unemployed, then crossed the Atlantic for New York and Los Angeles where he wrote and translated screenplays. His career as a once great filmmaker seemed to be long gone. As a youngster, Bunuel had often joked to his friends that he wouldn't be seen dead in Mexico, but by the mid-40s that was the only place where he'd stand a chance of directing another film.

Reluctantly, he drifted south to Mexico City which had become a haven for Nazi's, spies, communists, anarchists, and intellectuals of all stripes who had been hounded out of their own countries. Mexico's non-involvement in World War II meant there was plenty of money around, and wealthy film producers still remembered Bunuel and his surrealist classics like Un Chein Andalou and L'Age D'Or, and it was Oscar Dancigers who finally offered him the opportunity to get back behind the camera. After helming a couple of cheap programmers (Gran Casino and El Gran Calavera), Bunuel had dispelled the ring rust and felt ready to tackle something more substantial. The result was Los Olvidados.

After escaping from a reform school, El Jaibo (Roberto Cobo) returns home to the shanty towns of Mexico City where his loutish behavior gains him a reputation. Young street waif, Pedro (Alfonso Mejia) looks up to him with a nervy respect until Jaibo sleeps with his mother, Marta (Estela Inda). An infuriated Pedro then dobs him in to the police for killing a member of a rival gang, and so Jaibo seeks revenge.

Bunuel combines his love of surrealism with Italian neo-realism for Los Olvidados, and keeps the former to a subtle minimum whilst embracing the latter to stunning effect. He dispensed with the norm by hiring a largely professional cast (Inda and Cobo, and also Miguel Inclan as the blind beggar), and found it difficult to resist injecting his trademark flights of fancy (producer Dancigers had to talk him out of hiring a 100-piece orchestra that would play in the background of the scene where Jaibo kills Pedro). It's a hard-hitting film for its time, a tale of low-life criminality and all-consuming lust that leads to anger, death, and despair.

The script was based on Bunuel's own observations during his time spent in Mexico City, and also on real case studies from reformatories which he used to cement his screenplay in its realism. The film was shot in the director's typical haste in just 21 days, well ahead of schedule, despite some troubles during production, with crew members objecting to the harsh subject-matter and quitting. The film's hair stylist objected to a scene in which Marta refuses to feed Pedro ("No Mexican mother would do that!"). Bunuel stuck to his guns though, and refused to change anything in the script.

Indeed, the film's unflinching depiction of abandoned kids having to fend for themselves in a cruel world devoid of any kind of moral guidance was always going to be controversial. And when Los Olvidados premiered at the CineMexico, the critics were outraged that their city and its inhabitants had been depicted in such a harsh and unflattering way. Bunuel was criticised for perpetuating misery on the citizens, some of the actors who appeared in the film were so scared of the hostile reception that they fled the city, and producer Dancigers, who had invested a large amount of money in the film, felt intimidated enough to remove it from circulation after only two days (it premiered on a Thursday and was withdrawn on the Saturday). Of course, Bunuel was no stranger to this type of thing, some of his earlier films had provoked organised riots in the cinema, and he seemed to take the whole debacle in his stride; just another day at the office!

The tide turned, however, in the following year when Los Olvidados played at Cannes to a rapturous reception. It seemed the French had missed the enfant terrible (it had been more than two decades since L'Age D'Or and his controversial documentary, Las Hurdes), and the Spaniard was bestowed with the Best Director Award, and had that much needed career resurgence.

Los Olvidados has since become an accepted classic, with its gritty template being passed down the decades, with filmmakers as diverse as Hector Babenco (Pixote), Alan Clarke (Scum), Ulrich Edel (Christiane F.), Walter Salles (Central Station), and of course, Larry Clark and Harmony Korine (Kids), all willing and proud to display their influences. As for Bunuel, Los Olvidados marked the beginning of the third part of his career after his promising start in Paris, and 20 years spent mostly in limbo. This fresh new start lasted for the rest of his life where he made 26 fascinating films in 27 years, securing his reputation, once and for all, as one of the most important filmmakers of all time.

LOVE TO KILL (1993)

(Orig title: Ai zhi sha; aka Nue zhi lian)
Dir: Siu Hung Cheung and Kirk Wong /Hong Kong

Anthony Wong is in typical psycho nutjob mode here as Sam, a cruel, controlling, and possessive husband who subjects his wife Keung (Julie Lee) to brutal rape in their apartment. He likes to suffocate her with a polythene bag while doing it. She manages to fight him off and runs outside into the rain where a passing cop, Hung Lee (Danny Lee, the good cop in John Woo's The killer) protects her and savagely assaults Sam.

When Sam leaves the hospital, he escapes prosecutution because Keung is too afraid to speak out against him or press charges. The police give him a rollicking but have no choice but to let him go free. Back at home, Sam pathetically tries to make it up to Keung by massaging her feet and being nice to her, but this just has the effect of making her feel even more depressed and uncomfortable. Keung's mother is ill in hospital with cancer and she just about manages to get permission from him to got and visit her, but on condition that he escorts her.

Keung's heartache at seeing her mother in intense pain and being heavily addicted to opium sees her attempting to suffocate mum with a pillow. Now it's the time for the police to give her a rollicking, but they also remember her from the incident with Sam and accuse her of 'liking it rough' due to her not pressing charges. This pushes Keung over the edge and she slashes her wrist with a piece of broken mirror.

Cop Hung Lee takes pity on her and Keung eventually confides in him that she is terrified of her husband and is afraid for her son's safety. Lee immediately organises a van and he takes Keung home to collect her son and pack some belongings - He also takes an interest in her panties - Sam arrives home just in time to see them leaving in the van.

Keung and son move into the cop's apartment with his girlfriend Jenny. Meanwhile, Sam stays behind and fantasizes on revenge. He stalks Lee as a way of finding info on his wife's whereabouts. Lee finds himself increasingly drawn to Keung and finds it impossible to stop lusting after her, especially when she does the housework. And just as things look to be calming down and Keung is starting to rebuild her life, Sam turns up to spoil all the peace and harmony.

He checks her mother out of hospital and holds her hostage at their apartment. He orders Keung to come home or she'll never see mum again. And of course, when she gets there, Sam reaches full-on psycho mode. He teases her with a cutthroat razor, accuses her of sleeping with the cop, scrubs her in the bath tub, and chains her to the wall. He then goes out and frames Lee for police brutality. And while the cop is in custody, he takes a visit round to his apartment and brutally beats, rapes, and suffocates the cop's girlfriend Jenny, and takes off with his son. Hung Lee rushes to the hospital to find Jenny bloody, bruised, and in a vegetative state on a life support machine. And the scene is set for a bloody showdown...

This is a surprisingly subdued take on extreme domestic violence that in other hands may have become just another sleazy CAT III shocker (Herman Yau, or especially Billy Tang would have had a field day depicting the awful crimes in this film). Don't get me wrong, this film was made purely for the exploitation market but at least takes the time to acknowledge just how despicable the human animal can be without resorting to a dramatic 'fun-time' sleaziness like Yau's Ebola Syndrome or Billy Tang's Red To Kill, for example.

There's very little of the usual slapstick scenes (although there are some comic interludes, such as Lee's lusting after Keung while she does the cleaning, and his awkward relationship with his high-maintenance girlfriend, Jenny).

Anthony Wong is at his scummiest and best here as the psycho husband who subjects his wife to a miserable existence. His brutal sexual fantasies (actually, they're probably flashbacks) of the horrendous abuses on his wife are stemmed from his own childhood traumas; as a child, Sam's father savagely beat his mother and attempted to hang the little boy, but the rope breaks. And by the end of the film we can see how this evil behaviour is passed down the generations (Sam's own son witnesses much of the domestic carnage), and although the film refuses to suggest that the little boy will continue in his father's and grandfather's evil footsteps, you can't help but think that much damage has been done.

If this all seems a bit sensitive for a CAT III title then don't dismay; the film's finale is extremely violent - There's a brutal decapitation, a gruesome and repetitive face-smashing with an axe, a character beaten with a lump of wood that has six inch nails sticking out of it, a near-decapitation on a broken window pane, and some nasty nail-gun mayhem, with one character shot through the eye. Unmissable.

LUCKER THE NECROPHAGOUS (1986)

Dir: Johan Vandewoestijne / Belgium

The subject of necrophilia has cropped up over the decades in many horror films, albeit in mostly tame and metaphorical terms, with the works of people like Mario Bava, Roger Corman, and Jean Rollin all hinting at the twisted sensualities of death. In the 1970s when the gates of excess were thrown wide open, and almost every taboo you can think of were explored by filmmakers willing to obliterate the boundaries, still there was no one brave enough to tackle the subject in a blunt and literal fashion (Marijan Vadja's creepy and morbid Mosquito The Rapist was perhaps the closest thing to necrophilia we saw in 70s horror). A few years later and Joe D'Amato's Biou Omega came closer still to a full-on depiction of corpse fucking, but it wasn't until the early 80s that this most enduring and disgusting of taboos was finally broken with Gerald Kargls Angst, in which a young woman is murdered and subsequently raped.

Later that decade a pair of rancid videotapes started floating round Europe via mail order; Jorg Buttgereit's Nekromantik and Johan Vandewoestijne's Lucker The Necrophagous. And although both of these films have been known to induce actual physical vomiting in their audiences, Buttgereit's film is an arty shocker with warm sweeping music and
soft-focus photography which somewhat softens the blow, whereas Vandewoestijne's Lucker dispenses with the glossiness and gets down and dirty with the cadavers, and culminates in one of the most repulsive sequences in cinema history.

The film kicks off with Lucker on a mad killing spree after a failed murder, suicide attempt, and escape from a mental institution. He stores away his young female corpses and allows them to mature for a while (like a fine wine?) before he samples the earthly delights. And this sets up the unforgettable sequence in which Lucker cuts a woman's throat and watches her bleed to death before covering her with a sheet. We then spend the next week or so with the slobby psychopath as he kicks around in his squalid apartment biding his time...

Eventually he returns to the bed and uncovers the corpse, but the body laid out before him no longer resembles that of a young woman, but a bloated, discoloured stiff riddled with maggots (you can almost smell it). Undeterred, an aroused Lucker strokes the corpse between the legs, his fingers becoming slimy with the putrid residue of rotting flesh, and then proceeds to lick and suck the ghastly death juice from his hand. It's a scene that is guaranteed to sicken even the hardiest of extreme movie devotees, but that isn't all; Lucker then climbs on top for a bit of penetrative sex... The term 'Viewer discretion is advised' has never been so apt. But of course, this murderous necrophile can't continue with this kind of craziness for very long, and it's only a matter of time before death itself catches up with him...

Nick Van Suyt as the title character does a serviceable job of conveying the depravity of a sick maniac, though I very much doubt he put this on his CV when looking for further work. He deserves a ton of respect for having the balls to go ahead and get 'stuck in' to such a scuzzy role. He reminded me of a down-market version of Pep Tosar (of Aftermath fame) in his willingness to disregard everything for the sake of sleaze. And to my knowledge he hasn't appeared in any film since... Hold on a sec, maybe he did put Lucker on his CV...

Lucker is not a good film, in fact quite the opposite. There's some awful acting, bad framing, and needless time-padding in the film's rather short 74 minute running time. On the plus side, director Vandewoestijne shows some visual flourishes with lighting, spatial composition, and mood, but the very limited budget curtails any serious attempts at style. He also admirably rejects the idea of traditional attempts to try and understand the killer; a nice move considering how alienated this film is from the rest of cinema, and how alienated Lucker himself is from the rest of society. 'Why is it so important to know what makes him tick?' the filmmaker seems to be asking us, 'Lucker just is'.

The film has had a troubled history; the producers destroyed the original negative, the director gave up filmmaking altogether, and the film's commercial prospects were extremely limited. Nevertheless, a tape did the rounds on the grey market in a 74 minute cut with Dutch subtitles, and this was the only option available for years until Synapse released a Director's Cut on DVD in the mid-00s. This version is copied from a rare VHS due to the non-existence of the original source materials. And although it looks terrible campared with other Synapse releases, it is at least uncut and trimmed only of a few needless bits of padding by the director himself.

MADE IN BRITAIN (1982)

Dir: Alan Clarke / UK

After the BBC refused to broadcast Scum in the late 70s for being "too realistic", director Alan Clarke (along with writer David Lelend) was given another opportunity to explore the dark side of youth a few years later when he was invited to film a project for a short-lived TV series, Tales Out of School.

The result was an episode entitled Made In Britain, a no less realistic depiction of a rebel without a cause, featuring a powerhouse performance from Tim Roth as the troubled Trevor, an angry skinhead with a Swastika tattooed on his forehead. The film follows this deeply disturbed kid on his destructive path as he hurls racist abuse, vandalises homes and businesses, and crashes a van into the local police station. His social worker tries desperately to calm him down and plays on the boy's intelligence but to no effect. Trevor seems determined to spiral even further out of control, and sinks deeper into his own rotten sense of hatred before his rampaging behaviour lands him in police custody.

With its stylish mix of neon-lit streets and natural daylight, director Alan Clarke shows more willing this time around to experiment here than with his previous Scums, even trying out Steadicam for the first time to stunning effect. The way the camera prowls along, keeping up with the fiercely energetic Trevor has the effect of turning even the most ordinary scenes into provocative and poetic flourishes (he would use Steadicam later on in his career for The Firm and Elephant).

Actor Tim Roth in his first role is absolutely superb as the young Trevor spiraling out of control. Roth went on to carve a pretty decent career for himself on the fringes of Hollywood, working with such luminaries as Peter Greenaway and Quentin Tarantino, and has always been willing to offer a leg-up to up and coming filmmakers such as Buddy Giovinazzo when Roth agreed to play a role in his film, Life Sentences. But nowhere has he found a more meatier, grittier role than as Trevor in Made In Britain, one of the most honest and compelling of all young rebel movies.

One of the most fascinating scenes in the film shows Trevor in debate with a youth worker who scribbles his warnings on a blackboard about the dangers and idiocies of a life spent in the criminal justice system. What's so extraordinary about the scene is that the film doesn't choose sides, and both sides of the argument have their own understandable (if disagreeable) logic, and both are passionate and ring true. The youth worker literally spells out to Trevor that if he continues the way he is he'll find himself going "round and round" the system with no escape, and Trevor retorts, accusing the youth worker of being just as racist as him but hides it because he's a coward. Now, with the undercurrent of racism that existed in Britain during that time (and perhaps things haven't really changed too much since), Trevor could indeed have a point there. It's interesting how the youth worker doesn't explain to him how racism is stupid and wrong but instead simply sighs "No one cares about your little protest, Trevor".

Regardless of the racist subject matter (they could have been arguing about politics or football, or music or women, etc), this scene represents a classic case of young versus old. The older man has probably come into contact with many tearaways like Trevor in his time; his pleadings for a quiet life of order and stability constantly falling on deaf ears. And Trevor is the youth whose misguided and chaotic passion is outraged by the fact that he feels surrounded by cowards who are too afraid to fight his cause. It's the idealism of youth and the 'anything-for-a-quiet-life' of age that are at loggerheads in this scene, and it is one of the finest of its kind in the history of film.

With a slim running time of 73 minutes, Made In Britain is one of the finest TV movies ever made; it's gritty, honest, provocative, but full of style, courage, and compassion in everything from the camerawork and performances to the script and overall message: I'm sure most of us have had our Trevor moments in our pasts where we've been insanely passionate about things we cared about, whether it be football, movies, or a girl, etc, and Clarke shows us that 'growing out of it' isn't always a matter of maturity, but more often a case of having to take responsibility and make compromises just so that we can live a 'quiet life'.

The film also ends on an interesting note: For all the trouble that Trevor has caused he was never physically hit; he took some harsh bollockings from the people around him who were trying to steer him onto the straight and narrow, but he was never given a hiding. At the end of the film, however, when Trevor finds himself in police custody, his mouth infuriates one of the policemen who promptly wacks him with his truncheon. Trevor has no answer for that, he seems a bit stumped for the first time in his life. And it's there that the film ends. Make of that what you will.

MAITRESSE (1976)

Dir: Barbert Schroeder / France

Young man, Oliver (Gerard Depardieu), arrives in Paris and breaks into a building to discover that the place is a brothel. He gets into a relationship with Arian (Bulle Ogier), a professional dominatrix who owns the house. Pretty soon he finds himself assisting her in her work and becomes uneasy with the differences between her relationship with him and her clients. Inevitably, he decides he should take her away from it all. But will she go?

Maitresse is an unlikely love story, and a blackly comic look at the world of sadomasochism. Director Barbert Schroeder, the man behind Single White Female and Reversal of Fortune, presents this ice-cold romance as a painful and destructive affair with a heavy emphasis on the rituals of S&M, and is not recommended to the squeamish. The film was shot in a real brothel and portrays real clientele going through real acts of painful submission under the authority of S&M queen Bulle Ogier. And this makes for some unforgettable scenes of unashamed masochistic ecstasy. Ultimately though, it's a film which forces viewers to face up to their own relationships, with the material on screen serving as nothing more than an extreme form of the furtive mind games and power struggles that exists in the most normal and everyday of relationships.

In America Maitresse went X rated, but in the UK it was initially banned in its entirety in October 1976. The film was re-submitted to the censors five years later and heavily cut, mostly on scenes depicting real footage, like nipple piercing, genitals being needled, heavy spanking, and most notoriously, a penis being nailed onto a chair. The BBFC have always been outraged by the idea of consensual mutilation (and it's still against the law in the UK), with films like Blue Velvet, The Story of O, and Cronenberg's Crash being the subject of much controversy over the years. But even in its censored form, Maitresse proved to be too much for some viewers. In 2003 it was finally passed uncut with an 18 certificate.

MANIAC (1980)

Dir: William Lustig / USA

Frank Zito (Joe Spinell) is a very sick man. He stalks, murders, and scalps young women. He is not necessarily guided by particulars either, any will do; prostitutes, nurses, couples on the beach or on lover's lane - anyone who catches his eye is in serious danger. He lives in a crummy basement flat surrounded by his beloved mannequins, and often falls into deep depression, struck by guilt for his awful crimes. But his resentment and mad urges to kill just won't go away... He strikes up a relationship with beautiful photographer, Anna (Caroline Munro), and they genuinely like each other, but Frank can't hide his sickness from her for very long...

If you're a fan of 'fun-time' slashers like Halloween and Friday The 13th, then William Lustig's Maniac may come as something of a shock to the system. It's about as much fun as being stalked through a deserted subway after dark. Instead, we're invited to join the company of a miserable, self-loathing psychopath who prowls the seedy streets of New York's red light district in search of his next kill, or sulks around in his squalid flat, mumbling to himself whilst nailing the scalps of victims onto the heads of his mannequin collection. It's a grim, nasty, and unsettling film, but also perhaps one of the finest slasher movies ever made. I just wish there were more films like this that refuse to glamorise the killer and is prepared to get down and dirty with the harrowing bleakness of what happens behind the headlines in serial murder.

Inspired by the panic and paranoia of big city life, Maniac boasts the greatest sequence in slasher movie history in which a young nurse (Kelly Piper) is followed down into an empty subway station by her killer and is slaughtered in the toilets. It's a long and painfully protracted scene that will leave you with clammy hands thanks to some superb pacing and editing techniques, before the payoff when Zito rams his 'chete through her spine (this sequence is said to have influenced Alexandre Aja for the public restroom scene in Haute Tension).

An earlier scene in which Frank visits a prostitute is difficult to watch because it's played out so unsettlingly straight. It's easy to imagine a real life murder taking place in an almost identical way as the scene in which the hooker (Rita Montrone) begins servicing her client, only to be thrown down onto the bed and strangled. And it's here that Frank takes out his hunting knife and proceeds to cut away at her scalp, taking his souvenir with him from the crime scene.

Jay Chattaway's downbeat score adds to the bleak and harrowing nature of the film, as does Tom Savini's gruesomely realistic special effects (although Savini himself is said to have felt uncomfortable being associated with the film after it grew and generated its notorious reputation). Trivia fans will be interested to know that the character Frank Zito was named after director William Lustig's friend, Joseph Zito, who directed a couple of nice slasher movies himself around that time, Bloodrage (1979) and The Prowler (1981). But neither of those comes close to the urban nightmare that is Maniac, a film so ruthless and bleak it sent many a movie-goer leaving the cinema in fear, especially those who were planning on taking the train home.

William Lustig was a frequenter of the Deuce and the grindhouses of 42nd Street; he would skip class and soak up as much sexploitation and import horror as he could. He made his directorial debut in 1977 (under the name Billy

Bagg) with The Violation of Claudia, a porn effort. He eventually teamed up with executive producer Judd Hamilton and actor Joe Spinell to make their masterpiece, Maniac. His career ran steadily throughout the 80s, offering up genre classics like the Maniac Cop series and Relentless before he retired from directing to concentrate on releasing his favourite grindhouse movies on DVD with his label, Blue Underground (much in the same way as fellow New Yorker Frank Henenlotter, who gave up filmmaking for his own label, Something Weird Video, although he did return to the director's chair for the insane Bad Biology in 2008).

When Maniac was released in the early 80s it was accused of being symptomatic of everything that was 'sick', 'grim', and 'irresponsible' about modern horror films. Even many horror fans at the time felt that the film had gone too far in its depictions of cold-blooded murder, but in recent years with films like John McNaughton's Henry-Portrait of a Serial Killer and Gerald Kargl's Angst gaining reappraisal, even exploitative shockers like Maniac have had a partial acceptance with special edition DVDs and red carpet treatment on Blu-Ray. For many though, Maniac still remains a sick no-go area.

MAN BITES DOG (1992)

(Original title - C'est arrive pres de chev vous)
Dir: Remy Belvaux, Andre Bonzel, Benoit Poelvoorde
/Belgium

A spoof documentary in which a group of student filmmakers follow a racist, sexist, homophobic, and all round opinionated serial killer called Benoit. He cracks jokes, mocks the public, recites dreadful poetry, and is also a rapist. For all its sharp satirical humour, the film succeeds in wiping the smiles from our faces about two thirds of the way in during a scene of unbelievable debauchery; and it's then that the film attacks its audience, turning uneasy laughter into abysmal horror...

Benoit ogles the camera for most of the running time, giving tips on how to weigh down a corpse, and expressing his views on every subject imaginable between his acts of cold-blooded murder. Nobody is safe from this psychopath, men, women, children, the elderly, everyone is a potential victim. He doesn't stick to a particular murder method either; hence shootings, beatings, strangulations, suffocations, and even the blackly comic act of scaring somebody to death, is all paraded before our eyes. Benoit is soon calling the shots and even using his own cash to fund the impoverished production when funds are running low. And it's only a matter of time before the filmmakers are roped in to helping Benoit in his crimes until there's no difference between student filmmaker and calculating killer.

Shot in hand-held black and white, Man Bites Dog is a chilling parody on the Reality TV format which would pollute the world's airwaves for years to come. The filmmakers wanted to expose how easily the appearance of a film crew can alter the behaviour of those being filmed, and how the 'reality' of the film's subjects are nothing more than a performance designed to entertain the viewers. In Man Bites Dog that entertainment factor is taken to disturbing extremes, guiding the viewers through its farcical set up and becoming increasingly unsettling as it reaches its conclusion.

As if to confuse the line further between fact and fiction, the cast members appear on screen using their real first names, including Remy, the psychotic moron who is driven into participating in the crimes with dreams of fame and fortune, and director Andre who begins with a strict journalistic distance from Benoit but is eventually joining in on the mayhem too. And it's here that Man Bites Dog turns against its audience for liking and expecting to be thrilled by the exploits of serial killers. It's this latter element that puts the film into the company of John McNaughton's Henry-Portrait of a Serial Killer and Michael Haneke's Benny's Video and Funny Games; films which take on a similar stance and present us with amoral thrills before pulling the nasty carpet from beneath our feet. And like those films, Man Bites Dog also succeeds in presenting us with a cracked mirror which reflects on the cynical world view that panders to dumb arseholes (especially nowadays with the real life exploitation of reality TV which glorifies, condescends, and mocks its performers whilst swelling its producers' bank accounts).

Man Bites Dog cast a large influential shadow over the subsequent years. Whether directly or indirectly, the power of this Belgian arthouse favourite has made its presence felt in everything from the cheap and shoddy farce-fests of the crudest examples of reality TV, to the big screen skin-crawling horrors of The Blair Witch Project and The Last Broadcast (compare the last shot of Man Bites Dog with that of Blair Witch, for example).

In America, the film emerged unrated (except for Blockbuster Video who demanded one of their infamous re-edit jobs to make the film palatable to their customers), and in the UK it was passed uncut for both cinema and video. One of the chief censors at the BBFC later admitted that if they had known how popular the video would become they would have snipped a couple of scenes. Luckily for us it didn't happen, and Man Bites Dog escaped untouched from their clutches and reached cult classic status before its notoriety would return to haunt the censors.

MARTYRS (2008)

Dir: Pascal Laugier /France

In an introduction on the American DVD of Martyrs, writer/director Pascal Laugier makes an apologetic plea to his viewers concerning the film he has unleashed on the world. He berates himself for the damage the film may cause to those who are unprepared for the cruel imagery and deeply troubling philosophical ramifications therein. He openly invites his audience to hate his guts.

The film itself opens on a scene of a half-naked girl in utter distress running through an abandoned industrial estate. When the police finally pick her up, she is unable to disclose of any details about her mysterious incarceration. Medical inspections indicate that she hadn't been raped but her body is covered in scars and bruising. The police track down the place where she had been held captive, an old slaughterhouse. A thorough search of the place fails to yield any clues as to why she was held there, nor who was responsible.

Fifteen years later and the young girl, Lucie (Mylene Jampanoi), has grown into a beautiful but unstable woman, and has befriended Anna (Morjana Alaoui) in a home for abandoned youths. The two women break into a family home and viciously murder the occupants in the belief that the parents had something to do with Lucie's childhood ordeal. However, a monstrous assailant who has been terrorizing Lucie for years appears in the house and inflicts some nasty damage on the young woman. And this leads Anna to question further the mystery of Lucie's dark past...

To reveal any more about the plot would be unfair to those who haven't seen this, but suffice to say it succeeds in in pulling off three major shift changes in the narrative, with the above synopsis serving as nothing more than a hint of the horrors to come. It's the kind of movie that puts you through the meat grinder of shock horror and despair unlike anything since the days of Cannibal Holocaust and Irreversible. It's quite simply the closest thing to an emotional holocaust ever filmed.

Emerging as part of a new wave of extreme French horror, with the likes of Haute Tension, Frontier(s), and À L'intérieur, dazzling and horrifying an entire generation of film fans around the globe, Martyrs marks the zenith (or nadir, depending on your stand point) of that fresh new movement in the way it finds new ways to make an audience crumble under the enormity of its weighty ideas. Rarely has a horror film divided its audience so much, with some accusing director Laugier of gratuitous and unjustified bloodshed, and others rightly pointing out that the horrendous imagery is essential to the film's success. To label the film as 'Torture Porn' is completely off the mark, because although the extreme violence and tortures are quite graphic, not for a moment is the film leering or salacious in its depictions; it has an urgent catharsis that is absolutely necessary before the final revelations in the film.

Stylistically, Martyrs is as equally faultless as any film of its era. The rough and ready camerawork and rapid editing push the narrative into a steady pace, with the 92 minute running time passing by in a breeze. The film's colour palette juxtaposes cold blues, stark whites, and fiery reds, all reflecting the turmoil in the heroine's minds. And this is helped by a couple of stunning performances from Jampanoi and Alaoui whose raw emotions and exhausting shooting schedule reminded me of the torments that Marilyn Burns went through during the making of Texas Chainsaw Massacre. Kudos also goes to special effects artist Benoit Lestang who created the visual shocks which accentuate the ideological horrors on display, and who sadly committed suicide before the film achieved its global recognition as one of the most harrowing movies ever made.

MATADOR (1988)

Dir: Pedro Almodovar /Spain

A lurid cocktail of sex and death, Pedro Almodovar's Matador opens with morbid bullfighting instructor, Diego (Nacho Martinez), jerking off to violent video clips from Mario Bava's Blood and Black Lace and Jess Franco's Bloody Moon. Apprentice matador, Angel (Antonio Banderas in his least macho role), is a closet homosexual who faints at the sight of blood. He attempts to assert his masculinity by forcing himself on Diego's girlfriend, but this rape attempt turns farcical. Later, a guilt-stricken Angel hands himself over to the police and confesses to a series of murders of which he is innocent. His lawyer, Maria (Assumpta Serna), sees through his lies when she learns that he is haemophobic. She, however, just so happens to have a thing for blood and death, and despite her veneer of elegance and her important profession, likes to indulge in a bit of sexualised murder herself, striking like a black widow spider and inserting a long hairpin into the necks of her victims the moment they reach orgasm. Maria recognises a kindred spirit in Diego, the man who is actually responsible for the murders, and together they consummate their passion in a suicide pact for the ultimate orgasm...

  Matador is a tribute to the stylish giallo/slasher movies of Mario Bava and Dario Argento, injected with a dose of Almodovar's usual kinkiness and dark humour for a slice of chic erotic horror. The humour is apparent in the scenes where Angel tries to rape Diego's girlfriend and fumbles around with a swiss army knife, threatening her with a bottle opener before finding the blade, and later when he goes to the police station to confess, the girl's crazy mother tells him "Don't bother, you've done enough already". The film is also awash with ludicrous coincidences, such as Maria being Angel's lawyer whilst at the same time being in cahoots with the real perpetrator (this perhaps another nod towards Dario Argento whose Tenebrae includes an absurd sequence where a pretty victim is chased by a vicious dog, ever so conveniently, right into the killer's lair).

Generally though, Matador is a much more serious and sombre effort than Almodovar's earlier work, and has more going for it than just a stream of sick jokes. Angel's mother, for example, is a stone-cold religious maniac who has clearly instilled much poisonous guilt into her son's troubled psyche, and even goes as far as to try and persuade Maria that he is anything but innocent, and fails to see that his 'confessions' stemmed from a fractured frame of mind.

More tributes abound, such as the amusing catwalk scene which is clearly indebted to Bava's Blood and Black Lace, and also the climax which owes a lot to King Vidor's Duel In The Sun, in which Maria and Diego kill each other in an elaborate plan of sex and death, with their pursuers distracted by a solar eclipse.

MAY (2002)

Dir: Lucky McKee / USA

May is a troubled young woman; raised by an unstable mother, and afflicted with a lazy eye, her only friend is a glass-encased doll which makes her social engagements awkward to say the least. Her attempts to build friendships and relationships constantly go wrong after a short while and she finds herself spending a great deal of time alone. Her isolation gradually twists her mind and she eventually comes to the conclusion that the reason why her social life is in ruins is because the people she knew weren't really friends at all, but each of them did at least have one or two features that could be considered best friend qualities. She then goes on a killing spree, literally deconscructing her past acquaintances with the idea of taking away her favourite body parts and reconstructing them into her idea of the perfect best friend.

May is a modern-day Gothic fairytale for grown-ups that does an excellent job of holding the viewer's attention. Angela Bettis does a fine job in the lead role and helps the film to shift gears from sad and touching, to darkly comic, to downright frightening. And due to the film's dreadful ad campaign, it has relied almost entirely on word-of-mouth to find itself a willing audience. But this film, along with Brad Anderson's Session 9 and Larry Fessenden's Wendigo, remains one of the finest direct to video oddities of the early 00s.

For all the wonders of this fast-growing cult favourite, the most interesting scene is the finale, so if you still haven't seen it then skip the rest of this review as it's gonna get spoiler-heavy. To my mind, May doesn't really create a 'Frankenstein's monster' out of her old friends, she simply fantasizies about doing so. Notice how, because of her immaturity, she bases her best friend requirements purely on physical parts like hands, neck, tattoos, etc, and no emotional traits or characteristics are considered.

In the final scene, May lays out her compilation corpse inert beside her on the bed. She offers kind words of reassurance and caresses the stiff. She even puts her ear to its chest to check for a heartbeat. She's slow to fully embrace the corpse as her best friend because she knows that something is missing. The body she has stitched together is dead meat and cannot appreciate her, cannot see her. She breaks down in tears at this; "You're not looking!" she cries, "See me! See me!" With one final sacrifice May plucks out her own eyeball with a pair of scissors and places it into position on the corpse, and then waits for a reaction...

Now, the significance of this scene relates to the psychopath's vanity; the point being that she wants her perfect best friend to see her with her own eye. She wants to admire herself as another, but also - and more crucially - as herself. This is why I believe the slashing and hacking episodes to be imaginary; the 'murders' were pure fantasy, a selfish and psychopathic disregard for the living embodiment of her fellow human beings. As a youngster, Jeffrey Dahmer clobbered a friend unconscious with a baseball bat "to stop him from running away", and to keep him close by in order to control and possess him. A limp, unconscious body was all he needed, his imagination did the rest. And this relates to May in the final scene; as she rests her head next to the body, the corpse raises its hand and strokes her face. Her own hand. May, her own perfect best friend. Many viewers were disappointed that the film ended so suddenly on that note, but for me the ending was perfect.

MEN BEHIND THE SUN (1988)

Dir: T.F. Mous / Hong Kong/ China

Not to be confused with your typical CAT III entry, Men Behind The Sun reaches a whole new level on the shocking and disturbing meter and is easily one of the most repulsive movies you'll ever see. The film was made by Chinese director T.F. Mous partly because he wanted to draw attention to a barbaric era of Japanese foreign policy during the 1930s and throughout World War II, where Chinese and Manchurian citizens were considered sub-human by their Japanese invaders, and were subjected to horrendously cruel experiments involving the dissection of live humans, the inducing of hypothermia, bubonic plague, and other nastiness, all as a test to discover the extreme limits of human endurance. The experiments were led by General Shiro Ishii at the notorious Unit 731, and even to this day the Japanese remain in denial as to what exactly went on at that place. Mous' film, however, attempts to expose the ugly truth, for better or worse.

The plot centres on a group of teenage Japanese conscripts who arrive in Manchukuo, a Japanese puppet state in north-eastern China. They're freezing cold, hungry, and homesick, but their destination doesn't live up to its promise - They were assured that food and warmth would be plentiful, but when they get there they discover the conditions to be just as harsh as the rest of the empire due to the ongoing war effort. What the boys get instead is brutal discipline, indoctrination into the evils of fascism, and first-hand accounts of one of the most barbaric episodes in history. The rest of the film plays like a catalogue of atrocities.

One of the boys makes a run for it to escape the miserable place. A Japanese soldier opens fire on him with a machine gun and the kid runs into an electrified fence that surrounds the compound. He drops his ball and it rolls down the hill in the snow as he is burned to death. The young conscripts are told very little about the true nature of Unit 731 but gradually discover that something evil is going on. They become friendly with a little mute boy who is often seen over the fence. They throw the dead kid's ball back and forth to each other. Meanwhile, a train load of Manchurian citizens arrive at the unit; a woman has her screaming baby taken away from her and it is buried alive in the snow. The head of the squadron, Sgt. Kowazaki, begins indoctrinating the youths on the Chinese and Manchurians; they are to be considered worthless and sub-human. From now on the kids are ordered to refer to the foreign prisoners as 'Maruta', which literally means 'material', and the youths are driven to such frenzy that they gang up on a lone Chinese man and beat him to death with clubs. One man has been injected with bubonic plague three times - Those running the experiment decide to open him up to discover why he hasn't died.

The Chinese prisoners at the lab try to ascertain what's going on and why they've been held captive, and what would be the best escape plan. Outside in the freezing conditions, a woman is kept in -35 degrees temperature for ten hours and has ice-cold water poured onto her hands and arms. She is then taken back inside to an audience of officers and the Youth Corps, and then has her arms dipped in warm water. General Ishii himself slashes her down each arm and then literally rips off the skin from her limbs like he's removing elbow-length gloves to expose the skeletal stalks beneath. A man is then brought into the room and the audience are informed that his arms have been frozen at -196 degrees; his limbs look like grey blocks of ice. Ishii then starts to chop away at the arms with an iron bar and the frozen flesh and bone shatters into pieces. Some of the new recruits at the Youth Corps buy in to the twisted ideology and tow the line in both word and deed (but whether they act this way out of fear or a genuine support for the cause is not explored in the film). Others are not so cold and heartless though, and they are weary and questioning the whole barbaric idea behind the place.

The technicians succeed in creating plague-infected fleas with the idea of inserting them into bombs and dropping them from planes onto Japanese enemies. But there's a problem; due to the high temperatures that results from exploding bombs, most of the fleas will die before they get the chance to infect anyone. General Ishii comes up with the cunning idea of inserting the fleas into porcelain capsules instead so that they can be easily contained, but also when dropped from a height will be much more effective at spreading death and destruction. When he reveals his idea on the 'porcelain bacterial bomb' to an assembly he is given an ecstatic ovation with cries of "Bonzai!"

Another 'experiment': Dozens of Maruta are taken out into a field and tied to posts that are strategically placed at specific distances from a bomb that sits in the middle. The bomb is then detonated. And when the smoke clears a group of boffins inspect the damage; some are clearly dead and blown to pieces, others are still alive and in agony with legs hanging off by a strip of tissue and eyeballs loose from the sockets. The idea behind this pointless experiment is to calculate how close to an exploding bomb a man can be without dying (yep, not very close, apparently).

The next sequence in the film I thought was real the first time I saw it but I later learned that it's actually a very impressive special effect that took days of painstaking and tricky work to get right. A naked man is placed into a decompression chamber and the dial is cranked up to full power. He collapses to the ground and his intestine literally unravels from out of his anus and shoots across the floor. It's such a crude and realistic sequence it has an awful air of reality about it (footage really was taken of the experiments and sent back to Japan for study but none of it has surfaced since).

A Russian woman and her young daughter are encased in an air-tight glass container and gassed. The young recruits surround the box and look on as the pair succumb to the deadly fumes. What the inductees are supposed to be learning by watching these atrocities is unclear. Perhaps the idea is to inure them to the suffering of these people so that in the future they can partake in the experiments directly without feeling any sorrow for the Maruta.

Sgt. Kowazaki orders the young Ishikawa to go and bring the little mute boy into the compound. He carries out his orders assuming the kid will be given a medical check-up. But what happens instead is that the boy is stripped, laid onto an operating table, put to sleep with a cloth of chloroform, and then dissected alive. The way the flesh separates as the scalpel cuts through it exposing the yellowish fat beneath the skin is very real. After years of rumours concerning the authenticity of this scene, it was no real surprise when director Mous confirmed that the footage did contain real elements. With the permission of the parents and the local police, Mous filmed the autopsy of a young boy, and some of that footage was inserted into the fictional film. The strange thing here is that the real footage came from a dead child but in the finished film the mute child is alive while the dissection is carried out. Thus we see that the heart is still beating when the rib cage is opened up, which makes me wonder how on earth he did it. Presumably he must have been granted permission to interfere with the autopsy procedure (it is already known that the coroners agreed to wear the uniforms that Mous provided so that they would match the actors in the film, so what was to stop him from pushing a little further to secure the shots that he wanted?). It seems obvious that some kind of apparatus was used to artificially pump the dead child's heart so that it gave the impression of a living breathing human for the footage he needed for the film. But whatever the truth is, it's all a bit morally suspect really, especially in an action-packed exploitation movie like this. I also suspect that if the parents of that dead child ever saw the finished film they wouldn't be happy about having their son's remains paraded in an action/horror film for the entertainment of others (it would be interesting to know how Mous convinced the parents to allow him to shoot that footage). The heart is still beating as it is removed and placed into a jar of formaldehyde.

Ishikawa discovers what has happened to the mute boy and organises a revolt among the Youth Corps. They confront Sgt. Kowazaki in the disinfectant showers and they severely beat him with planks of wood. But oddly, this scene of violent insubordination is then forgotten about, and the film just carries on as though nothing has happened; the boys are not punished for the attack, and Kowazaki is later seen going about his business unscathed.

General Shiro Ishii drops a cat into a pit of starving rats as a way of demonstrating how power in numbers can defeat a larger opponent. The cat is slowly eaten alive (and this horrible scene is very real and difficult to watch). The Chinese prisoners start rioting in the cells and the Japanese soldiers put an end to this by cutting them down with machine gun fire. When Ishii finds out about this incident he is furious about losing so many Maruta ("precious experimental material") in the massacre.

More Maruta are taken out into the field and tied to stakes for another close-range bomb test (like the results weren't pretty conclusive the first time round; bombs kill and maim people at close range - Case closed). This time, however, one of the prisoners isn't secured properly and he manages to untie himself and helps to free the others. This infuriates the Japanese and they hunt the escapees down in their jeeps and motorcycles whilst firing at them. For a while things become chaotic with lots of action and stunts; the Chinese hit back, collecting weapons from injured soldiers and returning fire. The heroic Chinese are outnumbered and heavily out-gunned, and their brave stance is ultimately short-lived as they are all either run down by a vehicle or shot dead at the scene. Their corpses are then taken down to the incinerator that is run by an old drunken Japanese man who hacks up the bodies like firewood into small pieces to feed the fire whilst he sings traditional songs.

News filters through to the compound that the Soviets have declared war on Japan and that the Americans have dropped atomic bombs on Nagasaki and Hiroshima. The war effort and dreams of empire are over and Japan is on the verge of surrender. Ishii orders that all remaining Maruta be exterminated, all buildings in Unit 731 be destroyed, all documents and evidence burned, the Youth Corps be sent back home to Japan, and all officers are ordered to commit suicide.

Ishii's right hand man pleads with him to not be so rash, and argues that the data collected is too precious to be destroyed and that the officers deserve the opportunity to make it home alive. Ishii relents on the latter but insists on the destruction of all evidence that Unit 731 ever existed. The compound immediately falls into chaos;

officers who disobey orders are shot dead on the spot, the Maruta are gassed in their cells, labs are destroyed, offices detonated with explosives, other buildings catch on fire, soldiers loot the rooms for money and anything of value, hundreds of corpses are thrown into a huge hole in the ground and torched, the lab rats catch on fire and scatter around in flames in all directions (symbolic?).

The film ends with the soldiers and their families leaving on trains with an onscreen text revealing how they got back home and what happened to Shiro Ishii (he was later arrested by the Americans and agreed to hand over his collected data in exchange for his freedom. He was also suspected of being involved in the biological weapons programme in the Korean War. He died in 1959).

Men Behind The Sun is basically a catalogue of carnage. We're presented with scene after scene of increasingly ruthless and disturbing behaviour (including the immoral decisions of the director himself), and this does come at the expense of the narrative and plot developments in the film. It was shot in glorious 35mm celluloid and the music score is a strange throwback to old skool Hollywood adventure films of the 50s and 60s with its big brass sections and smoochy clarinets making for a bizarre and discomfiting mix. Indeed, the plot of the film and the way it is played out and presented is as a conventional Hollywood action film of old, but the disturbing contents, images, and subject-matter are the only things that lift it out of its time warp and convince us that the film wasn't made at least 25 years earlier.

People often ask where the film stands in terms of legitimacy; is it an exploration of those cruel times, or is it just a piece of crude exploitation? Strangely, I believe it to be a bit of both. Throughout his career in film, T.F. Mous has continually explored and exposed the cruelties of the Japanese during World War II, he obviously feels very strongly about that time in history and has done much to draw attention to those times and educate others on the facts, even uncovering important documents from Russia and America. But even with the best will in the world, his filmmaking skills are basic at best; his style reeks of classic Hollywood of old, and this, combined with his crude and disturbing imagery, gives his films a clumsy and morally reprehensible edge (where in any Hollywood film have you seen a real autopsy carried out on a little boy, or real footage of a cat being fed to hungry rats?). His directorial skills were not sufficient enough to tackle such weighty themes as the ones explored in Men Behind The Sun (or indeed his later film, Black Sun - The Nanking Massacre, which serves as a loose prequel that concentrates on the Japanese invasion of China in the 1930s), and this is perhaps the main reason why the whole thing comes across as a piece of exploitational trash.

The film's producer, Fu Chi, grew up in Northern China and he witnessed first-hand the atrocities committed by the Japanese during the war. He had very personal reasons for investing in the film, and he did so knowing he would probably never get his money back, let alone see a profit, as the film was never going to be commercial. I think it's safe to say that if the film fails as a piece of historical documentation, it's not because the people behind the camera didn't have the right intentions at heart. In fact, T.F. Mous perhaps took things a bit too far in that respect in the way he crossed the moral line himself in order to get his point across.

The aforementioned scenes of the autopsy, the cruel killing of the cat, and the needless burning of rats have for many viewers ruined any chance of this film being treated seriously as a legitimate work of cinematic art. Indeed, Mous' eagerness to present us with a picture of sheer evil and cruelty loses its moral high-ground the moment he starts to engineer real atrocities to put his point across. It's a bit rich to commit morally reprehensible acts in the making of his film to underpin that which he is railing against, and it's these scenes which most obviously bring on the accusations of exploitation. Ok, no humans were killed or tortured in the making of the film, but a dead child's body was violated, and animals were unnecessarily killed. It reminds me of how Italian filmmakers like Ruggero Deodato and Umberto Lenzi filmed the cruel slaughter of animals in order to address the moral vacuum of the West in their cannibal epics; it just doesn't wash.

Despite all this moral indignation, Men Behind The Sun definitely works as a nightmare vision of modern barbarism. Shiro Ishii was one of the most evil men of the 20th Century, and at least his awful crimes haven't been watered down for the sake of 'cinematic manners'. Ishii's character in the film is every bit as cruel and loathsome as the real person whose exploits have been speculated on for decades. Unlike the Nazi 'Angel of Death' Josef Mengele, who seemed to be propelled by his own sadistic drive, Shiro Ishii gave the impression that his experiments were conducted with a dogged devotion to collecting data that would benefit the Japanese war effort. To be seen to be indulging in the pure sadistic drive for its own sake may have been considered shameful and ignoble by Ishii, and so perhaps he concealed his sick urges under the guise of national duty. Who knows. One veteran member of the Youth Corps who was stationed at Unit 731 during the war gave a speech to university students and explained to them that Mous' film doesn't even begin to address the barbaric acts that were carried out at the compound - A chilling thought.

Men Behind The Sun has been banned and censored the world over, but it was in the Far East where the film caused the most controversy. At a screening in China in 1997 there were mass walk outs and a few viewers even fainted. According to Mous himself, 16 people have died of heart attacks while watching his film in the cinema. Much of the factual information in the film came from witness testimony as some of the fleeing Japanese soldiers were captured and put on trial in Soviet courts. The film was met with hatred in Japan and has only ever been screened in that country once. It wasn't the nastiness or gore which upset the Japanese, it was the film's taunting as a political hot potato which angered the conservatives and led to right-wing groups threatening to burn down all the cinemas in the country if the film was ever screened again. Mous received numerous death threats and had to flee Japan.

MEN BEHIND THE SUN 3 - A NARROW ESCAPE (1994)

(aka Maruta 3 - Destroy All Evidence; orig title - Hei tai yang 731 si wang lie che)
Dir: Godfrey Ho /Hong Kong

Godfrey Ho returns with a second unofficial sequel to T.F. Mous' Men Behind The Sun, and offers more of the same with a story very loosely based on fact, a dull and uninvolving melodrama, and more of the usual mondo footage as a way of boosting the exploitational shock factor.

It's 1945 and Unit 731 is in turmoil; Japan is losing the war, and the soldiers are frantically destroying all evidence of the evil experiments that were carried out there. They intend on decimating everything before the Soviets arrive. One group of prisoners are machine gunned in their cell, another are gassed in theirs. Documents are burned, labs are destroyed (including the sight of a Jap soldier accidently cutting himself and being exposed to the lethal chemicals), before the whole compound is blown up with dynamite. General Shiro Ishii addresses his men one last time and then hops onto a plane and leaves them to it. The rest of the soldiers board a train for their retreat through China, and this is where most of the drama takes place. These defeated troops are on a long journey home and this gives them the time to reflect on their experiences of working within the most barbaric hellhole of the 20th Century. The idea behind the story is an interesting one but it's handled so badly, and in the end we're left with nothing but a few gruesome flashbacks and a doomed love story between a soldier and an army nurse. When news reaches the train cabin of Japan's surrender, one soldier immediately commits Harakiri with his sword, and another drinks cyanide. The remaining troops take it in turns to reflect on their harrowing memories of the events at Unit 731 which have clearly traumatized them and filled them with guilt. And their long road home is racked with defeat, deprivation, and disease.

Even by Godfrey Ho's standards this is a ludicrous exploitation disaster. Who on earth was this film made for?

The Japanese detest the whole idea of having this shameful slice of their history displayed on the big screen, as was made pretty clear by their reactions to the first film in the series. The Chinese and Manchurians no doubt would have been offended by the idea of watching Japanese soldiers reminiscing on their journey home from one of the cruelest and most horrendous atrocities ever committed on Chinese soil. There has always been a cult in the West for Ho's chop-socky Ninja movies but I'm sure most of them would be appalled by the grim spectacle on view here. I can only assume that everyone involved in the making of this film was on drugs or something; even the original Men Behind The Sun wasn't even successful enough to break even financially, never mind warranting a bloody franchise!

Speaking of drugs, there are some moments in this film that bring on an odd hallucinatory vibe, especially to those who are familiar with the work of Alejandro Jodorowsky; we see scores of extras doing bizarre synchronised things like jumping from a bridge into a river, or wearing boiler suits and gas masks and marching in unison, or being buried alive in a huge hole in the ground, and other such grotesqueries filmed in scope that look like deleted scenes from The Holy Mountain.

Flashbacks include the sight of hundreds of enemy captives being obliterated with machine guns, dozens more being buried alive, another bomb test where a group of unfortunates are tied to poles in a field and a plane glides overhead dropping those infamous 'porcelain bacterial bombs' onto the ground, infecting the trussed up victims with bubonic plague, a woman having her arms frozen at -200 degrees and having the skin ripped off, a man having his frozen arms broken, and a bloody gun battle with Chinese troops. Mondo footage includes a graphic autopsy on a little girl. Most of the stock footage is shown in the first ten minutes with the usual autopsy scenes (with one body having its leg sawn off for some reason), and major surgery sequences. The intro credits are accompanied by sepia toned archive war footage, a la The Devil's Nightmare.

MISSISSIPPI BURNING (1988)

Dir: Alan Parker /USA

Two young white civil rights activists and their black co-worker are driving down a road in Mississippi and are pulled over by the law. After being referred to as "nigger lovers" the three men are then shot dead by members of the Sheriff's department, in a barbaric act of mindless hatred made worse by the fact that the murderers use their powerful positions within law-enforcement to conceal their nocturnal activities as high-ranking members of the Ku Klux Klan.

Alan Ward (Willem Dafoe) and Agent Rupert Anderson (Gene Hackman) are sent down from Washington to investigate the disappearance of the three activists, and are immediately made the targets of small-town prejudice. Former Sheriff, Anderson, doesn't seem to take the situation seriously at first; he makes jokes and sings Klan songs on the drive down, much to the annoyance of his partner Ward, a more sensible and by-the-book investigator. However, it isn't long before Anderson realises just how serious and dangerous the situation is when everyone they try to speak to ends up badly beaten and their homes burned to the ground.

Their investigation leads them higher and higher up the social ladder, with some of the most responsible folks of the town implicated in the deep-seated racism and intimidation being carried out on the black citizens; churches are burned, black men are kidnapped and severely beaten or killed by masked men, and a church congregation of black worshippers is attacked by men with bats and clubs. Ward and Anderson gather enough evidence to charge three white men with beating a black kid half to death, but the court case turns into a farce due to the judge being just as racist as anyone else in the town and who sentences the three men to five years suspended sentences.

Meanwhile, Anderson has been sweet-talking the Deputy's wife (Francis McDormand), and she seems sympathetic to the investigation, even informing him of the whereabouts of the bodies of the three activists. This crucial piece of info carries the investigation towards its end, but the two agents decide to employ some pretty nasty tricks of their own to see justice at long last.

Those familiar with the real life case of James Chaney, Mickey Schwener, and Andy Goodman, three civil rights activists who were murdered in Neshoba County in 1964, leading to the biggest manhunt in FBI history, will be left scratching their heads throughout much of this film, as director Alan Parker takes a free-form artistic licence and bends the facts to suit his own vision. On the one hand, Parker can be accused of treating the events as if his own dramatic drive was more important than history, but on the other, he does a remarkable job of re-creating the time and place of Neshoba County of the mid-60s; it's a scary place, and whether you're black or white or in any way different, or have a mind of your own, you seriously wouldn't want to have lived there during those times. That place with its burning crosses, burning churches, and authority figures wearing silly white costumes with pointy hoods and dealing out brutal retributions and death on anyone who isn't just like them - It's a vision of hell on earth. And for a studio film that was made in the late 80s, Mississippi Burning does not spare viewers from the truly disturbing and frankly evil goings on of that town; the violence is so one-sided and viciously cruel, and it's agonising to see these ugly scenes unfold, knowing that whatever else happens on screen for the next couple of hours, it's certainly not going to be for the faint of heart or the easily offended.

  No studio would have the balls to unleash a film like this in today's PC climate. And it's a shame because if you are in any way racist in your own heart, this film sure has the power to make you look deeply into yourself and reconsider your own prejudice. It's a film which does much to show how insane things can become when small-town attitudes are allowed to grow unchecked out in the wilderness.

Director Alan Parker, whose previous work includes Midnight Express and Angel Heart, films which take on a somewhat leisurely pace, but here with Mississippi Burning we're treated to a much more tightly constructed film which flies by at a ferocious tempo. Hackman is superb as Anderson, the world-weary Agent who deals with his grim profession with an equally grim sense of humour, and Willem Dafoe as his strait-laced partner who eventually dispenses with common procedure in order to bring justice down on the town. Also look out for a young Michael Rooker as a hick sheriff, Brad Dourif as a hick deputy, and R. Lee Ermey of Full Metal Jacket fame as Neshoba's hick mayor who is subjected to one of the film's most satisfying acts of revenge.

MOLESTER'S TRAIN: DIRTY BEHAVIOUR (1995)

(aka Birthday)
Dir: Hisayasu Sato / Japan

A young misfit, Yuu (Yumika Hayashi), has perception problems that stop him from recognising his surroundings in three dimensions, and this flat uninvolving view of the world has caused him to become isolated and detached. He resorts to documenting his surroundings on video camera, and while riding on the train he meets a young drifter, Kei (Kiyomi Ito of Lolita Vibrator Torture), and together they discuss their lives and pasts in between bouts of sex as a way of trying to re-connect with the world.

Even during the sexual act with Kei, Yuu finds it difficult to recognise anything beyond his perceived "poster" image of her. Kei tries to correct this by kissing him on the lips and manually inserting his penis inside her. Yuu suddenly becomes overtaken with lust, and he lays her down and fucks her, but he still seems quite distanced from her in the way that his arms are rigidly holding up his own body weight and his eyes stare blankly ahead, not even looking at her as he finishes the deed.

Yuu and Kei spend their days hanging out in a tent and by the docks, and on the trains that pass through Tokyo. Kei pulls out a bundle of dynamite sticks from her rucksack and announces that she intends to blow herself up on her 20th birthday. Meanwhile, perverts lurk on the trains molesting young women on the busy carriages. Yuu captures one such incident on video camera in which the woman seems to be enjoying the sexual intrusion, and he later reveals that the woman in question is in fact his sister. He then plays Kei a selection of home videos that he recorded on the trains documenting his family members; his sister is a masochist and when she can't find a boyfriend who is sadistic enough for her tastes she resorts to self-mutilation; his father suffered from an irrational fear of returning home, and has since vanished; his older brother also disappeared to join a strange sex cult; and his alcoholic mother suffers from blackouts and memory loss (talk about 'meeting the family'!).

Yuu turns to drastic measures in order to experience some kind of sensation at any cost and put an end to his depersonalization by asking Kei if he can join her in a suicide pact. On the night of her birthday they sit in the tent and strap themselves with the dynamite and count down the bad years of their lives before Kei lights the fuse...

Running for just 55 minutes, Molester's Train is an odd, dream-like film typical of its director. It's also perhaps one of Sato's most personal efforts in the way it deals with detachment and alienation in a much more open and honest way than many of his other works. Ironically, it's the depersonalized and isolated nature of this film that seems to get to the heart of the director's raison d'etre; Brainsex, The Bedroom, and Survey Map of a Paradise Lost are just a few examples of films which deal with similar themes, but none of them did so in such an open manner. With Yuu we have a character who expresses the reasons for his neuroses and voyeurism in no uncertain terms; by documenting everything on camera he hopes to make a connection with the world around him and to try to experience something to escape the numbness and isolation in his mind. It's a frustrating endeavor because, in the end, watching videotapes of his daily experiences takes him even further away from the real sensation, not closer. And thus, his attempts to connect with the world become increasingly extreme and desperate; for Yuu, a suicide pact is the last chance - only by experiencing death can he hope to feel something, anything - even his own obliteration strikes him as a fair deal.

Perhaps Yuu represents a part of Sato himself. Like many other characters in Sato's films, Yuu doesn't necessarily experience the things he is documenting, and this is a crucial point because this is one of the main ways the director chooses to express alienation; Yuu witnesses many things on the trains, but even the molestation of his own sister barely registers anything of a response from him because he's not there; he's on the train in their presence, but he is so emotionally distant that the incident doesn't affect him in the way it should. Even when he has sex with Kei, the experience does more to isolate him psychologically than to serve as an emotional connection (which is what Kei intended to show him). The sex act itself is all rather selfish on Yuu's part; not once does he look at her or caress her while he's on top; he just concentrates on thrusting his hips, faster and faster, until he shoots his load - Psychologically he's no 'closer' to her than if he was jerking off over a picture (or a flat "poster" image) of her.

    The train molestation scenes were mostly shot on crowded passenger trains in Sato's usual guerrilla-style, so that the ordinary Tokyo citizens, who weren't even involved in the making of the film, are seen in the background while the crimes are happening; the women are exposed in various states of undress, and they moan with just as much pleasure as protest, and the ordinary commuters look on, sometimes directly into the camera lens while the women are ravished in their presence. It makes for an odd viewing experience to say the least, and this kind of thing adds to the verisimilitude of the film. Even the names of the two lead characters, Yuu and Kei, are shortened forms of the actor's real names, Yumika and Kiyomi.

    Perhaps Sato's films as a whole are an attempt for him to deal with his own sense of depersonalization, and not just that of socicty as a whole. The verite and guerrilla shooting style works, not just because of the low-budget and the way it exposes the reactions of ordinary commuters to the potential abuse of women in their midst (and that they react like bemused and desensitized idiots), but because in this sense he resembles many of the voyeuristic characters he portrays in his films. He's the one standing on the train shooting scenes of molestation, not just the character Yuu. It's just as much Sato who flits around with his camera trying to document everything in sight with an increased sense of perverion and urgency (throughout his filmmaking career Sato has touched upon almost every perverion known to man, be it S&M, rape, fetishes, and bestiality, but he doesn't seem to favour any one of them, and is happy to re-visit a particular perversion in later films or abandon it entirely). And in his often prolific output of films over the years, he never seems to be emotionally involved.

MONDO CANE (1962)

Dir: Gualtiero Jacopetti and Franco Prosperi / Italy

The shockumentary, or 'Mondo' movie has existed since the dawn of cinema itself, and these films have outraged viewers worldwide for as long as films have been exhibited. It's certainly not a recent phenomenon. The word 'mondo' derives from the Italian for 'world' and became the by-word for a genre of fact-based shock movies and documentaries made by Gualtiero Jacopetti and Franco Prosperi that flourished in the 1960s. But in truth, the mondo movie can be traced back as far as 1900 to Thomas Edison's glimpses into the forbidden in a couple of his one-reelers which show a public hanging and an elephant being electrocuted.

The 1930s saw the first heyday for this kind of fare when sideshows would screen all kinds of this stuff; alongside Todd Browning's Freaks, the paying punters could lay eyes on all manner of sensationalist films, such as William Campbell's En Gaji (directed under the name William Alexander) which ended with real footage of natives sacrificing a member of their tribe to the gorilla god, En Gaji. Armand and Michela Denis Among The Headhunters was a film made by a husband and wife collaboration that also spent time with the natives, and these films made a fortune.

By the early 60s Jacopetti had written the narration for Mondo Di Notte (World By Night), a documentary exploring the weird and bizarre from the exotic parts of the world. It was quite successful, and this encouraged Jacopetti to take the format further. He teamed up with filmmaker Franco Prosperi, and together they travelled the world documenting the strangest rites in the most far flung cultures. The result was Mondo Cane in 1962.

"All the scenes you will see in this film are true and are taken only from life. If often they are shocking, it is because there are many shocking things in this world. Besides, the duty of the chronicler is not to sweeten the truth but to report it objectively". This quote is from a caption that appears on the screen at the beginning of the film. A dog is led into a pen that contains hundreds more dogs who seem quite hostile, and is then set free from its chain and allowed to wander inside the enclosure to check out the other hounds. And this probably serves as a visual metaphor for the journey we the viewers are about to take. The next sequence shows an 'appreciation ceremony' where a man called Brazzi inherits Rodolpho Valentino's fortune. He visits New York and is mobbed by adoring women.

Then we head to the jungle of East New Guinea - We witness a tribal pig feast where the animals have their heads beaten in with lumps of wood. A pet cemetery in California, then to an East Asian island where the locals eat dog meat. Back to Italy where it's Easter season and hundreds of chicklets are warmed in the ovens and are then dipped in coloured ink. In Japan, farmers massage the buttocks of bulls and make them drink 6 litres of beer per day, apparently it makes the meat taste better. In Africa, native women are fed in a fattening process. Back in America, we visit a gym for elderly widows who want to lose weight so that they can re-marry. To Hong Kong next where the locals basically eat any animal they can get their hands on, even crocodile. Rattlesnakes, muskrats, bugs and worms are also eaten. And this stuff is then sold to New York restaurants where the rich wine and dine in their plush surroundings.

Snake is the national dish of Singapore, and this seems like a good excuse to show them being skinned alive in the market place and sold to the punters in little brown bags. Next we head to a place called Calabria in Northern Italy where a ceremony is taking place in which the local men hit and scrape their legs with sharp 'Battienti', wooden discs lined with pieces of glass as a way of representing Christ's flagellation. Sydney coast guard babes parade through the streets and to the beach and demonstrate the rescuing of men from the sea. This sequence is very bizarre, especially when the girls then start to demonstrate their CPR techniques which are all synchronised with the others into a strange and thoroughly rehearsed unison.

Next we get to check out the effects of atomic radiation on the wildlife and environment in the South Pacific. Then we see an immense underwater cemetery where the ocean bed is covered with hundreds of human skeletal remains on the coast of Malay. On land, the natives hunt sharks for their fins. Not surprisingly, many of these folks are missing limbs, presumably from their past experiences of messing around with sharks. Their way of catching these big fish are to put poisoned sea urchins into the shark's mouths.

Next up we visit a Roman ossuary where old corpses are dressed in hooded robes and strange men dressed in similar garb wander around the dank surroundings tending to the bodies. Then over to Europe for the giddy goings on at a German beer house that soon turns nasty and violent. At dawn the stragglers stagger off home, pissing and puking and sleeping and fighting in the street (much of this footage is often used in documentaries on The Beatles, especially from their early Hamburg days). Then back to the Far East for the bizarre 'luxuries' of a Japanese massage parlor where business men are pampered in rude and violent ways, including having jets of ice-cold water blasted in their faces and the masseurs jumping up and down on their spines. Staying in Japan for the time being, we're presented with the embalmers applying makeup onto corpses. The next bit of footage was allegedly filmed in secret, and this is a brief scene shot in a home for the terminally ill in Singapore. Cars are crushed at a huge junkyard and are then displayed in an art gallery where the car blocks are the main exhibition.

This is quite a tame 'documentary' compared to the modern standards of the shockumentary, but many scenes in Mondo

Cane must have been quite an experience for audiences in the early 60s. There's little rhyme or reason between the footage here to link it all together other than having bizarre cultures and ceremonies from across the globe paraded before our eyes. But it isn't over yet. Next up we get a glimpse into the world of Czech painter Yves Klein, who has naked models rub themselves in his favoured blue paint and then make body prints onto a huge canvas. Adventures in Honolulu next with some American tourists, then Gurkha soldiers in drag, then bulls being decapitated with swords. Then it's over to Portugal for the annual 'Forcada' bull runs. Cue much amusement as people are chased down and gored by the bull horns (if you ask me they deserve all they get). The vocal sound effects of victims yelping are also very funny and were obviously overdubbed in post-production. Finally we reach the end of the film with a look at the 'Cargo Cult', a group of aboriginals who would observe from a distance how Westerners built runways and had food and supplies delivered to them by plane. The abo's were very impressed, and deep in the jungle they built their own runway complete with a control tower fashioned from bamboo. They assumed that constructing a runway would encourage the flying bird gods to come down from the sky and deliver them some food. How cute!

   Mondo Cane was a sensation. Shot in full colour in beautiful scope, and featuring a grand score from Riz Ortolani (the man responsible for the classic 'soap opera' theme of Cannibal Holocaust), the film was a pure spectacle and made a fortune. It's a gleefully leering and voyeuristic tour around the world that distorted reality any way its makers saw fit. It caused outrage among the critics who generally dismissed it as a vile form of sensationalism, and of course, having read this condemnation in the press, the punters came thick and fast to see this film that everyone was complaining about. Italy has always been a land of imitation as far as cinema goes, and filmmakers from that part of the world were soon churning out their own mondo movies, such as Mondo Freudo, Mondo Balordo, Malamondo, and Women of The World, where every bizarre activity known to man was exploited on film. But it was Jacopetti and Prosperi once again who steered the genre to where it needed to be when they released their official sequel, Mondo Cane 2.

POSTSCRIPT: THE MONDO MOVIE AND SHOCKUMENTARIES

Most of the mondo movies that flourished in the 60s had one thing in common; they all had scenes that were staged for the effect of the film. The filmmakers wanted sensationalism, and if they couldn't find it in the 'reality' of the things they were filming, they would simply create the shocking material themselves. Truth wasn't always stranger then fiction when it came to the mondo film. Pretty soon, the Americans jumped on the bandwagon and produced their own entries that documented the hippy movement with the same familiar air of crude sensationalism in the free-love and drug havens of the late 60s. But all this led to the saturation of the genre, and it was Jacopetti and Prosperi, as conscious as ever of the fast-changing world, who came to the rescue once again and offered Africa Addio in the late 60s. They instinctively knew that the old format of the mondo movie had run its course, and they decided to up the ante as a way of presenting things that were forbidden on television.

Africa Addio went further than any mondo film before it, and ultimately dispenses with the fun and light-hearted feel of their earlier films, and instead shows us a grim and pessimistic view of hell on Earth. Rumours circulated that the filmmakers had organised a real execution for the sake of the film, and the critics were once again outraged as they had been with the release of Mondo Cane almost decade earlier.

As the 70s progressed, the mondo film became increasingly extreme, making their 60s predecessors look almost tame in comparison. Savage Man Savage Beast was cut to ribbons by the British censors who objected to the animal violence in the film. Strangely, scenes of wild animals catching and feeding on their prey were cut on the advice of the RSPCA, but scenes depicting the practice of fox hunting were passed unscathed. Elsewhere around the world, the film became notorious chiefly for the scenes which supposedly show a man being eaten by lions in a zoo, and mercenaries castrating a native. It was later confirmed that both of these scenes were in fact dramatic reconstructions made purely for the exploitative factor. The film was made by Alferdo and Angelo Castianalli, who along with Mario Mora, overtook Jacopetti and Prosperi and became the new leaders of the genre. Their work also includes This Violent World, Sweet and Savage, and Shocking Africa. The latter is to this day still widely regarded as one of the most unpleasant films ever made. Other mondo-flavoured titles came along which reveled in gruesome death and explicit sex, such as Shocking Asia parts 1 and 2, and This Is America. And the public's fascination for death and disaster was also catered for in Days of Fury.

The 1970s also saw a rise in popularity of the sex education film. Filmmakers were keen to exploit the fact that sex films that served to educate the viewer could be much more explicit than would be acceptable otherwise. Shaun Cunningham's The Art of Marriage and The ABC's of Love and Sex were both tremendous box-office draws before hardcore porn became popular. But this type of fare had a negative effect on genuine sex education films, as they were all treated as exploitational garbage, particularly in the UK where the Swedish production, The Language of Love, was banned.

Faces of Death came along in 1979, and was the single most successful mondo film since Mondo Cane in the early 60s. This international hit was a co-production between American and Japanese financiers, and wallows in footage shot at a kosher slaughterhouse, the eating of monkey brains, autopsies, and death by electric chair. Like the earlier mondo films, many of the scenes here were faked, but it isn't always easy to know what is real and what isn't. My guess is that most of the footage is genuine but is not as graphic as you would assume. For the record, it's safe to say that the electric chair sequence was probably faked, and the eating of monkey brains was most certainly staged.

Faces of Death was huge in Japan, it was a bigger hit than Star Wars. In the UK the film got caught up in the video nasties debacle and was banned for years (even today the UK DVD is missing a couple of BBFC cuts to remove the sight of a dog fight and the killing of a monkey). The film also spawned numerous sequels, cash-ins, and rip-offs, such as The Shocks, and Death: The Ultimate Horror.

The success of Faces of Death and the rise of home video in the 80s led to a renewed interest in the genre, with sequels to the Mondo Cane series appearing on video along with sequels to Shocking Asia and This Is America. The Japanese and American financiers collaborated again for the production of The Killing of America as a way of trying to ape the success of Faces of Death. But this film is actually a different breed from the usual mondo stuff; The Killing of America is a genuinely uncomfortable look at the state of the modern world, and serves as the high water mark of the genre. And unlike the previous mondo entries, all of the footage is as real as it gets.

Home video allowed the mondo movie to flourish in cheapo productions where the staged sequences were banished altogether in series like Faces of Gore, Traces of Death, and Banned In America. These direct to video abominations took the exploitative factor to unprecedented levels, and feature bizarre voiceovers that mock the carnage on display. But there were others who took the genre elsewhere, such as the rare and barely seen Army Medicine In Vietnam, which stands as a serious look at the botched surgery of marines, including one soldier who has his face blown off, pieced back together, and then after recovery he is sent back onto the front line.

In the mid-90s the Brits added their own entry in the field with Executions, a video release that caused outrage in the press but was unbelievably passed uncut by the BBFC. I remember begging my parents to rent the tape for me but they wouldn't even entertain the idea, and I vividly remember reading the lurid tabloid headlines and scare stories about the film (which I took as recommendations!). According to the papers, Executions showed footage of people having their heads drilled. I eventually did get to see it and it's actually a serious intended documentary exposing the barbarity of the death penalty. As a youngster I could watch all of this stuff and it didn't bother me, not at all. But as I've gotten older I'm much more aware of my own mortality and much more sensitive to the suffering of others. Many of these films I find difficult to watch nowadays. I recently re-visited Executions for the sake of writing this piece, and although it's certainly not an easy film to watch, there's very little there footage-wise that can't be shown on broadcast news reports. The ending, however, shows a guy being machine-gunned in the face at close range. It takes him a long time to die and the camera never flinches from the gruesome horror on display as he takes his dying breaths. I love horror and gore movies as much as anyone, but the real stuff like this is something different; a boundary has been crossed here. I had to look away from that scene this time around.

THE VIDEO DIARY OF RICARDO LOPEZ

The most recent shockumentary I saw was The Video Diary of Ricardo Lopez. In this DIY mondo oddity we follow the last few weeks in the life of Bjork obsessive Ricardo Lopez. He was confident and articulate, but his world is turned upside down when he discovers that his favourite pop star is dating a black guy. He then sets about documenting the last moments of his life on video in his New York apartment, and we follow every step of the way as his mind disintegrates.

He refers to Bjork as a "nigger lover" and relates his own race theories in which he explains that white women make up only 5% of the world's population, and that white women are too precious and unique to be going with black guys. He purchases a vat of very strong concentrated acid with the aim of making an acid bomb that he hopes will be opened by Bjork herself. He mails it to her (the parcel was intercepted by the police). And then, like a real life Travis Bickle, he flips completely, and shaves his head, paints his face, and blows his brains out on camera.

The Video Diary of Ricardo Lopez is an extremely disturbing and humbling viewing experience. Lopez, for all his faults, was a bright kid; he was only 19 but his mannerisms and intelligence gives the impression that he could be at least ten years older. The film as a whole stands as a chilling look at the fragility of the human mind, and that of the obsessive stalker personality. But also, one can't help but feel some sympathy for Lopez; he had quite clearly lost his marbles, and the last shots of the film which sees him sitting with the gun in his hand are especially powerful. He barely utters a word throughout this long sequence, but his facial expressions tell their own story; as he contemplates the end of his life he seems afraid and perhaps even remorseful. He hadn't touched his medication for weeks and yet there seems to be a moment of clarity right at the end; it's as if he doesn't want to pull the trigger, but at the same time he realises the enormity of his crime; whether or not Bjrok opens the package he has sent to her is irrelevant in the eyes of the law. He knows that there's no turning back for him, and even if he had doubts about ending his life, he also seemed to be driven by demons that were ultimately beyond his control.

The police recovered the tapes when they raided his apartment and the footage was kept by the FBI for a number of years. Copies of the tapes were made and given away to those who requested the footage (and this in itself says something about our jaded sensibilities when we have to contact the FBI for our latest DVD fix). This casual distribution of such sensitive footage has caused much criticism of the FBI and those hoping to cash-in on the tragedy. Indeed, even watching films like this nowadays feels like an intrusion for me. There's something borderline obscene about watching this stuff; Lopez, like many other victims in these films, was somebody's son, somebody's loved one. He had dreams and aspirations. Yes he was a flawed individual, but most of us are.

Having said that, I still believe that more than any other type of documentary style of film, the mondo movie, in its many and varied forms, is a powerful medium for information. And for that reason alone I refuse to condemn them completely. No matter how crude or uncomfortable they may be for us to watch, they are only a reflection of the world we live in. And if they are offensive, then we must look back at ourselves and change the way we live. As the caption says at the begining of the original Mondo Cane, "The duty of the chronicler is not to sweeten the truth but to report it objectively".

MOSQUITO THE RAPIST (1976)

(aka Bloodlust, aka Mosquito The Desecrater)
(Orig title - Mosquito der Schander)
Dir: Marijan Vadja /Switzerland

Mosquito The Rapist tells the tale of a deaf mute who is fixated on death. He has a job in an office where his co-workers show nothing but open contempt for him. In a series of flashbacks we discover how this man has been victimised throughout his life; the death of his mother at a young age, abuse from his alcoholic father, bullying at school. His death obsession leads him to take nocturnal trips to the local mortuary where he defiles the corpses and drinks their blood through a glass straw.

The film has a grim and morbid atmosphere similar to Joe D'Amato's Biou Omega and Augustin Villaronga's Tras el cristal (both of which were made after Vadja's film). Mosquito returns to the mortuary and removes the eyeballs from a female corpse. He is also obsessed with dolls; a necrophiliac's substitution? People in the town are warned to stay away from the creepy Mosquito, but one young woman (played by Birgit Zamulo) flirts with him occasionally but he more or less ignores her. Back at home and Mosquito puts the eyeballs in a jar of formaldehyde and adds them to his collection.

Werner Pochath's performance as the title character reminded me of Carl Bohm's outstanding role in Michael Powell's Peeping Tom; his smart appearance, quiet nature, and icicle features all giving the impression, on first glance, that something is not quite right about this person; his antiseptic cleanliness concealing the murky waters beneath.

He just cannot keep away from the mortuary. His next visit ends with him stabbing another corpse. Mosquito's behaviour becomes increasingly erratic when a policeman catches him snooping around. He strangles the copper and escapes. Zamulo, the flirty dancey girl, falls from the roof of a building and dies. He seems afraid of sex, or more accurately, uncomfortable with human intimacy (his collection of body parts and dolls perhaps a way for him to have companionship on his own warped terms). This aversion to human intimacy is a big frustration for Mosquito and he trashes his room.

After Zamulo's funeral, he returns and caresses her corpse. The warped tragedy of the film is that Mosquito (billed here as 'The Man') can only allow himself to become intimate with her once she's dead (and thus non-threatening). It's only during this scene that we realise how much The Man liked and cared about her; her beauty, her careless attitude, and free spirit something he admired and perhaps even envied - He genuinely mourns that loss. And after that sad encounter, Mosquito seems to lose control altogether and sets his sights on living victims with his trusty straw, reaching a full-on Ed Gein mode.

If you're a fan of dark, morbid cinema then Mosquito The Rapist will have you transfixed for the entire 90 minute running time. Funny thing is, there's no rape in this film at all; Mosquito The Vampire, Mosquito The Necrophile, or Mosquito The Bloodsucking Corpse Raider would all have been more accurate titles (the German DVD release shortened the title to Mosquito). Made around the same time as George Romero's Martin, this film shares in the sympathetic depiction of a vampiric ravager, and also offers a darkly romantic lullaby theme courtesy of Dafydd Llewelyn, that adds to the cracked innocence and strange morbidity of the film.

Loosely based on a true story of a deaf and mute worker in Nuremberg who drank the blood of corpses and who eventually turned to murdering women to satisfy his blood thirst in the early 70s, and clearly a big influence on the filmography of Jorg Buttgereit, the film continues to captivate unsuspecting viewers to this day. Look out for some fine performances from Pochath and Zamulo, and the unflinching graphicness of a particularly troublesome flashback in which Mosquito's young sister is groped very unnecessarily by their fucked up father. This lone gem from Switzerland has left legions of fans and future filmmakers with new and darker paths to explore.

MS.45 (1981)

(aka Angel of Vengeance)
Dir: Abel Ferrara / USA

One of the finest urban revenge movies of all time, Ms.45 finds director Abel Ferrara dispensing with the macho vigilante likes of Charles Bronson and instead opting for the silent flower of Zoe Tamerlis. The results are frankly mesmerizing.

Young mute Thana (Tamerlis), is dragged into an alley and raped and robbed by a masked assailant (played by Ferrara himself under his pseudonym Jimmy Laine). Bloody and bruised, Thana arrives home only to be attacked again by an intruder. But this time she fights back and ends up killing the scumbag by bashing his head in with an iron. Rather than call the police, Thana drags the corpse into the bath tub and saws it into little pieces that she then wraps into paper packages and attempts to dispense into the waste bins of New York City. But her plans for disposal are risky and her pretty looks draws much attention from the male members of society. Unable to cope with the stress any longer, Thana snaps and goes on a killing spree, culling the male population of Manhattan. By the film's finale, Thana dresses as a nun and attends a work party with a loaded pistol and a bloody massacre in mind...

MS.45 was Ferrara's follow-up to Driller Killer, and like that previous film it got caught up in the video nasties panic and was banned in the UK due to the 1984 Video Recordings Act. It became an urban classic and one of the most hotly debated titles of the 80s. Even with its grubby roots mired in exploitation, the film was taken deadly seriously, not only because it was played out so straight and convincingly as a piece of cinema, but because it also played a key part in the 'gender wars' of cinema. In her book Men, Women, and Chainsaws, feminist academic Carol Clover cites MS.45 as introducing the notion that "we live in a 'rape culture' in which all males - husbands, boyfriends, lawyers, politicians - are directly or indirectly complicit and that men are thus not individually but corporately liable".

Personally I don't think that the film really has that much of a deliberate feminist stance other than the fact that the one doling out the punishments just happens to be female. At the end of the film she is systematically destroyed for her attempts at playing God. The final scenes at the party show that she was clearly insane and was unloading her pistol indiscriminately on both men and women, perhaps 'blinded' by her rage to the point where she had lost sight of who the real perpetrators are.

   MS.45 is often compared with Martin Scorsese's Taxi Driver and Michael Winner's Death Wish, but the film is actually much closer in spirit to Eurohorrors like Repulsion and Thriller: A Cruel Picture. Joe Delia provides the squawky jazz score that kicks in at the most dramatic points, and the film is also awash with surprising touches and interesting visual ideas. The true star of the show is Zoe Tamerlis (nee Zoe Lund) who was just seventeen years old at the time of filming, and whose assured performance made her an instant icon among lovers of cult movies. She later teamed up with Ferrara once again more than a decade later when they collaborated on the script for Bad Lieutenant (in which she also made an appearance as Harvey Keitel's junky lover). Tragically, her career was cut short when in 1999 she died of heart failure, leaving us with a precious few films in her back catalogue. As the angel of vengeance in MS.45, it's perhaps her most iconic moment.

   Ms.45 was cut by one minute and 42 seconds by the BBFC. The first rape loses shots of Ferrara undoing his trousers and then pulling down Thana's panties. The second rape loses shots of the intruder bashing his gun against the floor as he ejaculates. Shots were also removed from the scene where Thana dismembers his body in the bath tub, including an expression of pleasure on her face while she does it. The use of nun-chucks were removed from the scene with the gang of would-be rapists. In America, the film was subjected to similar cuts, but the uncut version was leaked into circulation when Warner Brothers' Maverick Collection accidently released the full version. The tapes were quickly removed from the shops after a week, but a number of them were sold and can be identified by the duplication date code on the sleeve; 082897.

MURDER COLLECTION V.1 (2009)

Dir: Fred Vogel /USA

The idea behind this film is to present a bunch of fake murder and death clips in a faux-documentary style. Web cams, home movies, and CCTV are all used to create a realistic effect, but most of the clips aren't convincing at all, and the 'ransom' scene at the end is a major disappointment to say the least...

It's a great idea for a film but is badly executed for the most part (sorry). First of all, the grisly details of the deaths are always conveniently kept out of frame (except for a nice decapitation scene), the father whipping his son with a belt is more humorous than horrifying. The scene with the cheating wife is a highlight, and this sequence would make a great stand-alone short film in its own right. But even this impressive scene is let down by things like bad acting and an obviously fake rubber axe, etc. Making a fake docu-style horror movie is much more difficult than people think; Vogel and co may have startled viewers with their verite flavoured August Underground trilogy, but the horror in those films came from the gross and lewd antics within, not because anyone thought they were real and bought into the whole 'found footage' legend. When making a film like Murder Collection, the tiniest details give the game away. Not only does the violence and gore have to be spot-on, but the performances must also be perfect otherwise they're not convincing at all. The smallest mistake ruins the whole.

The Japanese autopsy footage looks the most convincing until we see close-ups of the fake rubbery 'flesh'. The 'Grummer' sequence boasts some impressive performances and for a while achieves that awkward air of impending ugliness to come, but when the knife comes out it all goes to shit, and we're left with the standard Blair Witch-type hysterics. It isn't the worst of the Toe Tag films, but after the likes of August Underground's Mordum and Redsin Tower, Murder Collection V.1 is a major disappointment. A wasted opportunity then, I'd be very surprised to see a volume 2.

MUZAN-E (1999)

(Muzan-E: AV gyru satsujin bideo wa sansai shita!)

Dir: Daisuke Yamanouchi /Japan

A lady reporter investigates snuff films, and her journey leads to the web where we are bombarded with disgusting images of fetish porn involving menstruation. She interviews a bunch of perverted porn peddlers and we're shown more clips of brutal and violent sex tapes (with the obligatory 'digital blurs' which conceal the offending pubic hair as is customary in Japan; heaven forbid the Japanese seeing a muff on screen). A young woman is kidnapped, abused, and humiliated on camera before a caption appears on screen warning us about some forthcoming nastiness (perhaps influenced by Gaspar Noe's Seul Contre Tous), and then the girl is disemboweled with a machete. And in a scene indebted to Evil Dead Trap, the lady reporter tracks down the location of the snuff tape by recognising a brief glimpse of a building in the background on the tape. But when they arrive at the location, she is captured while her film crew are butchered on the spot. She then finds herself tied to a chair in her own snuff movie hell, but there are a couple of odd surprises at the end...

  Shot on video for the booming AV market in Japan, Muzan-E has never seen an official release outside of its native country and is almost impossible to find without resorting to downloading it off the web (which seems rather apt in this case). Following on from the Guinea Pig tradition, this type of mock-documentary style horror runs just over an hour and was an obvious influence on Mariano Peralto's Snuff 102. Muzan-E, for all its disgusting and lurid details deserves credit for trying to do something different with the 'oh so serious' type of pseudo-snuff garbage by throwing us a curveball ending and playing like a postmodern, self-referential entry in the Guinea Pig series, and at least remains much more engaging than amateur crap-fests like Tumbling Doll of Flesh.

NAKED LUNCH (1992)

Dir: David Cronenberg / Canada

"It's impossible to make a movie out of Naked Lunch. A literal translation just wouldn't work. It would cost $400 million to make and would be banned in every country in the world"

- David Cronenberg

    One of the most difficult and introverted studio films of the 90s, Naked Lunch is essentially a hit and miss affair, exploring the life and work of underground cult hero William Burroughs.
    Former bug powder junky, William Lee (Peter Weller), works as an exterminator and lives with his wife Joan (Judy Davis) who lures him back into the squalid world of addiction. Whilst under the influence of the powder, Lee hallucinates that he is a secret agent for a disgusting horde of giant beetles who order him to kill Joan and flee to Interzone. With an increasing dependency on the powder, and his grip on reality loosening further still, Lee meets some oddball characters, his typewriter mutates into a metallic talking insect, and he indulges in more exotic substances.

Naked Lunch is an amusing and often grotesque concoction, and Cronenberg sidesteps the trouble of bringing an 'unfilmable' text to the screen, and instead concentrates on events and incidents from Burroughs' personal life, combined with Cronenberg's own ideas on the sometimes painful process of creativity itself. The result is a fascinating mess of a film, virtually incomprehensible on first viewing but offering at least a few nuggets of interest on repeat viewings.

On the plus side, Naked Lunch is a demanding film that also stands on its own as a personal creation in its own right, boasting some of the most impressive and imaginative hallucinatory imagery in Cronenberg's career. It's also an allegory on the battle against personal demons that vividly expresses the nightmare of drug addiction. The very antithesis of mainstream entertainment, the film nonetheless offers fine performances from Weller, Davis, Ian Holme, and Roy Schneider. The downside is that there's no room for audience participation in the film; it's very egotistic and introverted. But perhaps the biggest flaw is that Cronenberg doesn't explore what Burroughs wrote, and instead seems more content to ask 'Why did he write?' And according to the director, he wrote because he shot his wife. And in this decision Cronenberg fails to shed light on the text that graced the pages of Burroughs' books, and thus fails to make clear just what it was that made Burroughs such a giant of 20th Century literature.

The scene that re-enacts the incident where Burroughs shot and killed Joan in a game of 'William Tell' stands as nothing more than a gimmick in Cronenberg's hands. As fascinating as Burroughs' life was, these biographical elements are less interesting than the contents of his texts. Burroughs' work had never been sufficiently explored in the cinema before, so it was exciting for fans to discover that Cronenberg - who cites Burroughs as one of his major influences - would be making a film based on The Naked Lunch. The film, however, is not an adaptation of the book but rather a snapshot of biographical elements combined with Cronenberg's own personal flights of fancy. Burroughs' fans were less than impressed.

Another misstep was Cronenberg's rather tame handling of Burroughs' most notorious character, Dr. Benway. Benway is generally considered to represent Burroughs' own dark side; he is a cruel, destructive, power-hungry manipulator whom the author allowed free reign in the safe form of penmanship whilst acknowledging that those negative characteristics were present in him too. Cronenberg, however, restricts Benway to only a couple of disappointing scenes.

Naked Lunch was originally intended to be shot on location in Tangier, but those plans were quickly dashed after the outbreak of the Gulf War. And this halt to proceedings left the director with no choice but to re-write the script (he is no stranger to this kind of pressure though; he basically wrote the screenplay for Scanners on set). The major problem was how to deal with Interzone, the international free zone in Tangiers that was a mecca for artists and bohemians of all kinds in the 50s, and is a place where Burroughs spent much of his time in those days. Cronenberg eventually settled on the idea that Interzone would become "a hallucinatory state of mind" for the film, and this meant that indoor sets had to be built to replicate the exotic Moroccan settings for a shooting schedule in Ontario, Canada. These unforeseen problems in the film's production led to the project becoming even more introverted. I think it's safe to assume that if Naked Lunch was shot in Morocco as originally planned, we would be watching a very different film today.

Initial audiences were dumfounded when the film first hit the screens, and many still are today. But with the subsequent releases of Crash and eXistenZ, fans and critics were more willing to put Naked Luch into context as being a part of Cronenberg's latest phase, following on from his 'humanist trilogy' that includes The Dead Zone, The Fly, and Dead Ringers. Those new to Cronenberg are advised to start elsewhere (try Shivers) as Naked Lunch is deliberately off-putting for the most part.

A NIGHTMARE ON ELM STREET (2010)

Dir: Samuel Bayer / USA

What a disaster. The opening diner scene was decent but from there on in it all goes tits up. The characters and acting are terrible, but as a long-time viewer of slasher movies, that kind of thing can be overlooked, but there is also zero tension or suspense, and we are ambushed with 'jump-scare' overload, or more accurately, jump-scares that don't make us jump. The film is filled with unconvincing elements obviously engineered by someone who has no real interest in the genre and doesn't have a clue how to execute even the simplest, creepy scenes.

Director Samuel Bayer made a Nirvana promo years ago. He has no experience in feature film, especially horror. Platinum Dunes picked him up to direct this piece of shit and I'm not sure why; he just doesn't have the credentials. Maybe they hired him knowing they could push him around and that he would follow orders, no questions asked, just happy and greatful to be working on a 'big' film and allowing his reputation to take a severe battering. Bayer seems like the kind of guy who would sell his own grandmother to get a shot at the Hollywood big time, and as for the execs at Platinum Dunes, well, those cunts sold their own souls a long time ago.

Nancy in the original was an interesting character (annoying but engaging), but here she's just a bland moron; as soon as she appeared on screen I wanted her to die a stupendous death. The new Freddy Krueger character is a joke; empty, bland, monotonous. He's supposed to be an anti-hero, the archetypal boogeyman, but here he's just a bore. His droning voice is enough to put you to sleep. Even his new style of make-up is crap - He looks like someone has smashed him in the face with a cheese pizza...

When Freddy (in his human incarnation) gets cornered by the lynch mob, that scene could have been a real show-stopper, but as it is, it looks rushed like no one could be bothered to think it through, or even that no one involved in this money-making caper understood the significance of that scene (or perhaps they just didn't give a shit). The burning of Freddy is one of the most interesting areas of the whole Elm St. series; it's a diabolical idea that was only hinted at in the original film, the fact that Freddy Krueger was a paedophile and child killer, and the good, decent, hard-working parents of the local area took it upon themselves to hunt him down and burn him alive. This time around the filmmakers opted to explore this legend in a flashback, and it should have been the centrepiece of the entire film, but ultimately in Bayer's hands the scene turns to nothing; just another excuse for a quick 'jump-scare' and some flashy CGI bollocks.

Freddy as a human is depicted as a pathetic character - just a harmless and mentally-challenged handyman whom everyone mocked and made fun of. But when he returns as the dark dream avenger, suddenly he's very smart and cunning and 'on the ball'. There's no link between his pathetic human form and his evil post-death slasher form; it's a terrible contrast, and it just goes to further cement the suspicion that no one behind the camera gave a shit about this film. And that's another thing - It's not even made clear in this remake whether Freddy Krueger really was a paedophile or not; he is chased and attacked by the furious parents who are baiting for his blood, and the audience are left confused not knowing if Freddy is even guilty of the crimes or not! And the kids themselves can't even remember! I would imagine it being difficult to forget if you were sexually abused as a child... To imply that Freddy Krueger was an innocent victim of mob mentality is a stupid move and obviously can't hold much weight for long because he soon starts carving up the kids in their sleep!

I would only recommend this to those cinema sadists who enjoy embarrassingly bad performances and disasters on film, of lovers of CGI shit storms only.

NIGHT OF THE LIVING DEAD (1968)

Dir: George Romero / USA

Often described as the first truly modern horror film (although a case can be made for the early gore films of Herscell Gordon Lewis), George Romero's Night of The Living Dead began a turning point in genre filmmaking and introduced thousands of movie-goers to verite ambience for the first time. But horror fans often need reminding that THIS MOVIE IS NOT PERFECT! It was a cheap, low-budget B-movie with a non-professional cast and largely inexperienced crew who just so happened to catch Vietnam and the civil rights struggle on TV news reports, and set about creating lurid documentary-like images for a true nightmare on film.

Barbra and her brother John visit a cemetery to place flowers on a relative's grave; but they are attacked out of the blue by a lumbering zombie. Barbra flees to a farmhouse where she meets a group of survivors, and together they are forced to put their differences aside if they are to fend off the hordes of flesh eaters who are trying to force their way in, before the shockingly casual and nihilistic ending.

Barbra isn't a tough heroine ready for battle against the undead, she spends much of the movie in an almost catatonic state; this being Romero's way of taking away viewer control - By focusing on a surrogate character who sinks into a helpless state, Romero succeeds in irritating the viewers and making them feel uncomfortable by not being able to control what's happening on screen. And when Barbra does finally pull herself together and finds the courage to take a stand against the ghouls, she is rather ironically eaten by her zombified brother. This was a real break from the norm in horror films at the time. With this film the floodgates of modern horror were opened - Heroes, heroines, and good people of all kinds are just as likely to be killed as anyone else, everything was not going to be okay in the end, our fellow humans could be just as monstrous as the monsters. The film's bad guy, Harry Cooper, insists on having everyone hide in the basement in the farmhouse, but the black hero, Ben (Duane Jones), refuses to be holed up down there - an understandable decision - But this turns out to be a big mistake later on. The bad guy is later proved to have made the right choice by offering to barricade everyone into the basement.

Perhaps Romero's central message was that WE ARE THE ZOMBIES, you and I, our friends and loved ones. On DVD be sure to stick with Romero's original version and avoid at all costs the 30th Anniversary Edition which includes a terrible synth piano score and some dreadful extra scenes that were shot 30 years later and do nothing but obstruct the story.

Also contrary to popular belief is the fact that although Night of The Living Dead is one of the greatest and most influential horror films ever made, it didn't have an immediate impact on the zombie movies that followed in its wake; Tombs of The Blind Dead, Messiah of Evil, Shockwaves, The Living Dead At The Manchester Morgue, Sugar Hill and Her Zombie Hitmen, etc; all of those films differed radically in zombie lore from Romero's shuffling rotting corpses of NOTLD. It wasn't until Romero unleashed the 2nd part of the series, Dawn of The Dead, a decade later did we see other filmmakers following suit, with Lucio Fulci's Zombie Flesh Eaters (released in Italy as an unofficial sequel to Dawn), City of The Living Dead, and Jean Rollin's Grapes of Death and Zombie Lake willing to promulgate Romero's basic vision of the zombie as a walking corpse who dines on warm human flesh. But still, even after Dawn of

The Dead, other filmmakers continued to take the myth elsewhere - Fulci with The Beyond and Gary Sherman with Dead and Buried, for example.

Over the years NOTLD has been rejected, celebrated, over-analysed, discovered, rediscovered, colourised, remade, extended, re-released, sequelized, ripped off, and spoofed to such an extent that it's difficult to make sense of its initial impact. The film is widely accepted now as a bona-fide genre classic, but for many years it was accused of having a negative effect on viewers. Produced for less than $150,000 and rejected by Columbia because it was in black and white, and rejected by AIP because it had no love story and a downbeat ending, NOTLD was then relegated to playing at matinees where it scared the crap out of an entire generation before showing up on the midnight circuit, becoming one of the most successful indie movies of all time.

964 PINOCCHIO (1991)

Dir: Shozin Fukui / Japan
Brain-modified sex slave, Pinocchio, can't get an erection and is thrown out by his horny female owners. Lost and vulnerable, he meets Himiko, a seemingly friendly face who offers him food and shelter. Himiko teaches Pinocchio how to walk and talk, but on their heels are the inventors who are in charge of the sex slave industry, and they must capture Pinocchio in order to repair him and spare the blushes of the company. This very odd couple are forced to live in the shadows and they spew forth all kinds of bodily secretions before Himiko reveals her true motives...

Borrowing heavily from the early work of Shinya Tsukamoto, both visually and thematically, writer/director Shozin Fukui creates a volatile cyberpunk nightmare that includes high-powered androids, slimy body horrors, and frantic set-pieces, all shot in a ferocious hyper-kinetic style. This is disorientating stuff, visually astonishing, tirelessly inventive, and includes just about every body fluid there is. Due to the film's low budget, many scenes were shot in guerrilla-style, with the normal everyday citizens staring into the camera lens and probably wondering what the hell they are witnessing as Pinocchio staggers through the streets dragging along with him a silver pyramid.

The only downside to this film is that the characters are so cliched and predictable; we have the inventor who will stop at nothing to protect his investment, the flirty secretary who will do anything for her boss, Himiko who is clearly much more sinister than she lets on, and also the agents who are chasing Pinocchio; they resemble your typical cyber-boffins who are willing to sacrifice anything for the sake of their important research.

On the plus side we get a director at the height of his directorial powers who wears his varied influences very much on his sleeve; we get elements of Tetsuo The Iron Man and Tetsuo 2 - Body Hammer with the faded comic-book-style colours, frenetic camera work, and the climactic robot march through the city. The scene in which Himiko gets violently ill in the train station and literally vomits everywhere is clearly modeled on the classic scene from Andrzej Zulawski's Possession. Fukui returned with Rubber's Lover in 1996.

9 SONGS (2004)

Dir: Michael Winterbottom UK

This sexually explicit film is set over a twelve month period charting the story of young couple, Matt and Lisa, whose love for live music is equalled only by their love of sex. The BBFC granted the film an uncut 18 certificate, making it the most sexually explicit mainstream film ever released in the UK. Actors Margo Stilley and Kieran O'Brian's sex scenes are all clearly unsimulated, and Margo requested that director Winterbottom refer only to her character's name in press interviews about the film. The soundtrack throws up an assortment of indie/rock tunes from the likes of Primal Scream, Dandy Warhols, and The Black Rebel Motorcycle Club, but overall it's not a great film, and the curiosity value wears thin quite quickly.

In New Zealand 9 Songs was given an R18 rating and moralist groups lobbied to have the film banned, but has since been broadcast on pay-per-view TV. But it was in Australia where the film caused the biggest fuss when it was initially slapped with an X rating only to be lowered to an R, causing much concern for moralist groups. In South Australia the X rating still stands.

NOIR ET BLANC (1986)

Dir: Claire Devers / France

This black and white arthouse oddity appeared in the UK surprisingly uncut. Films which deal with the subject of sadomasochism are notoriously frowned upon on these shores by everyone from critics, to censors, tabloid papers, and politicians. But Claire Devers' directorial debut seems to have completely bypassed the kind of moral panics which greeted Just Jaeckin's The Story of O, David Lynch's Blue Velvet, and Barbert Schroeder's Maitresse. The reason for this may be because Noir et blanc looks at first glance to be a mild and non-explicit depiction of submission. But make no mistake, this film certainly takes its themes of pain and pleasure to fatal extremes, and leaves very little to the audience's imagination.

Very loosely based on a short story by Tennessee Williams called Desire and The Black Masseur, Noir et blanc centres on a young office worker who is drawn into a masochistic relationship with, uh, a black masseur. Their desires become increasingly extreme and destructive as the pair reach into the realms of lethal eroticism.

Claire Devers won an award at Cannes in '86, but the film's risque reputation kept it away from any kind of English language distribution until the early 90s when a subtitled print appeared uncut in American arthouse cinemas. Devers' public profile continued to grow with her next film, Chimere, earning a Palm D'Or nomination at Cannes, and in 1994 Noir et blanc was passed uncut for home video in the UK. Unfortunately, this vital release did little to bolster the film's reputation, and which remains much talked about but barely seen.

OF FREAKS AND MEN (1998)

Dir: Alexei Balabanov / Russia

Of Freaks and Men tells the tale of immigrant worker, Johan (Sergei Makovetskii), who deals in slap and tickle photographs to the denizens of St.Petersburg in the early 20th Century. After a local engineer dies of a heart attack, Johan worms his way into the life of the wealthy daughter and coerces her into modeling for him in some spank-happy movies as the cinematograph has overtaken the photograph. Meanwhile, Johan's creepy friend, Victor (Victor Ivanovich), has managed to sleaze his way into the home of a blind widow and taken some lurid snapshots of the widow's adopted siamese twins. Pretty soon both respectable households begin to disintegrate.

Having caused a bit of a scandal in his native Russia with his gangster film, Brother, which was criticised for its moral ambiguity towards the criminal underworld, Alexei Balabanov's follow-up, Of Freaks and Men, takes a stunning detour to a no less controversial reception. With its combination of perverse subject-matter (including early pornography, sex with siamese twins, and general sleazy behaviour), a healthy literary vibe, and a murky sepia tone, Balabanov's film is Dostoevskian in its breadth, and serves as a pastiche of primitive cinema and as a critique on Russia's capitalist drive since the collapse of the Soviet state.

Banned in Ireland and generally treated cautiously elsewhere, Of Freaks and Men is a grim black comedy which nonetheless borrows aesthetically from Peter Greenaway's perfected artifice and parallels with David Lynch's The Elephant Man in the siamese twins story, making for a strange but genuinely original film.

100 TEARS (2007)

Dir: Marcus Koch / USA

A psychotic killer clown leaves the fairground and embarks on a killing spree with a huge meat cleaver and searches for his long lost daughter. Tracking him down are the police and an odd couple of amateur sleuths who are hoping to get the scoop of a lifetime for their local tabloid paper.

This is an extremely violent and graphic slasher movie; heads are cut off and split in two, limbs are hacked off, torsos are sliced open to reveal the sloppy innards. People are also shot, stabbed, and strangled thanks to some superb special effects courtesy of the great team at Odditopsy FX, helping to earn the film an NC-17 rating in America. The body count rises higher than most movies of this type in the first 20 minutes, and by the end credits the number of mangled corpses this film leaves behind is almost astronomical. The acting isn't great but the script is sharp, witty, and quite clever for this kind of thing. It sure beats other low-budget indie efforts like the first August Underground and The Gateway Meat.

Directed by the unfortunately named Marcus Koch with much love and respect for the genre, it's good to see a fanboy-type horror film that doesn't get bogged down in overdoing the 'ironic' and self-referential crap that plagues so many of these types of films. Here the director concentrates on more important things like making a decent script and casting a couple of leads who gel together quite well on screen, despite the fact that there isn't much chance of a sex scene between the two (she's a stunningly beautiful brunette, and he's a fat, flatulating ogre). The film's most impressive aspect though is definitely the extreme gore, so if you are squeamish you may want to avoid.

On the soundtrack there is a distorted chime from a musical box that sounds identical to Christopher Young's score for the first couple of Hellraiser films; it may have been taken from the soundtrack CD. The music also includes crappy techno during some of the killing scenes, and this type of music has never worked in films and doesn't work here at all. Also, the killer clown is a bit miscast and doesn't really pose a very menacing presence, but these are only minor criticisms as the film certainly delivers on the slasher essentials: A bunch of idiots get slaughtered in extremely nasty and graphic ways!

The 'Tears' of the title refers to the killer's MO which involves drawing teardrops on the wall using the blood of each of his victims, and the 100 gives you some idea of the excessively large body count.

OUT OF THE BLUE (1980)

Dir: Dennis Hopper / Canada

Tagline - "Her dad's in prison... Her mom's on drugs... The only adult she admires is Johnny Rotten".

Troubled teen, Cebe (Linda Manz), finds life difficult with a drug-addled mother and alcoholic, sexually abusive, ex-con for a father. She finds solace in the night life and seething nihilism of the local punk scene in Vancouver.

Dennis Hopper, god rest his soul, was always a contrary so and so; a man whose remarkable talents both in front and behind the camera were constantly off-set by his wild and self-destructive behaviour through drink, drugs, and pretentions, and whose steps up the filmic ladder were often met with sudden falls from grace. So much so that many times throughout his career he was considered basically unemployable by producers and directors, and Hollywood would often avoid him like the plague. The fact that he was also capable of a well-timed genius, combined with his engaging personality, offered him many 'second chances' that mere mortals like us could never hope to be granted. And right up until his death in 2010 he was always a firm fan favourite.

Hopper's career began in the 50s alongside James Dean in Rebel Without a Cause and Giant. This bright start soon drifted into improvisational chaos and 100-take madness that infuriated those around him, and banished him from the Hollywood hills. He returned in the late 60s with the low-budget Easy Rider which made a fortune and catapulted him to stardom, becoming one of the most bankable icons of the counter-culture era. But all of that success came to an end when he committed a second career suicide by heading deep into the jungle to make The Last Movie, with too much booze and drugs, but very little in the way of a script, or plan, or cohesion. By the late 70s he was referred to as "that photographer nutcase from Apocalypse Now", and his once promising career seemed to be well and truly over.

Surprisingly, another comeback was on the horizon in 1980 during the making of Out Of The Blue. Hopper had originally signed up to play Cebe's depraved father, but after writer/director Leonard Yakir jumped ship, Hopper was entrusted to take over the reins of the project, and much to everyone's surprise, he took to the helm with a sane and sober professionalism, managing a re-write of the script which incorporated his own dark vision, and remaining even-tempered throughout. He delivered the film on time, in budget, and with no complaints. The producer's gamble had paid off, and this independent Canadian feature was a hit with critics, despite its grim tones and punk aesthetics.

Hopper was rewarded with a Palm D'or nomination at Cannes, and for a while seemed to be back in contention. But for all the modest success of Out Of The Blue, he still hadn't fully purged his demons, and it wasn't until a few years later when he made yet another comeback as the psychotic Frank Booth in David Lynch's Blue Velvet did he finally reach some kind of contentment in his life and embraced the straight and narrow.

Out Of The Blue was described by Time Out magazine as "A film about extremes directed by an extremist", and indeed the film opens with Hopper crashing a truck into a bus load of school kids, and culminates in his daughter Cebe embracing the wreckage of human life in the city's punk clubs. The heart of the film lies in its cathartic energy, a destructive cry of anguish in the face of boredom, banality, poverty, and domestic hell; where the obliteration of self-destruction and a raw passion for noise and chaos is preferable to the quiet misery of trying to fix a broken home. Something Hopper could no doubt relate to (he certainly had no trouble in filling the role of the drunken wretch of a father!). An important and much overlooked gem.

PEEPING TOM (1959)

Dir: Michael Powell /UK

Critically reviled on its initial release for its morbid and disturbing voyeurism, Michael Powell's Peeping Tom is now held in very high regard as one of the finest British movies ever made. A psychologist (played by director Powell himself in a knowing bit of casting) subjects his young son to nightmarish experiments in his studies on fear. Inevitably, the child grows up to become a voyeuristic cameraman/serial killer (Carl Bohm) who stabs his pretty young victims with his spiked tripod and films the terrified expressions on their faces at the moment of death. He then goes home and watches the footage over and over again. Bohm conceals his derangement with a polite manner and clean-cut appearance, but it isn't long before his neighbour's suspicions encroach on his personal space.
  This film is much more restrained than its reputation suggests; none of the overtly gruesome bits are displayed on camera. Horror fans who are more accustomed to the latter day excessive bloodletting of the sleazy 'stalk and slash' formula will probably be disappointed with the steady pace and lack of graphic dismemberment, which is ironic considering that Peeping Tom played a big part in kick-staring the slasher boom of the late 70s/early 80s.

Peeping Tom was also one of the first films to depict a somewhat sympathetic killer, and this aspect has been imitated over the years in everything from Martin, Mosquito The Rapist, and Henry-Portrait of a Serial Killer. The stunning Eastmancolour photography with its bold and punchy colour palette has been much imitated too, as has Gordon Watson's creepy piano score. Director Donall Cammell paid homage to the film in his 1982 horror classic, White of The Eye, and also Italian horror auteur Dario Argento touched upon many similar themes in his excellent late 80s shocker, Opera.

Michael Powell deserted the earlier grand qualities which earned his reputation with Emeris Pressburger in the preceding years when the pair produced such classics as The Red Shoes and A Matter of Life and Death, and instead turned his attentions onto something altogether removed from the pleasantries of his earlier output. In one scene he goes as far as casting Moira Shearer, the dancer in The Red Shoes as a whore who gets stabbed to death by Bohm, and he even casts himself as the deranged psychologist whose sadistic experiments turns his son into a twisted murderer. The choice of casting himself in the role was clearly designed to express the obsessive and ruthless nature of all great artists, and also as a comment on the scoptophiliac nature of cinema-goers themselves, with Otto Heller's 'killer's eye' camerawork imitated to death ever since.

Unsurprisingly, the critics were not impressed. They didn't just dislike the film, they actively hated it and decried everything about it. Peeping Tom premiered in March 1960, just three months before Hitchcock's Psycho, and it was immediately panned. Derek Hill of The Tribune suggested that "The only really satisfactory way to dispose of [the film] would be to shovel it up and flush it swiftly down the nearest sewer". Some other loser called it "The sickest and filthiest film I remember seeing". The film's hostile reception brought its theatrical run to an immediate end when it was pulled from cinemas. And like Todd Browning before him, whose Freaks had been met with a similar outraged reception in the 1930s, Michael Powell's career effectively came to an end as a direct result of all the negative press. Alfred Hitchcock seemed to take an important lesson from this, and he rather wisely released Psycho without a preview press screening - Smart move.

In America the film played in a black and white version that was cut down to 86 minutes. But even in this shoddy form Peeping Tom managed to gain a cult following around New York's Alphabet City district in its limited theatrical run. Film student Martin Scorsese was suitably impressed and his dogged devotion to Peeping Tom helped to save it from oblivion, even providing his own full-colour 35mm print for future screenings and a DVD release. "I have always felt that Peeping Tom and 8 1/2 say everything that can be said about filmmaking", he said, "about the process of dealing with film, the objectivity and subjectivity of it and the confusion between the two. 8 1/2 captures the the glamour and enjoyment of filmmaking, while Peeping Tom shows the aggression of it, how the camera violates... From studying them you can discover everything about people who express themselves through film".

PERDITA DURANGO (1997)

(aka Dance With The Devil)
Dir: Alex de la Iglesia /Spain/Mexico

David Lynch was the first filmmaker to adapt the work of novelist Barry Gifford to the big screen in 1990 with Wild At Heart, a psychotic road movie which incurred the wrath of both the censors and critics. A few years later and Gifford's work was once again at the centre of cinematic controversy when bad boy Spanish director, Alex de la Iglesia, adapted his follow-up novel, 59 Degrees and Raining: The Story of Perdita Durango, and centres on the gun-toting title character (who was played by Lynch's partner, Isabella Rosselini, in Wild At Heart), this time played by Latino beauty Rosie Perez. Rising star Javier Bardem plays Durango's demonic lover, Romeo, and we're also treated to a supporting role by blues legend Screamin' Jay Hawkins...

Iglesia's previous films, which include Accion Mutante and Day of The Beast, were still on the fringes of cult, but here was the opportunity for him to hit the big time; he had a Hollywood-sized budget, a Hollywood star in Perez, and a hot-property in writer Barry Gifford (who also helped out with the screenplay). Mainstream acceptability were his for the taking... But when Perdita Durango hit the screens in the late 90s, that Tinseltown calling card went up in smoke. The result is a film which is sure to offend everyone at some point - Americans, moralists, the squeamish - as Iglesia's incendiary movie tackles such sensitive subjects as kidnap, rape, and murder in a fun, comic book mode of pitch black comedy. Unsurprisingly, Iglesia has never made a Hollywood movie to this day.

Whilst scaring away strait-laced blokes on the US/Mexican border, Perdita Durango teams up with charismatic criminal Romeo, and together they hit the road and indulge in occult ceremonies, wild sex, and rampant crime. Romeo talks her into human sacrifice, and they kidnap a teenage American couple whom they intend to offer up in a bloodletting. Meanwhile, Romeo is being pursued by a relentless DEA Agent Dumas (James Gandolfini) due to his connections with crime lord Santos (Don Stroud) who has him smuggling a truck load of fetuses across the border to be used in the black market of the American cosmetics industry. The chaos all comes to a head in the bright lights of Vegas for the final bloody showdown.

Perdita Durango is even more outrageous than Iglesia's previous films, and he seems to be enjoying himself misbehaving with his movie camrea. The cast are all resolutely excellent, including Hawkins whose silly antics and bemused mumbling is genuinely funny. But it's Javier Bardem who steals the show as the free-spirited wanderer, Romeo, who makes a stunning transition from his previous roles as a lady magnet in Jamon Jamon and Live Flesh, becoming a lady magnet of a more dark and dangerous kind in Perdita Durango. Indeed, Bardem's rise to the Hollywood A-list over the subsequent years has been an interesting journey watching him do it his own way with roles in the Coen's excellent No Country For Old Men where he plays a relentless and amoral hitman (the lucky devil also married Penelope Cruz). Also on the casting front, look out for Heather Graham's sister, Aimee, as the pretty blonde hostage, and Repo Man helmer, Alex Cox, as agent Dumas' partner.

Perdita Durango took almost three years to reach American audiences due to a seemingly endless string of distribution and legal tangles, and censorship. The film was cut to shreds for an R rating, dispensing with some potentially under-age nudity, and also violence. Added to this was the cutting of the climactic finale which sees Romeo's destiny merging with that of Burt Lancaster in Vera Cruz. Iglesia's crucial and innovative merging of the two films makes for a heroic and touching scene, but it was removed because of legal wranglings. The Americans also re-titled the film to Dance With The Devil. The film didn't fare much better in the UK where around 36 seconds of risque footage was dropped thanks to the BBFC. The cuts were mostly on the scenes where the kidnapped teens are deflowered by Perdita and Romeo, an experience of rape which the youngsters later appreciate as an ice-breaker for their own sexual relationship; a big no no as far as the British censors were concerned. The German DVD by Planet Media presents the full uncut version in a gorgeous anamorphic transfer.

PHILOSOPHY OF A KNIFE (2008)

Dir: Andrey Iskanov /Russia/USA

Running just shy of four and a half hours, Philosophy of a Knife is an 'artistic representation' of factual events that is said to have occurred at the infamous Unit 731, a Japanese camp based in Manchuria during the Second World War. Those looking for a documentary account of the barbaric practices that went on there will get what they're looking for, provided they're willing to sit it out and wade through all the dramatised footage, because despite the loose feel and lengthy grotesque sequences, the film does stay very close to a factual depiction. Those looking for a narrative-based drama, however, are advised to look elsewhere because Philosophy of a Knife shows director Andrey Iskanov taking full advantage of the artistic license the subject-matter affords him, and the end result comes across more as part documentary, part bizarre music video, and very little in the way of a conventional narrative-based drama.

Disc 1 starts with the voiceover of a freelance medical nurse who mourns the end of the war and who makes plans for a retreat back to Japan. Mostly in black and white with the exception of video footage of Russian Anatoly Protasov offering an engaging history lesson on the subject, the next two and a quarter hours of the first part of the film mixes archive footage of the war years with experimental videos depicting the awful goings on at Unit 731. The intro sees a man being escorted outside into the snow and beheaded with a sword.

A man with an English accent serves as narrator and he gives us some historical backstory including the Russo-Japanese war, the Russian Revolution, Japan's struggle to combat the spread of Communism, etc, all set to archive footage. The film boasts excellent use of sound design with weird drones and repetitive chimes and wonky electronic and industrial music typical of Iskanov's films. But the sound effects, as impressive as they are, have the annoying habit of drowning out some important scenes where its inclusion tends to ruin the mood of the film, such as the scenes where Anatoly Protasov discusses openly on camera his experiences in Manchuria during the war; his invaluable insight and frankness of his recollections are almost swamped by Iskanov's insistence on including layers of unnecessary drones on the soundtrack. These sound effects suit the other parts of the film much better but in the scenes with Protasov it seems almost disrespectful for him to drown these important factual insights with this experimental music. He even manipulates the audio to sound very clean and stark with the treble controls turned up very high in the mix. It all comes across as very childish, it's like he can't trust his audience to sit and listen to the old guy's tales and so he starts messing around with the audio as a way of 'livening things up'. It's a bad move that ruins much clarity in the film. Overall though, it remains Iskanov's most accomplished and coherent work to date.

Unit 731 was hell on earth for those unfortunate enough to have found themselves there; the human captives were subjected to horrendous experiments with the data collected being used as a way of helping Japan's war effort. A common practice at the camp was to conduct animal blood transfusions in humans - especially with horses. Horse urine would be injected into the human bloodstream and the effects would be documented in detail. The Japanese wanted to have the power of wiping out their vast enemies with something much simpler and effective than the usual military combat of guns and bombs, and with bacteriological research they had found their answer. At Unit 731 they produced anthrax, dysentery, cholera, and bubonic plague by the kilogram. They had produced enough bacteria to wipe out the entire population of the planet, and they were intending on using it too. It's a good thing they were stopped when they were.

   The film eventually settles into a prolonged depiction of the experiments; in one hyper-stylized sequence a pregnant woman has her foetus surgically removed while she is fully conscious. One experiment used humans in long and sustained exposure to X-ray to study the damage it causes to human organs. A young Russian man is subjected to this test.
Experiments to see how much physical pain a human can withstand before losing consciousness; a woman has her teeth ripped out, one by one, without anesthetic. After removing the entire bottom row of her teeth with pliars, she remains conscious (and screaming a lot), so the boffins then start on the top row. Men are contaminated with venereal diseases like syphilis and they are forced to rape captive women so that the boffins can check each stage of the infection and its effects. One young man is forced to rape a girl and infect her, and when he's done he is then taken to the gas chamber and timed on how long it takes him to die. It takes seven agonising minutes, and his face literally disintegrates. One person has his arteries opened up and is timed how long it takes him to bleed to death. Another is shot in the throat at point-blank range and also timed.

   Unit 731 seemed to be a kind of natural evolution of the way that science and philosophy had been heading in the last one hundred years or so; philosophers became atheists, scientists became amoral, and politicians put theories to the test on a grand scale. The Hitler-Stalin Pact meant nothing when German troops invaded the Soviet Union, Stalin would invent his own crimes so that he could have those he disliked executed after staging 'show trials', millions of Jews were being exterminated in Europe in a 'purification' of the Ayrian race, the Americans were testing atomic bombs in the deserts of New Mexico with the assistance of angelic figures like Albert Einstein. Trust, loyalty, pacts, and alliances had gone out the window and were replaced by fear, treachery, distrust, and wholesale destruction. The whole world had gone mad under a Godless sky, and Unit 731 was just the tip of the iceberg. That little camp based in the puppet state of Manchukuo seemed to encapsulate everything that was going on in the world at the time; the amorality, humans in a worthless form literally reduced to fodder, the innovations and scientific breakthroughs used as tools of destruction, etc. When looked at in this light, the atrocities of World War II seem like a desperate attempt at uniting the world; as ludicrous as it sounds, it was a way of trying to make order out of all the chaos and uncertainty.

 A young man who looks suspiciously like the same actor who had already been killed in the gas chamber earlier in the film is brought back for an experiment in phosphorous - He is strapped down onto an operating table and has chunks of the stuff placed onto his face. Phosphorous is an evil substance that ignites at room temperature (the Americans used their own version, known as 'Agent Orange' in the Vietnam War), and before long the poor guy's face lights up in a fireworks display as it melts his skin, and we can hear the screams of pure agony. In another 'test' cockroaches are infected with leprosy and inserted into a woman's vagina. The bizarre music throughout the film is industrial and repetitive; imagine Philip Glass on speed and you're on the right track.

 The Russian guy, Protasov, explains how he was caught picking mushrooms in the woods near Unit 731 and was only spared his life because he could speak Japanese and had studied at Harbin University. Part one ends with the freelance nurse (Yukari Fujimoto) writing a letter home.

With the second disc we're thrown right back into the action with nothing to explain what's going on. It's an odd move because part 1 finished with its own end credits, and part 2 has its own title credits, so really these are two seperate and distinct films but they also play back-to-back with no set up at the start of part 2. We get the same black and white footage, the same type of music, and the same snowy weather and blizzards. We also have the first sign of rebellion here as one testee jumps up during an experiment and attacks one of the boffins. This brave stance doesn't count for much though as he is beaten unconscious. The boffin is hurt and ties a tourniquet around his upper arm to stop the flow of blood. In the next scene some guy is literally butchered alive - He is dismembered while he is restrained and fully conscious. A pregnant woman is strapped to a chair and a doctor digs deep into her vagina with huge surgical instruments and aborts her baby, limb by limb.

The English narrator returns for another history lesson, and then we're presented with 'Frostbite experiments'.
Yoshimura Hisato was in charge of these tests and he later received an Order of The Rising Sun for 'innovations in modern science' in 1978. A naked young man is walked outside into the freezing air, is tied to a post, and then has buckets of ice-cold water poured on him. In the coldest months in Manchuria the temperature often reached -40 degrees. The man is kept there until he passes way beyond hypothermia; his body becomes almost frozen solid. He is then taken back inside and gradually warmed up with the intention of discovering whether the human body can recover after being exposed to such extremely cold temperatures. Not surprisingly, the kid doesn't make it on this occasion.

A woman is strapped to a seat and has her head skinned. Disease carrying cockroaches are attached onto her head and the skin is clumsily re-attached. Photos are taken, and then she is carried down into a basement and dumped there with hundreds of other corpses. Another woman is laid face down on an operating table, and she has the skin of her back removed. The boffins shock her with high voltage electrodes, and meat hooks are used to tear out pieces of her vertebrae. After some 'plague treatments' we're shown an experiment in 'the bends' whereby victims are used in decompression experiments; by artificially inducing deep sea conditions, we watch as the victim's blood literally boils, eyeballs pop out of their sockets, and the organs explode from the body.

The film wraps up with another history lesson concerning the end of the war. Americans capture the island of Okinawa, and the Japanese are ordered to fight on to the last man. Mass suicide breaks out across the Japanese empire. A 15 megaton atomic bomb is dropped on Hiroshima, and then a 20 megaton device is dropped on Nagasaki causing widespread destruction. The Soviets declare war on Japan, and this spells the end of Unit 731 as the people running the place know that it was only a matter of time before the Red Army came along to spoil all their fun. The place is decimated and destroyed, and the remaining test subjects are killed by cyanide.

The Americans captured Shiro Ishii but he was later allowed to go back to Japan after striking a deal. It's interesting how the data that was collected at Unit 731 has seemingly vanished. But according to the best authorities on the subject, the data did survive and made it into the hands of the Americans and Japanese. And if you consider how America and Japan dominated the post-war years in terms of medical breakthroughs, perhaps the main reason for their successes in this field was due to them having access to this data.

PIECES (1982)

Dir: Juan Piquer Simon /USA/Spain/Puerto Rica

A young boy kills his mother with an axe and cuts her body into pieces after being caught with a nudy jigsaw puzzle and porn mags. The police assume the killer to be some madman who has fled the scene, so the kid gets away with murder. Forty years later and there is a chainsaw-wielding maniac on the loose at a college campus, slicing and dicing the pretty students and collecting their body parts. But who's responsible?

   This is one of those so-bad-it's-good type of early 80s slasher movies; we're bombarded with bad acting, a boring police investigation, and all kinds of bizarre and insane moments that appear out of nowhere ("BAS-STAARRRD!!!"). There's also the usual share of cat-out-of-the-bag jump scares, but I've never seen any who know Kung Fu, until now. The film's real saving grace though is the extreme violence and gore, and we're treated to a nice amount of the red stuff in the film's numerous graphic slayings.

   There are also many blatant tributes to Dario Argento and giallo movies that are spread liberally throughout; shades of Deep Red and Tenebrae (the latter was made around the same time), the reliance on childhood sexual trauma as the springboard for a psychopath, the stylized POV shots of the black-gloved killer who seems to be omnipresent, stalking and slashing his victims (usually beautiful young women), the red herrings and heavy bloodshed (the stabbing on the waterbed is textbook Argento). But not even the great Dario had a chainsaw-swinging maniac his films. Even the music is Goblin-esque - Tension building bass notes and swirling synths.

Although shot in Spain, Pieces is also very much an American slasher movie of its time. Teens, sex, nudity, slaughter, and a boring police investigation (Christopher George of City of The Living Dead fame plays the film's detective, Bracken), it's all here. There's some hilarious goofs and cringe-inducingly bad acting on display (look out for Jess Franco regular Jack Taylor who plays a smug professor), but you can't miss it if you're a fan of slasher movies.

Director Juan Piquer Simon is no cult favourite like a Jess Franco or even a Joe D'Amato; the rest of his filmography is absolutely dire with the godawful likes of The Pod People, Cthulu Mansion, and Arachnid (ugh!). Only his late 80s effort, Slugs, can live up to the deranged promise of Pieces.

PIXOTE (1981)

Dir: Hector Babenco / Brazil

Shot on the mean streets of Sao Paolo, Pixote (pronounced 'pee-shot') is a bleak and harrowing depiction of the lives of a group of Brazilian street kids, many of whom were non-professional actors from the shanty towns. Over the three decades since the film was made little has changed in the country's treatment of its wayward youths, despite Brazil's economic boom in the last few years. Directed by Argentina-born Hector Babenco whose previous film, Lucia Fladia, caused a scandal due to its portrayal of Brazilian death squads; this later effort was no less controversial.

In Pixote we get a harsh snapshot into the lives of homeless street kids. A judge is murdered, and armies of young delinquents are herded into a reformatory. One of the new inmates is Pixote (Fernando Ramos de Silva), a young boy who bares witness to the murder suspect being executed without trial, and a pair of homosexuals murdered for no other reason than their sexuality. Pixote joins a gang and together they escape their incarceration and pretty soon they're back on the streets committing petty crimes. The lure of the money encourages them to get involved in pimping and drug dealing, but after they are ripped off, they seek revenge. The boys become friendly with a prostitute (Marilia Pera), and she helps them to get organised as a crime unit and eventually becomes Pixote's lover. A brief spell of happiness follows before the bleak denouement.

The first choice actor for Pixote missed a rehearsal, so eleven year old de Silva stepped up and won the lead role, becoming an icon among lovers of off-beat cinema. His savvy nature and mature, no-nonsense performance seems to have stemmed from his own experiences as a homeless street waif, which demanded an instant growing up and an assured confidence which helps to cement the film in its effective documentary realism. The gritty style was also helped tremendously by Rudolph Sanchez's impressive camera work. Director Babenco once again took a text by Jose Lozero (after his previous Lucia Fladia), and adapted its plot structure with an urgent, hand-held immediacy, giving the proceedings a grim air of authenticity.

International censors were not too kind to the film; in the UK the BBFC cut Pixote by 27 seconds under the Protection of Children Act to delete the scene which shows a child in the same frame as a sexual act taking place. The cuts were similar to those imposed on Larry Clark's Kids more than a decade later, and whose writer, Harmony Korine, was hugely influenced by Babenco's films. When Pixote premiered in Brazil, a retired court judge requested that Babenco be held to account under the law of national security for condoning the use of drugs, encouraging the corruption of children, and undermining social institutions. Most tragic, however, is the true story of what happened to the young actor Fernando Ramos de Silva; having made such an impressive impact in Babenco's film, he was later shot dead by Brazilian police in a bungled armed robbery. A grim fate indeed, and one which continues to haunt viewers three decades later, as the gun-toting eleven year old pimp in his trademark woolly hat igniting the screen and bringing the grittiness of Babenco's film crashing into reality.

Pixote is not for all tastes, but those looking for something as tough as nails and with no hope of redemption, will find much to be enthralled and appalled by here.

POISON (1990)

Dir: Todd Haynes / USA

A controversial, narratively complex triptych of tales that introduced Todd Haynes' work to a wider audience beyond the gay community. Taking its inspiration from celebrated French author/convict Jean Genet, this fiery feature debut does much to create an increasing sense of discomfort while wearing its intelligence on its sleeve.

The first story, 'Hero', is a faux-documentary in which neighbours and family members discuss Richie, a troubled seven year old boy who is said to have murdered his father and then quite literally flown away out the window, never to return. The second story, 'Horror', mimics the style of a 50s black and white sci-fi movie, and features Dr. Graves (Larry Maxwell) who succeeds in isolating the human libido into a handy serum, but accidently doses himself and mutates into a dangerous and infectious monster. And finally 'Homo', the most obviously inspired by Genet, tells of the obsessive John (Scott Renderer), a thief whose life in prison is turned upside down with the arrival of Bolton (James Lyons), an object of his desire since their days in reform school.

The three stories are assembled together in a challenging and innovative way, and the disturbing build-up of the scenarios seems to affect viewers on a subliminal rather than a more obvious, narrative based level. And this results in curious afterthoughts as the film slowly settles in viewers' minds long after the movie has finished. The stories vary in their styles and are linked very loosely in their themes of persecution, alienation, and sexual anxiety, and uncovering the film's intriguing and enigmatic connections is left very much up to the viewer to decipher. Rather than allowing the audience to be spoon-fed by a more obvious and traditional narrative style, Haynes' film actively demands its viewers to engage with the action on screen in a subjective manner. If the film has a 'message' it's very much up to you to work out because Poison is by no means an explicit polemic.

Poison opened to much hostility when far right religious groups expressed their displeasure at the film receiving funding from tax payer's money. And this had a crushing effect on the next generation of filmmakers as many funding bodies, such as the National Endowment For The Arts, had their government funding withdrawn as a direct result of the protests, leaving many young filmmakers without a pot to piss in, financially. The film did, however, find much favour with those who actually bothered to sit down and watch it (as opposed to those who just stood outside waving their accusatory fingers), and it eventually picked up the Grand Jury Prize at the Sundance Film Festival.

Director Todd Haynes first made a splash with Superstar - The Karen Carpenter Story, a short biographical piece played out with Barbie dolls. It won the Best Experimental Short Award at the USA Film Festival before Karen's brother Richard had the film prosecuted and banned in a lawsuit. Poison was his first feature film, and despite the controversy was successful enough for him to continue in his chosen medium throughout the 90s and beyond with films like [Safe], Velvet Goldmine, and Far From Heaven. None of his subsequent efforts showed the same degree of challenging innovations as his early work, nor sparked such notoriety, but they did at least bring some much deserved attention to Poison, a provocative gem steeped in technical virtuosity.

PORNO HOLOCAUST (1981)

Dir: Joe D'Amato /Italy

This goofy piece of exploitation trash from the uber-prolific Joe D'Amato mixes monster mayhem, hardcore porn, and sunny beach locations, but ultimately fails to satisfy on any level. The horror fans hated it, the raincoat crowd took it as a sick joke, and anyone else who saw it probably thought they were on drugs. However, believe it or not, it does have a tiny cult following among those who can't resist its sleazy, exotic charms.

A group of male and female 'scientists' travel by boat to an island to investigate radioactivity. Their research doesn't go as planned though as these people just seem to spend their time fucking on the beach. And unbeknownst to them, they're also being stalked by a radioactively mutated monster who goes on a killing spree and rapes the women!

Still unavailable to this day in any kind of legitimate English language version, Porno Holocaust was shot back to back with Erotic Nights of The Living Dead, using the same cast (with the notable absence of Laura Gemser), crew, and location. This has led to more than a few film guides and filmographies confusing the two. The sex and horror sequences are measured out fairly equally but monster fanatics will probably be bored to tears because the creature doesn't makes its appearance until well over an hour into the film (it does manage to wipe out all but two of the cast members though). The sex scenes are long, dull, and boring as hell; we get a crappy lesbian scene, and then two black guys on one white woman (and this section will always be remembered for one of the guys who stays limp throughout the whole scene!). And when the monster does show up it's a disappointment because it's basically a black guy with a bit of dried porridge stuck onto his face. His first scene is pretty cool though as he drowns a man in the sea and then coerces the girlfriend into giving him head! The monster continues on its rampage, smashing a man's head in with a rock, and another with a lump of wood. Dead bodies are eventually found scattered across the island, and when the captain has finished doggy-styling his lady friend he decides to investigate...

   The action is played out to a backdrop of sickly sweet pop music and disco tunes courtesy of D'Amato's regular tunesmith, Nico Fidenco (of Black Emanuelle fame). The Anthropophagus monster himself, George Eastman, is responsible for the script and he seems happy to appear in the film but wisely stays away from the hardcore stuff (as he did in Erotic Nights). Those of you who first encountered the film on dupy bootleg video will be astonished by the German DVD from Astro. Picture quality is crisp and colourful, and the somewhat exotic feel of the film (which was lost on the murky VHS versions) is fully restored here. It's also uncut and runs for the full 110 minutes. It's just a shame the dub tracks are in German and Italian only.

THE POUGHKEEPSIE TAPES (2007)

Dir: John Erick Dowdle / USA

Not a bad docu-style horror/slasher but is let down by some ridiculous acting and a corny twist ending... Police raid the home of a suspected serial killer. They don't find him but they do find more than 300 hours of video footage of the killer going about his business. The resulting film is put together mostly from those video tapes. It still hasn't been officially released in any form but was leaked online. And if it does eventually make it onto video shelves it will probably be trimmed down a little first as the leaked version looks to be a rough cut and outstays its welcome by a good ten minutes or so. There are some great individual set-pieces throughout, including stalkings, abductions, murders, and his bizarre treatment of his captives, and general weird behaviour. On the downside, some of the performances are incredibly bad, such as a forensics guy who discusses what kind of weapons the killer may be using; it's one of the most ridiculous performances you'll ever see. Also, the police-woman at the makeshift grave site looks like she has stepped right out of drama school in a performance of a lunchtime. My main quibble though is that the film never attempts to address the psychological motivations that leads some people to take pleasure in the destruction of children, and just seems content as a grim exploitation piece.

QUID PRO QUO (2008)

Dir: Carlos Brooks / USA

A well-behaved melodrama posing as a challenging and thought-provoking film.

Radio host Stahl has been confined to a wheelchair since he was a youngster due to a road accident which killed the rest of his family. He's on a quest to learn about a group of people who want to become parapliegic; they have been known to offer surgeons huge amounts of cash to physically disable them. Inevitably he meets Fiona, an attractive, mysterious weirdo who may hold some answers.

This kind of typically dull drama wouldn't be out of place on some daytime TV movie channel for bored housewives. Stahl even bags himself a pair of magical shoes that help him to walk again (magic realism? You should be so lucky!). The film takes an interesting and un-PC idea (healthy people who want to become cripples for lifestyle or even sexual purposes, and will do anything to have their wish), and turns it into the most bland, boring, and sorry excuse for a drama. It's as if the film's makers were so terrified of offending anyone and causing controversy that they pussyfoot and skimp around the idea like regular members of the PC brigade.

The strange subculture element was done much better in Cronenberg's Crash, and also in Brian Evenson's superb novel, Last Days, which centres on a detective who is sent to infiltrate a bizarre religious cult whose members hack off their own body parts in order to feel closer to God. But in Quid Pro Quo we're expected to follow the most dull and boring lead character in a long long time. The script is clumsy and it constantly takes the moral high-ground at every opportunity; it never really attempts to understand the psychological motivations of those who want to become parapliegic (which is funny considering the whole film is about a man trying to find out why). We also get your typical Hollywood tradition of the main character being the squeaky-clean perfect moralist (and in a film with this kind of subject-matter, it's like he's stuck between a rock and a hard place). There's almost a zero sense of humour either; absolutely no attempt to try and lighten the mood or characters. I can't be too harsh on the actors though, they did what they could with a lousy script.

My main criticism is that the film poses an interesting question and then spends the next 70 minutes trying to avoid the answers, leaving us to tag along with stupid cardboard characters who have absolutely nothing to say.

RABID (1976)

Dir: David Cronenberg / Canada

Following the scandalous triumph of Shivers, writer/director David Cronenberg extended his cold, detached vision on sexualised horror in the following year with Rabid. But this time instead of focusing on the residents of an enclosed apartment block, we're invited to follow the deadly STD through the wintery streets of Montreal.

Employees at a medical clinic witness a motorcycle crash, and one of the accident victims, Rose (Marilyn Chambers), undergoes radical surgery at said clinic involving new techniques in tissue regeneration. But when she awakens from her coma, she is in an agitated state, seemingly hungry for something. We soon discover she has developed a strange vaginal cavity in her armpit from which a spike protrudes to pierce her victim's flesh and feed on their blood. Rose then wanders the hospital trying to 'seduce' everyone in sight, and each of her victims develops highly contagious rabies. It isn't long before the outbreak reaches epidemic levels, with the dazed and lumbering diseased foaming at the mouth and attacking the public in violent frenzy. The National Guard are called in to try and quell the epidemic and bring back some law and order, but the situation spirals even further out of control, and the city becomes a battleground with survivors trying to fend off the infected and stay alive.

David Cronenberg first wrote Rabid as a tale of modern-day vampires called Mosquito, but due to his own misgivings about the project (his producer Ivan Reitman had to talk him out of scrapping the whole idea), Rabid altered form a couple of times before he was entirely happy with the script. The Canadian Film Development Corporation once again financed the film, even though his last effort, Shivers, caused much controversy in the press. The result is another for the pantheon of 70s horror and remains one of the most nightmarish and action-packed films of his career. He has a field day showing us a series of grim, disturbing, and darkly humorous imagery, such as the persistent frothing at the mouth that spells immediate mayhem, a Santa Claus getting machine gunned in a busy shopping mall, monsters preying on their victims in a bizarre form of sexualised 'intercourse', and Rose's visit to a porno cinema which seems to encapsulate the director's raison d'etre in a single extraordinary scene.

Reitman suggested the casting of porn legend Marilyn Chambers as her name alone would secure distribution for the film worldwide. Incidentally, Chambers (who had starred in the hardcore classic, Behind The Green Door) was looking to appear in something more mainstream, and although her performance in Rabid is pretty good, she returned to porn immediately after the film wrapped up production. Cronenberg returned with more body horror mayhem in 1979 with The Brood.

RAMPAGE (2009)

Dir: Uwe Boll Canada/Germany

Rampage follows a very pissed off young man as he plans a city massacre. He kits himself out in bullet-proof armor that resembles a paintball protection suit, and hits the streets armed to the teeth. The difference here from all the usual shooting sprees in the movies (and in the headlines) is that this troubled kid ain't planning on a suicide mission; he intends on getting away from the atrocity a free man. He also has other little agendas to settle, like burning money, dealing with the population bomb, and ...well, I don't want to spoil things, but those paying close attention should work out his cunning stroke of genius by the hour mark.

As in his previous work, writer/director Uwe Boll doesn't seem too interested in character development or actors (the great Dario Argento was always the same), and this results in some less than stellar performances (just check out the scene around the family breakfast table at the beginning). We also get Boll's trademark handheld 'photography'- cold and probing, some would say nauseating - But Brendan Fletcher's central performance is accomplished and believable, even if he seems far too normal and likable a person to be committing such crimes.

The film's biggest asset though is the rampage itself; a seemingly endless blitz of cinematic bliss. Mostly shot in real time, we're right there as Brendan squeezes the trigger on everyone he comes across. It's quite simply one of the best killing sprees in cinema history. After conquering the streets, getting revenge on the owner of a coffee shop, and - even better - unloading round after round in a beauty salon, Brendan enters a bingo hall and has a bite to eat! He sits there eating a sandwich and catching a breather whilst surrounded by a dosy mob of geriatrics who are completely oblivious to what's going on. It's a moment where even the ordinary and mundane brings on an oddly surreal tone. After this strange episode, however, we're right back into the action.

The way Boll tells his stories I find very refreshing. He has a careless juvenile attitude to both writing and directing, and I mean 'juvenile' in the best possible sense - Enthusiastic, eager, provocative, and even positive (in this sense Rampage reminded me of Stephen King's early novella, Rage). This film comes on like an angry student's knockabout screenplay, full of rage, idealism, and a call for social change. And that's no bad thing as far as I'm concerned.

Rampage is far more visceral and disturbing than Boll's earlier shooting spree movie, Heart of America (which also stars Fletcher), and if you do get the 'Boll bug' then be sure to check out Rampage as it's an essential part of his wacked-out filmography.

RAPE! 13TH HOUR (1977)

Dir: Yasuharu Hasebe Japan

Hasebe's most controversial film follows a bored shop assistant who tags along with a fugitive rapist and helps him in his crimes. And that's basically it. They rough 'em up, rape and rob them, and then move on to the next victim. The kid does have pangs of conscience here and there but one sight of the opposite sex and he can't control himself, and he's onto them, with or without consent. Some of the women enjoy the experience and even take control of the situation for a bit of reverse cowgirl! One woman even hands over a wad of cash and asks them to come back very soon! The rapist is also being hunted down by a posse of homosexual vigilantes, and the film ends with a nasty and violent poetic justice.

Rape! 13th Hour is a trashy piece of misogynistic mayhem that is at least completely honest in its exploitational triumphs and doesn't try to justify itself unlike many similarly themed Western movies of the time. The downside is that, because of this approach, the film dispenses with any kind of insight into the psychological effects of violence and rape on the victims, and instead serves as a lewd, crude, and shameless comic book caper, for better or worse.

Emerging as part of Nikkatsu's Roman Porno series, Rape! 13th Hour was the final film in Hasebe's 'Violent Pink' trilogy which kicked off with Rape! and continued with Assault! Jack The Ripper. It's a film which almost single handedly helped ruin the Nikkatsu Corporation with many critics complaining that the film "went too far" in its outrageous fun. Personally, I think the previously released Assault! Jack The Ripper is just as twisted as this but the Japanese critics saw nothing wrong in that film's depiction of a deranged couple who are aroused by bloody murder.

When approached by Nikkatsu and asked if he would make violent pink movies, Hasebe famously replied "Are you sure you want me? You must be aware - My craft is very bloody". But Nikkatsu were adamant that he make a trilogy of films that would push the boundaries of rape and misogyny. Well, Hasebe certainly delivered there, and the execs were very happy with the results until the scandal became too much. Nikkatsu found themselves taming down their future releases for a while until the success of Koyu Ohara's Zoom Up: Rape Site in 1979.

As for Rape! 13th Hour, it remains one of the key texts in the violent pinky genre, throwing in all the ingredients that make these films so compelling for cinema miscreants everywhere - Beautiful photography, beautiful women, lively soundtracks, oddball characters, and of course rape and gleeful sleaziness.

RED TO KILL (1994)

(Orig title: Yeuk Saat)
Dir: Billy Tang Hin-Sing / Hong Kong

Unbelievable. This film keeps up the CAT III tradition of taking lurid tabloid headlines and exaggerating the nasty, sensationalist bits for some big screen sleaze. CAT III movies are still criminally overlooked in the west, even among cult movie circles. But this is a good place to start if you're thinking of getting into the sleazy side of celluloid; even many jaded Hong Kong cineastes regard this film as utterly sick and repellent.

The film is set in a hostel for the mentally handicapped, and opens with a scene where a mother, unable to cope with her a retarded son, takes him in her arms and jumps out of a high-rise window to a splattery death. Meanwhile, while all this commotion is going on, a sex maniac drags a mentally handicapped girl into the attic and brutally rapes her - This sequence is played out with relish as the madman howls out his orgasm to a ludicrous and blackly comic effect.

Under these intense circumstances, Ming Ming (Lily Chung) is placed into the care of the hostel after the death of her father. She's quiet, shy, innocent, and doesn't really understand what's happening. Social worker, Miss Cheung (Money Lo), stays around to keep an eye on her and makes sure that she settles into her new home okay. The soundtrack has a slushy sentimental synth ballad that plays at regular intervals, and is very typical of Hong Kong cinema of the time. The local residents in the area are constantly complaining and protesting outside the doors; they suspect that a local 'sex lupine' who has been attacking the women is a resident at the hostel and are trying to have the place closed down ("Don't sympathise with the handicapped, they're not worth it"). Later that night a young girl who can't be older than 12 years old is sexually harassed by 'Uncle Chubby', a resident of the hostel. She knees him in the balls and raises the alarm, to which the whole neighbourhood come running out of their homes with sticks and clubs, and poor Uncle Chubby is severely beaten (this scene also includes the hilarious subtitle "You pervert, I'll crash your penis and take to cook shop"). It soon becomes obvious though that the culprit isn't Uncle Chubby but the hostel's manager, Mr.Chan (Ben Ng).

While Ming Ming practices a dance routine her skirt floats up and Mr. Chan catches a glimpse of her red panties. He can barely control the waves of lust that hit him in the groin - Here we cut to a traumatic childhood memory where Chan witnesses his mother sleeping with another guy, and then his father coming home and catching them in the act, to which the guy slashes him with a knife in the struggle. Dad's blood splashes across the window and this becomes a nightmare image that haunts Chan for the rest of his life. His mum then starts systematically hacking up daddy's corpse with a meat cleaver whilst growling malicious insults. She then trips and lands onto the sharp end of the cleaver which almost completely severs her head - So Mr. Chan understandably has a few problems 'upstairs', and whenever he sees the colour red, it triggers a violent sexual frenzy in him that he cannot control.

Poor Ming Ming is then brutally raped in an extended sequence that is almost unbearable to watch but also blackly hilarious, with Chan playing up to the camera, gleefully chewing the scenery for maximum shock effect. After he has finished he blames Ming Ming for her ordeal, and in her confused and broken mind she seems to accept it. He then rapes her again whilst whispering things like "We make a great couple. We should have a baby. If it's a girl I'll still be happy". By this point Ming Ming has sunken into a near catatonic state. The next scene shows her in the shower, weeping, and trying to cleanse herself of the ordeal, scrubbing her vagina and even using a blade to shave away her matted pubic hair, and cutting herself in the process. Even during such a harrowing scene, the camera lingers on her naked body for maximum exploitation value. Tut tut.

Social worker Miss Cheung discovers Ming Ming in a bad state and eventually gets the truth out of her, "Painful...

Painful..." she cries, "Mr. Chan touched me". What follows is one of the most insane court scenes in movie history when Chan is faced with the charges ("The witness is mentally retarded, this is a special case"). Ming Ming is faced with a barrage of ruthless cross-examination from Chan's barrister ("You enjoyed it didn't you... Did you have an orgasm?"). The case is thrown out when Ming Ming has a breakdown in court and is unable to reasonably state her case (she has an IQ of a ten year old for chrissakes!). So, back at the hostel Mr. Chan continues to torment the traumatised girl in his position of power. Miss Cheung catches him in Ming Ming's room, and this is when he turns his attentions onto her. Cheung then sets out a plan of revenge whereby she will use Chan's own neurosis against him... But Mr. Chan is onto her game and he shaves his head for one of the most joyously fucked up showdowns you'll ever see.

Wow, what were they thinking? Red To Kill is easily one of the most tasteless and sleaziest films in this book. It was directed by Billy Tang, the man behind Brother of Darkness (which also features Money Lo), Doctor Lamb, and Run and Kill. All of those films are extreme in their own right, but Red To Kill is undoubtedly head and shoulders above them in terms of sheer shock factor and in its gleefully un-PC attitude. In its own way this film is second only to Men Behind The Sun for being the most fucked up movie ever to come out of Hong Kong; yes, even moreso than The Untold Story and The Underground Banker. As you can gather from the above synopsis it certainly isn't a great work of art as such; it's cruel, it's cynical, it's ludicrous and tasteless, but it's also strangely engaging. It was shot straight up like any number of Hong Kong films of the time and kind of emulates the typical Hollywood 'erotic thriller' template of the late 80s, with its noirish angles, loathsome characters, and an uncaring social framework. But unlike those Hollywood epics, Red To Kill tackles some very sensitive subject-matter and injects it with the kind of leering, exploitative fun that is designed to entertain and even titillate its audience! The result is unlike anything you've ever seen.

Lily Chung is passable as Ming Ming but she is never really convincing as a mentally handicapped woman. The other residents of the hostel (all played by 'normal' actors) are more believable as mentally challenged characters, but it's Ben Ng who steals the show as the 'sex lupine', the seemingly sane and sensible manager of the hostel who transforms into a crazed sex monster at the sight of red. His frenzied performance out-does Anthony Wong in The Untold Story and Simon Yam in Doctor Lamb; the sequence at the end where he has shaved his head and subjects Ming Ming and Miss Cheung to much violence and sexual abuse is genuinely creepy and his leering grin is not easy to forget.

Director Tang continued his one-man assault on the boundaries of taste and decency with such inferior offerings as Brother of Darkness and Sexy and Dangerous before going 'straight' with a number of socially conscious dramas, beginning with Chinese Midnight Express, featuring Ben Ng and Hard Boiled's Tony Leung Chiu-wai.

RETRIBUTION SIGHT UNSEEN (1993)

(aka 3 Days of a Blind Girl)
Dir: Wing-Chiu Chan / Hong Kong

Retribution Sight Unseen is a glossy CAT III thriller that serves as a more twisted version of Fatal Attraction with a bit of Crazy Love For You thrown in. Anthony Wong is great as the intruder who enters the home of the gorgeous Veronica Yip who has undergone eye surgery which leaves her unable to see for three days. Wong poses as a friendly handyman at first but can't conceal his insanity for very long. He gradually becomes more and more sinister and perverted and psychotic as the film progresses, subjecting Yip to all kinds of foulness and control-freak behaviour until the tables are finally turned... There's lots of silly slapstick humour courtesy of Wong (look out for the shower scene, and his way of dealing with a pretend intruder), lots of eye candy courtesy of Yip, and lots of your typical CAT III mayhem. This doesn't reach very high on the shocking and disturbing meter compared to other CAT III titles, but is well deserving of the rating, especially at the end when the violence kicks in proper.

ROBOTRIX (1991)

(Orig title: Nu ji xie ren)
Dir: Jamie Luk Kim-Ming / Hong Kong

This silly piece of sci-fi mayhem from Hong Kong was sexy and brutal enough for it to be awarded with the CAT III rating. Life-like androids from across the world are demonstrated at an expo. The German robot and American Robot have a fight in a battle of supremacy. Both robots malfunction but the American goes ape shit and starts murdering the spectators. Then Eve R27, the Hong Kong robot somersaults into action and beats the crap out of the Yankee droid and saves the day. The Sultan of some middle eastern country is in attendance and the police show up to inform
him that his son has been kidnapped by a disgruntled Japanese robot maker, Ryuichi Yamamoto. This Yamamoto character is a bit of a crazed genius and has managed to fuse his own thoughts into a new android that is fully sufficient and is causing a lot of trouble in the city. The remaining scientists give Eve an upgrade by transferring the thoughts of a recently killed police woman into the machine, and then it is sent out to track down and destroy Yamamoto's driod, and save the Prince.

Heavily influenced by Hollywood action movies like The Terminator, Robocop, and Universal Soldier, Robotrix ups the ante on the sex and violence front, and we're treated to some superb stunts and set pieces. The scene where Yamamoto's rogue android brutally rapes a hooker until she bleeds internally and then ruthlessly throws her corpse out of the window is extremely nasty, and made even moreso by its inclusion in such a routine actioner as this. And a later scene depicts the brutal and casual killing of a policeman that is not easy to forget. Popular actress Amy Yip (of Erotic Ghost Story) plays Eve the sexy cyborg, Japanese AV sensation Chikako Aoyama (of Edo Rapeman) plays Eve's trusty sidekick, and both provide plenty of T&A, and CAT III regular, Billy Chow (of Escape From Brothel and Horrible High Heels) plays the evil robot. All in all it's a fun piece of hokum, an unrelenting and gleefully gratuitous slice of sleaze that mixes sex, violence, and slapstick into a nice little time-killer. But beware, there is a cut version doing the rounds that drops the rape scene.

ROMPER STOMPER (1992)

Dir: Geoffrey Wright / Australia

Geoffrey Wright's Romper Stomper opened at Leceister Square in the early 90s and was surrounded by controversy when the Anti-Nazi League gathered and protested outside. In an eerie air of deja vu, a similar reception greeted

A Clockwork Orange 20 years earlier, and like Kubrick's film, the morally outraged protestors had not even seen the film that they were so adamant would encourage imitative behaviour. Those who actually sat down and watched the movie saw nothing that could in any way label it as a pro-Nazi picture, and the wide-spread controversy in the end created a firestorm of publicity, thanks to the tabloid frenzy and the misguided lemmings, and Romper Stomper became something of a hit.

The film follows a gang of neo-Nazi skinheads led by Hando (Russell Crowe) who beat and bully the local Vietnamese. They also get into a tangle with the father of a rich white girl (Jacqueline McKenzie), and she runs away to be with Hando, and becomes witness to an array of nasty goings on, and is lectured on the 'ideologies' of Hitler's Mein Kampf. After a night of sex, violence, and debauchery, the thugs discover that their local pub has been sold to a Vietnamese man. They then converge on the place and brutally assault the new landlord's two sons ("Let's break some fingers!"). A third son manages to escape unseen, and he phones his friends for back up. And before long, cars and van loads of Vietnamese show up brandishing baseball bats and iron bars. A mass brawl breaks out at the back of the pub, and Hando's heavily out-numbered skinheads flee the area, leaving their casualties behind to face their ugly fates. The gang are chased through the backstreets of Melbourne to their dilapidated hideout, a barbed wire fortress where they intend to make a last stand. But the sheer number of enemies forces them to escape through a roof hatch instead as the Vietnamese clobber their way inside and set fire to the building. The skinheads commandeer a nearby warehouse and set up their new base, but the damage is done, and the gang turn on each other as Hando's bully-boy antics spiral out of control, leading to treachery and murder.

Russell Crowe's first lead role is a tour de force in seething hatred as the shaven-headed Hando, and he is also backed up with some solid support from McKenzie as Hando's spoilt brat lover, Gabe, and Daniel Pollock as Hando's second-in-command, Davey, whose secret love for Gabe and his own German heritage adds another angle to the drama, as these things only seem to effect Davey's conscience once the madness has reached irrevocable levels. The thrash punk soundtrack was created by members of Screwdriver, and the oily tunes like 'Fuhrer Fuhrer' and 'Fourth Reich Fighting Men' adds to the gritty excitement of the chaotic fight scenes. None of the musicians would accept licensing fees or royalties for their work on the film. The excitement though is ultimately quashed by a sense of dismay for people like the characters in Romper Stomper; all the violence and hatred stemming from the sad fantasies of grown men who cannot even take charge of their own destinies let alone a neo-Nazi movement.

Romper Stomper found itself mired in controversy once again in 2000 when the psychotic British prisoner Robert Stewart battered to death his Asian cellmate while he slept, only days after watching the film. Stewart idolised Hando and also Alex from A Clockwork Orange, and the numerous letters he wrote contained much hatred and racism. But I think this awful tragedy says more about the failings of the Feltham Young Offenders Institute than it does about the film's supposed racist and amoral stance. The fact that the actions of a psychotic young prisoner, who was already known for being racist before he committed the crime (he had a Swastika tattooed on his forehead) can be used as a further ploy to call for a banning of the film beggars belief. The nutcases of society (and in the prisons and young offenders institutes) can be led to extreme violence by watching Cartoon Network if they're that way out, so the argument that Romper Stomper can cause imitative behaviour among normal members of society is either moral cowardice, legal chicanery, or plain old stupidity, as far as I'm concerned. Besides, the skinheads in Romper Stomper are depicted as a group of dumb and selfish bullies who all turn on each other at the first signs of anyone taking a stand against them; hardly character traits that anyone in their right minds would aspire to. Like it or loathe it, Romper Stomper is here to stay. Director Geoffrey Wright has much to say on the subject of racism, and on its travels across the globe, Romper Stomper, despite all the controversy, got people talking about racism and its effects on individuals and on society as a whole. And that can only be a good thing.

SACRED FLESH (2000)

Dir: Nigel Wingrove / UK

Despite the abundance of flesh on display, Nigel Wingrove's surreal throwback to British softcore and Italian nunsploitation flicks is a crushing bore, and has more in common with Bill Zebub's experimental disasters like Frankenstein The Rapist rather than the sultry textures and decadence of filmmakers like Tinto Brass and Ken Russell.

Coming on like a 72 minute music video, Sacred Flesh revives that old tale of a Mother Superior who is believed to be possessed by Satan because she lusts after the sisters in the nunnery and masturbates a lot. Cue lots of near-static shots of actress Sally Tremaine rolling around on the floor, playing with herself whilst dressed in the heights of sister chic!

Regardless of Tremaine's beauty, the film outstays its welcome by a good half hour or more. Undoubtedly, this kind of material has a growing fanbase with Wingrove's labels Redemption and Salvation offering a range of similar, shot on video fare, along with full-colour illustrated books all catering to this kind of sexual fantasy. It's the kind of film which may have been a real doozy (or at least watchable) if it had been directed by someone with an eye for gothic decadence, human frailty, and sensual shenanigans like a Jean Rollin (whose previous works have been released through the Redemption label). But as it stands, with its reliance on a glossy modern promo style, fake tits, and outfits that look like they came from Anne Summers, it's not really up to much.

On the plus side, the film does deliver the blasphemy in spades, and we get to witness some intense visions as Sister Elizabeth's carnal desires spin out of control. And this kind of fun didn't go down well with the folks at the BBFC who promptly cut the film for its initial release, only to reinstate the footage a few years later.

SALO, OR THE 120 DAYS OF SODOM (1975)

Dir: Pier Paolo Pasolini / Italy

Towards the end of World War Two in Fascist-controlled Northern Italy, a pack of sadistic libertines coerce a group of young teenagers into a nearby castle where a bunch of equally ruthless women 'entertain' them with tales of sexual debauchery. Any kind of sexual activity is forbidden without the libertine's permission, and the often naked captives are used in a series of cruel and degrading social experiments, such as an ugly marriage ceremony, a disgusting dinner banquet, and other unpleasant past times.

Salo is one of the most shocking, disturbing, repellent, and subversive movies ever made, and marked the end for director Pier Paolo Pasolini whose mutilated body was discovered on the outskirts of Rome just days before its premiere. The film's initial release was overshadowed by lurid tabloid headlines and sensationalist photographs of the director's corpse. A rent boy confessed to the murder but circumstantial evidence suggested the involvement of others, possibly right wing extremists threatened by his Marxist leanings and open sexuality. And whilst the confusing and mysterious nature of his death would continue to be debated for decades by fans and conspiracy theorists alike, the film itself was almost universally reviled by critics and the Italian government first time around.

Based on an equally controversial book by the Marquis de Sade with its relentless detailing of the most extreme and disgusting sexual fantasies reaching an almost nullifying effect, Salo is a stomach-churning experience but stands as an essential classic of world cinema. It's certainly not family viewing, but the camerawork, music (by Ennio Morricone!), and stunning performances more than make the trip worthwhile. Often compared both favourably and unfavorably to films like Liliana Cavani's The Night Porter and Lina Wertmuller's Seven Beauties, Salo has an ice-cold approach to sexuality; there are no conventional characters, there's no psychological angle, no realism as such. Instead, Pasolini seems determined to unveil all the niceties conferred upon sexuality in romance, erotic softcore, and plain old pornography, and presents everything - including nudity, sadomasochism, and sexual sadism - in a way that is both sensually reductive and stunningly subversive. He also rather crucially shifts the historical setting of Sade's original to the 20th Century in order to exemplify further the targets of his transgressive masterpiece. The insatiable greed of the powerful is brutally satirised in the 'Circle of Shit' segment in which manufacturers force consumers to dine on industrial food; namely crap.

   Pasolini claimed that Salo was his first film about the modern world, and indeed it is an unflinching look at the new Fascism of neo-capitalism and takes Karl Marx's warnings about the commodification of man to an almost literal extreme as characters in Salo are reduced to nothing more than slabs of meat to be exploited by members of the 'establishment'. The film's finale adds further to the subversive nature of the project when the libertines use binoculars to view their victim's excruciating rape and torture. This violent massacre merges the view from the binoculars with that of the camera lens, thus merging our gaze with that of the sadists, and uniting our voyeuristic complicitness with degradation and death.

Now of course this did not go down too well with international censors, and Salo has been banned and cut to ribbons the world over. Only in the mid-00s did the BBFC finally lift its thrity year ban and pass Salo uncut for home viewing. But elsewhere the film has been treated even less favourably, especially on home video; a gay bookstore in America was famously raided by police when the uncut version was discovered to have been on sale there. Funny old world isn't it.

SAVAGE GRACE (2007)

Dir: Tom Kalin Spain/USA/France

Based on the true story (Natalie Robin and Steven M.L. Aronson's book of the same name), Savage Grace charts the history of the Baeckeland family, from the birth of the son, Tony, in the 40s to the death of the mother Barbara in the 70s. They were a very wealthy family (the grandfather invented a commonly used plastic, Bakelite), but they were also easily bored and had too much time on their hands, which culminated in them creating their own dramas for everyone to see - adultery used as a spiteful weapon of revenge on a whim, an increasing alienation between father and son, the father stealing his son's girlfriend, incestuous threesome frolics, the emotional instability of all concerned, etc. But first time director Tom Kalin concentrates most of his efforts on showing how all of this behaviour has affected the son, Tony. He also takes a few risks as a filmmaker, and this makes it worth seeing for that reason alone.

It's beautifully shot and offers up some fine performances (the brilliant Julianne Moore is as game as ever in her portrayal of mother Barbara). It's also a mixture of darkness and light in terms of both aesthetics and subject-matter, and producer Christine Vachon presents us with yet another interesting drama which involves unorthodox social themes and demented sexuality. Not the most extreme movie you'll ever see, but is much better than the many bad reviews would have you believe.

SCREAM BLOODY MURDER (1972)

Dir: Marc B. Ray / USA

A young boy, Matthew, runs a bulldozer over his father, killing him. He then falls from the seat and has his hand crushed beyond repair in the vehicle treads. Ten years later, and Matthew returns home from a mental institution with a hook in place of his mashed up hand. But his Oedipal rage starts anew when he discovers that his mother is now remarried. Matthew murders his mamma's new hubby with an axe, and when mother intervenes, he throws her to the ground and she bashes her head on a rock and dies (presumably). Matthew flees home and hits the road accepting a lift from a young couple. He hallucinates that the girl is his mother - hallucinations which continue to torment him throughout the film - and of course, he ends up killing them too. The movie continues to follow Matthew on his murderous journey; an artist/prostitute, a sailor, housemaid, a pet dog, an elderly woman, a house caller - Everybody gets it. The plot steers into other areas in the second half of the film, exploring kidnap, mental abuse, and sexual intimidation.

This is a pleasingly nasty and violent little film considering it was made in 1972 and I'm surprised it doesn't have a much larger cult following. There's lots of gruesome death scenes filmed with trippy wide-angle lenses and hosts a tense, downbeat ending making it top-of-the-range exploitation. Matthew isn't a glamorised and unstoppable killing-machine like Freddy, Michael, or Jason; he's a pathetic, single-minded mamma's boy who deflects all of his own problems onto others (like many real life killers), and it's these lurid qualities that make the film all the more interesting to watch, as far as I'm concerned.

The UK video version loses a small cut during the axe murder scene, and is also trimmed of the aftermath of the pet dog butchered with a meat cleaver. The American video version (which is also available in an awful looking transfer on cheap horror DVD box sets) is fully uncut. This film is in desperate need of a proper DVD release, so until then, happy hunting.

SCUM (1979)

Dir: Alan Clarke / UK

The violence and fear of borstal life is explored in Alan Clarke's extraordinary Scum which began life as a TV drama only to be shelved by the BBC for being "too realistic". Clarke and co remained undeterred in their attempts to expose the abuse and corruption in British institutions, and instead remade that caustic drama a couple of years later for the big screen. The result was unlike anything else seen in British theatres.

Young thug Carlin (a very young Ray Winstone) is sentenced to imprisonment at a young offenders institute. He is immediately assaulted by officers and beaten up by the 'Daddy' of A-wing, Pongo. Initially Carlin steers clear of trouble and takes his abuse on the chin, but once he gets to know the ropes and understands whom he can trust and whom he can't, he sets about a violent rise to the top, wiping out Pongo and his cronies one by one (including the use of snooker balls in a sock as a weapon, which has been imitated in other films over the years). Once Carlin proclaims himself Daddy of A-wing, he takes over Pongo's cut of the drug deals and other contraband, and protects the few friends he has made on the way. However, his new authority doesn't reach high enough to deal with the officers whose abuse and neglect crosses the line when a young inmate commits suicide after being raped. A full-scale riot ensues...

With largely the same cast who appeared in the BBC Scum, this later version is no less unnerving in its depiction of a brutal authoritarian system that seems utterly unconcerned with reforming the young inmates. It was also shot in Clarke's usual stark and grounded style that would typify his later works such as The Firm and Rita, Sue, And Bob, Too. Ray Winstone's performance as Carlin is assured and totally believable as the first of many big-screen roles to come, and he's also aided by the superb Mick Ford who plays Archer, a much more ingenious rebel who devises many non-violent ways of making life as inconvenient as possible for the screws, such as pretending to be vegetarian in order to disrupt the prison menu, and then showing an interest in converting to Islam in the presence of the chief warden who happens to be an intolerant idiot and devout Christian. The film is also very unflinching in its violence and disturbing details, with the desperate suicide of a young man being difficult to watch due to its gritty realism. The film's most notorious scene though is the rape in the greenhouse which was trimmed by the BBFC for its initial release and early home video editions. It has since been passed uncut by the board.

During preparations for the TV version, Alan Clarke and writer Roy Minton spent six weeks researching on borstal life and spent time visiting the institutions and interviewed many ex-inmates in order to construct as real a drama as possible, and many of the stories and tidbits of information gathered were worked into the script, not only forming the narrative but also serving as a damning indictment in the troubled 70s. It's no surprise that the BBC refused to broadcast the result until the 90s, by which time this latter version had secured its reputation as being one of the finest and harshest British films of the 70s. Thank goodness that important research didn't go to waste.

SEED (2007)

Dir: Uwe Boll /Canada/Germany

Typical of Uwe Boll, he makes another film that is simultaneously shocking, disturbing, and crudely inept in equal measure. There's a manhunt for a serial killer known as Seed. His modus operandi is to lock people in a room (including in one scene, a young toddler) and film them as they starve to death. He keeps the camera rolling for months while the bodies decompose. He then sends the videos to the police as a way to shock and taunt them. When he is finally captured the electric chair fails to kill him, so the authorities decide to secretly bury him while his heart is still beating. A very bad move as Seed manages to break out of the grave and continue on his killing spree...

   Many of these types of slasher movies tend to glamorise the killer too much, but Boll admirably keeps things restrained in this film, and goes for a much bleaker approach. Don't get me wrong, there are a couple of murders that could have come from a Friday The 13th movie, such as the scene where Seed kills a victim from under the bed. Boll also borrows elements from post-Saw killer movies, but generally, the 'coolness' of the killer is played down. And I don't know about you, but I like that in a film; had Seed been depicted as some unstoppable killing-machine, a la Michael Myers or Jason Voorhees, much of the impact of the film would have been lost. And instead we're treated to an evil psychopath who represents the worst of human nature. Also, be warned - The opening segment contains real footage supplied by PETA of animals being killed in the most appalling ways - You might want to keep the skip button at hand.

On the downside, the film is cut together quite badly and the 70s setting is not very convincing at all (they probably chose the 70s simply as a way of keeping the electric chair in the plot). For the police scenes it looks like Boll has gone for a noirish style but it doesn't work on digital video, just makes everything look flat and dull. On the positive side, the scene involving the woman, the chair, and the hatchet is superbly brutal; this extended scene was shot in one take and rivals Herschell Gordon Lewis in the leeringly gratuitous sweepstakes. Also, be prepared for the ending as it's one of the cruelest and most cold-blooded in the history of film, I shit you not, and makes it a must-see for that reason alone.

With Boll's promise to donate 2.5% of Seed's profits to PETA, you can buy the DVD knowing you have committed a good deed for the day.

A SERBIAN FILM (2009)

(Orig title: Srpski Film)
Dir: Srdjan Spasojevic / Serbia

Shock Corridor was a cinema show broadcast on Serbian television. Its presenter, Aleksandar Radivojevic, encouraged homegrown filmmakers to be more gory, more perverse, more violent, and have more Takashi Miike moments in their films. The result was a slew of provocative pictures from that part of the world, including The Life and Death of a Porno Gang, Zone of The Dead, and most notorious of all, A Serbian Film. And judging by these efforts, it's clear that Serbian filmmakers were indeed taking notes from Shock Corridor.

The plot of A Serbian Film centres on Milos (Srdjan Todorovic), a retired porn star who agrees to make one last film with the mysterious artist Vukmir (Sergei Trifunovic) as a way to make money to support his family, but he has no idea of the true nature of the film's production, and when he does discover what's going on, he has no chance of escape...

This is a near masterpiece of extreme cinema, full of tragic ironies, solid production values, well-developed characters (insert your own joke here), and is very well directed. It's a film that is very much deserving of its notorious reputation as it goes places where very very few films are willing to go. It permeates a dark and grim atmosphere throughout; the atrocities don't come at you straight away, and the audience does have the opportunity to relax on occasion, but nonetheless, A Serbian Film weaves a ghastly spell that is designed to unsettle its viewers from the outset.

Around forty minutes into the film is when things get weird, and around ten minutes later it gets totally sick, and I mean truly TRULY sick. There are at least three scenes here that are very shocking, graphic, and utterly disturbing, and have caused no end of trouble with fans, critics, and censors around the world. Many reviews of A Serbian Film have given away all the grim and gruesome details of the plot but I'm not going to do that here because the element of surprise is of vital importance to the overall effect of the film (although there are some predictable cliche moments, here and there). But suffice to say, if you're a fan of the darker side of horror then Srpski Film is a must-see.

The genesis of the film stemmed from pure bloody-mindedness; Radivojevic had become angry and disillusioned with the whole Serbian film scene who he felt were ignoring real filmmakers and instead saw bureaucratic funding going to "Boring, pathetic, politically correct films done by people who don't know the first thing about cinema". He used his platform as the presenter of Shock Corridor to propose his ideas for a new direction for Serbian films, in which he called for filmmakers to be more daring and provocative. In the end he decided to practice what he preached and teamed up with like-minded director Srdjan Spasojevic, and together they set up their symbolically-titled production company, Contra film, and began launching their bloody crusade.

SEX: THE ANNABEL CHONG STORY (1999)

Dir: Gough Lewis / USA

Young, smart, attractive, and a hardcore porn star to boot, Annabel Chong became infamous in the mid-90s for her appearance in The World's Biggest Gang Bang, an event which saw her have sex with 251 men in ten hours, breaking the world record (a feat that has since been shattered by Jasmin St.Claire with 300, and Kimberly Houston with 620).
In this fascinating documentary she visits her parents who have no idea about her chosen profession, and explains to them exactly what she does for a living, and why.

Released around the same time when a number of fictional films appeared using explicit, unsimulated sex scenes as a tool of feminine empowerment (Romance and Baise Moi, for example), Sex: The Annabel Chong Story was the first to attempt a non-fictional account of the same. Ironically, even with the word 'sex' gracing the title as an obvious come-on to its target audience, The Annabel Chong Story is not a sexy film. In fact, it's a sad, depressing study, but is also oddly compelling for those reasons.

Filmmaker Gough Lewis follows Chong from her gender classes at USC where she voices her opinions and lets it be known that her antics are empowering and an attack on the traditional ideas of patriachy, to the porn world where she works. And Lewis doesn't flinch in presenting the reality of the industry. However, it soon becomes apparent that Chong is deeply troubled and less in control than she lets on. She admits to being gang-raped while in London, and expresses her anxieties concerning her parents (who live in Singapore) finding out about her true occupation. And it's here we learn that her real name is Grace Quek, and that she seems more compelled by self-hatred than emancipation. She was only 22 when she appeared in The World's Biggest Gang Bang (which was also filmed by porn director John Bowen and released on video). She was led to believe that all 251 men had taken AIDs tests, which turned out to be untrue, and she never received her full pay for the stunt, insisting that money was never really the point in the first place, and that she was willing to die for her cause anyway.

Chong/Quek is almost like two different people (perhaps a symptom of Bipolar?); Chong is self-assured and articulate, whereas Quek is a self-loathing mess. Whether she's frolicking around uninhibited, spouting post-feminist rhetoric, or allowing herself to be filmed while she cuts her arm with a blade, her exhibitionism exposes nothing but contradictions, making her more of a psychoanalyst's wet dream than an aggressive liberator.

The film was released to mixed opinions, with some championing its feminist stance while others appreciated it more as an expose on the degradation of the adult film industry. If you consider that director Lewis was sleeping with Quek during the making of the film, the whole production collapses into hypocrisy. He shot the film with a critical eye on the porn lords and their exploitative rackets, yet 'Mr. Squeaky Clean' Lewis was banging his subject behind the scenes!

SHIVERS (1975)

(aka The Parasite Murders; aka They Came From Within)
Dir: David Cronenberg /Canada

> "I love sex, but I love sex as a venereal disease. I am syphilis. I am enthusiastic about it but in a very different way from you".

So said David Cronenberg on his rationale on his first commercial feature, Shivers, which caused an almighty stink in his native Canada but has since become regarded as one of the highlights of 70s horror. It's original, inventive, controversial, ironic, dangerous, and caused an instant notoriety. The film unfolds entirely in and around a luxury apartment block as the residents therein are infected by slug-like parasites that invade the human body, turning the hosts into sex-crazed maniacs. These creatures invade through any bodily orifice available - usually the mouth, but in a scene featuring scream queen Barbara Steele, the parasites are happy to make entrance through more private areas too. Of course, mass panic ensues as the uninfected try to escape and hide away from the hordes of horny homicidal sex addicts who run riot through the corridors and apartments, and Cronenberg has a blast playing against society's sexual taboos.

Shivers is as much Cronenberg's ironic comment on society as it is a horror film, laced with gross black humour and clever invention. It also displays his usual themes which would crop up again in his later work (and in that sense the film is similar to George Romero's Night of The Living Dead). His previous underground films like Stereo and Crimes of The Future were also brimming with his warped body-horror ideas, but Shivers took those obsessions and unleashed them on a mainstream audience. The film's isolated setting brings on a claustrophobic edge, and the 'monster' represents our own sexuality which was definitely a break from the norm at the time (and this also relates to Night of The Living Dead in which the monsters in that movie was our fellow man; even our neighbours, or loved ones, or ourselves). Cronenberg toys around with the antagonistic characteristics of the movie monster to an unsettling effect, and he's clearly having a good time subverting our biological needs. Even in today's climate of remake mania in Hollywood, no one has yet attempted an updating of Shivers; if a remake was done correctly, it would no doubt cause just as much controversy now as the original did back in the 70s.

Cronenberg struggled for years to find financing for the project and had almost given up on the idea and was preparing to go to Hollywood to work with Roger Corman when the Canadian Film Development Corporation (as they were then known) stepped forward and offered the relevant funding. However, even before the film had been released, Cronenberg found himself and his film in hot water as Shivers became a scandal in the Canadian press and would remain his most controversial film until Crash caused a similar stir in the British tabloids a couple of decades later.

The trouble started when film critic Robert Fulford was invited to a preview screening of the film as a gesture of goodwill by the producers at Cinepix. They had hoped for some mainstream acceptance for their exploitation title by having a renowned critic provide a review prior to its official release. The move horribly backfired when Fulford (under the pseudonym Marshall Delaney) wrote a damning piece entitled 'You should Know How Bad This Film Is. After All, You Paid For It', where he accused Shivers of being the most despicable and repulsive film ever made. He also pointed out that tax payer's money had financed the film and that it was a completely unacceptable way to spend public money. This moral panic spread like wildfire, and other so-called film critics attacked Shivers for similar reasons in the Toronto Globe and Mail, and the Montreal Gazette (who, to be fair, did allow Cronenberg to publicly defend his film in print). The scandal reached parliment, Cronenberg became a celebrity, and Shivers became the most successful home-grown movie in Canadian history. When people learned that Shivers was the only film funded by the CFDC that actually turned a profit for the taxpayer, the furore quickly died down, making Cronenberg the most bankable director in the country. And this allowed him to explore his obsessions further in projects like Rabid and The Brood, each with a more generous budget than before.

There were exceptions to the bad press though, Cinema Canada published a glowing review praising Shivers as a masterpiece of horror, and Cronenberg himself managed to turn the tide of criticism in his favour when asked to account for his work, "The true subject of horror films", he said "is death and anticipation of death, and this leads to the question of man as body as opposed to man as spirit".

Shivers has since been accepted as an innovative genre classic, with its daring and unflinching probe into social-sexual taboos of the time - promiscuity, lesbianism, homosexuality, and even paedophilia and incest - The film can also be seen as a journey through the historical evolution of the horror movie as a legitimate artform in its own right. On home video it has more or less managed to stay intact in most territories. The best option is the Region 0 DVD from Image; it's uncut and presents the best looking transfer of the film so far.

SHOCK (1977)

(aka Beyond The Door 2)
Dir: Mario Bava /Italy

Dora (the beautiful Daria Nicolodi), her new husband Bruno (John Steiner), and Dora's young son, Marco (David Colin Jr.) move into a new house where she recovers from having a nervous breakdown. Things don't go to plan though as the young boy is easily bored and quite a prankster in the household. Turns out Dora's ex-husband was a heroin addict who committed suicide seven years previously, and new hubby Bruno is keen to keep the cellar door locked... Meanwhile, Marco's pranks become increasingly disturbing and perverted; he invades his mother's bedroom drawers, cuts up her panties, and utters casual sentences such as "Mama, I have to kill you..." Has her son been possessed by the evil spirit of her ex-husband, or is Dora simply having another breakdown?

A Bay of Blood may have been more graphically gruesome, Rabid Dogs more claustrophobic, and Black Sunday more influential, but Shock is easily Mario Bava's creepiest and most disturbing film. A masterpiece of psychological horror that boasts a career-best performance from Nicolodi, a superb and haunting theme tune by I Libra, and a tightly woven script by Dardano Sacchetti. Just like Joe D'Amato's Buio Omega, Shock was also released on dreadful pan-and-scan VHS copies that looked awful and muggy, and this led to many fans and critics dismissing the film. The DVD release by Anchor Bay, however, is a revelation (but currently out of print); the colours and image are fully restored, adding to the unsettling mood of the film.

Bava was aided in this his last film by his son, Lamberto (who went on to direct Macabre and Body Puzzle), and the pair offer up some of the most effective scares of their careers; there's the sequence near the end where little Marco runs towards his mother on the landing, and I guarantee that scene will scare the crap out of you. That scene alone has had a clear influence on Japanese scare-monger, Hideo Nakata, whose Ringu, and especially Dark Water, are loaded with similar chills. There's also the very creepy scene where the little boy softly strokes his mum while she sleeps, and then the camera cuts to his perspective, or perhaps the perspective of her deceased husband, Carlo, whose large rotting hands caress her neck... The scene with the wardrobe is reminiscent of Roman Polanski's Repulsion, and the ambiguities relating to Dora's mental health relate to that classic American horror, Let's Scare Jessica To Death. Dora's hallucinations are all expertly done and produce quite a chill. Whether her son is possessed, or if she is insane, or if Bruno is helping or harming her, are never really made clear, and the ambiguities are admirably kept at a knife edge until the very end of the film.

The hint of possession led to the film being re-titled Beyond The Door 2 for its Stateside release, implying that it was a sequel to Ovidio G Assonitis' Beyond The Door, a cheesy Exorcist clone, and of course this did Bava's underrated classic no favours at all.

SHOWGIRLS (1995)

Dir: Paul Verhoeven / USA

Bad boy of flash-trash cinema and intellectual Dutchman Paul Verhoeven once again teamed up with the equally trashy but not so intellectual writer Joe Eszterhas after their box-office success with Basic Instinct, and together they wallow in the Hollywood gutter, offering big-screen sleaze, lurid exploitation, and just about every tacky and tasteless cliche possible. The result was almost universally despised by the critics but became an instant cult phenomenon as gobsmacked cineastes struggled to make sense of the multi-million Dollar monstrosity which unspooled before their eyes.

Showgirls centres on Nomi Malone (Elizabeth Berkley), a lowly stripper who finds that becoming a showgirl often goes hand in hand with the seedier side of life. She makes it as a 'private dancer' at the Cheetah Club before making it to the big time in a casino show called Goddess. En route to this ambitious wish-fulfilment we follow Nomi's lewd antics backstage where she flits between night club owner Zack (an almost comotose Kyle McLachlan) and out-of-work songwriter James (an atrocious performance from Glenn Plummer).

It's a bloody awful film but it's also understandable how it became such a cult favourite; like an ensuing car crash you just can't look away. Director Verhoeven is no stranger to adding a bit of gratuitous and sleazy entertainment value to his Hollywood epics, be it the excessively violent gunning-down of Murphy in Robocop, or the three-titted whore in Total Recall ("I sometimes wish I had three hands!"), or Sharon Stone flashing the gash in Basic Instinct, but in Showgirls he takes that cheeky fan-boy attitude and pushes it to unprecedented levels. The film's adult orientation, tacky sex scenes, and revealing dialogue earned it an NC-17 rating in America, with many provincial cinemas refusing to screen it (and this led to one of Variety magazine's all-time great headlines, "Stix Nix Naughty Pix"). Verhoeven had anticipated some flak and he even generously refused to accept his $6 million pay packet until the film turned a profit (which it didn't, it flopped quite badly). Eszterhas wasn't so kind, and he was attacked mercilessly in the press for his screwball screenplay which includes such priceless lines as "I'm not a whore, I'm a dancer". Madonna and Drew Barrymore were originally wanted for the roles of Gina Gershon and Elizabeth Berkley, but fortunately for them, they declined. In a panic at the critical mauling the film was being subjected to, United Artists re-promoted the film for midnight screenings in LA as a way to try and generate the same campy following of The Rocky Horror Picture Show and the like, with gangs of drag queens parading cue cards and free lap dances for the audience.

Out of 14 of the UK's leading critics, only one enjoyed the film (well, only one dared to admit he liked it), in America it was 2 out of 34. It has been described as "Shallow", "Prurient", "Voyeuristic", and "Exploitative", but in the right mood those kinds of accusations can become attributes. Indeed, there's something undeniably appealing to many viewers in its misguided ethics: The voyeuristic sleaze which the film purports to expose and condemn is simultaneously exploited for cheap thrills and giggles in the audience. Overall, the only thing to be exposed really was Verhoeven's hypocrisy (he just couldn't resist, could he?).

SICK GIRL (2007)

Dir: Eben McGarr / USA

Perfect for a triple-bill with Katiebird and Header, Sick Girl is a film that will test the patience of those who dislike micro-budget horror and those who are uncomfortable with kid-on-kid violence and murder, but does offer a few nuggets of interest to those who are willing to overlook its cheap origins and lapses in taste.
 Izzy (Leslie Andrews) boards a school bus, beats up and then pisses on a nun. She then calmly murders a couple of louts in a nearby field. Turns out that Izzy is an orphan (we never find out what happened to her parents, maybe she killed them too?), and is homicidally protective of her younger 'brother' who is a constant target for school bullies. Izzy's ways of dealing with said bullies is to unleash a barrage of cruelty and sadism in her calm and collected way, and this often leads to some spectacularly brutal set-pieces. But all this countryside mayhem leads to some harsh consequences later on...

Much more technically proficient and atmospheric than the usual SOV crap that has polluted video stores in recent years, Sick Girl nevertheless has been labeled as 'torture porn' in some circles by those quick to judge its relentless abuse of characters as simply gratuitous and for the sole purpose of entertainment. Alas, they're wrong; it's definitely not torture porn, there is so much more going on here for it to be pigeon-holed into that category (the 'torture porn' label was a term coined by someone who despised that particular sub-genre anyway, so it's ironic how horror fans still use it often, even as a term of recommendation!). That's not to say that Sick Girl is an easy ride; no doubt some viewers in the age of post-Columbine were shocked and outraged by the attitude and imagery on screen, but you're just as likely to find fans of the film who appreciate the dark humour, gritty shooting style, and nods and winks to the horror genre as a whole. Look out for 80s horror icon Stephen Geoffreys (of Fright Night, 976-Evil, and Evil Ed fame) who plays Izzy's anxious teacher, and who provides a very interesting interview on the Synapse DVD. Also check out the film's homage to Andrew Birkin's The Cement Garden, and some very tawdry twists on Oliver Twist that will never seem innocent again.

SILIP: DAUGHTERS OF EVE (1986)

Dir: Elwood Perez / Philippines

Unlike many modern shock movies that display a cynical edge to the cinematic extremes they delight in showing us, Silip is a whacked out movie hailing from a time when the shocking material on screen was depicted quite innocently.

This little known gem is the perfect movie to show those who think they've seen it all; a bizarre blending of cheesy melodrama, steamy sex, and gratuitous violence. It's like a tawdry old soap opera gone very very wrong.

In an isolated salt-making community under a baking hot sun, a group of children desperately plead with the local stud Simon (Mark Joseph) to spare a buffalo from being slaughtered. Simon ignores their cries and proceeds to beat the buffalo's head in with a club before skinning it and preparing lunch. The kids are so distraught at losing their pet in such a brutal way that one young girl is induced into having her first period. Simon spends his off-time sleeping with the local women in the village, and when happy-go-lucky Selda (Sarsi Emmanuelle) returns from a trip from Malta with her American boyfriend, she also tries to get him in the sack.

Meanwhile, Selda's devout sister, Tonya (former Miss Philippenes Maria Isabel Lopez), runs a bible class for the kids and punishes her own feelings of sexual desire by rubbing handfuls of salt onto her cooch. And it isn't very long before the eccentric little village is torn apart by uncontrollable lusts, brutal bloody violence, gang rape, and misguided mob justice.

If Alejandro Jodorowsky and Fernando Arrabal were to remake The Wicker Man with a bit of Who Can Kill a Child? thrown in for good measure, chances are it would look something like this. A couple of scenes stray very close to hardcore but this is not a straight-up sex movie, it's far too bizarre and disjointed for that. Sarsi Emmanuelle steals the show as the Westernised and outspoken Selda, whose promiscuous dalliances cause the delicate mores of the village to collapse. Lopez is also fantastic in her role as the devout Tonya, with her hysterical preaching and patronising ways coming across like Dr. Quinn Medicine Woman on drugs. Her warning to the young girl who has just started menstruating typifies the crackpot mentality of the whole film:

Tonya - "We all reach the age where we're easily tempted. The Devil is constantly around us. He is always waiting for a mistake so that he can... so that he can tempt us into... into committing a mortal sin. And the ones that he tries most to tempt are girls having their first period, like you."

Girl - "But how do you know who the Devil is?"

Tonya - "He appears in the form of a young man. Those with large organs are devils, that is the true source of the Devil's evil powers here on Earth."

Girl - "Huh? Does that include my father too?"

Made at a time of relaxed censorship in the Phillippenes under the rule of Imelda Marcos, Silip, along with better-known titles like Scorpio Nights and Snake Sisters (also starring the beautiful Lopez) were being churned out by filmmakers who were given the green light to explore the seedier side of life in their movies. Bizarrely, the profits gained from those sleazy epics were channeled into funding various cultural schemes throughout the country.

The film barely saw any distribution outside of its native land except for a scarce VHS release that was dubbed into English, but very few people saw it before it sunk into oblivion. Mondo Macabro released it on DVD in the late 00s in a nicely framed transfer that restores the rich colours, the original language with English subs, and also Lutgardo Labad's original score for the film, all of which were lost in that horribly brown, VHS pan-and-scan job. The DVD also includes the hilarious dub track; just check out the scene where Selda's American boyfriend has a fight with Simon and then storms back to his shack and demands a blowjob from Tonya - Absolutely priceless dubbing.

THE SINFUL DWARF (1973)

(aka Abducted Bride)
Dir: Vidal Raski / Denmark

The sleaziest dirty dwarf movie ever made. This film follows the depraved title character (former kids TV favourite, Torben Bille), who lives in a crummy, dilapidated boarding house with his equally messed up mother. His favourite past-time is to lure young women into the house (including a teenage girl who is taken against her will after following a wind-up toy puppy to her doom). Once the women are inside, he strips them, locks them in the attic, gets them hooked on smack, and then pimps them out to a group of shady clients. Meanwhile, a young couple have booked a room at the place, and when wifey disappears, it's up to the husband to find out what the hell is going on in the house of horrors...

With a title that is both crude and accurate, The Sinful Dwarf has been an underground video hit for years, enticing and amusing jaded horror and sleaze buffs for the best part of three decades. And the film itself doesn't disappoint in the way it lives up to its salacious name and sick reputation. Bille is spot-on as the titular dwarf who procures the unwilling smack whores with a leering cheeky-chappy smile on his lips. The other cast members aren't so good, but most of 'em are only there to writhe around naked, suffering withdrawals and rape. The set 'design' works perfectly; the dirt, decay, and overall grimness of the boarding house reflects the whole premise and mindset of the film (why anyone would pay to spend the night in that shit hole is beyond me). These aesthetics of filth were later replicated in Joel M. Reed's Bloodsucking Freaks, especially the scenes featuring the caged women who look like they've just stepped out of Raski's film, with the same grubby lighting and dirty decor.

After a luke-warm reception in its native land, The Sinful Dwarf was picked up by exploitation legend Harry Novak for a stateside release under his company, Box Office International (under the new title Abducted Bride).Whether the film's original makers saw a payday from the American drive-in theatres is unknown, but Novak was notorious for ripping people off, so I wouldn't bank on it.

Something Weird Video released the film on DVD-R because apparently it proved to be too outrageous to be released as part of their official stock. Severin released two versions of the film; the original cut, and also a hardcore version that runs for an extra four minutes and includes some very unattractive body-double shunting (this version was also released in Denmark as a 2 disc set). In the UK the film simply went under the radar, freaking out many a viewer when it was broadcast on cable TV in the mid-00s.

SNUFF 102 (2007)

Dir: Mariana Peralto / Argentina

Snuff 102 is about a hot young student reporter (Andrea Alphonso) who is investigating the existence of snuff movies and winds up landing herself a starring role in one. There are also other sub-plots along the way showing how the other women found themselves in snuff hell, including a pregnant drug addict who is lured to a horrendous death by a man whom she trusts.

This film is, without a doubt, one of the most disturbing I have ever seen. It's right up there with Men Behind

The Sun and Nekromantik 2 in terms of its sheer onslaught of nightmare imagery and sick ideas. First we get an intro card that reads: "WARNING. Torture scenes documented in this film are real. Caution is recommended to sensitive viewers". And although the film isn't real per se, there is some very nasty stuff here including some genuine pics and clips. The intro was simply a way to make the audience feel uncomfortable and on edge (Blair Witch, Snuff, and The Texas Chainsaw Massacre all deployed similar tricks in an effort to make us believe the events depicted were real).

The film opens with a scene of a lab monkey being fed on something (don't know what), grainy 8mm black and white footage of a rotting corpse in a bath tub being cut into pieces by a man with a saw, some real animal killing and cruelty (a squealing pig is dragged outside by farmers and has its throat cut), some still images of murder and accident victims that look definitely real. The film is so well put together in terms of creating that gritty realism of bits of scrap footage cobbled together, it's hard to tell what's real and what isn't. I even asked myself the question that most extreme movie devotees will ask themselves at least once in their lives: What the hell am I doing watching this? Forget August Underground's Mordum, this is the real deal sick shit.

Borrowing a riff from Japanese AV shocker Muzan-e, we eventually fall into a narrative with the young lady reporter who is investigating some brutal killings of prostitutes in the local area. Her quest leads inevitably to the web where we get to see more footage that looks just way too real (might even be real); a man having his throat cut wide open with blood gushing out, fingers hacked off, an S&M clip of a woman having her nipples nailed to a table... The woman then interviews some local expert on snuff. This expert sounds like he has read his Jean Baudrilard and kind of serves as a commentator for the atrocity exhibition on screen (much like Baudrillard himself, when he was alive, calmly picking away at the fault-lines of our modern culture).

To see a guy punching a woman in the face about fifteen times would be off-putting in any other film, but here it's actually a relief, because it's so lame and unconvincing you know it isn't real. The very next scene, however, features someone having their fingers cut off one by one, and it puts you back on edge again because it looks like it could be real. The special effects are generally outstanding in this film and they blend in so perfectly with the mondo shock footage that it becomes very difficult to ascertain real from fake footage. Only when we're firmly established in the viewing experience do we find our feet and know what's what.

There is also another plot-line concerning the pregnant drug addict who is lured to her death, and I won't even mention what happens to her (apparently, viewers at the Mar Del Plata International Film Festival were so outraged at this sequence, thinking it was real, a man in the audience took action and beat the crap out of director Peralta while the film was still playing). I should mention though that it's the editing and camera angles that give the game away and confirm to us that it isn't real (this is not a documentary style film, although it does feel that way early on). Still, this is a devastating film. If you want to have your face shoved into the abyss then this is for you.

SOCIETY (1989)

Dir: Brian Yuzna / USA

Many film directors start out in the horror genre as a way of making an immediate impact, and once their credentials are in place they often move on to bigger things, or at least projects that are different (Sam Raimi, Stuart Gordon, Abel Ferrara, et al). Brian Yuzna, however, has always been a true lover of horror films and has always stubbornly stayed within the mushy template of the genre. Even his lesser projects like The Dentist and The Dentist 2 show an unpretentious admiration for the simple mechanics of old skool horror, combined with his love for deranged - but also often sympathetic - monsters, and bold, primary-coloured day-glo aesthetics. He is chiefly remembered today for his racy sequels to Re-Animator which heaped on the twitching body parts and sick laughs, but even in his darker films like Necronomicon and Return of The Living Dead Part 3, his desire to break new ground is always perfectly balanced with a strange satire and morbid sense of fun.

Yuzna's most extraordinary film was his directorial debut, Society, one of the many highlights of 80s horror but which remains a much overlooked gem. The plot of Society centres on former Baywatch boy Billy Warlock, whose alienation and increasing paranoia makes him afraid and weary of his own family. His friend Blanchard (Tim Bartell) is just as suspicious as Billy, and sets about snooping around the family mansion and gathering audio recordings which seem to suggest that some kind of incestuous orgies are going on. But when Billy's friend dies in a nasty car wreck, the film's hero must continue on his journey to find out exactly what is going on, during which he will discover the literal meaning of the word 'butthead' and will get to the guts of the matter as people are literally pulled inside out...

Society is a film which plays on the nightmare of teenage angst, and those feelings of paranoia, persecution, and alienation; not just in society at large, but within the family unit. The film should have propelled Yuzna to the horror A-list but it didn't happen, perhaps because Society is also an unashamed attack on bourgeois appetites and the cliquiness of the Hollywood elite. The special effects were created by Screaming Mad George (of A Nightmare On Elm Street fame) whose show-stopping finale has left many viewers gagging in delight and disgust as he graphically obliterates the line between pornography and horror. Surreal, metaphorical, and visually astonishing, this sequence was only made possible with the aid of gallons of KY jelly and tons of special effects goo, and one truly warped imagination. Enjoy!

SOMBRE (1998)

Dir: Phillip Grandieaux /France

If you're looking for some big screen sleaze in the manner of William Lustig's Maniac, built on thrills, spills, and spectacular human suffering, then I'd advise you to look elsewhere because in Sombre, director Grandieaux simply refuses to play that game. Instead we're offered almost two hours of character study of a man (Marc Barbe who looks a bit like Mark E. Smith) whose mad urges to kill are shattered by his own tortured sense of guilt and fractured state of mind. Similar to Henry-Portrait of a Serial Killer in mood and in the way most of the murders are off-screen, this is a bleak and harrowing film where the desolate surroundings seem to reflect the killers mind. His emotional baggage and traumatic mysterious past have led Jean to the killing and disposing of prostitutes. It's dull and pretentious in places and is more likely to make an audience feel depressed rather than excited (so fans of Friday The 13th should look elsewhere for their kicks). The killer himself is a shell of a man, a useless waste of space, and it's a credit to the filmmakers that he didn't become some overly sympathetic 'tragic figure'. That's not to say that Sombre is an easy going; some viewers no doubt will find it too much to take.

   The killer becomes friendly with a girl called Claire, despite the fact that he has attempted to kill her sister, and she tags along with him on his murder spree. A mutual dependency seems to bond the pair based on Jean's 'seeing the light' in Claire's innocence, and Claire seeing Jean as a person in need, a man whom she can attempt to save. Sombre has caused much scandal with critics over the years because in Claire's character there seems to be a part of her that yearns to be a victim herself. But director Grandieux refuses to confirm or deny this idea. He also chooses to avoid a traditional backstory to explain the roots of Jean's sickness; indeed he seems to refuse the whole idea of psychology altogether in his film, and it's left very much up to the viewers to work out what's going on in the heads of these tragic characters. Faces are often blank and expressionless, the dialogue is kept to a minimum, and all physicalities are limited to the basic human functions of consumption, sex, and violence. In this respect, Grandieux as an artist is treading similar territory as people like Wyndham Lewis and Bret Easton Ellis, both of whom view the world and its people in terms of exteriors and surfaces, language and body language, and the disinclination to delve directly into the workings of the mind. And Grandieux's lack of emotion in his portrayal of moral decay perhaps stems from an outraged morality (as it does with Bret Easton Ellis), a feeling of despair in a world full of numbness where the only way to truly experience anything is by way of murder and death itself.

SPLATTER: NAKED BLOOD (1996)

(Orig title: Nekeddo buraddo: Megyaku)
Dir: Hisayasu Sato / Japan

A young crazy genius develops an endorphin called 'My Son' and injects it into the young women at his mother's medical lab who are involved in contraceptive research. The serum has the effect of turning pain into pleasure and sadness into happiness, but young Eigi totally miscalculates how dangerous the potion can be when the med lab girls begin to show some alarming behaviour; one of the girls takes body piercing to fatal extremes, and another quite literally eats herself to death. Eiji's mother eventually discovers the truth and watches as her boy injects the rest of the serum into himself. Mother and son then get it on for a bit of incestuous 'bump n grind' whilst hooked up to a bizarre kind of dream stimulating machine, a place where extreme violence is the ultimate pleasure...

Naked Blood doesn't really heat up until after the half hour mark, but when it does get going it doesn't let up. It's very similar in style to the films Sato made in the 80s like Wife Collector, Brain Sex, and Genuine Rape (which this film just happens to be a remake of), and shares with those films the themes of alienation, voyeurism, isolation, and perversity. But here Sato also adds a welcome dose of Cronenbergian outlandishness and body horror to the mix. The scenes where the girl deep fries her own hand, plucks out her own eyeball, and then proceeds to eat both are perhaps some of the most deranged imagery in the director's ouevre. His films remind me of the work of Jean Rollin in the way he has a knack of turning micro-budget filmmaking into dark lyrical dreamscapes on film. His movies are best watched at night in a hazy frame of mind where the quiet build-up leads to maximum effect.

Naked Blood is one of the better examples of the Ero-guro sub-genre (or 'erotic-grotesque'), a Japanese filmic trend which infuses sexual themes with potent body horror. On its travels around the world, Sato's film has been clearing the aisles with its extreme material being too much to handle for some. Most notoriously, the Canadian premiere at the Pacific Cinematheque in Vancouver where less than a third of the audience made it through to the end credits. The gruesome special effects were created by the great Yuichi Matsui who went on to work on the Ringu series, and also Audition, Imprint, Ichi The Killer, and Kill Bill Vols. 1 and 2. Filmmaker Noboru Iguchi paid tribute to Naked Blood with the deep fried scene in Machine Girl. High praise!

STOIC (2009)

Dir: Uwe Boll /Canada/Germany

I'm starting to like Uwe Boll more and more. As a director he leaves a lot to be desired in terms of technicalities and aesthetics, but he instinctively knows which stories are worth telling. Stoic charts the aftermath of a prisoner's suicide. His cellmates take turns at explaining the events that led to the tragedy - But what is true and what is bullshit? At first, the surviving cellmates seem genuinely upset and sorry for their 'friend', but when we learn of the harsh victimization this young man went through before his death, it leaves us wondering whether they really give a shit at all, and suspect that they're actually just passing the buck to save their own skins, morphing the truth, Rashomon-style.

Most of the film takes place entirely in the prison cell with the four characters, and it's a lonely place. It's their whole world for 23 hours a day. The boredom that breeds the violence and humiliation they inflict on the weakest of the group. Devil makes work for idle thumbs and all that. The man is forced to eat a full tube of toothpaste and drink coffee mixed with salt and pepper. But it gets worse; when he vomits, he is forced to eat it all up again, and then he is pissed on, badly beaten and raped. Another inmate (Ed Furlong) then rapes him in the arse with a mop handle while he's laid out semi-conscious. Around the hour mark the situation becomes even more intense when the prisoners decide that the young man should hang himself before he gets the chance to report to the authorities...

John Hillcoat's Ghosts...Of The Civil Dead (1988) explored similar themes but was never as intense and claustrophobic as this. Both films share the same message too, that the prison and judicial systems are fucked and do more harm than good. Towards the end of the film the inmates turn their attentions to the next lowest in the pecking order, and it's quite clear that he's next for some similar treatment.

STOP THE BITCH CAMPAIGN (2001)

Dir: Kosuke Suzuki / Japan

A couple of disgruntled losers decide to use the services of a bunch of schoolgirl street whores and run away without paying, causing a major street war between the whores and the pussy swindlers! Based on the Manga by madness and rape-loving Hideo Yamamoto (the man who created Ichi The Killer), Stop The Bitch Campaign is outrageous fun from start to finish. The Boss (played by Kenichi Endo) is superb as the out-of-control rapist; the scene where he deflowers and tortures a first time whore is dark, misogynistic, and funny as hell! The soundtrack throws up 60s style retro garage rock, classical choruses, and country pop shit, all adding to the mayhem on screen. The crazy opening credits feature all kinds of sex, torture, and S&M in a rapid montage style, and the chaos never lets up. A fast-paced sleaze fest of guilty pleasures. Enjoy!

STOP THE BITCH CAMPAIGN 2 - HELL VERSION (2004)

Dir: Kosuke Suzuki /Japan

The mayhem continues with a ragtag band of perverts who are blindfolded and driven to an exclusive brothel where they get to indulge in their wildest fantasies. Cue much hilarity as we get to witness Baby perv, 'Michael' perv, Rape perv, and Vegetable perv do their thing. But the fun doesn't last for long as dead bodies are found, and it seems there is a killer on the loose killing the whores... The brothel is run by the beautiful Sori Aoi, a survivor from Part one. She seems a bit paranoid and constantly on edge about what is going on under her roof, and she is plagued by nightmarish memories of the scary make-up man from the previous film (actor Kenichi Endo who stole the show in part one also plays the vege-perv in this sequel). But when the shit hits the fan, it's up to Aoi to save the day... Less of a 'Whodunnit' and more of a tacky and tasteless sleaze fest, Stop The Bitch Campaign 2 runs just less than an hour and passes by in a flash, leaving you wanting more. There's no blood or gore, unfortunately, but is a highly entertaining shitfest nonetheless.

THE STORY OF O (1975)

Dir: Just Jaeckin /France

This softcore classic was banned in the UK for 25 years and was only deemed fit for consumption in the year 2000 when it was the subject of some illegal screenings in this country. The BBFC were then forced into making a decision, and like The Texas Chainsaw Massacre, which had been outlawed for a similar length of time and had also been screened without a certificate, both films were then passed uncut by the board.

The Story of O followed in the footsteps of director Just Jaeckin's previous film, Emmanuelle, which was a big hit and helped secure some mainstream acceptability for softcore sex, and spawned countless sequels, cash-ins, and foreign rip-offs. But whereas Emmanuelle was a delicate adaptation of Arsans cult novel, Jaeckin decided to up the ante the next time around by focusing on Pauline Reage's scandalous tale of a woman's journey into sexual awareness through the dangerous pleasures of sadomasochism. By taking another explicit novel, Jaeckin hoped to ape the success of his previous film, but instead it was banned outright by the British censors who accused it of being "Utterly filthy".

It's not a great film, but it does stick quite closely to Reage's text (except for the ending which sees O commit suicide in the novel). The film's strength lies in its beautiful soft-focus visuals and the fact that former fashion photographer Jaeckin adds a sweeping and epic quality to the story and is quite an ambitious and audacious attempt to break away from the run-of-the-mill softcore erotica which was being churned out en masse during the 70s. The film was quite popular with audiences (despite one critic who famously complained that it bared so much flesh he was considering vegetarianism), and has become a landmark in softcore, finding echoes in later works like Stanley Kubrick's Eyes Wide Shut and (more explicitly) in Catherine Briellat's Romance. Indeed, it was successful enough to warrant a sequel in 1984, Story of O 2, which the less spoken about the better. Reage even followed up O with Return To Roissy, which was very loosely adapted for the screen by Japanese provocateur Shuji Terayama in the early 80s for the unforgettable Fruits of Passion, which goes to show that there was still much life in the legend yet.

Mysteriously, the BBFC still hasn't made it clear why The Story of O was banned in the UK for so long. It's no more explicit than Jaeckin's other work like Emmanuelle and Lady Chatterly's Lover, both of which suffered some slight trims by the censors. One can only assume it was the sadomasochistic angle which offended the board. The British have had a long and difficult relationship with the idea of consensual mutilation, with real life scandals like the Spanner Case in the 90s and the filmic misadventures of Barbert Schroeder's Maitresse and David Cronenberg's Crash all provoking the wrath of the authorities on these shores. This in contrast with the French whose main objection to the film was in its depiction of women, with France's First Minister for Women's Affairs criticising Jaeckin and his film for presenting a harsh and stifling depiction of feminine sexuality; which is ironic considering how liberal the film is compared with Reage's book.

SUBURB MURDER (1992)

Dir: Jeng Kin-Ping / Hong Kong

British rule in Hong Kong had always forbid filmmakers from attacking their imperial majesty and from depicting their rulers in a bad light. Suburb Murder, however, looks to have escaped the scandal sheet perhaps because it's a tale based on a true story, but the finished film can barely disguise its resentment, and does little to sugarcoat its anti-colonialist stance, and pushes as far as the rule of law will allow.

A young woman and her grandfather stumble upon a mutilated body while jogging in the hills and they report their discovery to the local police. The body is that of a young white woman who looks to have had her face smashed in and her nipple bitten off. An investigation is launched. A tip-off leads the police to the hideout of a wanted gang, and a gun battle ensues with the gang members desperate to escape. One young rogue is captured and beaten by the police. In custody he is beaten some more and interrogated, and he agrees to tell the police the full story of his crimes in exchange for a cigarette. Cue a lengthy flashback as the kid explains his side of the story, a la Daughter of Darkness and The Untold Story.

Kang's only childhood friend was Chi, a chubby kid who was taken by his father to live in America. Kang plays truant one afternoon and goes home to witness his father catching mum fucking another guy. The guy jumps out of the bedroom window and escapes in his underwear. Mother is slapped and thrown out of the house, and young Kang is also thrown out on his ear and told never to return again. And from then on the kid must fend for himself on the streets.

As a young adult, Kang works as a dishwasher at a restaurant but his boss is an arsehole and is constantly looking for an excuse to dock his wages. Kang and his co-workers have formed a gang and they go out looking for trouble; they find a young couple and beat the boyfriend and gang-rape the girl. They then head back to work and beat the crap out of their boss. A passing policeman sees the incident and gives chase but the boys make their getaway on foot. Kang bumps into his old friend Chi who is back in Hong Kong after the death of his father. Kang takes him back to his living quarters but the other boys are in the middle of a sex sesh with a couple of young women, and Chi is shocked by the unabashed coupling on display. The arsehole boss sends out some heavies to attack the gang with clubs and iron bars, and a mass brawl ensues in the middle of the street.

The gang go to have some fun at a whorehouse and one of the older hookers turns out to be Kang's mother who he hasn't seen for years (this only becomes clear after two of his friends have slept with her). Kang feels upset and betrayed, and his resentments start to simmer under the surface. He and his old friend Chi make a pittance by washing cars, one of which belongs to his father who looks him over like a piece of garbage and throws a couple of Dollars in his face. Kang's father looks to have done well for himself over the years since he severed all ties with him and his mother; he drives a nice car and wears an expensive suit. Kang's humiliation continues when he helps a white woman with her bag from the boot of a taxi but she refuses to give him a tip. He shouts abuse at her and then he is arrested by a white man for begging offences. In custody he bumps into his father yet again who looks to be employed by the city, but he refuses to bail out his son.

Kang later gets himself a girlfriend, Kitty, and on her birthday the gang have a little party for her and get drunk (everyone seems to drink San Miguel in Hong Kong). Whilst walking her home, they stop by at King's Park for a drunken sing song; Chi decides he wants some wine and heads off to the shop, Kang and Kitty stay behind and have a smooch, but the merry mood is spoiled when a pair white thugs show up and beat Kang before raping Kitty. Chi returns to the hills to see what's going on and he attacks the thugs with a stick, but he is beaten with a rock and left paralyzed. Kitty runs into the middle of the road and is run over by a passing van and killed.

From now on Kang is like a time-bomb ready to explode, and when he and his gang get drunk and go roaming the hills at King's Park, they spot a young Western couple sitting on the grass. The boyfriend is badly beaten, and then his hands are tied and Kang finally explodes; he takes a tree branch and repeatedly beats the guy's head in with it. He then approaches the others who are gang-raping the woman, and he pushes them aside and then beats her head in with the stick and even bites her nipple off in a psychotic rage. The others have to drag him away. The girl's lifeless body is then thrown into the tall grass and they flee the area.

After a violent robbery at a gambling den with the use of guns and machetes, the boy's days are numbered. Their pictures are broadcast on the news and they fall out and turn on each other. One of the gang members, Hairy, is captured by CID and he later informs officers of the gang's hideout. And the story comes full circle when the police show up for a blazing gun battle.

This downbeat tale from Hong Kong is atypical of the usual CAT III madness in that it is played unsettlingly straight; there's none of the usual dark humour or hammy psycho performances or bold candy coloured lighting effects to be found here. What we get instead is an absorbing and believable study of encroaching madness brought on by a string of humiliations and bad luck, and has more in common with Fu Lee and Chu Yin-Ping's Angel Heart than Herman Yau's The Untold Story. It still offers the obligatory CAT III sex scenes and a steady build-up to a grim and violent finale, but at the same time it feels completely out of step with the works of Yau and Billy Tang, and Bosco Lam, et al. The rape scenes are as graphic and exploitative as most Hong Kong titles, and the killing of the young woman at the end is extremely nasty and disturbing; Kang's resentment has reached such a fever pitch of discontent that even to see an innocent couple spending some time together in the park is enough to make his blood boil and sends him completely over the edge. And director Jeng Kin-Ping should be commended for depicting the seething resentments that simmer under the surface of society in a completely honest and brutal fashion. It's certainly not a film for everybody, and those new to the CAT III phenomenon will be turned off, but for those of you who are more familiar with these films may find it a refreshing change from the norm.

SUSPIRIA (1977)

Dir: Dario Argento / Italy

Suspiria is a dose of vintage Italian terror from the king of modern horror, Dario Argento. Shot in the late 70s in the aftermath of his international breakthrough hit, Deep Red, and anticipating his later shockers such as Inferno, Tenebre, Opera, and The Stendhal Syndrome, Suspiria is a sensory overload of black magic, madness, and death. It's a film which dispenses with his earlier giallo preoccupations and instead plunges the viewer into a dazzling technicolour nightmare where the irrational and supernatural evils are given free reign. Little wonder then that Argento has since become widely regarded as the quintessential Italian horror auteur.

The plot of Suspiria is deceptively simple; an American student, Suzy Banyan (Jessica Harper), arrives in Germany to enrol at the Tansakademie, an internationally renowned ballet school, where she eventually discovers that the place is run by an evil cabalist organisation headed by the 'Black Queen' Helena Markos. But it's the way Argento tells the story that makes the film so daring and innovative. The fluid and intoxicating camerawork, the extreme expressionistic style, and bold primary coloured lighting scheme lead the viewer mesmerized through a labyrinth of stylish sets and beautifully balletic murder set pieces. It's a film in which the character's physical realities are less important than their psychological states which are echoed in the meticulous set designs.

After the success of Deep Red, Dario Argento had become an avid reader of H.P. Lovecraft whose tales of cosmic terror were often linked with the author's own expansive mythology. A recurring theme for Lovecraft was an array of extremely powerful beings whose practice of the dark arts had led them to the outer realms from where they would inflict insanity, mutation, and chaos in the human and material world. Argento had never planned on bringing Lovecraft's work to the big screen, but after listening to stories from his wife (actress Daria Nicolodi) about her grandmother's troublesome experiences at a school with occult connections, Dario put two and two together and the stage was set for his most ambitious film to date...

Suspiria was radically different from the horror hits of the time in that it lacks the rationalist social minutae that was the backbone of other supernatural sagas like Stephen King's early novels, Carrie and Salem's Lot, and William Friedkin's The Exorcist (also that film's original novel by William Peter Blatty). Those tales prided themselves on creating everyday characters set in realistic backgrounds, ensuring that the sceptical reader/viewer would go along with the outlandish elements once firmly planted in the normal, everyday settings. Well, Argento certainly banished that idea (as did Stanley Kubrick a couple of years later with his adaptation of King's third novel, The Shining), and we're plunged almost immediately into the cinematic storm in Suspiria, where magic and menace is quite literally everywhere.

Music is also a key element in the film's audio-visual delirium, with Argento encouraging the prog rock group Goblin (credited as 'The Goblins' here) to freak out, resulting in one of the most memorable soundtracks in horror history. It's a tinkling nursery rhyme that builds with a mocking voice imitating the tune, and then reaches a crescendo of metallic drums, scary synths, and agonised screams. It's a perfect melding of sound and vision, and perhaps one of the film's greatest achievements overall, with the camera hungry for images that can match the heightened threat of the sounds. A sensory overload that strives to attain that "rational derangement of all the senses" that French poets like Rimbaud and Baudelaire were so fond of.

The all-female coven are in complete control, and all the male characters in the film are missing something (which amounts to a symbolic castration according to some of the characters); a young male dancer with no money is at the receiving end of cruel gossip and bad jokes, handyman Pavlos has no teeth due to a bout of gingivitus that Miss Tanner (Alida Valli) seems suspiciously amused about, pianist Daniel (Night Train Murders' Flavia Bucci) has no vision because he's blind ("Can't you see that?!"), and Little Albert, the young boy, seems to have no voice. The film as a whole lacks that male rationality that so typified the giallo in previous years (altough it did come under threat from Daria Nicolodi's character in Deep Red). In Suspiria, it's the feminine irrational that rules, and is considered for the most part to be destructive of the individual and of social structures as a whole. Men have absolutely no power in the film and at the same time it is unflinching in its depiction of feminine evil.

Whilst many are quick to pick upon gender issues relating to Argento's films, very few are willing to acknowledge the magical beliefs which adorned his work around this time. Gender studies and psychoanalysis are the critic's main tools of deduction when deciphering a film. However, they often come unstuck in their attempts to analyse the unruly mysticism in films like Suspiria and its follow-up, Inferno (also Kubrick's The Shining which left many scratching their heads when Jack Torrence's character is freed from a storage room by a ghost, thus dispensing with the idea that all ghostly apparitions and 'bumps in the night' can be blamed on everyday 'rational' occurrences like hallucination and mental illness, etc). Maitland McDonagh's book on Argento, Broken Mirrors/Broken Minds is a case in point; here she completely ignores the conversation between Suzy and Mandel (played by The Exorcist's Rudolph Schundler) in which he talks about the power of the occult: "They're malefic, negative, and destructive. Their knowledge of the art of the occult gives them tremendous powers. They can change the course of events, and people's lives, but only to do harm". This kind of dialogue is blasphemy for those devout materialists who rely on rational explanations in order to make sense of anything.

Overall then, Suspiria is a tremendous achievement, a feast for the eyes and ears, so full of mystery and wonder: Why is Miss Tanner smiling all the time? Does she know something we don't? Was that really red wine that Suzy poured down the sink, or was it something more sinister? And what's the deal with that beam of light that is shone into Suzy's face and causes immediate migraine and eventual collapse? Who knows. It's a film in which every door and curtain leads to more darkness and more mystery, and we're treated to some of the most extravagant murders in film history as Argento continues his obsession into the beautiful and sacrificial destruction of human bodies and minds.

A rare hit in the US for Argento, Suspiria was released by 20th Century Fox in an R-rated version that was trimmed of some of the violence. It became a collector's item in the 80s with the Venezuelan VHS and Japanese laserdisc both uncut. Magnum Entertainment later released the complete version in a widescreen transfer (it has since been released by Anchor Bay in a definitive 3 disc set). In the UK it wasn't passed uncut by the BBFC until the 90s.

SVIDD NEGER (2003)

(Burnt Nigger)
Dir: Eric Smith Meyer /Norway

Sporting a deliberately provocative title but containing nothing in the film that could label it as racist, Svidd Neger is nonetheless an outrageously black and bizarre comedy. It tells the story of a small group of neighbours who live in small huts and caravans out in the middle of nowhere. A hard drinking father (who looks a bit like Slavoj Zizek) wants the very best for his daughter, and to him that means she should marry a strong man and give him a grandson (he drowned his ex-wife and baby). The neighbours are just as fucked up and eccentric - the fat son who masturbates a lot and thinks he's the right man to impregnate the daughter, an incestuous mother who sits around reading magazines all day, and an adopted black kid who smokes a lot of dope, sleeps with a picture of Dolly Parton, and communicates with his natural father in Africa by putting messages in bottles and throwing them out to sea (!). Also living nearby is a Saami who is another admirer of the beautiful blonde daughter; problem is, he's just as crazy as the rest, and the situation all comes to a head of hillbilly debauchery with lots of explosions, violence, and gore, northern Norweigan style.

No plot outline can do this film justice though, and don't worry, no black people are burned either (maybe one or two whities). Many have compared the film to the work of David Lynch, but it actually bares a closer resemblance to the whimsical surrealism of Jim Jarmusch crossed with the slapstick sensibilities and creative camerawork of Sam Raimi.

The film caused much controversy even before it was released; the title alone brought accusations of irresponsibility and racism, and led to the film being reported to the European Court of Human Rights. And although Svidd Neger is very un-PC in places and boasts lots of twisted dark humour, it's actually a parody of how small-minded country folks expect a black person to be. The cast and crew who made the film are a multicultural group themselves. If you liked Taxidermia then you'll probably enjoy this too.

SWEET SWEETBACK'S BADASSSSS SONG (1971)

Dir: Melvin Van Peebles / USA

In the early 70s, a new strain of exploitation movies found their way into the grinders. And unlike the short-lived genres of yesteryear, like beach party flicks and biker epics which played mostly at drive-in theatres, this new breed of films played almost exclusively within urban areas. Blaxploitation had arrived with its kick-ass brothers and sisters, pimps, pushers, and super studs. Audiences flocked to the grindhouses excited to see black heroes finally make it to the big screen. The white middle class critics were scared shitless by these films, and they were also frowned upon by many in the black community who accused them of playing up to racial stereotypes and conveying the wrong type of messages. Nevertheless, for the next few years Blaxploitation dominated the inner-city screens with its funky threads, soul music, and 'kill whitey' revenge scenarios.

There had been a few forerunners to the genre, such as The Black Klansman and The Bus Is Coming, Honky, but things really kicked off in 1971 with the release of a couple of films that, although seemed to attract a similar audience, were very much polar opposites in terms of their origins and overall messages. One was MGM's Shaft, a slick detective yarn starring Richard Roundtree as a black crime fighter and boasted a supercool soundtrack by Isaac Hayes. The other was much more raw, angry, and confrontational; Melvin Van Peebles' Sweet Sweetback's Badasssss Song.

Written, directed, produced, and starring Peebles himself, and dedicated to "All the Brothers and Sisters who've had enough of The Man", Sweetback opens with the title character working in a brothel doing live sex shows. He is hassled by a couple of cops and witnesses a fellow black man being abused. He decides to take action and attacks the cops, bashing their heads in before fleeing on foot. The rest of the film follows Sweetback on the run through the backstreets and urban decay of Ghettoville, USA.

When the film made it into theatres audiences were dumbfounded. They had seen nothing like it before. Peebles didn't sugar-coat the film at all; it's a grim, gritty, angry, and unrelenting tirade and a call for social change. And there's nothing in the style or performances or overall message that even attempts to lighten the blow. This uncompromising stance was rewarded with an X rating from the American censors ("An all white jury" as the ads put it) who were threatened by the fact that a black anti-hero had brutally attacked the police and then successfully crossed the border into Mexico at the end, his crime going unpunished. The epilogue warns us to "Watch out... a badasssss nigger is coming back to collect some dues". It was the first in a new wave of Black Rage films and audiences were lining around the block to see it.

This ground-breaking film raked in more than $10 million in its first year (a profit margin which outstripped its big-budget counterpart, Shaft, which managed $12 million), and became one of the most financially successful indie movies of all time, prompting producers to embrace black actors and turn them into screen heroes with a healthy box office kerching making it all worthwhile. Thus Blaxploitation was born, but none of the subsequent productions (often starring icons such as Jim Brown, Jim Kelly, Pam Grier, and Fred Williamson) could quite live up to the original double-whammy of Sweetback and Shaft. The main reason being that Sweetback was for real, it was a film that came from the heart of Peebles, not from a lust for profit, unlike the other films in the genre. He washes the screen in pain in order to move audiences into action, and announces that black militancy has reached your neighbourhood and that the times they are a-changing.

The British censors passed Sweetback uncut and it remained that way for three decades until 2003 when the docudrama Badasssss! was released. Peebles had written to the BBFC assuring them that a scene in which a young boy loses his virginity to a prostitute in Sweetback was played by a man called Hubert Scales who was over eighteen at the time. However, Badasssss! makes it quite clear that it was actually Melvin's son, Mario, who played the part, and he could not have been older than fourteen at the time, thus putting the film in breach of the Protection of Children Act. The BBFC had no choice but to review their rating, and on the advice of a lawyer, they cut the scene to keep the film within the bounds of UK law.

TAXI HUNTER (1993)

(Orig title: Di shi pan guan)
Dir: Herman Yau / Hong Kong

In this CAT III shocker, Anthony Wong stars as a successful insurance agent who has endless trouble with the local taxi drivers. The skip him, rob him, and even kill his wife and unborn child! Something snaps in him and he goes on a killing spree, wiping out the scumbag cabbies (I'm not making this up!). The detective investigating the murders (Man Tat Ng) is a kick-arse cop with Jackie Chan-worthy stunts, and he just so happens to be an old drinking buddy of Wong's. So when he suspects his friend of committing the crimes, he is torn between sympathy for his buddy and his duty as a cop...

As with many CAT III titles, Taxi Hunter starts out as a broad comedy but darkens as it progresses. The action and violence is strong, bloody, comical, and absurd (there's also an amusing tribute to Scorsese's Taxi Driver where Wong does his own take on the "Are you talkin' to me?" speech). This was also filmed on a bigger budget than usual; here we have some highly choreographed fight scenes, stunts, crashes, shoot outs, and a superb car chase.

He makes for a clumsy and awkward urban avenger in his shirt and tie, but Wong is a CAT III superstar, king of the genre, and this is perhaps one of his most underrated performances. Wong himself has said it was his favourite role to date, "I think it is my best piece of work because that role involves a humanised character". He was relieved to play a good guy at last (well, at least a character whom the audience can cheer for) after years of being typecast as the bad guy due to the widespread racism in the Hong Kong film industry (Wong is mixed race, with a Chinese mother and British father).

As for director Yau, Taxi Hunter sees him at the top of his game. It's not quite as outrageous as his later efforts like The Untold Story and Ebola Syndrome, but shows much promise and hints strongly at the shock horror elements that would prevail in much of his subsequent work.

TENEBRAE (1982)

(aka Unsane)
Dir: Dario Argento / Italy

Best-selling crime author Peter Neal (Anthony Franciosa) arrives in Rome to promote his latest novel, Tenebre, but soon receives a threatening phone call and learns that there is an obsessed killer on the loose using his book as a blueprint for a string of murders. Inspector Germani informs him that a young shoplifter (the gorgeous Ania Pieroni) has been found with her throat cut and pages of his book stuffed into her mouth. Meanwhile, the killings continue to mimic events in the novel and Neal receives pictures of the murder victims in the post with quotes from his own work. His agent, Bullmer (exploitation legend John Saxon), and his assistant Anne (Daria Nicolodi, Argento's wife at the time) try to persuade him to leave town, but Neal decides to stay put and help out with the investigation. Even when the killer is finally dispatched, there still seems to be no end to the bloodbath.
   Seemingly constructed from a mountain of ideological influences, Tenebre actively demands its viewers to engage in subjective interpretation. Such a challenging assortment of interpretative texts is unheard of outside of art movies - Freudian angst, perception, psychoanalysis, gender studies, identity, an awareness of the work of Michelangelo Antonioni, etc - And it's interesting to note that Argento's creativity only started to dwindle once his films were taken seriously by intellectuals.

The word 'tenebre' literally means 'darkness', but the film itself is brightly lit with sunny outdoor locations and light modern interiors. Dario was referring to the darkness of the mind, or the subconscious, in the film's title (the bright aesthetic and colour schemes were also designed so that the victim's blood would be as visible as possible). And again, as with his previous work, Argento prefers to construct stories which self-consciously embrace the process of deduction and interpretation, and in the process anticipates the viewer's and critic's own analysis as it goes, subverting the thriller/giallo conventions and playing around with our preconceptions of gender and misogynous screen violence; victims scream and moan aloud as if they're having orgasms while they are cut, stabbed ('penetrated'), and strangled in stylish hyperreality, and the film is awash with surreal symbolism.

One of the greatest psycho movies ever made, Tenebre reunited Argento with DP Luciano Tovoli who lensed Suspiria, and Claudio Simonetti of Goblin who composed the catchy soundtrack. Argento was inspired to write the script after receiving threatening phone calls from a fan while in Los Angeles. And, as is the way of any artist of the macabre, he took that basic premise to its most startling extremes for a nightmare vision on film. His usual technical invention is also in full force here with a single crane shot that anticipates a double murder scene in which the camera ascends a builing, peers into the windows at the lives of the future victims, travels over the roof, and then descends down the other side. It's an audacious move and very typical of Argento at the time.

In the UK, the film was swept up in the video nasties controversy and banned in the mid-80s. It was passed by the BBFC in 1999 with cuts, and then passed completely uncut in 2003. In America it was badly truncated and even re-titled Unsane by the film's stateside distributers for a limited release. The Anchor Bay DVD is fully uncut.

TETSUO: THE IRON MAN (1988)

Dir: Shinya Tsukamoto / Japan

By pure coincidence 1988 saw the release of two unrelated Japanese films with characters called Tetsuo who mutate into oblivion; Katsuhiro Otomo's cult anime Akira, which became the first 'Manga movie' to achieve international recognition, reached its chaotic finale with delinquent teen Tetsuo bloating into a gigantic mess of oozing liquified body-mass, almost filling an Olympic-sized sports stadium with his blob-like enormity. It was Otomo's speciality: Body-horror for the wayward teen, and animation as a legitimate filmic art. The other was a no less delirious horror weirdy, Tetsuo: The Iron Man, a brutal and perverse meeting of technology, sex, and violence.

Shot in a rough and ready style on scraps of black and white 16mm film, Tetsuo The Iron Man makes up for its tiny budget limitations with a hyper-kinetic style and an inexhaustible imagination. The confusing 'plot' concerns a quiet salaryman (Tamoroh Taguchi, who later showed up in the Guinea Pig entry, Android of Notre Dame) who is freaked out by visions of transmutation, and who apparently killed a child in a hit-and-run accident. He tries to deal with the troubling memories by engaging in strange sex practices with his girlfriend (Kei Fujiwara, who would go on to direct a couple of her own cyberpunk entries with Organ and Organ 2). It soon becomes apparent that the kid survived the accident and has passed on a highly infectious disease which infects human flesh, transforming man into rampaging machine. And before long, Taguchi mutates into a metallic killing machine with a huge drillbit for a penis that he uses on his girlfriend in a gruesome sex attack before hitting the streets in a war with the now grown-up hit-and-run victim... or something like that.

Director Shinya Tsukamoto, who appears in the film as the self-mutilator who lives in the junkyard and inserts metal tubing into his open wounds, is clearly in his element here. It's a labour of twisted love with its hyperactive camera and rapid editing techniques. He also presents us with wild and unruly montage sequences made painstakingly with stop-motion animation techniques for an insane barrage of twisted nigtmarish imagery.

Tetsuo seems to take its inspiration from a wide variety of disparate sources; the most obvious reference points are perhaps as a heady mixture of elements from Eraserhead, Robocop, and The Evil Dead, with a heavy dose of Cronenberg and Jan Svankjmajer thrown in for good measure. But Tsukamoto takes these elements and mashes them into something completely delirious and original. The resulting film re-ignited the fledgling cyberpunk movement and became a midnight favourite in Tokyo before sweeping the globe and capturing the imagination of cult film fanatics the world over. So, if you're in the mood for fetishistic visual overload, the lack of a traditional linear plot, and a pure cinematic experience, then Tetsuo is for you.

TETSUO 2 - BODY HAMMER (1992)

Dir: Shinya Tsukamoto / Japan

The international success of Tetsuo The Iron Man awarded Tsumamoto with something resembling a budget this time around for a sequel-cum-remake. And like Sam Raimi's Evil Dead 2, Tsukamoto was ready to do it all over again in epic proportions for Tetsuo 2 - Body Hammer. This time, however, he also presents to us a backstory which helps explain all the chaos...

Borowing plot elements from Cronenberg's Scanners, Tetsuo 2's premise sees a visionary lunatic pitching his rival sons together in a war based on mind power. Tamoroh Taguchi returns as the 'salaryman' who is attacked by a pair of scary looking fellows who belong to a subterranean sect of shaven-headed followers who are prone to mutations. The two men shoot Taguchi in the chest with an infectious rivet gun and kidnap his little boy. In a fit of desperation, he chases the bad guys up onto the roof of a tower block where the kidnappers taunt him by dangling his child over the edge. Taguchi's fears and fury reach boiling point and he begins to mutate, and a strange gun breaks out of his chest. And in his attempts to finish the bad guys, he accidently shoots his own child, leaving nothing behind but lots of blood and a pair of tiny hands being held by one of the cackling kidnappers. Having to go home and explain all this to his wife understandably puts their relationship under severe strain. And when the kidnappers return and take off with her too, Taguchi's transmutations reach overdrive as he gradually becomes a human tank who is prepared to put his own loved ones in jeopardy in order to get even with his rivals. The underground sect, meanwhile, sees a new leader (Tsukamoto himself) who forces his way into power, and this man happens to be Taguchi's long lost brother who is no less adept at sprouting firearms from his body. And the war continues...

This time around, director Tsukamoto shot the film in colour with a murky comic book tint; in some scenes (especially the ones played out in broad daylight) he employs a shade filter over the lens giving the shots a strange orangey glow. For such a small budget film the visuals are no less than stunning throughout. He also resumes his love for the busy hand-held photography, rapid cutting, and bizarre stop-motion sequences which are perhaps more impressive than those seen in the original Tetsuo film. And there's a blatant homosexual subtext made apparent in the scenes featuring the shaven-headed army posing and pumping iron and penetrating their fellows with metal pipes.

The emotional side of the story is also improved upon in Tetsuo 2 with the backstory adding depth and dimension to the main characters. Most impressive though is the exploration of fury and the desire for revenge that becomes so great that wiping out your entire family is perfectly fine if it means getting one over on those who put them in danger in the first place. It's a trait that pertains the human condition but is rarely explored to any degree in film (consider for example how during hostage situations the police often have to restrain husbands, fathers, and sons from gaining entry into situations where their presence would spell disaster for those captive family members whom they care about the most. It's a 'curse' of masculinity that many men are in danger of jeopardising everything in times of crisis due to feelings of helplessness and a lack of control).

Tetsuo 2 stands as a film unto itself and you don't have to be familiar with the original in order to get to grips with this one. However, if you were impressed by Iron Man then chances are you'll be amazed by this full colour offering. Tsukamoto returned with a third installment of the Tetsuo series in 2010 with Tetsuo: The Bullet Man. It was shot on DV in English with a largely Western cast. Tsukamoto this time casts himself as the mutating anti-hero, and the film is good fun, although overall it lacks the unruly spark of mayhem and epic quality of the first two films.

THE TEXAS CHAINSAW MASSACRE (2003)

Dir: Marcus Nispel / USA

Platinum Dunes has alot to answer to. This off-Hollywood comapany has been at the forefront of the 00s remake mania, re-thinking, or 're-imagining' horror classics with varying degrees of success. While some may accept these remakes as an interesting way of keeping horror in the multiplexes, others are not so tolerant, accusing Platinum Dunes and their likes of churning out soulless fodder with ready-made brand names (Dawn of The Dead, Halloween, Hellraiser, etc), and ready-made plots as a cynical ploy to squeeze cash from long-established cinematic legends; a simple lazy money-maker with a ready-made market to tap into.

The remakes of The Hills Have Eyes (2006) and The Hitcher (2004) are arguably more impressive than the originals, but Platinum Dunes cocked up big time with A Nightmare On Elm Street (2010) and The Texas Chainsaw Massacre (2003).

The film opens with a group of teens driving through Texas in a Scooby Doo van. They pick up a disturbed hitch hiker (so far so familiar); but this hitcher isn't some crazed goon like in the original, but a victimised young woman who has presumably escaped some extreme ordeal. We don't really find out much about her though because no sooner has she entered the van and she removes a pistol from her cooch and shoots herself through the mouth. With a dead girl on their hands, these fun-seeking teens are brought back down to earth with a bump and decide to contact the police... However, what they get instead is R. Lee Ermey posing as a Sheriff, who is actually the patriach of an inbred clan of twisted cannibals. Well, the day goes from bad to worse for the youngsters when they find themselves on the family menu...

This remake dispenses with many crucial elements that helped make Hooper's original such a terrifying experience, and instead serves as a nominal entry in the decade's craze for updating genre classics, and which can join the likes of The Omen (2006), The Amityville Horror (2005), and A Nightmare On Elm Street (2010) as an insulting and pointless time waster.

Among the unforgivable sins in this film is the portrayal of Leatherface; there is a scene where he pours salt into the wound of one of his victims, thus implying that he gets a sadistic kick out of torture. Anyone who saw the original Chainsaw will know that this scene is completely uncharacteristic; he was a hulking great retard who was brought up in a slaughterhouse with very little in the way of moral guidance, but he wasn't sadistic. In the original he slaughtered those teens because, in his own mind, he treated them like they were loose cattle, not because he was necessarily evil, but because he didn't know any better; in his life among such dubious company as his 'family', that was all he had ever known. So to see him inflicting unnecessary tortures on the youngsters in this film was clearly off the mark and left me wondering whether the filmmakers had even seen the original, or whether they even cared to get to grips with Leatherface's character. Indeed, in the original Chainsaw, after killing the first couple of kids, Leatherface sits in the living room nervously looking out of the window. Even with a flesh mask concealing his features, his eyes and posture give us the impression that he is worried, perhaps afraid of his father finding out that there are 'livestock' roaming around when it's his responsibility to do the 'chores' and slaughter them. Thus he was a killer through circumstance, not because he necessarily enjoyed it.

The original film was also very loosely based on the exploits of Ed Gein who was certainly no sadist - He was completely deranged, but he seemed to go about his dirty business with an air of innocence about him; he just didn't realise that what he was doing was wrong, much like Leatherface (in the case of Ed Gein, a policeman investigating a grave robbery walked into a bar and asked the patrons if they knew anything about the disappearance of the corpse, to which Gein piped up "Oh yes, I've got her up at my house!" Everyone, including the policeman, thought he was joking around, but he sure wasn't).

The remake also loses the verite ambience of the original, including the bright blue oblivious sky and scorching hot Texas vibe which accentuated the unforgiving horrors and isolation of the character's predicaments, and the finale is played out in a rain-soaked twilight which could have taken place in any American state. The soundtrack borrows those screeching notes from the original at the beginning, but soon gets bogged down with a typically cliched and uninvolving score that can be found in any number of New Line assembly line crap.

The remake also perpetuates that annoying trend of modern horror that insists on having an aura of viewer empowerment; whereas old skool horrors like the original Chainsaw, and also Wes Craven's Last House On The Left had a cracked fairytale edge in that when youngsters make even innocent mistakes they were sorely punished. But with the new Chainsaw, those harsh cautionary lessons are abandoned in favour of a 'can-do' exercise in overcoming adversary. Thus, we have young 'victims' ducking and rolling out of the way of the swinging chainsaw, and insulting their captors even when they are restrained and at the cannibal's complete mercy. It's bullshit and I didn't believe any of it.

Overall then, it's a million miles away from the 'final girl' situation of Marilyn Chambers who had quite clearly gone insane during her super-human (but also believable) escape feat at the end of Hooper's original. Here it's lead actress, Jessica Biel, whose fearless attitude and immense physicality make her a match for any boogey man, and she of course escapes the ordeal unscathed of any physical or mental damage. The end result is crappy watered-down horror for the masses, to make them feel good about themselves like any other mainstream genre; it's a direction which the horror film should not be heading in.

On the plus side, there's a particularly ghoulish treat where Leatherface takes the facial skin of one unlucky victim and wears it as a mask. It's a nice touch as he seems to strike a new persona, and the hapless heroes and heroines are forced to do battle with a monster who bares the twisted resemblance of a friendly face, with pube beard and all!

TITICUT FOLLIES (1967)

Dir: Frederick Wiseman / USA

Appearing in the early 90s after a mysterious 25 year ban, Frederick Wiseman's feature debut, Titicut Follies, is a documentary set in the Bridgewater State Hospital, Massachusetts, where the criminally insane go about their daily bouts of injustice and humiliation alongside the mentally ill. There's no structure to the film as such, no story to follow, no voiceover to tell us what's going on; just grainy black and white images capturing the incompetence and despair, fly-on-the-wall-style, in a mental institution.

There are some disturbing moments - a clearly distressed inmate gets naked and goes berserk in his cell, frank exchanges about mutual masturbation between inmates and screws, and what appears to be a deceased inmate propped up in a chair being shaved, presumably to smarten his appearance for the funeral. But there's nothing sensationalist or exploitative in the approach of the filmmakers. Alongside the sporadic hygiene of the institution, hunger strikes, force-feeding through tubes inserted down the throat, and general victimization, the patients and guards put on their annual show, the Titicut Follies, a musical play which offers a brief respite from the daily horrors.

The controversy started just prior to the film's premiere at the 1967 New York Film Festival when the government of Massachusetts tried to have the film banned on the basis that it violated the patient's privacy and dignity. In watching the film, however, one can't help thinking that it was the detached observations that served as a shocking indictment of the institution that was causing the real concern, not the welfare of those depicted. And the film was allowed to be shown. But in the following year, the Massachusetts' Superior Court ordered all copies to be removed and destroyed after a social worker complained of a scene which shows a naked man being tormented by a guard. Director Wiseman appealed against the decision and a compromise was reached whereby only doctors, lawyers, and healthcare professionals were permitted to view the film. Wiseman appealed again, this time to the Supreme Court, but he was basically shunned. This was the first time that a film was banned from the general public on grounds other than obscenity, immorality, or national security in America, with Wiseman frustrated that the court restrictions were "a greater infringement of civil liberties than the film was an infringement on the liberties of the inmates".

It wasn't until 1991 that the film was deemed acceptable for public consumption, by which time the damage had already been done. Whereas contemporary films like Cathy Come Home did a lot to change British attitudes towards poverty and the working classes, Titicut Follies could have had a similar impact on American attitudes towards incompetent institutions and the mentally ill, were it not for the powers that be being terrified of being portrayed in a bad light, and scurrying around trying to have the film banished so as to save their own reputations rather than their most vulnerable citizens. Shame on them. Indeed, had the film reached its rightful audience in the first place, there's a good chance that institutions like the Bridgewater State Hospital would have been either closed down for good or had their services dramatically improved. But as it were, the place remained open for decades, stacking up case after case of death and neglect; the most infuriating being the case of an inmate who, according to his representative, Steven Schwartz, was "restrained for 2 and a half months and given six psychiatric drugs at vastly unsafe levels", and who eventually "choked to death because he could not swallow his food". That's censorship for you; rarely makes things better, often makes things worse.

At least now the film has its rightful place in cinema history, with luminaries such as Nick Broomfield and Marc Singer accepting Wiseman's compelling film as a crucial document of its time, with Singer's 2000 documentary Dark Days taking inspiration from Wiseman's polemic and cementing its long overdue legacy for the downtrodden masses. Tough stuff then, but honest to a fault.

TOKYO FIST (1995)

Dir: Shinya Tsukamoto / Japan

Shinya Tsukamoto first hit global notoriety with Tetsuo The Iron Man and Tetsuo 2 - Boddy Hammer, films which combined hi-tech city-scapes and extremely twisted body mutations, and ignited the cyberpunk movement in Japan.
Tsukamoto's work was lauded in the west where fans and critics were dazzled by his 'Cronenberg meets Manga' madness, and was considered the 'Jimi Hendrix of film'. Hollywood were interested in signing him up to direct
Flying Tetsuo, a project which eventually came to nothing, and Tsukamoto stayed away from filmmaking for three years before he returned with his masterpiece, Tokyo Fist.

Moving away from the futuristic fantasies of his earlier work, Tokyo Fist centres on insurance salesman, Tsuda (Tsukamoto himself), who bumps into an old school friend, Kojima (Tsukamoto's brother, Koji), who is now a pro boxer. Kojima visits Tsuda's apartment while he's out and tries it on with his fiance, Hizuru (Kahori Fuji), who knocks him back. When Tsuda finds out, he takes a walk round to Kojima's place for a fight but is punched through the door by the boxer. This violence seems to impress Hizuru and she ends up moving in with the brute, much to the annoyance of Tsuda who takes up boxing lessons with a plan of revenge. Meanwhile Hizuru has begun experimenting with body piercing and tattoos, and seems to alleviate her discontent by pricking herself with needles and awakening her own masochistic desires. This deranged love triangle spirals seriously out of control, with Tsuda and Kojima joining in this brutal game of sadomasochism by re-arranging each other's faces before the film reaches its gruelling finale.

Tsukamoto extends his virtuoso style with a raw, hand-held edginess; we see fists breaking through the tissue of human faces with the camera mounted inside the character's heads. The colour palette is stark and intense, contrasting cold blues and black and white, with hellish reds and bold primary colours. Every scene in Tokyo Fist is shot from unusual angles and not once does it play by the rules of the conventional technicalities of cinema. The result is as astonishing as anything seen in the Tetsuo movies.

On the casting front, Tsukamoto does a fine job in the lead role as Tsuda, a mild-mannered salaryman driven to extremes by a raging jealousy and desire for revenge. His brother Koji is equally impressive as the self-assured Kojima, and Fuji is more impressive still as the self-mutilating Hizuru whose flesh serves as a canvas of scarification which maps the psychological disintegration of this doomed trio. Often surreal and sublime, Tsukamoto also presents us with the most brutal and emotionally exhausting boxing match in cinema history; a gruelling marathon of anger and pain that sees the characters pummel each other with no regard for their own increasingly unrecognisable faces. And this culminates in the final shots of the film in which the victor turns around to salute the audience, but the spectators react in repulsion and disgust as the champion's face is a battered and bruised mess with swollen cheeks and a broken jaw bone dripping with blood. Unmissable.

TOKYO GORE POLICE (2008)

Dir: Yoshihiro Nishimura / Japan

If you're one of those who despises CGI gore and bloodshed then stay well clear of this one as it gleefully unleashes the digital red stuff at 24 galons per second.

In the near future, the soaring rise of violent crime has resulted in the privatization of the capital's police force. The corporate-owned law enforcement groups are at liberty to unleash brutal (and often fatal) punishments on the city's criminal elements. The biggest offenders are a gang of mutant rebels called Engineers whose chaotic temperaments and near immortality hold the citizens of Tokyo in a grip of fear. It's up to Ruka (Audition's Eihi Shiina) and her deadly law enforcement squad, The Tokyo Gore Police, to hunt down and kill the marauding pests, but the 'key' to killing these creatures often hides within, and it's not always an easy task... She's also on the search for the person who killed her cop father, and eventually encounters the crazed scientist who is responsible for the creation of the Engineers.

Unsurprisingly, this shot on video splatter movie was directed by a special effects artist, Yoshihiro Nishimura, who had previously unleashed his bag of tricks in Sion Sono's Suicide Club. It's very rare for an FX guy to take to the helm and produce a film that is anywhere near satisfying (Tom Savini's remake of Night of The Living Dead is one such rare exception), but Nishimura handles the project well, delivering a solid slice of sordid comic book craziness, awash with an ocean of arterial spray, gruesome dismemberments, and cyberpunk posturing. It's a film that stands head and shoulders above other films directed by FX artists, such as Ryan Nicholson's Torched, and there are just as many glorious practical effects as well as the CGI stuff.

What is surprising is that the film was passed uncut by the BBFC. The UK DVD (2 disc set from 4Digital) is the one to go for as it is presented in a very nice transfer and is accompanied by a shed load of bonus features missing on other releases. Lookout for the Verhoeven-esque mock TV commercials ("Harakiri is suicide!" "New wrist-cutter design! To die for, yay!"). Also lookout for the mutant designs of some of the Engineers who look like reject Cenobites from the Hellraiser sequels. The film also boasts what is perhaps the bloodiest blowjob gag in movie history. Ah, the world would sure be a duller place without the extremes of Japsploitation. Enjoy!

TORTURA (2008)

Dir: Marcel Waltz and Michael Effenberger /Germany

A bunch of party girls find themselves stranded in town, but that turns out to be the least of their troubles as as a gang of sadistic cannibals hunt them down, one by one, to eat them alive... And that's about as close to a plot this movie gets. The first 25 minutes are boring as hell with godawful hip hop crap on the soundtrack, but as soon as cannibals make an appearance things get pretty tasty. We first make their acquaintance when they strap some poor dude onto a table and cut off his fingers, barbeque them, bite off his nipples, and put straws in his wounds so they can drink his blood. Oh, they also cut his leg off with an industrial sized handsaw, and one of the lucky girls is given the bloody limb as a treat. A slow start then, but once it gets going it's pretty much unrelenting to the end. The special effects are very good, the performances decent, and it's nice to see cannibalism added to the 'torture porn' mix. Tongues are ripped out, and eaten. Intestines are ripped out, and eaten. Spleens are ripped out and... you get the idea. The trussed-up victims are eventually forced to have a nibble and even kill each other, much to the amusement of the cannibal clan.

TUMBLING DOLL OF FLESH (1998)

(aka Psycho: The Snuff Reels; Orig title - Niku Daruma)
Dir: Tamakichi Anaru /Japan

Plain old crappy AV amateur time... A young woman agrees to do some porn sessions. In the first session she has one on one sex with a guy. The sex is explicit and unsimulated, but suffers from pixelation blurs of Japanese censorship (even pubic hair is forbidden to Japanese viewers). The scene goes well and afterwards they have dinner. In the second session things get a little rougher; she is tied up, and a couple of guys use dildos and vibrators on her, and someone else pours candle wax onto her arse and lower back (pretty sensitive areas, no?). Again, none of this is simulated. When it's all over, she makes her excuses to leave, but while she's putting on her shoes, one of the guys creeps up behind her and bops her on the head with a baseball bat, knocking her out. She wakes up tied to a bed, and here we have the third session (or 'snuff' session); she is tortured and killed on camera. End of story... None of the 'special effects' are even remotely convincing, this makes the Guinea Pig movies look like glossy Hollywood productions. Not good.

TURKISH DELIGHT (1973)

Dir: Paul Verhoeven / Netherlands

The censor's scissors are always at hand when Paul Verhoeven makes a new film, and his erotic drama Turkish Delight was snipped of around six minutes of offending footage by the British censors on its initial release. The problematic areas were in the many sexual encounters of Erik (Rutger Hauer), a young sculptor whose bed-hopping antics allowed him briefly to forget about his insecurities and broken heart due to the loss of his love, Olga (Monique van de Ven). Erik reminisces on their fractured relationship which ended in tragedy; Olga is involved in a road accident and Erik gently nurses her back to health in his flat. The couple eventually get married, but their happiness comes to an end when her father (Wimm van dern Brink) dies, taking his calm influence to the grave. Much heartache and arguments ensue, and the couple split. Olga emigrates to America and re-marries. They eventually do get back together, but Olga collapses and is diagnosed with a brain tumour. Erik decides to stay with her to the end.

This collaboration between Paul Verhoeven and screenwriter Gerard Soetman was a splendid meeting of minds; Verhoeven supplied the risque and plentiful sex scenes, and Soetman provided the bitingly satirical script targeted at the Dutch establishment. Indeed, Verhoeven would carry the mantle further in his future work, repeating the cheeky swipes at the rampant commercialism and the status quo in the 'news flash' clips and mock-ad propaganda in Hollywood hits like Robocop and Starship Troopers. Ultimately though, Turkish Delight is a touching portrayal of a loving relationship, despite all the casual sex and scatological madness on display.

If censorship wasn't enough of an obstacle for this modest gem to contend with, Turkish Delight opened in theatres in the same month as a trio of classics; Serpico, Papillion, and Westworld. Over time, the film has enticed a fair deal of interest and has been influential over the years; echoes of the doomed lovers can be felt in such arthouse triumphs as Lars Von Trier's Breaking The Waves. Steven Spielberg is said to have been so impressed with Verhoeven's previous film, Soldier of Orange, that he even recommended him to George Lucas as a potential director of Empire Strikes Back. He quickly retracted that enthusiasm though once he clapped eyes on Turkish Delight, a film much more in keeping with the Dutchman's sleazily evocative aesthetics. One can only imagine how different the Star Wars saga would have been had Verhoeven taken to the helm...

TWO THOUSAND MANIACS! (1964)

Dir: Herschell Gordon Lewis / USA

While driving out in the country, three couples end up in a strange town called Pleasant Valley where the whole community gives them a warm welcome and free lodgings. When the visitors begin to disappear, however, the remaining couple suspect that all is not well and begin plotting their escape. Turns out that the whole town is populated by Confederate ghosts of those slaughtered during the American Civil War, and who re-appear every one hundred years to exact revenge on the Yankee tourists.

Though technically more proficient than the earlier Blood Feast, Two Thousand Maniacs! holds back on the gore in comparison with Lewis' earlier outing, but there are still some wonderful murder set pieces here - The thumb-slicing and subsequent dismemberment with an axe isn't just graphic, the camera seems to linger on the scene for much longer than any other filmmaker would deem necessary. More sadism ensues with some poor guy being drawn and quartered between two horses pulling in opposite directions, another man is forced into a spiked barrel and rolled down a hill, and a woman is crushed to death by a huge boulder during a strange game of dare; and all of these atrocities are committed in front of the local yokels who clap and cheer the proceedings like enthusiastic parents at a school sports day gathering. With this film, HG Lewis chooses to build up to the murder scenes to give them more impact rather than bombard the audience with blood and guts, and the film is all the better for it. This time the horror is drawn-out and more disturbing, resulting in a vast improvement over Blood Feast.

THE UGLY (1996)

Dir: Scott Reynolds / New Zealand

A seriously creepy and unsettling mix of psychological horror and supernatural shocks, whose gradual ascent into the heights of the horror pantheon was almost solely down to word-of-mouth alone.

Famous psychiatrist Dr. Karen Schumaker (Rebecca Hobbs) is currently riding on the waves of publicity after securing the release of a convicted serial killer. She is invited to a maximum-security institution by another killer, the notorious Simon Cartwright (Paolo Rotondo), and she accepts, much to the annoyance of the head of the institution. Dr. Schumaker arrives and converses with Cartwright in an attempt to get to the roots of his sickness, but eventually discovers that he is driven to kill by the ghosts of his past victims.

With an array of flashbacks, disturbing jump-cuts, crash-zooms, and strange fantasy sequences, we gradually come to understand what makes Cartwright tick. The cruel abuse of his mother, the school bullies, and his social inadequacies as a young adult, bring on a brief but vivid picture of the killer's past. After killing his mother, Simon is tormented by her ghostly form, and he goes on to add more victims, who in turn become ghostly apparitions and torment him more and more. Simon is also much more intelligent and manipulative than Dr. Schumaker gives him credit for, and she gradually sinks deeper into the madness and is left questioning her own sanity.

It's difficult to talk about this film's influences because although there are some obvious reference points, The Ugly takes them into whole new territory. The sharp suited Dr. Schumaker questioning an incarcerated serial killer is reminiscent of Silence of The Lambs, and Simon's abusive past at the hands of his unstable mother, resulting in psychopathic traits relates to Hitchcock's Psycho. However, The Ugly is unlike either of those films and takes the screen serial killer into a lore of its own.

Writer/director Scott Reynolds appeared on the scene just as a couple of his fellow countrymen, Peter Jackson and Lee Tamahori, were being noticed in Hollywood. Both Jackson and Tamahori produced outrageous and grim pictures in New Zealand but immediately tempered their work once they hit Tinseltown; Jackson with his Lord of The Rings, and Tamahauri with his James Bond caper, Die Another Day. But judging by Reynolds' startling early short films, and his follow-up to The Ugly, Heaven, there's still hope yet that this remarkable talent will continue to tread the dark side. Only time will tell.

One of the most impressive aspects of The Ugly is the way Reynolds creates a psychological template; the film's visuals relate to the cracked state of the killers mind. Schumaker's bold red suit reflects the increasing rage Simon feels towards her, and the ice-cold blue of his cell reflects his isolation and inhumanity. And of course there are the ghosts themselves. The apparitions that appear throughout the film are genuinely creepy. Simon's dead mother appears over his shoulder in his cell with the camera zooming in on her twisted blue smile with blood dripping from her mouth. In lesser hands, that scene could have been comical, but Reynolds renders it perfectly to spine-chilling effect. Subsequent apparitions are no less effective, with these ghouls depicted in the same cold blue style which reflects Simon's mind. Indeed, throughout the film we're left wondering whether the ghosts are just a part of Simon's insanity, or whether they are a real and malevolent force independent of his psyche. And that ambiguity is held to the very end of the film.

Even with the extended scenes of bloody violence, the BBFC left The Ugly intact. The Metrodome DVD is therefore taken from the same transfer that first played at festivals around the world, gaining the respect of hardcore horror fanatics, and causing many a sleepless night. It's a masterpiece, and one of the scariest films of the 90s. I dare you to watch it alone at night.

THE UNDERGROUND BANKER (1993)

(Orig title: Xiang Gang qi an: Zhi xi xue gui li wang)
Dir: Bosco Lam / Hong Kong

CAT III movies, I love 'em! Anthony Wong plays long distance truck driver, Tong, who has just moved his family into a small apartment to ease their financial strain. Early in the film he is accosted by petty crims who claim to own the road where he parks, and they demand $200 for him to leave his truck there. Nicknamed 'marshmallow' because of his soft and jovial nature, Tong reluctantly hands over the cash. Later, while eating lunch at an outside cafe, a woman's body falls from a high-rise window and lands on his table. His workmate tells him that the woman probably owed money to the local triad boss, the 'underground banker'.

Tong's wife Chun (Ching Mai) bumps into an old sweetheart, Canner, who is now working for the triads. She takes him back to their apartment to meet Tong and their young son, Tak. Canner informs the family that they're living next door to the notorious serial killer Doctor Lam! The nervous family get to meet Lam (who was originally played by Simon Yam in Dr. Lamb, but here he's played in a less evil but more cryptic mode by Sex And Zen's Lawrence Ng), and he assures them that he is not a danger anymore. He then expertly kills a chicken with a cleaver for tea, and this does little to settle the nerves of Tong and Chun. Little boy Tak doesn't seem to mind though, and he spends a lot of time round at Lam's flat playing video games.

Tong feels insecure about his inabilities to satisfy his gorgeous wife and so he uses self-help audio cassettes to improve his technique and stamina, and this leads to a hilarious practical joke when his workmate gets hold of the tape. Meanwhile, Canner ropes Chun into investing on the stock market with the hope of easing the family's financial woes. And before long she inevitably finds herself losing the family savings. Canner tells her not to worry because his brother is an usurer and will lend her the money she needs.

With Tong not knowing about her gambling away all the money, she agrees to see Canner's brother for help. Canner's brother turns out to be Chao (Ho Ka-Kui, the psycho nutcase from Brother of Darkness), the underground banker, and he agrees to lend her HK$40,000 to be paid back in weekly installments. A week later she gives Canner 10,000 promising to pay the other 30,000 very soon. But Canner tells her that the debt has increased and that she now owes 48,000. She protests but realises she's been caught in some shady scam. Canner tries to reassure her that everything will be okay, and he gets very close and tries to kiss her. She backs off disgusted, and then Canner tells her that he has spiked her drink with an aphrodisiac. He then rapes her while she's in a delirious state. The rape scene is played for maximum titillation with that 80s chic day-glo lighting and soft drum-machine 80s rock on the soundtrack, and displaying Ching Mai's beautiful naked body in various positions; she tells him to stop but the drug has the opposite effect on her orgasmic moans and sensual body language. He then beats her.

Pretty soon Chun begins selling her body to raise money, and this sees her being tied up and spanked and doggy-fucked by a bunch of strangers with the William Tell Ouverture galloping along on the soundtrack, all making light of her desperate situation. Tong's prankster workmate even gets in on the action and sleeps with her, and this makes things awkward in a later scene when Tong brings him home for tea. His friend later confesses that he has slept with Chun but swears blind that he didn't know that she was his wife. Tong beats him up and leaves.

By now the ruthless triads have stepped up their campaign of intimidation, and begin threatening Chun's family. The outside of the apartment is vandalised with graffiti and the security gate at the front entrance has been chained up and padlocked. The fire brigade have to cut the chains to free the family. Chun enters Chao's office and begs for more time to raise money, and pleads for him to leave her family out of it. She is then drugged and gang-raped, but this time the incident is recorded on video and Chao informs her that videotapes will be handed out to all and sundry if she doesn't start making payments.

Chun's sister, Chi Kwan, is abducted, and Chao slaps and intends on raping her but she jumps out of the speeding van. She sustains injuries but she still manages to make it to Chun's flat and attacks her for getting her involved in the debt. Tong has to break them apart, and it's only now that he learns the full extent of the trouble that his wife is in. Chun tells him about losing their savings, and Chao, and the prostitution, and the intimidation. Tong feels he has no choice but to sell his truck. He gets 90,000 for it, and a colleague gives him a further 20,000 to help out.

He visits Chao's office with the 110,000 and offers to settle the debt in full there and then, but Chao instead has him crawling around on the floor in an act of humiliation to amuse his cronies. The triads then play the rape video and Tong is informed that if he wants to stop it from being seen by anyone else he should pay an extra 100,000. This devastating revelation sees Tong leaving in a huff and refusing to pay a penny. He is then robbed of his money outside by Canner's men on a busy city street and not a single person steps in to stop the attack.

That night while Chun and her young son are sleeping, Chao's men chain up their security gate and pour petrol through the mailbox. They then set fire to the place. Tong returns home to find their flat ablaze, with Chun and Tak screaming for their lives. He rattles at the security gate but it's no good, there's nothing he can do. The fire spreads, and Chun pushes her boy under the bed in a futile attempt at safety. She gets caught in an explosion and Tong can only watch in agony as his wife writhes around in flames and drops to the floor in a burning heap. It's a truly nightmarish scene rarely presented so graphically on film. Dr. Lam shows up with a pair of bolt cutters and opens the gate. Chun is dead but little Tak is rushed to hospital.

Outside, Canner appears and he teases Tong about the death of his wife, to which a normally peaceful Buddhist monk steps up and beats the crap out of Canner to much applause from the gathering neighbours of the block. In a heartbreaking scene, Tong visits the hospital to see his little boy - Tak is badly burned; his head is a bald mess of melted flesh and his face unrecognisable. Lam presents Tak with a gift, a Nintendo Gameboy, but the kid can't play it because his hands now resemble charred stumps of melted flesh. Chi Kwan is furious and swears revenge on the gang. Lam tries to console
Tong and offers to help him get some payback on the Triads. Tong the soft 'marshmallow' has doubts and is unsure of himself, but then a tearful Tak encourages his dad to "beat those bastards", and Tong's eyes burn with sorrow and vengeance...

What follows is a grim and glorious revenge attack on Chao and his cronies. It's an extremely violent finale which sees Tong pulling out a meat cleaver and shouting "I'll chop you and make BBQ pork buns" (an obvious reference to the bunman in The Untold Story), and Doctor Lam finds his bloodlust renewed bigtime. We get slicing and dicing, meat cleaver fights, dicks blown off, piano wire used as a garrote, and a nasty castration. Director Bosco Lam (who made A Chinese Torture Chamber Story the following year) teams up with Hong Kong's 'King of sleaze', producer Wong Jing, and together they have created an almost perfectly crafted piece of audience manipulation; by the hour mark you'll be screaming for the bad guy's guts as insult, rape, and death is added to the character's injuries. Anthony Wong is in fine form in a rare role as the good guy, and Ho Ka-Kui as Chao is also brilliant in his typecast role; he's such a mean and ruthless cunt, always ensuring that Chun's debt can never be settled. And Lawrence Ng as Doctor Lam adds an interesting ambiguity in the middle-ground between good and evil.

The film ends with a disturbing coda that shows Tong to have been radically changed by the ordeal, and not for the better; as the end credits roll he is seen setting himself up as the new underground banker, lending money to someone and laying down his rules for repayment. A classic.

THE UNTOLD STORY (1993)

(aka Bunman; Orig title: Bat sin fan dim ji yan yuk cha siu bau)
Dir: Herman Yau / Hong Kong

The first CAT III title to become an international hit, and the one that propelled actor Anthony Wong to cult movie superstardom, The Untold Story was directed by former cinematographer, Herman Yau, who used his years of experience in the film industry to fashion one of the most visually dazzling and explicitly graphic crime films in the history of Hong Kong cinema.

Based on a true story that happened in 1978 in which a restaurant cook, Wong Chi-hang, was accused of murdering his boss and his entire family with a meat cleaver, and then serving their body parts to unknowing customers in the restaurant, the film opens with Chi-hang (Anthony Wong) beating a man to death in an apartment and then burning the corpse. Eight years later, body parts are washed up onto the shores of Macau. The police, led by Danny Lee (of Doctor Lamb and Love To Kill, and who also served as producer on this film) is the police captain who always has a sexy hooker on his arm. There is lots of silly humour from the investigating officers, mostly at the expense of the only female cop who is ridiculed for having small breasts and looking like a tomboy.

Wong has drastically altered his appearance since the murder almost a decade previously, and is now running his own restaurant in Macau. He specializes in selling BBQ pork buns which go down well with the locals and with the investigating officers. But, of course, the buns are not filled with pork but with human remains. After a couple of brutal murders of people who have pissed him off in some way, Wong is eventually arrested. In custody, the police have very little evidence to pin on him so they resort to a long and sustained period of interrogation as a way of getting him to confess to the crimes. He is brutally beaten by both the cops and his fellow prisoners in the holding cell. He attempts a grisly suicide but is saved at the last moment. He is also kept awake for days on end and injected with water which causes painful boils to appear on his skin. Unable to handle the pressure for much longer, Wong breaks down under the mistreatment and agrees to reveal all of the gruesome details of his numerous killings...

If the film hasn't already pushed the boundaries in terms of graphic violence and bloodshed, Wong's flashbacks to the murders of his boss and his family certainly do the trick. There is also a very nasty rape scene and a desperate suicide attempt in a prison cell involving a rusty old slop bucket. The rape scene in particular has been the subject of much controversy over the years; Wong has openly admitted that he dislikes the film for this reason, and director Yau has made his own excuses for depicting the scene in a very crude and voyeuristic way, insisting that he wanted to capture the scene purely from the killer's deranged perspective. But basically, the rape scene is there for the sole purpose of exploitation; sure, Yau may not have intended to arouse the viewer's sexually with this scene, but there's no doubt that he lingers on the victim in her peril and even revels in displaying her naked body, complete with bush shots (which are a rarity even in CAT III titles) before killing her and mutilating her corpse.

The scene featuring the killing of the family is also a long and drawn-out one, and makes for some very difficult viewing. In excruciating detail we watch as they are tied up and graphically butchered, one by one; first the son has his throat cut, then the mother is killed, the father, and then the rest of the petrified children who are cowering near the dining table. One of the little girls is beheaded with the meat cleaver in graphic detail. All seven family members are massacred in this extended and harrowing sequence. Interestingly, Wong doesn't set about the killings in an out-of-control psychotic rage, but in a determined and methodical way which makes the scene all the more disturbing in his calm and pre-determined nastiness. Unforgettable.

VIDEODROME (1982)

Dir: David Cronenberg / USA

"I've got something I want to play for you". One of the most puzzling and extreme movies ever released by a major Hollywood studio, Videodrome sees director David Cronenberg continuing on his body horror themes and social satire that he had developed throughout the 70s, but this time he also adds a welcome dose of surreal, hallucinatory weirdness to the mix.

The plot of Videodrome centres on obscure cable channel entrepreneur, Max Renn (James Woods), who inadvertently stumbles upon a strange broadcast whilst checking a pirate satellite. The show, known as Videodrome, depicts women being tortured on camera by masked men, and Renn becomes obsessed with finding out the truth behind the mysterious channel - Is it real or fake? Who's behind it? And where does the signal come from? To find the answer to those questions leads him to a roster of dangerous characters, including kinky lover Nicki Brand (Debbie Harry), media commentator Brian O'Blivion (Jack Creley), his daughter Bianca (Sonja Smits), and eyewear tycoon Barry Convex (Lewis Carlson).

His fascination with the videodrome signal isn't necessarily based on any moral crusade to put an end to the abuses on screen, it's selfishness and greed that pushes him on with the lure of making a profit, until he discovers that watching Videodrome causes him to suffer bizarre and often violent hallucinations and bodily mutations. Turns out, Videodrome is a corporate enterprise, a secret TV broadcast that causes its viewers to develop brain tumors that can be used to control perception itself, all hidden behind images of extreme pornography. The idea is to create a society that is completely dependent on the signal, a nation of TV addicts who are enslaved to whatever agendas the corporate powers see fit. Thus, Max Renn eventually becomes an assassin and is used as a pawn by warring factions to do their dirty work, before the violent and baffling finale.

Released in the UK in 1983, Videodrome coincided with the emergence of home video and the fast transformations of television itself at the time. Channel 4 appeared in 1982, and we had breakfast TV for the first time ever. The home video explosion was well under way with VCR's being sold in this country at twice the rate of America, but this private home viewing also had a negative effect on those who wanted to control what we saw on those machines. The video nasties fiasco was just around the corner, with uncut and unregulated videotapes widely available in the nation's stores, such as Cannibal Holocaust, The Driller Killer, and I Spit On Your Grave, with fears that those tapes, with their grim content and salacious sleeves, would have a negative effect on the nation's youth. Suddenly, your television wasn't safe anymore, and the powers that be decided that those videos needed to be legislated against. That square box that sits in the corner of your living room was causing anxiety and was increasingly being treated as some sinister thing. So it was suitably ironic how Cronenberg's film - which ultimately rejects the idea of censorship - was subjected to censorship itself at the time, with fearful distributers cutting out whole chunks of the film to avoid the video nasties scandal.

The themes explored in Videodrome have become more relevant with the ensuing decades since the film was made, especially with the rise of the internet and the way it is slowly taking over our lives and creating a very public consciousness. The media conglomerates manipulating and controlling the populace with their not-so-subtle propaganda (sometimes amounting to an altering of consciousness itself in the process).

Back in the early 80s Videodrome was often dismissed as an eccentric take on the new video age, but if you consider his later film, eXistenZ, which was released in the late 90s (and also touched upon some similar themes as Videodrome), critics were accusing Cronenberg of losing his vision and running out of steam, it's hard not to conclude that it's the technology and mindset of our modern age that is slowly catching up with Cronenberg's vision, making his ideas seem less outlandish nowadays, or as Jean Baudrillard suggested - we are entering an age of "the implosion of science fiction", whereby the expanse of the human imagination will one day be eclipsed by the technological realities of our darkest dreams. Pretty scary nonetheless.

Indeed, Cronenberg's film is prophetic in many ways; notice how the character Brian O'Blivion seems to represent the modern-day web-savvy technocrat; he is a 'media expert' who only exists as a huge library of video cassettes through which he communicates with the world. With the internet, we are all media experts nowadays, we're all promoting ourselves online in one way or another, whether it be socially through Facebook, or globally on Youtube, our lives are more documented and exposed than ever. Even O'Blivion's name relates to the latter-day trend of online 'usernames', the pun-ladened alias' of anonymous web forum members.

Another example would be the growing sophistication of TV commercials over the decades since the film was made; the colours, the jingles, the psychological manipulation of the whole thing. Brand names with their logos symbolising 'the things you want in life', 'the things you NEED in life', the media and advertisers have learned how to seduce that part of our brains that compel us to go out and buy the latest 'thing', or to vote for this or that political party. The 'brand name' seduces the viewer, it plays up to their sense of being, their sense of wanting to belong, to fit in with a society that deems the brand name to be 'cool' and 'normal', and as such, it also plays up to our anxieties of existing in the world without those things, without the 'coolness', without that social acceptability. Actually, your TV has indeed become sinister, it has been made dangerous and unhealthy by the very people who outlawed the 'video nasties', and who regulate what we can and cannot watch 'for our own good'. And Videodrome picks up on both the seductive and repulsive aspects of this modern-day capitalist control. Even the so-called 'balanced' and unbiased reporting of the BBC News is ultimately a crock of shit; just like any other corporation they have their own agendas to push forward; the only difference is they rely exclusively on public money to do so. Notice the health warnings that are everywhere; everything is suspected of causing cancer nowadays - the very products and gadgets and 'telly addict' lifestyles of late capitalism radiated from our TV screens - the fast food, the mobile phones, the comforts and inertia. It's suitably ironic how Max Renn develops a brain tumor after being exposed to the evil corporate signal of Videodrome.

This exploration of the seduction and repulsion of the TV lifestyle is symbolised perfectly in the scene where Max is lured to his throbbing television screen by Nicki Brand. Sex has always been a big selling point in advertising, a way of gaining an audience's attention. The sex appeal aspect of television plays on the viewer's desire to bypass the threshold of possibility; the screen lurches out at you with its seductive images, it invites you along ("C'mon Max, come to me"). To be absorbed by the TV screen and transported into the world of perfection and sex and splendor has become one of the true motivators of mankind. But of course, Nicki isn't really there luring Max along, it's just an image, a hallucination. Regardless of Renn's altered state of mind brought on by his brain tumor, the image on his screen isn't real; the image is actually made up of thousands of electronic dots, or 'cells' through the manipulation of quantum mechanics and digital processing which, in their entirety, results in an approximation of an image, BUT NOT THEE IMAGE (and we the viewers who are watching Videodrome are under the very same illusion because we're also just watching events that are being played out on a screen).

And yet, Max's brain finds no obstacle here to stop him from being sexually aroused. A strange but everyday perversion then becomes apparent; basically that Max is being turned on and sexually stimulated by a machine that sits in the corner of his living room. And if you think that's an odd notion, just consider exactly what it is you are doing the next time you place a porn movie into your DVD player - After a while, out pops your hardon, and you can fast forward or rewind to the sexiest footage with which you can synchronise your ejaculation; there's no actual 'love-object' in your presence, no actual 'love-object' on your TV screen either, just an approximation of such built up by the electronic cells that dot your screen. This kind of postmodern wank amounts to nothing more than a strange kind of illusion or hallucination; namely, psychic sex with the electronic box that sits in the corner of your living room - your TV set.

Interestingly, you can forget that you're in fact watching a digital image, and the TV screen then presents to you the desired 'love-object' or porn star, and assume that somehow the picture is genuine; or more accurately, you will not assume anything - to you the picture is real. And it's fascinating how we allow ourselves to be so easily duped like that by machines. Nay, we even actively pursue this deception because the sexual fantasy (in relation to the porn film) is more effective if we try to submerge ourselves into the screen as much as reality and our minds will allow. And it's interesting how this notion brings up a whole locust-storm of fallacy in our brains when it comes to our desires and lusts. And it teaches us another lesson about 'reality' itself in accordance with post-modern thought: that 'rationality', 'logicality', and everything we consider sacred and FACT as a species is all shaped and compromised by our desires - And more crucially in relation to Videodrome; the desires of others. But I digress.

With Videodrome, Cronenberg is clearly taking his subject-matter much more seriously than in his previous work. He even dishes out some just deserts on his negative characters, EC Comics-style.Of all the supposed 'bad' guys in Cronenberg's films up to Videodrome, none of them were truly evil. Dr. Emil Hobbes of Shivers was definitely a madman, but he genuinely believed his experiments with parasites would help mankind; Dr. Hal Raglan of The Brood was shrewd and arrogant, but he was also driven to make up for his mistakes. And Scanners' Darryl Revok was motivated by a justified vengeance. Barry Convex, on the other hand, the implaccable corporate manipulator of the Videodrome signal seems to be Cronenberg's first truly negative character with not a shred of human decency. The director relishes the opportunity to give him an awful and gory death. But was Convex real or just another hallucination emanating from Max's damaged mind?

This confusion and ambiguity concerning the levels of reality explored in Videodrome can also be found in the work of one of Cronenberg's major influences; writer William Burroughs. In his books and other experiments using film, tape recorders, and 'cut-up' texts, Burroughs (along with friend and cohort Brion Gysin) demonstrated the idea of reality being a construct (or 'Reality Film') which can be manipulated in the minds of others for good or bad. This theoretical terrorism encouraged readers to conduct their own experiments with drugs and tape recorders as a way of slashing and discombobulating reality itself ("Cut the words and see how they fall"). Thus Videodrome is more Burroughsian than his own future adaptation of Naked Lunch a decade later.

Rick Baker provides the outstanding special effects work with throbbing TV screens, a stomach opening into a gaping vaginal cavity, and the extended death sequence of Barry Convex which almost out-does the exploding head scene in Scanners. DP Mark Irwin lends his usual cold and sardonic eye to the proceedings, and Cronenberg's regular composer, Howard Shore, contributes the dark and eerie synth organ score. The film was cut by the MPAA for its theatrical release but has been left fully intact on all DVD editions. Another masterpiece from Cronenberg then. Essential viewing.

VISIONS OF SUFFERING (2006)

Dir: Andrey Iskanov / Russia

In this insanely experimental horror film from Russia, a man is attacked and tormented by dark suited ghouls who emanate from his dreams. But that's only half the story as much of the film also centres on an S&M type of nightclub with scantily clad women cavorting and taking drugs...

Boasting wildly inventive camera work, bizarre fetishistic fantasies, and outlandish animation effects, director Andrey Iskanov is perhaps Russia's answer to Shinya Tsukamoto. There's a great nightmare sequence (actually, the whole film comes across as a drug-induced nightmare on screen) where a man is handcuffed to the branch of a tree, and a masked figure is approaching him, cutting through the tall grass, gradually gaining ground, and the man is unable to escape or defend himself. It's an effective nightmare scene shot in muddy yellow and shows so much promise; it'll make your toes curl. The film is littered with similarly impressive vignettes like watching a series of avant-garde shorts running back to back. The only downside to this style is that much of the film is very repetitive, especially the nightclub scenes, and there is so much strobe lighting which becomes irritating after a while. But if you're in the mood for a delirious night in front of your TV then you could do a lot worse than this, as Iskanov seems to thrive on rejecting traditional narrative storytelling and opts to embrace a much more earthly, improvisational approach.

WELCOME TO THE DOLLHOUSE (1995)

Dir: Todd Solondz / USA

An excellent, if excruciating, depiction of the horrors of high school life, Welcome To The Dollhouse won the Grand Jury Prize at The Sundance Film Festival thanks to its bleak but brilliant humour, and helped rejuvenate the filmmaking career of writer/director Todd Solondz after his disastrous debut. The plot centres on 11 year old Dawn Wiener (Heather Matarazzo), an awkward and unpopular school girl who is a constant target for bullies. Due to her lack of social skills, she often finds herself in some desperately embarrassing situations, and her home life isn't much better; her brother and sister are both smarter and more talented then she is, and she struggles to win the affections of her parents. She develops a crush on her brother's band mate Steve, and this ends in another emotional setback when she attempts to get close to him. Worryingly, she later allows herself to be coerced into sex by a rough tearaway kid who has his own emotional insecurities to deal with.

This is a refreshing and insightful black comedy, but it's also painful to watch; throughout the film, Dawn remains an engaging figure, even with her nerdish look and awful taste in dresses, you really feel for her and hope that her situation will improve. Whether your own childhood can relate to Dawn of not, I'm sure most of us will be reminded of some uncomfortable memories from our own childhood as the film unfolds. And this effectiveness is helped immensely by the performances of the young cast; none of them put a foot wrong. Director Solondz keeps the proceedings fiercely unsentimental throughout and presents a flash of genius with dialogue and individual set pieces that would later crop up en masse in his later masterworks such as Happiness and Storytelling.

Welcome To The Dollhouse is often wrongly thought of as Solondz's feature debut; he'd actually made an earlier film, Fear, Anxiety, And Depression, but the experience had been so painful and disappointing for him that he walked away from directing for a few years and took up a career as an English teacher before a friend encouraged him to get back into the helmer's seat. With the relevant funding in place, and a script he was happy with, Solondz felt ready to make amends for the nightmare experience of his first feature, and began touting the screenplay around New Jersey. He felt dismay for the parents of potential child actors who described his script as "delightful", and felt more relieved and trusting of parents who referred to it as "sick" and "depressing"; the latter he took as compliments because, after all, that was how he felt about the world he was portraying. One of the true masterstrokes was the casting of 11 year old Heather Matarazzo, whose astonishing performance shows a talent far beyond her youthful years, and who won an Independent Spirit Award for Best Debut Performance.

People often accuse Solondz of wallowing in the darker side of life in his films, whether it be dysfunctional families, child abuse, or loneliness. Most of his characters seem to harbour dark secrets, and his films are often darkly funny. But he actually uses humour to express the horrors of life because it's the only way he can adequately cope with the torments of the modern world and all its unlovely people.

WENDIGO (2001)

Dir: Larry Fessenden / USA

Something must be seriously wrong when big-budget dreck like Ghost Ship and Jason X are given international theatrical releases, but lower level productions which offer a genuine creepiness and originality, like Wendigo and Session 9, are shuffled off onto the direct-to-video market.

Larry Fessenden's Wendigo is a film which deals primarily with childhood fantasy. The isolation, the sinister locals, and brooding darkness that surrounds the country cabin has an unhealthy effect on the youngster's mind. Miles is the only child of Jake and Kim, New York city dwellers who head upstate to the Catskills for a weekend vacation. Jake's busy lifestyle means that he's not always there for his son, and this looks to have caused Miles to become introverted (he also doesn't seem to have developed much respect for his father). Whilst driving through the woods they hit a deer. The family are then immediately surrounded by angry hunters who find their prized deer with a broken antler. The aggressive behaviour of the locals, and their abusive shouting and gun-waving terrifies the youngster into fantasy overdrive. Miles doesn't understand that the hunter's behaviour is simply brutish and uncultivated; he interprets their aggression as an immediate danger to the lives of his family, and doesn't
believe his father would be capable of protecting him and his mother if the confrontation were to escalate.

Much of the film is seen from the perspective of Miles, where both fantasy and reality combine in alarming ways (see also Claude Miller's La classe de neige for a more obvious example of disturbing childhood fantasies). When the family arrives at their secluded country cabin, the parents are angry and somewhat perplexed at that little episode, but they are not afraid, they do not feel threatened or in danger in any way; it's from the paranoid perspective of their son that the bumps in the night have a sinister edge. The subsequent fantasies are an attempt to arrange, decipher, and take control of the situation - all this stemmed from the mind of a young and feeble child who wants to reassure himself that there exists some kind of mythical force that can protect us from the terrifying nihilism of cold-blooded murder. His father, Jake, is not really hospitalised; it's the pure fantasy of Miles testing and exploring his anxieties. There's no vengeful monster either, that too is just a wishful blend of his hopes and fears combining to produce a fantasmatic protector - Strong, invincible, and awe-inspiring - The ideal father-figure perhaps?

WET WILDERNESS (1975)

Dir: Lee Cooper / USA

This sick little porn film pays homage to the sadism and murder scenes in Wes Craven's Last House On The Left, but those expecting a climatic rampage of revenge will be disappointed as this film wraps up on an unredeeming note.

A pair of hippy throwbacks take a wander through the woods and are accosted by a dangerous sex maniac. Armed with a machete and wearing a bright yellow and black ski mask, the madman forces the peace-loving stragglers to perform sexual acts on him and each other whilst waving his blade around like he's conducting some kind of depraved orchestra. One of the girls escapes but the other is not so lucky and she meets the sharp end of the maniac's weapon. The escapee returns to the scene with the aid of more cardboard characters who serve as nothing more but slabs of meat to be treated in a similar way. It's no spoiler if I tell you that all does not end pleasantly for the hippies. More nastiness, murder, and forced-incest ensues...

Made for spare change in the woods in a single afternoon, Wet Wilderness is a 'roughie' that lacks the zesty zeal of Widow Blue and the darkly comic tirades of Harry Reems in Forced Entry, but makes up for it in its casual and gleeful degeneracy. Daymon Gerard does an adequate job of playing the maniac, even though his face is hidden throughout the entire running time. The yellow and black ski mask seems almost illuminated among the dull and hazy foliage, and brings on a slight phobia in some viewers; but make no mistake, this backwoods killer is far more dangerous than any wasp or hornet, and he has one hell of a nasty sting in his 'tail'. The film's biggest let down is the 'gore' which amounts to some light plywood in the shape of a 'chete or axe glued to the victim's head or torso with a dollop of ketchup. But I suppose the FX are no worse than in Last House On The Left.

Another disappointment is that Wet Wilderness doesn't come close to matching the gruelling sadism of Craven's classic; the killer is a nasty piece of work all right, but he doesn't share quite the same array of sick ideas as Krug and Weasel and co. Maybe it's because in Cooper's film we're dealing with a lone psychopath and he doesn't have any evil buddies to help bounce ideas around?

Wet Wilderness appeared on a double-bill with Gil Kenston's Come Deadly (they were also paired up together on the Afterhours DVD), and played to some moderate success before shipping up on VHS by VCA. Now, the original soundtrack was loaded with uncleared music taken from the classic themes of Jaws and Psycho, and in order to get the film back into the public eye without facing legal action, the folks at Afterhours had to re-dub the entire audio track. And although this tampering isn't really much of an artistic violation, those who remember the original version of the film should bare that in mind (that version is still lurking around if you know where to look). But in terms of visual quality, the Afterhours DVD - though bedecked with speckles and print damage here and there - looks pretty good considering the film's origins.

WHAT IS IT? (2005)

Dir: Crispin Hellion Glover / USA

If you think Crispin Glover is a bit weird and a bit wrong in the head then that opinion will probably be exacerbated tenfold when you see what kind of films he produces when he's behind the camera. What Is It? is the first part of a planned 'IT' trilogy which continued with It Is Fine. EVERYTHING IS FINE! and will conclude with the as yet unfilmed It Is Mine.

The plot and even the premise of this fucked up little film is difficult to describe let alone make sense of (what the hell is it? You tell me!), but basically it's a very strange and disturbing mix of Fassbinder and Jodorowsky. The cast are made up almost entirely of folks with Down's Syndrome, and Glover himself appears as some central messiah.

Some have interpreted the film as a representation of Glover's mindset and the many different sides to his psyche and personas. His public persona, that of the Hollywood actor, is the side he seems the most uncomfortable with, and this is said to be represented by the black-faced minstrel who injects snails. The Nazi elements of the film (including an extremely racist song) are also said to express his hatred of his Hollywood star. The snails represent his regrets and broken dreams.

Some have said that each of the Down's Syndrome cast members represent specific parts of his psyche that he is unhappy with, but I'm not sure if I agree with that; these characters are often violent and lustful towards each other, but it all seems quite innocent. In interviews, Glover seems delighted to be making art with the mentally handicapped, and I very much doubt that their presence in the film is purely to mark out the negative parts of his own mindset; although if you think about it, the casting of a bunch of 'retards' is perhaps precisely what his more sinister side would do (after all, Glover's psyche was behind the making of the film, he was in charge of casting and also has said that he would only direct the film if he could cast those with Down's Syndrome). And in this regard, maybe the film is an attempt to consciously express how he unconsciously sabotages his own work? Glover sits on top of a stone pillar as the bewildered super-ego.

The film could also be seen as a way of pushing 'political correctness' to its most logical extremes where it goes so far that it comes out the other side as a deeply disturbing and troubling film that is sure to offend many who see it; and many will attack the film for expressing the very things that political correctness believes are good for society. Hence we have 'retards' doing 'normal' and everyday things like killing snails and being jerked off by big-breasted women in monkey masks. Lots of snails are abused, Shirley Temple is demonized as a Nazi, and Steven C. Stewart who had Cerebral palsy (and also appeared in It Is Fine, and who died shortly after) falls head-first from the stone pillar in a scene that will make you cringe in shock but is also darkly amusing.

What Is It? was originally conceived as a short film in 1996, but gradually grew into a monstrous feature production that took ten years to complete. Glover was always insistent right from the beginning that the majority of the cast members would be actors with Down's Syndrome. David Lynch hopped on board as executive producer, and before long the rumour mill began to spiral out of control with many stories going around that the film was about handicapped children killing snails. The on-set production went very well and according to plan with numerous shoots over a two and a half year period, but it was the technical problems with the film stock that delayed its premiere. And due to the ill health of actor Stewart, Glover also agreed to appear in the Hollywood production, Charlie's Angels, as a way of making the money he needed to complete the shoot of the second part of the trilogy, It Is Fine!

Audience reaction was generally split down the middle with some celebrating the taboo-breaking experiment as an insightful antidote to the Hollywood norm, and others criticising it as a piece of pretentious shock-mongering. Glover has yet to authorise the DVD distribution of either of his films, and instead travels the world screening them in roadshows where he also promotes his books and does Q&A sessions.

WIFE COLLECTOR (1985)

(aka Rotten City; Orig title - Hitozuma Korekuta)
Dir: Hisayasu Sato /Japan

Japanese society's passive attitude towards rape never ceases to amaze me, particularly when portrayed so openly in film: here in the West, where the crime is considered marginally less abhorrent than murder, the traumatised victim is, more often than not, depicted wreaking savage revenge with a variety of sharp implements (at least in the films I tend to watch); in Japan... well, let's say that the woman's reaction is often less bloody, but certainly no less shocking.

Wife Collector is a tale of a deviant taxi driver who kidnaps and molests young women and records his crimes on video. In one sequence a girl is raped by two louts out in the rain. Afterwards she takes a cab home and then masturbates in the shower. And if that isn't un-PC enough, the cabbie drives around playing his own rape tapes on a little monitor, and records himself molesting some chick in the back seat in full view of the passing traffic while wearing a gas mask! Two sisters find themselves competing over the 'affections' of the scumbag taxi driver, and the girls eventually find comfort in each other's arms...

Wow. This is one of Sato's better films of the Pinku eiga era that wraps up with the director's trademark 'guerrilla-style' street filming in which the everyday public become unknowing extras in a sleaze epic. With a running time of just over an hour, Wife Collector passes by in a brief but brilliant flash, and is sure to amuse those who think they've seen it all. The film also boasts an avant-garde jazz/rock soundtrack courtesy of Ginza Sound who sound like a cross between Can and The Fall, in Japanese.

THE WILD ANGELS (1966)

Dir: Roger Corman / USA

The biker movie was a short-lived genre which came roaring into the American drive-in theatres in the mid-60s and went crashing to a halt in the early 70s, leaving behind a brief but brilliant back catalogue of atrocities and a reckless amoral culture whose grubby outsider characters would often burn out in a blaze of nihilistic glory. Forerunners to the genre were everywhere, from studio releases (The Wild One), exploitational road movies (Faster Pussycat Kill! Kill!), to underground mythologising (Scorpio Rising). But with the publication in 1965 of Hunter S. Thompson's landmark book, Hell's Angels: The Strange and Terrible Saga of The Outlaw Motorcycle Gangs, the public's interest in these shady characters had elevated the gangs into pop heroes, and it was only a matter of time before some bright spark in the movie business came along and put their crude and dangerous exploits onto the big screen. Enter Roger Corman.

Perhaps the most important figure in the history of indie film, producer/director Corman and his AIP production house unleashed The Wild Angels in 1966. With its amoral anti-heroes, grim and gritty style, and overall unredeeming stories supposedly based on true events, the critics at the time labeled the film as dangerous garbage. The punters didn't agree though, and The Wild Angels was soon breaking AIP's box-office records and inspired a whole slew of imitators over the following years, but none of them could match the gruelling charm of Corman's epic which to this day remains the greatest biker movie ever made.

From its opening shots, The Wild Angels is a grim and nasty joyride with the film's only positive statement coming from its leading man, Peter Fonda ("We want to be free to ride our machines without being hassled by The Man. And we want to get loaded"). Fonda is the leader of his gang, The Heavenly Blues, a ragtag group of social misfits and psychos who tear through the land and get into fights with gangs of "Taco benders" and rednecks. A nurse gets KO'd, and there's much looting and dope smoking as the outlaw riders thrive on defying the authorities.

The film culminates in the outrageous funeral scene where Fonda's deceased buddy, Loser (Bruce Dern), is laid to rest amid bongo drum beats and sloshes of cheap plonk. But the service soon becomes a full-scale riot as the boys systematically destroy the church, sit Buddy's corpse up with a joint in its mouth, rape the poor widow, and beat the crap out of the priest before dumping his body into an empty casket.

On the casting front, Fonda stepped up for the role after first choice actor George Chakiris dropped out after refusing to ride a chopper, and he looks born for the part with his uber-cool line deliveries, backed up by his horde of delinquents in black leathers and sporting swastikas which add to the transgressive shenanigans on display. Bruce Dern is also great as Loser, a snarling scumbag who is shot by a cop and whose last words ("I just want to get high") would echo throughout the whole counter-culture movement. Lookout for Nancy Sinatra who seems to be around to confirm that she can't act for shit. And also Peter Bogdanovich helped out behind the camera, and who of course would go on to bigger and better things in the following years.

The film was unique for its time in that the entire movie is seen from the perspective of the gang members themselves with no outsider characters present to offer an objectified and/or moral counterpoint. Ironically, The Wild Angels played at the Venice Film Festival in 1966 as the only American film entry that year. And the film's box-office kerching meant that the floodgates were opened for a slew of oddball imitators, from the good (Hells Angels On Wheels, 1967), the bad (Angels From Hell, 1968), and the downright crude (Satan's Sadists, 1969).

The biker film was a passing fad which came and went, having given a leg-up to rising stars like Fonda and Dern, and also Jack Nicholson and Dennis Hopper, before revving off into oblivion. The posters and ad campaigns were aggressive and sleazy, the entertainment was built on wanton cruelty and debased behaviour, the anti-heroes were cool as fuck but also dirtball scumbags, but for the exploitation crowd it was filmic heaven. Those films prided themselves on violence, sex, and chaos, and delighted in driving a wedge between the fans and the mainstream of society. And that is something to be celebrated indeed.

WILD AT HEART (1990)

Dir: David Lynch /USA

Fans of David Lynch will already be familiar with the writer/director's many nods and winks in his films towards

Victor Flemming's The Wizard of Oz. That timeless childhood classic has fascinated Lynch since he was a youngster, and has continually wormed its terrifying beauty into his work. Wild At Heart still stands as Lynch's most obvious tribute to Flemming's classic fantasy, but ironically it also remains Lynch's most savagely violent film to date.

Loosely based on Barry Gifford's novel, Wild At Heart is a deranged road movie that propels through the savage underbelly of modern Americana. Murderous Sailor (Nicholas Cage, doing a permanent Elvis impersonation) and his lover, Lula (Laura Dern), are on the run from a gang of psychotic killers hired by Lula's crazy mother (Dianne Ladd, Dern's mother in real life). Their journey takes them through a series of surreal, violent, and darkly comic escapades, but will their mutual love carry them through?

An exuberant, funny, and disturbing film due to its many scenes of violence and death, Wild At Heart takes a detour from Lynch's previous Blue Velvet from the outset; whereas Blue Velvet centres on a couple of relatively normal characters who find themselves in a web of encroaching evil, Wild At Heart begins with the film's hero committing a brutal murder, and events soon become increasingly disastrous and apocalyptic from that point on. There's also a positive and optimistic message in the film that suggests even the most fantastical of fairytale endings really can become a reality, just so long as you're prepared to follow the yellow brick road...

Barry Gifford himself loved the film, describing it as "A wonderful thing, like a big dark musical comedy". Lynch called it "A film about finding love in hell" (a few years later the two men would collaborate on the astonishing Lost Highway). Many audiences disagreed, and Wild At Heart produced mass walk-outs from preview screenings. Lynch panicked and re-edited the film, removing gruesome scenes of torture and murder that were apparently leaving the
theatres half-empty due to people leaving in a huff. But even with these tempered scenes, Wild At Heart remains

well-known for its graphic violence; from the head-cracking opening, to the bungled bank robbery and nasty shotgun mayhem, that annoyed the hell out of the censors and led to critics complaining about film violence, yet again.

At the time of its release, the MPAA was reviewing its ratings system, and Wild At Heart was slightly trimmed. In the UK, however, the film was left untouched by the British censors, passing with an uncut 18 certificate.

An unofficial sequel followed in 1997, Perdita Durango, directed by Spanish maverick Alex de la Iglesia which caused even more of a stink for the censors and critics. As for Wild At Heart, lookout for the aforementioned references to The Wizard of Oz, listen out for Angelo Badalamenti's dark and achingly beautiful score, and marvel at the unforgettable roster of oddball characters who populate the film, such as Crispin Glover as Lula's strange cousin who keeps cockroaches down his boxers, stays up all night making sandwiches ("I'm making my lunch!"), and is supposedly abducted by aliens wearing "little black gloves". Willem Dafoe is also excellent and almost unrecognisable as the creepy hitman Bobby Peru. Freddie Jones, Calvin Lock Hart, David Patrick Kelly, and Mr. Eraserhead himself, Jack Nance all appear as the gang of killers, and Harry Dean Stanton as an unfortunate victim caught up in all the madness.

SUBVERSIVE! SPANISH HORROR UNDER THE FRANCO REGIME

In the 60s and 70s many prominent Spanish filmmakers turned their attentions to horror and exploitation. Many of these directors had previously established reputations in the arthouse scene and had never before gone anywhere near the exploitation genres. Usually, a filmmaker would start his career with a low-budget horror production to make a quick and easy impact, with the intention of moving onto more 'serious' works in the future, whereas these Spaniards turned to horror as a way of reaching the populace (both national and international), in an attempt to draw attention to life under fascist rule. By the mid-70s most of these filmmakers returned to the arthouse and/or political films, and their reputations continued to grow as they had done previously.

After the nationalistic victory in the civil war, the Spanish government was keen to expand the movie industry. Those in power hoped to "Europeanize" their cinema by making it innovative, modern, and with international appeal. However, these art films were only frequented by intellectuals and foreigners, and the filmmakers wanted to socially engage with ordinary working class filmgoers. La marca del hombre lobo (Mark of The Werewolf) was a big hit in 1967, and it was this film that encouraged directors to embrace popular genres as a way of communicating with both the Spanish people and international viewers about their plight under the Franco regime.

The horror film made it possible to address themes to a mass audience that would be unacceptable in other genres. A slew of exotic, horror and exploitation movies were then being produced in Spain by filmmakers who were considered to be serious artists, for the simple reason that these types of films were a good place to address strong political points without arousing the suspicions of the strict censors. Graphic sexuality, lesbianism, and other activities officially deemed as "perversions" by General Franco's government, flourished in horror and fantasy during this period.

Claudio Guerin Hill had secured his arthouse credentials with films like Los desafios and La casa de las palomas before he turned to the horror genre with La campana del infierno (Bell From Hell, 1973), a clear critique of the Spanish regime. This film explores the opposition between young and old in its characters. The young representing the new generation, and the old representing corruption, compliance, and the founding of the regime. The film starts with John, a young man who has just been released from a mental institution where he is ordered to report back in six days. But he rips up his appointment card as soon as he leaves the building, suggesting hostility to the authorities from the outset. In fact, it was his aunt who had him locked up so that she could spend his inheritance.

John's actions throughout the film are rebellious, and the mental institution is symbolic of the repression of the new and radical ideas of the younger generation. Indeed, the doctor is being bribed to keep John in the nuthouse, and he agrees to this, not from any medical ethics, but out of sheer greed and corruption.

Michel Foucault in his book, Madness and Civilization, suggested that 'reason' was deemed to be whatever the ruling members of society wanted it to be, and that 'madness' was everything which fell outside of this reason. The mental institution, then, is the cell into which all of those who don't recognise the accepted modes of behaviour are dumped. National pride, family values, and the Catholic Church represent the 'reason' in society, and everything else - which includes John - represents the 'madness'. When John returns to his home town, he sets about attacking those who represent the established order with fiendish practical jokes.

A clever move in Bell From Hell was the casting of Alfredo Mayo in the role of Peter, the building contractor on whom John seeks revenge. In the 1940s, Mayo played a number of roles linked to Franco, the most obvious of which was Raza (Race, 1941) which is allegedly based on the dictator's experiences. In Bell From Hell, Mayo is clearly there to evoke a connection in the audiences eyes between him and Franco. Even the costumes he wears are very similar to the ones worn by Franco in photographs taken on hunting trips.

It's also worth mentioning that Mayo and his fellow hunters in the film attempt to rape a young girl but are stopped when John shows up and terrorizes them on his motorbike. The same characters are later seen in the front row at church like respectable members of the community (and this scene looks just as much to be a homage to Straw Dogs as it is an attack on Franco and Catholicism as a whole).

Guerin Hill does a fine job of linking the narrative, the characters, and the ideology of the regime, and the Spanish censors didn't suspect a thing. Sadly, he died on the last day of filming by falling from the bell tower, and we'll never know if he could have gone on to even better things.

Bearing in Mind Foucault's Madness and Civilization, lets take a look at Juan Lopez Moctezuma's urgent cry for social revolt, The Mansion of Madness (aka Dr. Tarr's Torture Dungeon, 1972). A journalist visits a French sanitarium in order to write an article for a newspaper. But surprise surprise, when he gets there he eventually discovers that the lunatics have taken over the asylum.

Having the movie set in France was simply a trick used by the filmmakers to discourage the scrutiny of the censors (also, France was a relevant setting because of that country's rich socialist history which could be used as an encouragement for social change on the Spanish audience). When we reach the asylum, we can see that it's in a state of degradation, and this makes an obvious connotation to the state of Spain itself at the time. Of course, the asylum represents Spain as a whole, the lunatics represent the Franco regime, and the new leader, Maillard, with his clumsy speech and idiotic mannerisms, is clearly modeled on the generalissimo himself. There is much in the dialogue of Maillard that is ironic, macho, and obliviously self-mocking; he makes a fool of himself with his own words, is delighted with his own crap jokes, and waves his arms around hysterically when ordering his battalions to attack. The asylum guards represent the stupid, bigoted members of the Falangist guards - Their sadistic treatment of their captives, for example, and their allegiance to a social framework which puts them at a disadvantage, and their complete ignorance of this fact. The starving prisoners who are let loose from the dungeons at the end of the film represent the Spanish working class who immediately set out to overthrow the lunatics in a great revolutionary war.

There are so many examples I could give of this film's subversive hints, and to list them all would be unnecessary as almost every scene contains something at the expense of the Spanish authorities. During the final struggle a girl holds up a pistol and utters the words "Viva la revolution" and then shoots Maillard in the chest. In his death throes, Maillard muses briefly on life with a ridiculous comment for comedic effect; "Yes, the tree, the leaves, the roots... Can this be the end of Maillard?"

Director Moctezuma depicts the asylum as being run by a bunch of morons and that it would be easy to have them overthrown. He even blatantly advocates the assassination of Franco and does all he can to draw the viewers in to comparing the sanitarium with the situation in Spain itself. Contrary to the other directors covered in this article, Moctezuma didn't go on to make arthouse or openly political films when the regime collapsed. He instead found himself in Mexico where he continued in his experiments in the cinefantastique with the insane Alucarda and Mary, Mary, Bloody Mary, both of which cut back on the artistic qualities (although he kept the subversive edge with Alucarda, an unflinching attack on Catholicism), and ironically, his horror debut, Mansion of Madness, remains his most vital and powerful film.

Vincente Aranda, however, was a filmmaker who put his earlier experimental work on the back-burner while he too tried his hand at subversive horror cinema. The result was La novia ensangrentada in 1972 (the film later reached global cult status under the anglisized title, The Blood Spattered Bride). The encouraged machismo in Franco's Spain was the target of this scathing assault. The main character, Simon Andreau, expresses ideas, values, and beliefs of Francoist patriachy, and the audience is encouraged to be critical of these opinions.

One scene shows Simon and his wife taking a stroll in the countryside. When they embrace each other, Simon suddenly turns vicious and forces his wife to perform fellatio on him. He attacks her again in an aviary, and the bride surrounded by the birds represents the captivity of women at the hands of the male-orientated social conventions. Aranda was keen to show how sexual chauvinism was linked with political and national chauvinism. After the Franco regime, Aranda went back to filmmaking that was more directly political and has continued to do so since.

Eloy de la Iglesia was a member of the outlawed Communist Party and also chose to work for a while in popular genres. Le semana del assesino (aka Cannibal Man, 1971) addresses social injustice in Franco's Spain by showing horrific acts of madness and murder being a direct result of the repression and alienation of the working class. Aranda does an excellent job of showing how Spanish society was ultimately cannibalising itself, and his later works became more directly political after the end of the regime.

Juan Antonio Bardem was also a Communist Party member and a major force within the Anti-Fascist film movement in Spain. Most of his early films had a social conscience (Muerte de un ciclista and Calle Mayor, for example). In 1972 he directed The Corruption of Chris Miller, a psychological horror film about two women who are visited by a mysterious young man. The film explores themes of sexuality and power in a way that didn't incur the wrath of the regime because the themes were enmeshed in the fantastical trappings of the horror genre, and this allowed Bardem to push the envelope much further than he would have been permitted in a typical everyday drama. And of course, once the regime had fallen, he had the opportunity to confront political subjects in a much more open manner without fear of prosecution in films like The Warning in 1978.

The Franco regime attempted to present a liberal facade to the outside world, but eagle-eyed Spaniards and international audiences saw in these films a clear and subversive edge that was difficult to ignore. All the films mentioned in this chapter have a dark, grimy atmosphere light years away from the modern tourist's impression of Spain as a place of sun, sea, and sand, etc. Obviously, not all of the Spanish horror films of this era had a political agenda, but the ones I have talked about here are enormously subversive; and as a way of gaining further insight into the phenomena of cult cinema, it's useful to consider the historical context of these remarkable films.

IS CENSORSHIP STILL RELEVANT?

For many years, film censorship was the scourge of horror fanatics who felt that their favourite movies were persecuted by people who had no care or understanding of the genre. The more hardcore devotees would search high and low for the definitive uncut videotapes, often paying in excess of £100 per tape, even if the end product turned out to be a murky, washed out, pre-recorded duplicate. It didn't matter. The uncut version was like a trophy to video collectors, a one-up on the censors whose decisions to cut and/or ban these films was always held in disdain.

This video culture expanded tenfold with the rise of DVD and the internet. Nowadays anyone can locate uncut movies at the at the click of a button and have them delivered directly to their homes from anywhere in the world, with no need for any dodgy contacts (and they're also much cheaper these days). And this begs the question: Is film censorship still relevant today?

In the last few years, the British Board of Film Classification (BBFC) have gradually relaxed their rules on censorship to such an extent that only movies that contain images that effectively break the law will be subjected to trims. In fact, the censors nowadays are more likely to help distributers get around the law rather than dictate to them what should and what should not be passed according to their own moral views on such matters. It's interesting to note, however, that these huge steps forward have only come along in proportion to how easy it has become to locate uncensored material in the last few years. And it's easy to conclude from here that film censorship (including international censorship) has indeed become irrelevant, because of the simple fact that the censors are being made to compromise their efforts by fast developing technologies that are beyond their control, such as the internet.

It's similar to what has been happening in the music industry in recent times, with record companies and retail outlets having to compromise their business efforts by illegal download sites that offer their copyright products free of charge.

Remarkably, it is now the film industry itself who have become the main obstacle to freedom of expression, and who seem to be doing the censor's jobs for them, as we shall see... But first, let's take a look at some censorship troubles over the years as a way of putting this madness into some kind of context...

GRAPHIC VIOLENCE AND LUCIO FULCI

Thousands upon thousands of movies have been cut by international censors over the years, and graphic violence and gore has always been a subject of concern. The films of Lucio Fulci are the perfect place to start when discussing graphic violence and gore, because in his movies, excessive screen violence is the whole point; just like musicals break up the plot for song and dance numbers, Fulci's films break up the plot for long drawn-out scenes of violent set-pieces (see the spider attack in The Beyond, for example).

Lucio Fulci made his movies in Italy (except for the location shots mostly filmed in New York), but were sold oversees in an attempt to have a slice at the huge American market. Ironically, his films were so violent that mainstream cinema chains refused to screen them, and so his movies were relegated to playing the grindhouses, the only place where unrated films could find an audience. This kind of ousting of excessive films worked as a very non-subtle form of censorship in itself; by limiting the theatrical potential of such films, the industry effectively curtailed any financial success they may have enjoyed. By refusing these films a mainstream audience, and limiting the revenue of such fare, the industry succeeded in killing off the theatrical outlet of these gruesome epics.

However, it wasn't just on the theatrical front where Fulci's films were causing problems. By the early 80s home video was growing ever popular, with small distributers picking up low-budget horror films and releasing them uncut for home viewing. The splinter in the eye sequence in Zombie Flesh Eaters, the little zombie girl getting her head blown off in The Beyond, and the infamous head-drilling scene in City of The Living Dead were all widely available uncut for public consumption until the Director of Public Prosecutions (DPP) compiled his list of 'potentially obscene' tapes which eventually ushered in the Video Recordings Act, 1984, in which 70 titles were prosecuted and removed from video shops. It was a piece of legislation which affected us Brits for almost fifteen years.

VIOLENCE, MORALS, AND INCONSISTENCIES
Sometimes censors have a strange attitude when it comes to screen violence. For example, the Bruce Lee vehicle, Fists of Fury, which had scenes snipped out involving the use of nun-chucks as deadly weapons (an offence that has kept Jim Van Bebber's Deadbeat At Dawn banned in the UK for many years), but allows all fight scenes involving hand-to-hand combat to remain intact. Compare this to John Woo's action classic, Hard Boiled, in which all the scenes involving excessive gunplay ('excessive' being an understatement to describe this particular film) are allowed to flourish, while scenes depicting hand-to-hand combat, like knees to the chest and karate chops to the throat, were censored for being too violent.

There are so many examples of inconsistences in censorship that to list them all would be unnecessary, but I'll give you one more example: When Hellbound: Hellraiser 2 was submitted to the BBFC in the late 80s, the board decided to remove the scene where a distressed psychiatric patient uses a cutthroat razor to hack and slash at his own flesh, but they passed the scene in which a cenobite has nails hammered into his head. And, if that isn't confusing enough, they also felt the need to remove the sight of a pair of bare breasts.

VIEWER IMPLICATION
Movies that attempt to implicate the viewers in crimes taking place on screen are asking for trouble as far as the censors are concerned. There is a scene in John McNaughton's Henry-Portrait of a Serial Killer in which two killers force their way into a random family home and proceed to beat, rape, and kill the occupants (not necessarily in that order). The problematic area here becomes apparent when the camera pulls back, revealing the events to taking

place on a television screen, with the two said killers watching their own previous crimes on videotape that they had recorded themselves. Watching and enjoying it ("I want to see it again"), thus implicating the viewers who are watching (and at least seeking) entertainment through the degradation and death. Although the film has finally been passed uncut by the BBFC for home viewing, for many years this crucial sequence was re-edited for the British public and lost most of its voyeuristic and subversive power as a result.

Also of note is the original poster for Henry-Portrait that was banned for being too disturbing.

DISTRIBUTER CUTS

On occasion, films are tampered with before they even reach the censor's office. The films of Dario Argento have often been the victims of this kind of practice. His 1985 film, Phenomena, had more than twenty minutes of footage dropped by US distributers as a way of give the film a more acceptable running time (they also re-titled it to Creepers for the American market). The Bird With The Crystal Plumage, Deep Red, and The Stendhal Syndrome were treated with equal disrespect, resulting in films that made little sense to foreign audiences.

When Abel Ferrara's The Driller Killer was re-submitted to the BBFC in the late 90s after being banned in the UK since 1985, the distributers dropped some of the violent footage in order to stand a better chance of being passed. It was a frustrating moment for horror fans because the BBFC claimed that the full uncut version would not have caused any concern for the board and would have probably passed in its entirety had it been presented to them in its full undiluted form. The same distributers also removed a further six minutes of non-violent footage simply to fit the film onto shorter cassettes.

WHEN CENSORSHIP SPOILS THE JOKE

In the mid-90s those spoil-sports at the BBFC insisted on removing several scenes from Steve Ballot's The Bride of Frank. UK horror fans were particularly annoyed with their decision since one of the main cuts required was to take away the film's central joke; as the tagline says, "All Frank wants is true love. But you better not mess with Frank, because if he tells you 'I'll cut off your head and shit down your neck', he ain't kiddin". The BBFC demanded 74 seconds of cuts, including the sight of a man being "realistically fellated", a man having sex with the eye-socket of a woman, and the showstopper: Cuts to remove the sight of a man defecating down the neck of another. The BBFC offered the following statement as justification; "Cuts are made on grounds of potential harm and potential obscenity, for unjustified sexual detail, and sexual violence". But don't dismay, the uncut version is available on Region 1 DVD.

VIDEO NASTIES

Having already touched upon the subject of video nasties earlier in this chapter, let us now examine the fate of those titles and see where they stand legally in today's climate...

* Absurd (orig title: Rosso Sangue; aka Horrible) - Still banned in the UK

* Anthropophagous: The Beast - Released with around 3 minutes of pre-cuts under the title The Grim Reaper in 2002

* Axe (aka Lisa, Lisa; aka California Axe Massacre) Re-released uncut in 2005

* The Beast in Heat (orig title: La Bestia in Calore) Still banned in the UK

* The Beyond (Orig title: L'Aldilà; aka Seven Doors of Death) Re-released uncut in 2001

* Blood Feast was passed uncut in 2005

* Blood Rites (orig title: The Ghastly Ones) Still banned

* Bloody Moon was finally passed uncut in 2008

* The Bogey Man was re-released uncut in 2000

* The Burning was re-released uncut in 2001

* Cannibal Apocalypse (orig title: Apocalypse Domani) passed with 2 seconds cut in 2005

* Cannibal Ferox was released with around 5 minutes of distributer cuts and 6 seconds of further cuts in 2000

* Cannibal Holocaust passed in 2001 with 5 mins and 44 secs cut to remove most animal cruelty and rape scenes

* The Cannibal Man was passed with minor cuts in 1993

* Cannibal Terror passed uncut in 2003

* Contamination was passed uncut in 2004 with a 15 certificate

* Dead & Buried passed uncut in 2004

* Death Trap (aka Eaten Alive) Re-released uncut in 2000

* Deep River Savages (aka Man from Deep River) passed with cuts in 2003

* Delirium (aka Psycho Puppet) Released with minor cuts in 1987

* Devil Hunter was passed uncut in 2008

* Don't Go in the House passed with substantial cuts in 1987

* Don't Go in the Woods was released uncut in 2007

* Don't Go Near the Park was released uncut in 2006

* Don't Look in the Basement was passed uncut in 2005 with a 15 certificate

* The Driller Killer passed with cuts in 1999 then later re-released uncut in 2002

* The Evil Dead passed uncut in 2001

* Evilspeak - uncut in 1999

* Exposé (aka House On Straw Hill) was re-released with minor cuts in 2006

* Faces of Death was released with 2 minutes and 19 seconds of cuts in 2003

* Fight For Your Life is still banned in UK

* Flesh for Frankenstein (aka Andy Warhol's Frankenstein) passed uncut in 2006

* Forest of Fear is still banned

* Frozen Scream - Still banned

* The Funhouse was passed uncut in 1987

* Gestapo's Last Orgy is still banned

* The House by the Cemetery was passed uncut in 2009

* House on the Edge of the Park passed with almost 12 minutes of cuts in 2002

* Human Experiments was re-released with minor cuts in 1994

* I Miss You, Hugs and Kisses passed with over a minute of cuts in 1986

* I Spit on Your Grave was released with approximately 7 minutes of cuts in 2001

* Inferno was passed uncut in 2010

* Island of Death was released uncut in 2010

* Killer Nun escaped uncut in 2006

* The Last House on the Left finally passed uncut on the 17th March, 2008

* Late Night Trains was released uncut in 2008

* The Living Dead at Manchester Morgue (aka Let Sleeping Corpses Lie) re-released uncut in 2002

* Love Camp 7 was banned for a second time when it was submitted to the board in 2002

* Madhouse passed uncut in 2004

* Mardi Gras Massacre is still banned

* Mountain of the Cannibal God was released with around 2 minutes of cuts in 2001

* Night of the Bloody Apes was released with around a minute of pre-cuts in 1999

* Night of the Demon passed with almost 2 minutes of cuts in 1994

* Nightmare Maker (aka Butcher, Baker, Nightmare Maker) is still banned

* Nightmares in a Damaged Brain passed with cuts in 2005

* Possession passed uncut in 1999

* Pranks (aka The Dorm That Dripped Blood; aka Death Dorm) was waved with minor cuts in 2001

* Revenge of the Bogey Man was released with extra footage in 2003

* The Slayer passed uncut in 2001

* Snuff was passed uncut in 2003, but has yet to be re-released

* SS Experiment Camp was released uncut in 2005

* Tenebrae was re-released uncut in 2003

* Terror Eyes was released with over a minute of cuts in 1987

* The Toolbox Murders was passed with almost 2 mins of cuts in 2000

* Twitch of The Death Nerve (aka A Bay of Blood) Passed uncut in 2010

* Unhinged passed uncut in 2004

* Visiting Hours was passed with around 2 minutes cut in 1986

* The Werewolf and the Yeti is still banned

* The Witch Who Came From the Sea was passed uncut in 2006

* Women Behind Bars is still banned

* Zombie Creeping Flesh (aka Hell of the Living Dead) was released uncut in 2002

* Zombie Flesh Eaters was finally passed uncut in 2005

Of the 70 titles that appeared on the DPP's list in the mid-80s, most of them can be found uncut on the internet, usually on Region 1 or Region 0 DVD. Notice how many of the titles are still officially outlawed on these shores, but the reason for this is that many of the films haven't been re-submitted to the board since the video nasties era, and most would probably get through the censors office unscathed nowadays.

AVOIDANCE OF THE 'VIDEO NASTIES' LABEL
Not only did the Video Recordings Act have these films banned from our homes, but it also had a direct impact on future releases for years to come. Films like The Evil Dead and Dead and Buried were only freed from the censor's clutches once the distributers agreed to make extensive cuts. Had they refused, those films, along with countless

others, would have found themselves further prosecuted. It was this kind of ultimatum which affected home video certification in the UK for almost two decades.

THE DEVILS
One film which didn't make it onto the list of the DDP's list of tapes was Ken Russell's The Devils, probably because it has never been given an official home video release in any way shape or form since the inception of the medium. Although the film had been censored before its theatrical release in this country, it was the film's own financial backers who objected to it the most. When Ken Russell took the film over to America for a screening for the financiers, their horrified reaction was to label it as "disgusting shit". They promptly removed whole chunks of the film before sending it out in a limited theatrical run.

Russell's masterpiece was based on Aldous Huxley's 'true life' account of demonic possession in France in the 17th Century. It was Russell's only political film and called for a distinct anticlericalism. Oliver Reed delivers a career best performance as the rebellious priest Father Grandier who is burned at the stake after urging the citizens to resist the destruction of their city. The film boasts many blasphemous scenes and orgies involving the Ursuline nuns who believed to have had their bodies possessed by Grandier, encouraged by the visions of Sister Jeanne.

Film critic Mark Kermode was a good friend of Russell's and he spent a long time searching for the 'lost' footage which included the infamous 'rape of Christ' scene in which the nuns tear down an effigy of Jesus and pleasure themselves with it. After a long search, the footage later surfaced in the Warner Brothers' vaults. This restored director's cut was then screened at the National Film Theatre in London in 2004. Kermode also put together the excellent documentary, Hell On Earth: The Making of The Devils, in which the cast and crew were interviewed at length on the film's background and production. Both the film and the documentary were broadcast on Channel 4 with the BBFC giving the original version of The Devils an uncut certificate.

So we had the restored version of the film in a gorgeous 35mm print, and some invaluable bonus feature material which would make for an excellent special edition DVD release. But all hopes were dashed when the American backers put their foot down again and banned the film for a second time. The version screened on Channel 4 looked astonishing, it was a beautiful and pristine print of the film. The only version available nowadays is the one that has been leaked onto download sites which is missing the rape of Christ scene, and this version looks absolutely dreadful and should be avoided at all costs. It's a sad fate for one of the finest British films of the 70s.

NO PUBES PLEASE, WE'RE JAPANESE

The Japanese censor is often quite a fussy individual because the job is usually handed out to those who are eased out of the regular police force. And although it isn't law in Japan, there is an unwritten agreement that the censors should avoid showing pubic hair wherever possible, which often results in the use of those optical smudges, or 'pixelations' to blur out any offending pubes on display. It is also standard practice in Japan for censors to blur out the sight of penises on screen. But rather amusingly, in 1992 an animated feature came along entitled Legend of The Overfiend which found a clever way of avoiding the restrictions by having 50 foot tall super-beings sprouting strange phallic-like tentacles that would penetrate pretty young girls. The tentacles even had glans, but the censors were unable to do a thing about it. And, as if to rub the authorities' face in it, the sequel, Legend of The Demon Womb, seemed delighted with its notoriety and pushed its luck even further with the penis/tentacle ambiguity.

THE BLACK BLOOD MANOUEVRE
New Zealand filmmaker Scott Reynolds may have learned a thing or two from those extreme Manga offerings, as in his superb psychological horror film, The Ugly, he opted to use ink-black blood in order to be able to splash it around liberally without worrying how the censors would react (the same trick was also used earlier in Geoffrey Wright's skinhead flick, Romper Stomper, where the blood tone ranged from red to black to dark green). Perhaps inspired by Hitchcock's use of chocolate syrup for the shower scene in Psycho, Scott Reynolds knew that red blood would be too much for many to handle, and that by simply altering the colour of the 'claret' he could depict his violent scenes with much more freedom and graphic detail than he would have gotten away with otherwise. And it worked, because despite the often graphic nature of the film, it has played more or less intact in every territory in which it was released.

THE ALL-IMPORTANT R-RATING
Most mainstream movies dealing with problematic subject-matter nowadays must secure an R-rating at all costs. Failure to do so will result in having the film slapped with an NC-17 rating, or not much better, having it released unrated.

Cinema chains in America are now dominated by the multiplex, and these chains will only screen films that are certificated for large audiences, usually family viewing ($$$). R-rated movies are acceptable to the multiplexes because youngsters under the age of 17 can watch them as long as they are accompanied by an adult. Movies rated NC-17, however, are not accepted by the multiplexes, and this can cause the death knell of any film hoping to make a profit (the NC-17 certification does not allow anyone under the age of 17 into the theatre, regardless of whether they are accompanied by an adult or not). Unlike the UK, filmmakers in America can legally release their films without the need of censorship (unrated), but most cinema chains refuse to screen unrated material. The multiplexes will claim that the reason for this is a decision based on morality, but actually, the real reason is because these films have a hard time pulling in the punters, thus losing out on revenue. It's 'bad for business' and all that. So, movies are often tamed for an R-rating if they wish to reach the largest possible audience and to stand a chance of recouping the financial costs. And this makes studio bosses very picky when it comes to releasing adult-orientated films...

STUDIO CONTROL

Whenever a particular type of film has a run of success, studio bosses are quick to leech onto that success and create a winning formula which will help to bring in the big bucks. In the late 70s and early 80s moviegoers were greeted by a new phenomenon; the slasher movie sub-genre. John Carpenter's Halloween was released in 1978 and was a huge success, and studio bosses were quick to notice a gap in the market. Independent producer/director Sean Cunningham had previously worked in the porn industry (he also produced Wes Craven's debut feature, The Last House On The Left), but, inspired by the success of Halloween, he set out to make a violent slasher movie that would play across the drive-ins of America. That movie was Friday The 13th. Paramount picked up the film and gave it a full-on nationwide release with a large ad campaign that only a major studio could afford. It was a huge success.

If Halloween had borrowed elements from Black Christmas to update the slash 'em formula, Friday The 13th went further afield and borrowed its gruesome elements from Mario Bava's proto-type body count movie, A Bay of Blood. Encouraged by this kind of wining business formula (i.e. a movie that costs spare change to make can rake in a fortune at the box-office), Paramount were keen to ape the success by releasing sequel after sequel after sequel...

By the early 80s these 'stalk n slash' or slasher movies were being targeted and picketed by campaigners who objected to the idea that youngsters were being entertained by these types of films. And, under pressure from the media, the American censors (The Motion Picture Association of America, or MPAA) began tightening their regulations on screen violence. So now we had a situation where the studios wanted to continue making these financially profitable films whilst at the same time adhering to stricter controls, resulting in sequels that became tamer and more lacklustre with each passing year; all this to attain a safe R-rating (see also the Nightmare On Elm Street sequels which descended into pure comedy and pastiche rather than nightmares). Studio bosses had found their winning formular, and they'd be damned if any filmmaker let a little blood get in the way.

By investing in films like Friday The 13th and their like, it was the studios that dragged the underground up to the surface, where people who normally would have had no idea about the existence of these films now had no way of avoiding them. Had these original films been left alone on the drive-in circuits and grindhouses, much of the later strict controls of the mid-80s, I believe, would never have become necessary.

CONCLUSION
If censorship has indeed become irrelevant in recent years, this is mostly in relation to back-dated films which are easy to find in uncut form nowadays. The new problem is the way Hollywood itself is taming down its own films for the all-important R-rating. It's difficult to imagine a major studio allowing their products to go out with an NC-17 rating nowadays (recently, Alexandre Aja's remake of The Hills Have Eyes was threatened with an NC-17 until the bosses agreed to drop some of the nastier footage).

On DVD, however, uncensored material, even from major studios, are often released fully uncut with no problems or complaint. Ridiculously, the remake of The Texas Chainsaw Massacre boasted a superbly nasty scene in which an unfortunate victim is hooked to the ceiling and is literally cut in half down the middle by Leatherface's chainsaw. The odd thing about the scene is that it didn't actually appear in the film! That footage was never included in the finished film even though it was clearly shown in the trailer! The footage can only be seen on the 'Making of' featurette on the 2nd disc. Nothing like a good old exploitation tease, eh?

In the UK, the BBFC are more willing than ever to allow serious-intended films that happen to contain risque elements to flourish uncut on these shores. But when it comes to pure exploitation cinema, the censors still hold a nit-picky, nanny-state attitude to what we can and can't watch. Recent examples, such as Koji Shiraishi's Grotesque, Bruce LaBruce's L.A. Zombie, and Tom Six's Human Centipede 2 were all banned in their entirety in the UK for being utterly gratuitous. Well, this is all well and good for the do-gooders of society, but exactly what difference does it make if something like Baise Moi or Irreversible are granted certificates because those films have something other to say than to merely excite and disturb their viewers? Grotesque may not be a work of art but it's a bloody good piece of torture porn. Human Centipede 2 is crude, and explicit, but is jolly good fun nonetheless. And although Human Centipede 2 doesn't offer anything in the way of social commentary, it's a blackly funny horror show all the same.

What should it matter if none of those films have anything to say other than to excite and amuse their audiences? Why should these films have to justify themselves by adding a social and/or a historical context just to make them palatable to those who aren't even interested in horror films? It's a ridiculous idea, and the end result would be a sham; if Grotesque added a subtext showing how madness and murder are linked to some dubious political framework, then would this element make the film acceptable to the censors? Well, that's the way those in charge of censorship tend to think nowadays. But even if Grotesque did happen to have a subtext to justify the gruesome bloodshed on screen, it would be fake and phony. But that seems to be the way the censors operate in today's PC climate.

Sometimes the horror, sex, gore, and exploitation is reason enough to watch a film, and there's nothing wrong with that. Many of us have an interest in the dark side of life for its own sake and don't feel the need to justify our interests. I don't need some nitwit like Wes Craven to add some 'progressive aspect' to a film for me to enjoy it or to find value in it other than the nastiness on display. We don't muse on the troubles of the 70s oil crisis when we watch The Texas Chainsaw Massacre, do we? No, because ultimately it's irrelevant to what's happening on screen.

I genuinely believe that the real damage is being done by films that are completely unrestrained in churning out the most soulless and empty-headed garbage that proliferates the multiplexes nowadays. I'm thinking Transformers, The Fast and The Furious and its sequels, Adam Sandler abominations, etc. None of those films offer anything in the way of social value or 'progressive aspects' that seem to be oh so important to our moral guardians. They're the cinematic equivalent of the Big Mac; just pure unadulterated junk. Where's the restraint? Where's the health warnings against this kind of crap? If you have an IQ in the double digits these films will put you into a coma. But the studios who churn out this stuff don't give a shit, they're just happy to reap the financial rewards. These types of films are genuinely harming society by dumbing down the masses and turning them into mindless, materialistic fucking slobs, and yet nothing is being done about it. In fact, the situation is clearly getting worse as the years go by.

To my mind this is the true obscenity of modern cinema. And yet it's allowed to flourish unchecked because the major studios have the financial muscle to fight in the courts, whereas the small indie production companies don't. These films have also created a monopoly of the multiplexes, and if you go to the cinema nowadays you can't avoid this kind of crap. Unbelievably, it takes 10 screenwriters, a whole army of crew members, and dozens of 'test screenings' to perfect the nullifying wastes of time that are the modern blockbusters. The studios will argue that they are simply meeting demand and giving the people what they want. But if you ask the average filmgoer what he or she would like to see in the cinema, they'll tell you that basically they'll watch anything the studios are churning out ('whatever's on at Warner Village'). What the studios won't accept is any responsibility for the sorry state of modern society. And this is another thing; according to the censors, we're stupid and not responsible enough to make up our own minds when it comes to horror movies; but when it comes to the shittiest mindless blockbusters, all of a sudden we're considered completely responsible and entrusted to have our mindless and idiotic 'demands' met by the Hollywood studio system. It's a funny old world...

When all's said and done it comes down to control. A shady and sinister control that is in cahoots with big business and has very little to do with morality or decency. It's all a ploy to take charge of every cinema in the land, and to regulate every non-studio film so that nothing can flourish, so that no other important and vital avenues of film can be opened and explored. Everything has to fit within the accepted norms of studio control, otherwise it must be strangled at birth. And in that case, fuck the studios, fuck the MPAA, fuck the BBFC, and give me Human Centipede 2 any day; something fresh, honest, and invigorating - A true expression of the fucked up world we live in. Censorship is not only irrelevant, but it's also deeply troubling and, as a chief censor would put it, 'problematic'.

THE VANISHING POINT OF CINEMA

What Jean Baudrillard called the "vanishing point along the lines of music" is also happening in film. But before we examine its effects on cinema, let's take a closer look at Baudrillard's theory in music. We are all obsessed with the quality of music, not necessarily with how the songs are written or performed, but how they sound through our speakers. Take for example the young men who like to drive around in 'pimped up' sports cars; how many of them dedicate the entire boot of their cars to house powerful sub-woofer speaker systems where they can "mix, regulate, and multiply soundtracks in search of an infallible or unerring music". To these boys, the actual sounds of the music is less important than HOW IT SOUNDS (the 'transmission') after it has been fed through their channels and amplifiers, when it has been given a high-fidelity treatment. And this is what Baudrillard meant when he suggested that music "would disappear into its own special effect".

The speaker of any modern piece of hi-fi equipment is separated into sections; you can find up to three or four channels each transmitting a certain texture of the sound. Music is broken down into layers, and these layers are tweaked to increasing perfection, and they're all reunited in the environment as the musical transmission leaves the speaker. It seems today there is no more room for innovation concerning musical instruments, and that all future progress will be through increasing the sound qualities of recordings, and that music will slip away "into the perfection of its materiality, step beyond its boundary" as Baudrillard put it.

Consider how old albums are being constantly re-released in 'digitally re-mastered' versions where the original recordings are broken down and digitally re-built, and are made to glow anew as the soundtrack is coated in its own perfection. And this search for an unerring musical pleasure is no longer used solely to improve old recordings; in modern music, the recording process itself has become more important than the song craft and the performance of the songs. Take Radiohead for example; if you listen to the six studio albums to date, you'll notice a gradual progression from performance based, melodic pop/rock (Pablo Honey and The Bends), to more avant-garde performance based stuff (OK Computer), to the rejection of all performance and standard instruments, and the reaching of the very threshold of the disappearance of music (a couple of tracks on Kid A and Amnesiac). With these last two albums, Radiohead reached the dead end of musical minimalism (that's perhaps why on Hail To The Thief the band seemed more willing to embrace their past glories; they couldn't get any closer to the core of musicality without disappearing completely in the process).

With Kid A and Amnesiac Radiohead had gotten to the stage where they were less interested in chords and melodies than with WHAT TO DO in the studio with sound itself. How will it sound through the speakers? Regardless of what artistic or social/political comments the band were implying, transmission took centre stage. In Pulk/Pull Revolving Doors, traditional chords and melodies are left behind, and what we hear instead is a strange kind of groove built on fuzz and pops and crackles with looped piano notes and spacey synth sounds going nowhere. The vocals on this track are interesting because firstly, it doesn't even sound like frontman Thom Yorke; his voice has been altered so much that he actually sounds like an android or an extra-terrestrial creature. Secondly, there is no singing as such, at least not in the traditional sense, and instead we're presented with spoken lines that are unintelligable because of the way his voice has been filtered through various FX. So one line of the vocal is flat and dull, and the next line can echo with heavy reverb for a whole minute. The only way that this track can be heard is through a good quality hi-fi system because, unlike their previous performance based recordings (of guitars, bass, and drums, etc), this particular recording is grounded fully in the luxurious high-fidelity sound tests. Thus, to hear this track played through the small, tinny speaker of a laptop, or mobile phone, or wireless radio, would be to miss the point entirely of what Radiohead are offering. If you listen to this track on anything less than a 200 watt RPM stereo system, then YOU WILL NOT REALLY HEAR THE TRACK AT ALL.

The overall tone and depth and bass of so much modern music cannot be accessed by the listener unless he or she can upgrade to a decent hi-fi stereo system with several speaker channels. Modern music recording has made it essential for us to listen on constantly upgraded equipment, otherwise this music as such disappears.

So how does this vanishing point affect film? Well, I was recently offered the opportunity of watching a pirate copy of Spiderman 3 (which I declined, naturally); but sometime later I realised how interesting it would be to view the latest special FX-ladened Hollywood blockbuster, not in its anamorphic big screen glory with super-duper room shaking sound, but on a crappy little bootleg copy at home. Stripped of all the veneer that makes a modern blockbuster, I'm quite sure that Spiderman 3 would resemble nothing more than a lousy, meaningless, and loud mess. As I mentioned above, modern music fans cannot fully access music unless they have a hi-fi stereo system, so modern film fans cannot access the latest Hollywood blockbuster unless they visit the local multiplex (and concerning Spiderman 3, it's probably safe to say that even in a multiplex cinema it will resemble nothing more than a lousy, meaningless, and loud mess).

In the context of the vanishing point along the lines of film, the pirate DVD serves as a counter-irony to big screen entertainment; the way in which a huge glossy product is 'captured' by the dull senses of a handheld video camera (usually around 8 megs/50 megapixels), and uploaded onto a hard drive and onto the internet where viewers around the world can download it, burn it onto disc, and then 'enjoy' it at home whilst the film is still doing the rounds in the cinemas. I'm reminded of Theodor Adorno in Minima Moralia where he observes that a film which is already three months old is dismissed or thrown out like so much garbage, and that "the newest one is preferred at any price, even though this last one is not the slightest bit different... Every program must be sat through to the end, every 'bestseller' must be read, every film must be seen during its first release in the movie theatre", which echoes his earlier ideas with Horkheimer in the 'Culture Industry'.

The whole video piracy phenomenon is suitably ironic because every latest blockbuster movie is a 'must see' movie, even in the unwatchable form of a bootleg copy. With the video camera, the movie pirate takes a glossy product, breaks it down digitally, and then rebuilds it in a new and cheapened, accessible form. The Hollywood movie industry spends millions of Dollars on sounds and visuals only for the pirate to spend peanuts on breaking it down and giving it away for free. Here we have the opposite of a 'digitally re mastered' product; this is digital sabotage. The blockbuster movie is filtered through the pirate's unsuitable home equipment; a 50 megapixel video camera is incapable of absorbing the detail on screen, is incapable of recording the movie in identical form. The sound is muffled, the visuals lack the bright, clear sheen that radiates in the cinema, the colours are faded and washed out, etc. The result is often a drab imitation of a blockbuster movie (in the same way that blockbuster movies are a drab imitation of cinema itself).

Now let's take a closer look at the modern filmmaking process. We have already witnessed the gradual demolition of authentic movie sets and their replacement with CGI - This being the most obvious example of cinema disappearing into its own special effect. But what about the more intimate special effects in otherwise authentic movies staged on real sets? We have reached the stage where even single frames of celluloid can be digitally manipulated on computer after the shooting has taken place. In previous years, it was only the editor who worked on a film after the shooting schedule was complete. But now we have entered an era where THE WHOLE MOVIE IS TO BE CREATED AFTER THE SHOOTING TAKES PLACE. Films are now being made in digital laboratories rather than movie sets. Movie sets have now become just a blank canvas on which a director can test his imagination; or, to put it another way; the movie set is just another way for the filmmaker to keep notes, and is used in the same way as script annotations and storyboards.

In this sense, the movie camera itself is fast becoming redundant, and is perhaps why filmmakers are nowadays less concerned with what to point the camera at than with WHAT TO DO with the camera when it is pointed at something. Hence flashy visuals with optical lenses, fish-eye lenses, morphing effects, zoom effects, rotations, crane shots, dolly shots, busy MTV-style effects, steadicam, and so on and so forth. And perhaps Hollywood actors and actresses can sense this disappearance of cinema and feel themselves ripe for disposal too, and find themselves indulging in facelifts and plastic surgery in an attempt to harmonize with the fakery of their chosen medium, not just out of personal vanity, but to make themselves worthy of a fake cinema, even when the movie camera is nowadays more interested in itself than with the background players/mannequins. The filmmaking process has become more important than film itself, and is well into the process of slipping away into the perfection of its materiality.

APPENDIX: INTERVIEW WITH AUTHOR PHIL RUSSELL

This interview was first published at Make-Your-Offer.com

The next author stepping up to the plate and sharing with us is Phil Russell. Hats off to Phil for a very interesting interview. I look forward to more of these as time goes on.

Why did you get into writing?

I think the seed was my innate desire to communicate with people, and perhaps turn them on to things they may be unaware of.

What inspired you to write Beyond The Darkness?

I was sick and tired of seeing films I love being torn to shreds by the critics, and I just wanted to 'fight their corner' so to speak. That was the main inspiration. Not all the reviews in my book are positive though, far from it. I felt it was important to balance things up with a few not-so-positive reviews so that it wouldn't resemble some 'fanboy' geek type of book (which it could easily have been!).

The book started as a blog that I had running for a while; I originally planned to write a complete A-Z guide for horror, cult, and extreme cinema, but soon realised it was just mad ambition and would take forever to complete, and so I settled on around 180 films. The blog has since been taken down to keep the folks at Amazon happy. Writing the book was a joy, but of course some films inspired me to write more than others. There were a couple of difficult and frustrating moments in putting the book together, but on the whole it has been a very worthwhile experience...

What were the difficulties in writing your book?

Mostly factual/research stuff. Y'see, some of the films I covered are very obscure and finding information about them was sometimes difficult. Often the answers could not even be found at the usually reliable IMDB. The filmmakers themselves were difficult to contact and many of them don't speak English.

I interviewed the beautiful Asia Argento and it went really well. The phone call to Rome cost me an arm and a leg but it was worth it. She was polite, engaging, and seemed to be genuinely interested in the book. It was my first interview and I was so proud. But there was a problem; the device I used to record the conversation was faulty – either that or my laptop was the problem – and the recording is lost. Devastated! I can remember the gist of most of her answers but decided not publish the half-remembered interview as it would be a disservice, and I wouldn't want to misquote her.

Another frustrating moment was my attempted interview with Crispin Glover. Glover is best known as a Hollywood actor who has appeared in Back To The Future, Charlie's Angels, and Willard, etc. But in his spare time he likes to get behind the camera and direct his own films which are much more disturbing and challenging, and as far-removed from Hollywood as one can get.

One of his films features Stephen C. Stewart, an actor who suffered from cerebral palsy, and in one scene he falls head-first down some stone steps. Now, early in the interview I asked Crispin why he kept that footage in the final cut of the film – it was clearly an accidental fall and I very much doubt it was in the script – I was genuinely interested to know why he kept that scene in the film (and still am).

Maybe he was offended by my probing, or maybe he could sense my moral outrage at the inclusion of such a scene. I don't know. But for whatever reason, he hung up on me! Maybe he didn't expect to be held to account by a nobody like myself, or maybe there was a fault on the line (he was in the Czech Republic when I called). Who knows. But I didn't write the book so that I could kiss anyone's arse. I wanted facts, but oh well, it was a learning curve at least.

It wasn't all doom and gloom and frustration. My interview with Nick Zedd went very well. There are interviews available on Youtube with Zedd and in the past he sometimes gave interviewers a tough time, but he was completely honest, open, and forthright in his conversation with me. He was also happy to help out with stills assistance for the book for which I'll always be grateful. Zedd also inspired me to self-publish; the 'Do-It-Yourself' punk aesthetic has always fascinated me, and especially nowadays with the power of the internet, it seems the obvious thing to do...

Another good thing about my book that I must tell you about is that it reached NO.1 on Amazon's Bestseller rankings for a few days in the 'Reference/Encyclopedia' section, on both sides of the Atlantic. And I shall boast about that fact until the end of my days! The book has also sold surprisingly well in Germany which is still a mystery to me...

Another good looking book cover – how did you create it? If you paid someone to help – was it expensive?

Thank you. It is a pretty cool cover. The credit goes to my good friend Jenny Sinclair who created it for me. She used software that is free and easy to use online.

(Note: The cover has since been updated in June 2012)

What are your favourite books?

I like anything that is dark, challenging, disturbing. Anything from William Burroughs to Zola. I love horror fiction, novels, and short stories. Reference books on film, art, music, true crime, etc. Bizarro fiction. And more horror. My favourite authors are people like Jack Ketchum, Jean Baudrillard, Stephen Thrower, and Brian Evenson.

How many books do you have available for sale?

Just the one at the moment; BEYOND THE DARKNESS: Cult, Horror, And Extreme Cinema.

Do you have any plans to write more books?

At some point in the future yes. I have many ideas for novels, novellas, and shorts. Mostly horror fiction, but I will also try some black comedy at some point. I'm also a musician and at the moment it's my rock band that takes up most of my time and energy... There may also be a Beyond The Darkness Volume 2 in the future with more reviews, articles, and interviews – that is if anyone will talk to me!

Why did you decide to join MYO?

I think it's a great opportunity to be part of something new, not just as a self-published writer, but also as a booklover too. I always enjoy a good haggle when I'm out shopping, and MYO gives us the opportunity to approach authors with offers that are a bit lower than the RRP. MYO could be the start of something great; a community of booklovers who are free to create a platform and rally to a cause – of being proud independent writers. I feel so lucky to have been invited here and to be part of this. Let's just hope that this venture will blossom into a huge success.

But for that to happen we've got to spread the word and invite others along. I'm very excited about MYO, chiefly because we can all help and support each other in doing what we love to do. And also because this website is brand spanking new, and if there is ever a 'goldrush' at MYO, us lucky few members who got here first will never miss out on that kind of action! So thanks for this opportunity, let's make it happen!

Where do you do most of your writing? (Do you have a special place that you go to?)

I don't really have a special place to write. I suppose the good thing about writing non-fiction is that the usual setbacks – such as writer's block or a lack of inspiration, etc – don't usually apply. For example, in the case of my book, if I felt myself to be in a creative slump, all I had to do was watch a gruesome horror DVD and bingo! I had page after page of ready-made inspiration! When I eventually get round to writing fictional pieces I expect it will be a whole new ball-game of having to rely almost entirely on my own imagination. But I look forward to the challenge.

So although there's no particular place where I do most of my writing, I do have one rule; I must be alone when I write. If I get distracted by anyone, I will probably turn into Jack Torrence from The Shining and will hunt them down with an axe…

Printed in Great Britain
by Amazon.co.uk, Ltd.,
Marston Gate.